Modern Aspects of
Graphite Technology

Modern Aspects of
Graphite Technology

Edited by

L. C. F. BLACKMAN

BCURA Industrial Laboratories
Leatherhead, Surrey, England

 1970

ACADEMIC PRESS: London and New York

ACADEMIC PRESS INC. (LONDON) LTD
Berkeley Square House
Berkeley Square
London, W1X 6BA

U.S. Edition published by
ACADEMIC PRESS INC.
111 Fifth Avenue
New York, New York 10003

Library of Congress Catalog Card Number: 70-107934
SBN: 12-103350-3

PRINTED IN GREAT BRITAIN BY
THE WHITEFRIARS PRESS LTD, LONDON AND TONBRIDGE

CONTRIBUTORS

D. V. BADAMI, Turner Bros. Asbestos Co. Ltd., Rochdale, England.

A. R. FORD, Morganite Carbon Ltd., London, England.

E. GREENHALGH, Morganite Carbon Ltd., London, England.

J. M. HUTCHEON, United Kingdom Atomic Energy Authority, Warrington, England.

J. B. LEWIS, Chemical Engineering Division, Atomic Energy Research Establishment, Harwell, England.

H. H. W. LOSTY, The General Electric Company Ltd., Wembley, England.

G. A. SAUNDERS, Department of Applied Physics, The University, Durham, England.

P. K. C. WIGGS, Morganite Carbon Ltd., London, England.

PREFACE

The broad aim of this book is to present a balanced account of the main factors that concern the preparation, properties and industrial (non-nuclear) applications of commercial graphite. Nuclear applications form a highly specialized subject that is well covered by existing publications.

The industrial use of polycrystalline carbon and graphite has long preceded a thorough scientific understanding of the materials. During the past decade, however, the rapid increase in the number of research publications bears witness that graphite is now well established as an area for pure and applied scientific research. Thus, although the bulk of graphite used in industry is synthetic and of polycrystalline structure, our understanding of the behaviour of industrial composite material comes primarily from researches on ideal, or near-ideal, single crystals. These have generally been natural crystals, though in recent years important findings have resulted from studies of synthetic pyrolytic material.

The impetus for increased study of graphite arose from its use in the nuclear industry. The enthusiastic response from research workers had undoubtedly been sustained by the remarkable and often unique properties of the tightly-bonded carbon hexagon networks, whereby extreme stability is coupled with highly anisotropic structural, mechanical, electrical and thermal properties. Thus, for example, the thermal expansion normal to the hexagonal layer planes is some 30 times that in the direction of the planes; the electrical conductance is some 10,000 times higher along the layer planes than across them; the thermal conductivity along the layers exceeds that of metallic silver while in the normal direction the crystal acts as a poor insulator; in the layer direction the crystal is as soft as talc and is readily oxidized while in the basal plane the Mohs scale of hardness is reported as high as nine and the resistance to gaseous oxidation is also high.

It is no wonder that technologists are exploiting the diverse properties to produce tailor-made materials for industrial application. These materials are invariably composites, and as such exhibit a much lower overall degree of anisotropy depending on the method of preparation. But the precise value of the bulk anisotropy is generally of vital importance to industrial application, and accordingly considerable attention has been paid to the subject—sufficient to have added significantly to the basic understanding of anisotropic composites in general.

One area that may still be fairly regarded as something of an art is the actual process of graphitization—whereby graphitic material is obtained by the controlled heating of organic precursors. Studies of the changes in structure from elementary disordered clusters of carbon, through various stages of crystal ordering to something approaching the ideal hexagonal layer structure, have identified and interpreted many important factors in manufacture. But a rigorous understanding of the process is still far from established.

Though, as outlined above, it is the basic understanding of the graphite crystal that has to a large extent underpinned the advance in industrial exploitation, this book is not primarily concerned with the perfect crystal. Indeed, it is only in Chapter III, on the electron transport in graphites and carbons, that the basic crystal lattice receives explicit attention. The other six chapters are concerned mainly with the technology of industrial grade material.

BCURA Industrial Laboratories,   L. C. F. BLACKMAN
Leatherhead, Surrey,
England
April, 1970

CONTENTS

I. Polycrystalline Carbon and Graphite

J. M. HUTCHEON

II. Manufacturing Technology of Baked and Graphitized Carbon Bodies

J. M. HUTCHEON

III. Electron Transport in Graphites and Carbons

G. A. SAUNDERS

IV. Thermal Gas Reactions of Graphite

J. B. Lewis

V. Mechanical Properties

H. H. W. Losty

VI. Friction and Wear

D. V. Badami and P. K. C. Wiggs

VII. Industrial Applications of Carbon and Graphite

A. R. Ford and E. Greenhalgh

Chapter I

POLYCRYSTALLINE CARBON AND GRAPHITE

J. M. HUTCHEON

United Kingdom Atomic Energy Authority, Warrington, England

I. INTRODUCTION

Natural deposits of graphite are visibly crystalline and single crystals of some millimeters in size can be extracted from it. The synthetic pyrolytic graphite, however, can also exist as near-perfect single crystals of quite large dimensions. With these exceptions, all forms of carbon and graphite are poly-crystalline. There are profound structural differences between the various forms which is obvious from the wide range of physical properties apparent in the different forms of graphite. For example, the differences in hardness between natural graphite flakes, carbon black powder and metallurgical cokes are very obvious, as are also their differences in electrical and thermal conductivity.

Until comparatively recently the natural and artificial forms of carbon were regarded as either crystalline (that is graphite or diamond) or amorphous, but the first application of X-ray diffraction methods to the "amorphous" carbons led to the view that the latter were also graphitic with their apparently amorphous character arising from the very minute size of the crystallites.

A. THE GRAPHITE CRYSTAL

The structure of the graphite crystal was first established as a result of X-ray studies by Bernal (1924). The crystal consists of layers of carbon atoms in the form of fused benzene rings, each atom being symmetrically related to three nearest neighbours in the plane. The planar structure is stabilized by resonance and the mobility of the electrons in the plane results in significant electrical conductivity in the planar directions. In the direction at right angles to the layer planes bonding is by Van der Waals' forces, and the separation of the planes (the d-spacing) is $3 \cdot 354$ Å. Normally the relative position of the planes is such that alternate planes are in exact register (**AB** sequence) so that the structure is hexagonal. Displacement in the direction parallel to the layers is relatively easy because of the low van der Waals' attractive forces, so that stacking defects can occur. In particular, most synthetic graphites contain $10-30\%$ of a slightly less stable rhombohedral form (Lipson and Stokes 1942) in which the stacking sequence of the layers is **ABC** rather than **AB**. The proportion of the rhombohedral form can be increased by grinding synthetic graphite (Bacon 1952).

B. POLYCRYSTALLINE CARBON

The range of materials included under this heading consists of the products of pyrolysis of organic compounds at temperatures above about 700°C. This temperature is the minimum at which the product can in general be regarded as substantially pure carbon, although there may still in some cases be significant proportions of other elements, as discussed in Section VI. In common with graphite, polycrystalline carbons are largely made up of substantially plane condensed aromatic layers, stacked in roughly parallel groups, but may differ from graphite in the following important respects:

(i) spacing (d) and mutual orientation of the layer planes;
(ii) dimensions of the layer planes (L_a) and the number (N) in a stack, that is stack height (L_c);
(iii) defects in the layer planes;
(iv) mutual orientation of the layer plane stacks. This variation can also be expressed as a variation in the size, shape and total volume of the pores between the layer plane stacks;
(v) carbon atoms not incorporated in layer planes;
(vi) inclusion of atoms other than carbon in the structure.

These structural differences lead to considerable departures in the properties from those of graphite in respect of electronic properties, transport properties, surface properties and chemical reactivity. However, the elements of structure which these materials possess, although rudimentary for many examples, preclude the use of the term "amorphous" and such materials are best described, following Franklin (1951a), as "non-graphitic carbons".

To a greater or lesser degree the structure and properties of these materials are modified towards those of graphite by heat treatment at temperatures up to about 3000°C in vacuum or an inert atmosphere. When such a transition occurs to a significant degree, it is referred to as "graphitization" and the product is then a "polycrystalline graphitic carbon" or "a polycrystalline graphite".

C. CLASSIFICATION OF CARBONS

But not all carbons will undergo this transition. Those that are so capable are termed "graphitizing carbons" by Franklin (1951b) and the remainder are termed "non-graphitizing carbons". Examples of the former are pitch and petroleum cokes and the carbon derived from pyrolysis of polyvinyl chloride; examples of the latter are the carbons derived from polyvinylidene chloride, from cellulose and from sucrose. Franklin (1951b) distinguishes the two types in terms of the relation between crystal height and crystal diameter on heat treatment (both of these quantities being obtained from analysis of the X-ray diffractogram), as indicated by Fig. 1 which is taken from her paper. In this figure the non-graphitizing carbons are heat-treated up to 3000°C but the data for graphitizing carbons refer to materials with a maximum heat-treatment temperature (HTT) of 1720°C.

Mrozowski (1956) uses the terms "soft carbons" and "hard carbons" as broadly equivalent to Franklin's "graphitizing carbons" and "non-graphitizing carbons". He has provided (1958) a useful general classification that "soft carbons" are formed from the liquid phase, "hard carbons" from

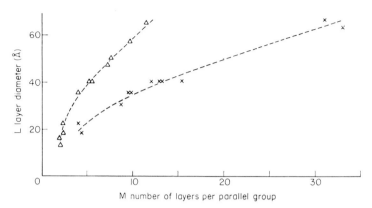

FIG. 1. Relationship between the layer diameter, L, and the number, M, of layers per parallel group for graphitizing ($\times$) and non-graphitizing ($\triangle$) carbons. (After Franklin 1951b.)

the solid phase, and carbon blacks, regarded as a third variety, from the gas phase, although for many blacks formation takes place through an intermediate liquid droplet stage.

D. EXPERIMENTAL METHODS

In the last thirty years an enormous amount of work has been done to elucidate these variations under the impetus of the technological importance to the coal and oil, carbon black, metallurgical, nuclear energy and aerospace industries. The experimental approaches can be classified (Ubbelohde 1966) as either analytical or synthetic.

1. X-ray Diffraction

The most used analytical technique is X-ray diffractometry, and most workers in the field have made use of this to obtain estimates of d, L_a and L_c. Essentially, the position of the diffraction lines permits an estimate of d and the width or shape of the intensity profile of a line leads to L_a and L_c. This, however, is a grossly simplified description; the interpretation of X-ray scattering data from non-graphitic carbons is a highly specialized subject, for a comprehensive treatment of which the reader is referred to the recent review by Ergun (1968). An important general point is that in order to get precise results measurements have to be carried out with great care and by comparison of results from several different lines in the spectrum in order to eliminate the purely geometrical broadening (which is a function of the X-ray equipment) and also strain effects which give rise to puckering and distortion of individual layers (Fitzer *et al.* 1966). Considerable differences may be found (Fitzer *et al.* 1966; Short and Walker 1963) in the estimates of parameters according to the procedure used. Hence, comparisons of results for different materials are likely to be misleading unless they are obtained by exactly analogous techniques. Moreover, the method becomes progressively less sensitive as the crystal size increases since practical considerations limit the precision of the determination of the d-spacing to about ± 0.004 Å (Fitzer et al. 1966).

2. Other Analytical Techniques

The X-ray technique has been supplemented by a wide range of other analytical approaches. Diffraction methods have been used (Section IIF) to study orientation as well as the degree of development of the structure. Direct observation of structure has been made by electron microscopy (Section IIG) and, for the coarser structural elements, by optical microscopy (Section IIF).

Information about the "free valencies" in the structure has been obtained (Pullman 1959) by study of the electronic properties including electrical resistivity (Bowman et al. 1958), magnetic susceptibility (Section IIK) and electron spin resonance (Ingram 1959; Cerutti et al. 1960). Estimates of layer plane size have been made from thermal conductivity measurements (Taylor et al. 1968). Elements other than carbon, including the particularly important element hydrogen, have been estimated (Section IIH) by classical methods. The different types of bonding of carbon atoms in the structure are reflected in differences in the rate of solution of carbons in liquid oxidizing media and this has been made the basis of one method of analysis (Section IIL) of carbon structures. The relation between neighbouring layer planes and the structure of the planes themselves has been inferred (Maire and Méring 1958; Ubbelohde and Lewis 1960) from a comparison of the ease of formation of intercalated lamellar compounds (for example with bromine, potassium and oxygen) by a range of carbons (Section IIM).

The mutual relation of the layer plane stacks has been inferred (Sections IIJ and IIIC) from studies of the properties of the microporosity between these stacks. Less direct inferences can also be drawn from measurements of mechanical properties (Hong and Mrozowski 1955), hardness (Simbeck and Kronenwetter 1963) and thermal expansion (see for example Okada 1960).

All these measurements, like those by X-ray diffraction, have been made for given materials heat treated to a range of temperatures and thus contribute to our knowledge of the evolution of structure on heat treatment.

3. Synthetic Methods

It is reasonable to expect that graphitizing carbons are more likely to be formed from molecules which already exist as large flat polyaromatic structures and which pass through a fluid phase where there is adequate mobility for stacking to occur. By a generalization of this type of argument information about the structure of carbons has been obtained by a consideration of the starting material and by following the changes occurring during carbonization by a variety of techniques, including direct observation of change of state, analysis of evolved gases, and analysis of residues by classical techniques, infrared spectroscopy, electron spin resonance, and other methods. These methods are discussed in more detail in Sections IIN and IIIB.

II. SOFT CARBONS

By contrast with hard carbons, the soft carbons are characterized by changes in all their properties on heat treatment from about 1000–3000°C and these changes have been extensively studied. The very obvious change in appearance of the diffractograms on such treatment, typified by Fig. 2 (kindly supplied

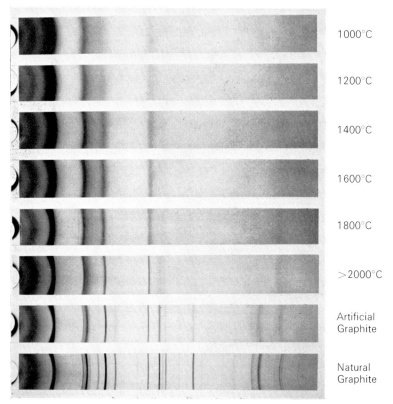

1000°C

1200°C

1400°C

1600°C

1800°C

>2000°C

Artificial Graphite

Natural Graphite

FIG. 2. X-ray powder photographs showing increase in size of graphitic crystallites in cokes formed from pitch at successively increasing temperatures. (By courtesy of Dr. H. P. Rooksby, Hurst Research Centre, GEC, Wembley.)

by Dr. H. P. Rooksby) is perhaps the most fundamental observation in the whole topic of carbon science. The key features are the existence of a line or band at, or close to, the [002] position for all heat treatment temperatures, indicating the existence of parallel layer planes in all the materials; the sharpening of this line and the appearance of lines in (00*l*) positions of higher *l* value, indicating the growth of the crystal; and the appearance of lines in (*hkl*) positions, indicating the emergence of three-dimensional ordering, as the heat treatment temperature is raised.

A. LAYER-PLANE SPACING

The first systematic X-ray studies covering a range of types of carbon were those of Hofmann and Wilm (1936), some of whose results are shown in Table I.

From the position of the [002] line or band it was already clear from this work that the *d*-spacing, except at the highest heat-treatment temperature, was greater than the characteristic value of 3·354 Å for graphite. Other

TABLE I

Crystallite Dimensions†

Carbon	Layer-plane spacing (Å)	Crystallite dimension (Å)	
		L_a	L_c
Ceylon graphite	3·35	∞	*ca* 200
Carbon monoxide carbon 700°	3·4	120	180
Carbon monoxide carbon 550°	3·4	150	160
Carbon monoxide carbon 420°	3·4	60	70
Carbon monoxide carbon 400°	3·45	40	35
Retort carbon	3·45	45	40
Acetylene soot	3·55	21	13
Acetylene soot calcined	3·55	26	14
Supranorit	3·5	18	8
Supranorit calcined	3·45	26	7
Sugar carbon	3·6	21	9

†After Hofmann and Wilm (1936)

measurements (Biscoe and Warren 1942; Franklin 1951) indicated that for many materials (particularly carbon blacks and petroleum or pitch cokes which had undergone heat treatment at a temperature in the range 1000–1500°C approximately) a spacing of about 3·440 Å was characteristic of a graphitizing carbon in the non-graphitic state. On heat treatment to 3000°C Franklin (1951a) found that this fell to a value which for the materials she

studied varied between 3·428 and 3·361 Å. The explanation for these variations, although also given by other workers, was brought out most clearly by
Warren and co-workers (Biscoe and Warren 1942; Warren 1956).

Noting that the existence of a line near the [002] position indicates the
presence of a parallel-layer structure, Warren examined the detailed shape of
the broad diffuse (hk) reflections visible in the diffractogram of carbon blacks,
and the manner in which modulations appeared in these traces as the blacks
were heat treated up to 2800°C. The characteristic shape of such a line is
asymmetric; a sharp rise on the low-angle side is followed by a gentle falling
away on the high-angle side, as indicated in Fig. 3.

This shape corresponds to a two-dimensional reflection and indicates that
the parallel layers are not stacked according to either the standard hexagonal
or rhombohedral modes, but that the crystals consist, according to Biscoe
and Warren (1942) "of a number of graphite layers stacked together roughly
parallel and equidistant, but with each layer having completely random

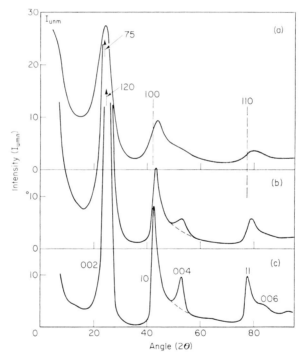

FIG. 3. Intensity curves for three carbon black samples. (a) Spheron grade 6 black,
unheated; (b) same black, heated 2 hr at 1500°C; (c) same black, heated 2 hr at 2800°C.
Radiation Cu Kα. For all three curves, the Compton modified scattering has been sub-
tracted. (After Biscoe and Warren 1942.)

orientation about the layer normal". For such a structure they coined the term "turbostratic".

With increase in heat treatment temperatures the modulations transform into symmetrical lines (cf. Fig. 3) corresponding to the appearance of the three-dimensional (*hkl*) reflections of the planes of atoms in the graphite crystal.

B. DEGREE OF GRAPHITIZATION

As noted above heat treatment of a soft carbon leads, for a given starting material, to the following changes in measurable crystallographic parameters.

(i) The structure changes from turbostratic towards graphitic (in general predominantly to the hexagonal (**AB**) form, although there may be exceptions (Pandic 1966)), with the appearance of *hkl* lines as noted above.
(ii) The *d*-spacing decreases from the turbostratic value of 3·44 Å towards the graphitic value of 3·354 Å.
(iii) The apparent layer diameter (L_a) increases.
(iv) The apparent layer plane height (L_c), or, alternatively expressed, the number of layers (N) in a parallel layer packet, increases.

Workers in this field have sought to define an index of crystal development which should have a more fundamental significance than heat treatment temperature and should, if possible, be independent of starting material.

1. Maire and Méring's g-Factor

One such index, the "graphitization factor" (g) proposed by Maire and Méring (1958, 1959, 1960) is simply defined from the apparent layer spacing $\overline{a_3}$ as

$$\overline{a_3} = 3·354g + 3·440(1-g) \tag{1}$$

So defined, g is a purely empirical quantity indicating the position of the material on a scale of which the two fixed points are the turbostratic and graphitic spacings. It increases, as expected, with HTT for soft carbons. Méring and Maire (1960) have published a curve showing this variation for the soft carbon derived from PVC. Their results, together with relevant data from Franklin (1951a) and Akamatu *et al.* (1956) are shown in Fig. 4.

2. Probability of Ordering of Adjacent Planes—the Franklin/Bacon p-Parameter

Given that the forces between the layer planes for spacings of this order are of the van der Waals' type, it is clearly physically reasonable that relative rotation of the planes to bring them into register should result in a reduction of the layer plane spacing and a relationship between the *d*-spacing and the

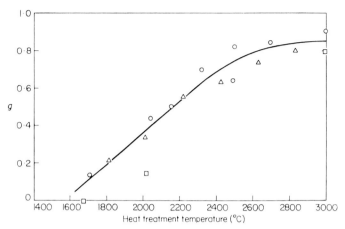

FIG. 4. Change of g-factor with heat-treatment temperature for PVC coke. ○, Franklin (1951a); △, Méring and Maire (1960); □, Akamatu *et al.* (1956).

degree of ordering is therefore to be expected. It is possible to proceed further on the basis of theoretical calculations of the intensity variation across a line for different degrees of order, and thus from line profile measurements to compare experimental values of an ordering parameter with experimentally measured values of the d-spacing. This was done in a classic set of experiments by Franklin (1951a) using the (112) line in the diffractograms to evaluate p, the probability that a random disorientation occurs between any two neighbouring layers. She worked with a range of carbons with measured apparent d-spacings varying between 3·359 Å and 3·418 Å and prepared from different raw materials with different heat-treatment temperature (HTT). Her results are reproduced in Fig. 5.

The assumption of a characteristic spacing of 3·44 Å for a turbostratic graphite carbon is seen to be well justified but the experimental results clearly do not follow a linear relationship.

Franklin explained this by postulating that in the ungraphitized carbon there were four types of spacing, namely the purely graphitic, the purely disoriented, that corresponding to reduced disorientation adjacent to an oriented group and the isolated disorientation spacing between two oriented packets (see Fig. 6).

This leads to the relation

$$d = 3·440 - 0·086(1 - p^2) \tag{2}$$

shown by the parabolic curve in Fig. 5.

Bacon slightly modified this equation (1951, 1958a) to account, *inter alia*, for the fact that the influence of an oriented packet will extend beyond the layers immediately adjacent to it. Bacon's modifications are particularly

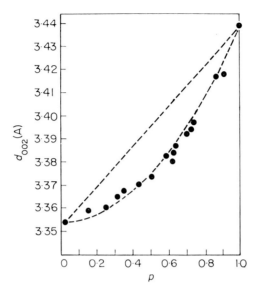

Fig. 5. Relationship between d_{002}, the apparent inter-layer spacing, and p, the proportion of disorientated layers calculated from the (112) line on the assumption of a random distribution of orientations and disorientations. The curve represents the relationship calculated assuming that there exist only three inter-layer spacings, 3·354 Å at an orientation or at a disorientation isolated between two orientations, 3·399 Å at the first disorientation on either side of an orientated group, and 3·440 Å at all other disorientations. (After Franklin 1951a).

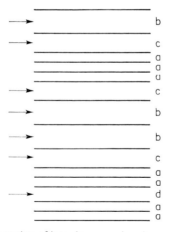

Fig. 6. Schematic representation of inter-layer spacings in graphitic carbons. (a) Orientation spacings, 3·354 Å; (b) normal disorientation spacings, 3·44 Å; (c) reduced disorientation spacing on either side of orientated group; and (d) doubly reduced, isolated disorientation spacing. The arrows indicate the positions of disorientations. (After Franklin 1951a).

significant for well crystallized graphites, where the Franklin equation anomalously indicates a zero slope for the curve at $p = 0$, and for the most highly disordered graphitic carbons.

Bacon's final equation, deduced theoretically, is

$$d = 3 \cdot 440 - 0 \cdot 086(1-p) - 0 \cdot 064p(1-p) - 0 \cdot 030p^2(1-p) \tag{3}$$

which gives even better agreement with the experimental data than eqn (2).

The value of p is thus an important characteristic factor for a polycrystalline carbon and is another index of graphitization.

With increasing heat treatment temperature for a graphitizing carbon the apparent value of d decreases and p falls from near 1 to near zero. Franklin's generally poorly graphitic materials covered approximately the range $p = 0 \cdot 2 - 0 \cdot 8$, as did Bowman's study of a petroleum coke with HTT from 2000–2800°C. For a standard electric furnace graphite Bacon (1958b) gives a value of $0 \cdot 15$ and for a range of rather less well crystallized near-isotropic graphites values in the range $0 \cdot 3 - 0 \cdot 5$ have been reported (Hutcheon and Jenkins 1966).

3. Warren's P_1 Factor

Warren (1956) used a similar technique to study intensity profiles for the two-dimensional reflections and lines in heat-treated carbon blacks, and defined P_1 as the probability that two adjacent layers should be *correctly* oriented. Warren's definition has been followed by other U.S. workers, notably Bowman (1956) who studied the evolution of the graphite structure in petroleum coke.

Bowman's d-spacing results appear at first sight to contradict those of Franklin and to give a linear relation with P_1 (or p) but when Bacon's correction is applied the remaining discrepancies are not clearly outside the range of experimental error.

4. Comparison of Different Indices

If the original Franklin form of the equation is used, the various equations can be rewritten (Ergun 1968) as

$$d = 3 \cdot 354 + 0 \cdot 086p^2 \quad \text{(Franklin)} \tag{4}$$

$$d = 3 \cdot 35 + 0 \cdot 09(1 - P_1) \quad \text{(Warren and Bowman)} \tag{5}$$

$$d = 3 \cdot 354 + 0 \cdot 086(1 - g) \quad \text{(Maire and Méring)} \tag{6}$$

For values of p between $0 \cdot 2$ and $0 \cdot 8$ Bacon's correction to eqn (4) are small. Hence, for eqn (6) to be consistent with eqn (4) we should find a relation

$$1 - g = p^2 = (1 - P_1)^2$$
$$P_1 = 1 - (1 - g)^{\frac{1}{2}} \tag{7}$$

to result from experiments in which P_1 and g were determined independently.

Maire and Méring (1958) and Méring and Maire (1960) determined P_1 (following Warren 1956) from the profiles of the modulated two-dimensional bands and d from the exact position of the 00l reflections. From their hypothesis that ordering should not occur until the individual layers had taken up the fully aromatic arrangement (see Section II) they expected to find a relation

$$P_1 = g^2. \tag{8}$$

The experimental results quoted in Fig. 7 reproduced from Méring and Maire (1960) agree well with this prediction. However, eqn (7) also gives a fair representation of the points. The references generally supply sufficient detail on experimental errors to permit a valid comparison of alternative theoretical interpretations.

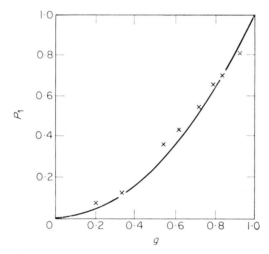

FIG. 7. The relationship between P_1 and g. The full line is for the equation $P_1 = g^2$. (After Méring and Maire 1960.)

C. LAYER-PLANE GROWTH

1. Relations between L_a and HTT

As Table I shows, L_a dimensions of the order of 10–100 Å are recorded by X-ray methods even for soft carbons at HTT below 1500°C. Up to this point the classical X-ray work suggests that the changes occurring consist in the main of two-dimensional polymerization (Méring and Maire 1960); it is only when an L_a dimension of 100 Å or somewhat less (Houska and Warren 1954) is reached that carbon blacks, for example, begin to show the modulations

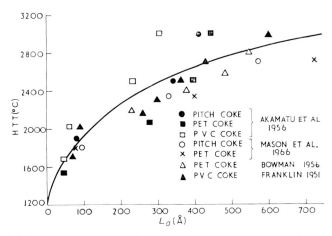

FIG. 8. Relation between L_a and heat treatment temperature for soft carbons.

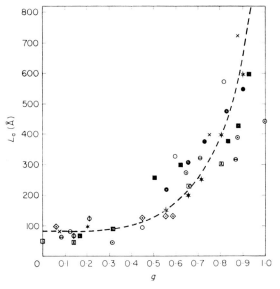

FIG. 9. Relation between L_a and g. Data from: Bowman (1956) ● Pet coke; Mason *et al.* (1966) × Pet coke, ○ Pitch coke; Akamatu *et al.* (1956) ⊙ Pitch coke, ⊠ PVC coke, ⓪ Cosmos black, ⊖ Thermax black; Franklin (1951a) ■ PVC coke; Maire and Méring (1960) ✳ PVC coke; Warren (1956) ◇ Carbon Black.

of the two-dimensional (hk) bands that signify the onset of graphitization. The further change of L_a with HTT is summarized in Fig. 8 which collects together a number of published results (Franklin 1951a; Bowman 1956; Akamatu et al. 1956; Mason et al. 1966).

Maire and Méring (1960) have expressed L_a as a function of g rather than HTT and an essentially similar relation has been proposed by Takahashi et al. (1965). Figure 9 shows the results of several workers (Franklin 1951a; Akamatu et al. 1956; Warren 1956; Bowman 1956; Maire and Méring 1960; Mason et al. 1966) plotted in the form suggested by Maire and Méring (1960) and includes the curve proposed by these authors.

Such a shape is indicative of a stage of comparative constancy of L_a at 100–150 Å while the ordering is occurring up to a value of $g \simeq 0.5$.

2. The Distortion Parameter δ^2

The distortion parameter δ^2 of the layers for pyrolysed PVC subjected to different HTT between 1600°C and 3000°C has also been measured by Bouraoui (1960), Maire and Méring (1960) and by Méring and Maire (1960). This parameter measures a mean deviation of the atoms in a layer from the median plane of the layer and can be obtained from the analysis of the X-ray diffractogram by methods used by Houska and Warren (1954) on carbon black, by assuming different median spacings, which can also be related by the methods described already to the graphitization parameter g. Maire and Méring observed that a spacing of 3·44 Å corresponds to a δ^2 value of 0·14 Å which they regarded as so high as to deprive the value 3·44 Å of any absolute significance.

They expressed their experimental results by the relation between δ^2 and g shown in Fig. 10 from which they deduced that (with some uncertainty) the parameter δ^2 remains constant until g reaches 0·5 and then sharply declines to zero as g goes to unity. Clearly the interpretation is not unequivocal.

3. Significance of L_a

The physical significance of the above conclusions is that they concentrate the attention on the imperfections within the plane rather than the distances between the planes. In particular the apparent increase of L_a with heat-treatment temperature is regarded simply as an "ironing out" of the plane by removal of imperfections within it, rather than an increase in radius of a perfect plane.

The stage of nearly constant L_a in Fig. 9 is associated (by Méring and Maire 1960) with the removal of curvatures (or discontinuities) in the layer planes over a range of tens of angstroms and the stage of rapidly increasing L_a to the straightening out of curvatures of the order of thousands of angstroms.

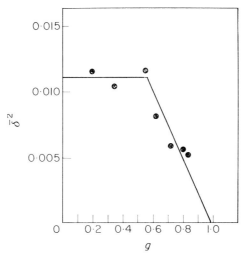

Fig. 10. Relation between δ^2 and g. (After Méring and Maire 1960.)

A maximum size of about 600 Å for the L_a dimensions of heat-treated soft carbons has frequently been reported (see, for example, Franklin 1951a; Bowman 1956; Mason *et al.* 1966) using materials such as petroleum cokes, pitch cokes, and polyvinyl chloride char. Since the line-broadening method is used, and for such large crystals the lines are sharp, this could be an under estimate.

Bouraoui and Méring (1964) criticized earlier estimates of L_a for soft carbon on the ground that different estimates are obtained by the line-broadening method according to which of the (hk) diffraction bands is selected for analysis. They proposed a treatment of the data for pitch cokes with HTT 1000, 1500 and 2000°C which led to a conclusion that the layer diameter is about 300 Å for all these temperatures, the effect of heat treatment above 1000°C being to remove distortions in the layers without increasing their size.

Eeles and Wilson (1965) studied the variance of the line profile for three commercial graphites which, by the normal Scherrer method, had L_a values of 200–500 Å. For two of these their variance technique indicated $L_a = 3000$–4000 Å. If their technique can over-rule in-plane imperfections, these results are in broad agreement with the views expressed by Méring and Maire (1960).

This concept of a large plane (some thousands of angstroms in diameter) containing gaps and imperfections, the dimensions of the plane being considerably greater than the dimensions of the areas over which the true polycyclic aromatic structure appropriate to graphite exists, is also supported by the analysis of Laue photographs (Steward and Cook 1960) who use the term "mosaic" to describe it.

D. INCREASE IN CRYSTALLITE HEIGHT ON HEAT TREATMENT

The change in L_c dimension is another property sharply distinguishing the soft from the hard carbons. Early work showed that for pitch extracts, "solidified" by heating to 450–500°C, further heat treatment first reduced the number of layers in the stack, as detected by X-ray measurements, from about eight to about four, probably due to disturbance of the stack by evolved gases, but beyond 800°C this number increased rapidly again (Riley 1947). At a heat-treatment temperature of 3000°C petroleum cokes, which are generally similar in behaviour to the pitch cokes and pitch extracts, reach

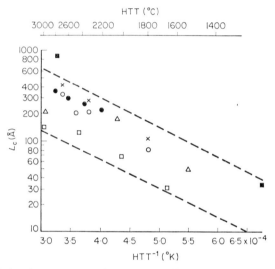

Fig. 11. Relation between L_c and HTT. Data from: Bowman (1956) ● Pet coke; Mason *et al.* (1966) × Pet coke, ○ Pitch coke; Akamatu, *et al.* (1956) △ Pet coke, □ PVC coke; Geller and Walker (1963) ▧ Pet coke.

L_c dimensions of about 300 Å (*ca* 80 parallel layers). For a petroleum coke Bowman (1956) found log L_c to depend linearly on the reciprocal of absolute heat treatment temperature (Fig. 11) up to an L_c value of 350 Å for one particular material, while other workers' results show a broadly similar pattern.

Méring and Maire (1960) also studied crystallite heights. They deduced that the layer plane packet increased in thickness up to about 60 layers for HTT = 2200°C ($g \simeq 0.5$) but that no further increase in height of the crystallite took place, although ordering continued up to 3000°C HTT (see Fig. 12). Their results, shown in Fig. 12, represent a continuation of those of Franklin (Fig. 1), shown to the left of the dotted line.

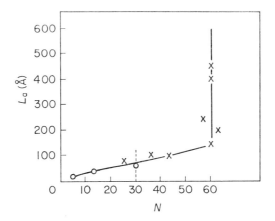

Fɪɢ. 12. Relation between L_a and N. (After Méring and Maire 1960.)

E. KINETICS OF GRAPHITIZATION

The type of relation shown in Fig. 4 implies that an equilibrium is reached in a time short compared with heat-treatment times, so that the state obtained is characteristic of the temperature rather than of the time at which the material is held at temperature. This slightly unusual phenomenon has interested research workers in this field for many years, and has recently provoked a good deal of detailed experimentation.

Okada *et al.* (1963) found that, for material previously heat-treated to 1200°C, further heating to 2800°C gave the same d, L_a and L_c parameters whether it was carried out at a rate of 1000°C per minute or at a rate of 1000°C per hour. Fair and Collins (1963) heated their specimens for up to 50 hr at 2000°C or 6 hr at 3000°C, and found that most of the change in d-spacing and in resistivity occurred in the first 1–2 hr. They confirmed that these properties were, for a given starting material, much more dependent on temperature than on time, although time effects were found. Broadly similar results for d-spacing have been obtained by Fischbach (1963) and Mazza (1964).

The phenomenon implies, as first pointed out by Franklin, that the activation energy of the process is not constant but increases steadily as the process proceeds until it reaches the point where it is greater at a given temperature than the energy available for driving the process. It is suggested (Mizushima 1960; Fair and Collins 1963) that ordering within a turbostratic crystal will take place from more than one nucleating plane in the crystal. At the early stages of this process ordering requires a rotation of only one or two planes in order to produce a small group of planes in the correct graphite hexagonal structure. But once these units begin to overlap within the crystal extensive rearrangement of the layer planes has to take place in order to impose a uniform pattern throughout the crystal, and this increase in the number of layer planes which have to move corresponds to the increase in activation energy.

Everett and Redman (1963) pointed out the analogy with the effect of temperature on the evolution of HCl from PVDC at temperatures up to 700°C. Like the graphitization process, this proceeds to a fixed level depending on temperature. The authors assumed that HCl evolution resulted from cross-linking, and that the free energy of activation increased linearly with the number of cross-links already formed. They obtained excellent agreement with experimental data.

Both for soft carbons and for the hard "glassy carbon" the application of pressures of 10,000 atm during graphitization was found (Noda and Kato 1965) markedly to accelerate the process, as judged by d-spacing measurements.

Recent kinetic studies (Pacault and Gasparoux 1967), in which L_a (and magnetic susceptibility—see section IIK2) were measured, showed significant dependence on time. For a range of temperatures between 1520 and 1929°C continued slow crystal growth was observed up to at least 120 hr, and even at 2030°C saturation had not been achieved at 48 hr. These authors found that by expressing L_a in terms of an equivalent time at temperature, the time-scale being adjusted to the temperature, they could superpose curves for different temperatures to obtain the unique curve shown in Fig. 13.

In this curve the abscissa is $\log k_1 D$ where

$$k_1 = 10^{14} \exp(-82,000/\theta) \qquad (9)$$

θ being the HTT in Å, and D is the heating time in minutes. At temperatures above about 2500°C, k_1 is large so that $\log k_1 \gg \log D$ for practical heating times and therefore $\log kD \simeq \log k$. For heat-treatment temperatures

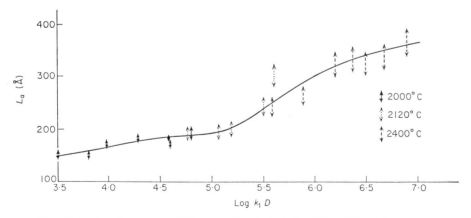

FIG. 13. Rationalized curve of L_a versus "equivalent time" for different temperatures. (After Pacault and Gasparoux 1967.)

around 2000°C, $\log D \gg \log k_1$ so that the abscissa is almost $\log D_1$, but the shape of the curve indicates that L_a changes only slowly with time. Hence these results do suggest that previously determined values of the L_a may differ somewhat according to heating time, but do not greatly alter the classical view that L_a depends chiefly on heat-treatment temperature.

F. ORIENTATION

Petroleum cokes, even when just "set" at 450°C, frequently show very clear intensity variations round the [002] ring when examined on X-ray photographs (Mrozowski 1956; Bacon 1956; Walker *et al.* 1959) and for these materials, but not for the "hard" phenol benzaldehyde char, lamellar bundles are visible in the electron microscope (Kmetko 1956).

1. *Optical and other measurements*

In many cokes, particularly those prepared at 450–500°C from pitch extracts, corresponding striated structures are visible in the optical micro-scope (Beutell *et al.* 1963; Brooks and Taylor 1965; Ihnatowicz *et al.* 1966; White *et al.* 1967) although the difference in scale of observation calls for care in interpretation. Indirect evidence of these structures comes from measure-ments of the shape (Hutcheon and Beirne 1956; Walker *et al.* 1963) of the particles produced by grinding such cokes.

Characteristically, the cross-section of a coke lump in the neighbourhood of a pore shows a filamentous structure following the pore circumference and a longitudinal section shows filaments running parallel to the pore axis (Grossman 1958). Types of coke showing this phenomenon particularly markedly are known in America as "needle" cokes. The thermal expansion coefficient of such cokes in the direction perpendicular to the striations is much greater (Pratt 1958) than that in the parallel direction.

Indirect evidence is also provided by the orientation of such properties as electrical resistivity in moulded or extruded carbons, which argues for a preferred orientation following the shape of the particles (since this is the only parameter on which the moulding or extruded process can act) and hence to planes of weakness in the lumps from which the particles are made.

2. *Origin of Orientation*

The origin of this near parallel stacking in the ungraphitized soft carbons has been associated (Kipling *et al.* 1964a; Kipling and Shooter 1966a, b) with the existence of a fluid phase during carbonization (in turn associated (Franklin 1951b) with a predominantly hydrocarbon source material). This provides the mobility which permits planar molecules to lie in the interface of a liquid gas surface (present for example when pyrolysis of a fluid material results in bubbles passing through the solidifying mass) and thus to stack into parallel layer packets. It is clear that, if at low heat-treatment temperatures, planes deviate only to a small degree from parallel alignment, then comparatively small movements of layer planes are sufficient to combine a crystallite with one "above" or "below" it with a resultant increase in particle thickness as measured by X-ray methods. Also, in these regions where contiguous layer plane packets formed in the solidifying material depart only slightly from coplanarity, although their a-axes may be randomly oriented, only small movements of layer planes are needed to bring the planes into register and thus produce a bigger plane as "seen" by the X-rays. Figure 14(a), due to Franklin (1951b), presents a schematic representation of the structure of a "soft" carbon (at HTT 1000°C), which illustrates the concept. This process has been followed directly (Akamatu and Kuroda 1960) by a combination of electron microscopy and selected area diffraction. Anthracites behave similarly, the orientation being here in relation to the bedding plane resulting from the geological origin. By contrast, for the non-graphitizing type of structure much larger movements of layer planes, and breaking of cross-linkages, would be necessary to build a crystal in this way.

In special cases, such coalescence can occur without fusion. The vat dyestuff flavanthrone forms a molecular crystal structure in which the individual molecules lie in parallel stacks. A shift of only about 2 Å for four flavanthrone molecules in this crystal can result in condensation to form a layer plane containing 32 benzene rings with a hole (the perylene gap) in the middle (see Fig. 14(b)) which would have an L_a dimension consistent with that observed experimentally (Stadler 1960).

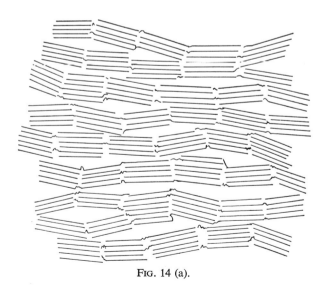

FIG. 14 (a).

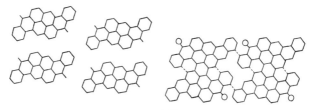

Fig. 14 (b).

Fig. 14. (a) Schematic representation of the structure of a graphitizing (but non-graphitic) carbon. (After Franklin 1951b.) (b) A suggested condensation position of four molecules of flavanthrone brought about by a slight compaction of the arrangement in the single crystal (shown on the left, in projection). The condensed molecule, after removal of the two central oxygen atoms, shows a "perylene gap". (After Stadler 1960.)

G. ELECTRON MICROSCOPY

With the aid of a specially developed microtome technique Dawson and Follett (1959) were able to prepare sections of reactor grade graphite suitable for electron microscopy. Their sections showed, for polycrystalline graphite, a grain structure analogous to that seen by optical microscopy on polished sections of metals. The approximate linear dimensions of the grains observed (all of which had their basal planes perpendicular to the viewing direction) were 3300 Å, that is considerably greater than those (*ca* 500 Å) estimated by electron diffraction.

Metal shadowing was used to measure the thickness of the grains and produced an estimate of 150 ± 25 Å, that is a stack of 44 parallel layers. Selected area electron diffraction indicated rotational stacking faults in the grains at a frequency of about one for four layers, which agrees well with the corresponding estimate of one for six layers made by Bacon from X-ray line-broadening measurements (1958a).

The boundary region between microcrystals was narrow—50 Å or less— except at points where three or more microcrystals joined. Here clear structureless areas, possibly pores, with diameters in the range 400–800 Å were found.

Dawson and Follett found dislocations in the basal planes from Moire pattern fringes but not in the pyramidal planes, although it is unlikely that their technique would have shown these had they been present. Speculative representations of these dislocations are given by these authors as indicated in Figs 15 and 16.

Later workers (Grenall and Sosin 1960; Hennig and Kanter 1960; Williamson 1960) have confirmed the presence of dislocations in the basal plane appearing in double lines about 1000 Å apart, indicating dissociation into partials, which are attributed to thin strips of rhombohedral packing within layer plane packets.

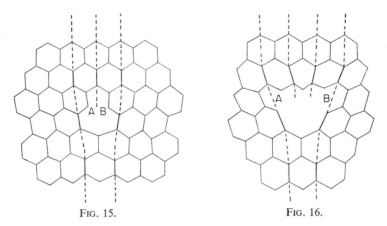

FIG. 15.   FIG. 16.

FIG. 15. Diagram showing an edge dislocation of Burgers vector [20$\bar{2}$0] in the hexagonal layer net plane in graphite. (After Dawson and Follett 1959).
  FIG. 16. Diagram showing an edge dislocation of Burgers vector [40$\bar{4}$0] in the hexagonal layer net plane in graphite. (After Dawson and Follett 1959).

H. CRYSTAL BOUNDARIES

1. *Theoretical Studies*

At the edges of layer planes we may expect (Bradburn *et al.* 1948; Coulson 1960) to find departures from the normal trigonal bonding corresponding to: (i) C—H bonds, (ii) aliphatic side-groups, and (iii) non-aromatic rings permitting packing of the planes. These three situations correspond in fact to different definitions of the plane size and it would not be surprising if different estimates were obtained by different experimental methods. Crystallographic line-broadening methods, depending on the degree of precision of the analysis, will give a lower estimate of size corresponding to periodicity of departure from the true polyaromatic plane. Chemical and microscopic methods will not detect puckering in a plane, nor distinguish readily between (i) and (ii).

2. *Hydrogen Content Measurements*

Digonskii and Krylov (1964) related the number of benzene rings in a plane, and hence the plane area, to the C/H atomic ratio, assuming all peripheries to be saturated by hydrogen atoms, and obtained the equation

$$L_a^2 = \frac{4S}{\pi} (1 + 3n(n-1)) \tag{10}$$

where L_a has its usual significance, $S(\simeq 5\cdot 2 \text{ Å}^2)$ is the area of a single benzene ring in a plane and n is the atomic C/H ratio. For large planes this reduces, to a satisfactory degree of approximation, to

$$L_a^2 = \frac{4S}{\pi} 3n^2 \qquad (11)$$

or

$$L_a \simeq 4 \cdot 5n. \qquad (12)$$

These authors obtained, by hydrogen analysis, an estimate of the crystal diameter of a soot in good agreement with the X-ray data; Cullis *et al.* (1966) similarly found results of the right order (compared with crystallographic data) for gas-phase deposited carbons, but the crystallite diameters did not vary with the C/H ratios as predicted.

For a petroleum coke heated to about 1500°C, Digonskii and Krylov (1964) estimated, by hydrogen analysis, a crystallite size of *ca* 1500 Å, which is at least an order of magnitude greater than that indicated by X-ray measurements. Mason and Owen (1966) reported a value of 50 ppm (by weight) as a typical hydrogen content for a U.K. nuclear graphite (PGA), while Redmond and Walker (1960) reported for an American nuclear graphite (TSP) a hydrogen content (estimated by degassing at 2000°C) of 0·07 cc/g (STP) equivalent to about 7 ppm. With the higher figure and the large value of n appropriate to these materials, eqn (11) leads to an estimate for L_a of approximately 6000 Å.

The latter figure, although much greater than the crystallographic estimate of about 600 Å (Mason *et al.* 1966) is of the same order as the value found (3300 Å; Dawson and Follett 1959) for U.K. nuclear graphite by electron micrography.

J. PORE STRUCTURE AND SURFACE MEASUREMENTS

1. *Density and Porosity*

As indicated above, heat-treated "soft" carbons contain gross adventitious porosity derived from the evolution of gases while the progenitor material was fluid. This porosity is not completely removed by grinding. Figure 17, due to Fialkov *et al.* (1964), shows pore size distributions for various coke types after fine grinding (*ca* 70% <50 µm, 50% <10 µm) and calcining to 1300°C.

In order to obtain a meaningful "real" density it is common to use helium as pyknometric fluid in order to obtain maximum penetration of the pores. When this was done for such "soft" carbons as those derived from PVC, polyvinyl acetate, polyacenaphthylene and dibenzanthrone (Kipling *et al.* 1964a, b; Geller and Walker 1963; Walker *et al.* 1959) in powdered form (20–40 mesh), the estimate of density approached the theoretical value for graphite as HTT was increased. For petroleum cokes (Asher 1961) the helium density is normally some 5% below the theoretical. The difference is attributed to "closed porosity". The results of Kipling *et al.* (1964b) are shown in Fig. 18.

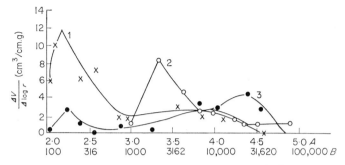

FIG. 17. Differential distribution of specific volumes ($\Delta V/\Delta \log v$) of macropores and intermediate pores in three types of heat-treated coke as a function of A, log pore radius (Å) and B, pore radius (Å). Coke: (1) pyrolysis, (2) pitch, and (3) cracking. (After Fialkov *et al.* 1964.)

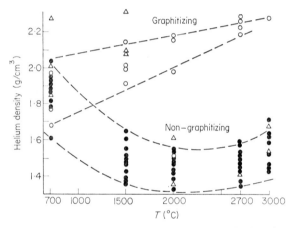

FIG. 18. Effect of temperature of preparation on the helium density of: ○, graphitizing carbons; ●, non-graphitizing carbons; △, non-graphitizing carbons from cellulose or a cellulose derivative. (After Kipling *et al.* 1964b.)

2. Origin of Closed Porosity

Mrozowski (1956) has predicted that because orientation of layer planes is only to be expected over relatively small areas, even for heat-treated soft carbons, and because the graphite crystal is inherently anisotropic in its thermal expansion, stresses will develop in polycrystalline graphites on cooling from graphitizing temperatures and that these stresses will be relieved by the formation of micro-cleavages parallel to basal planes. Such cleavages have been detected by low-power electron microscopy of commercial graphites (Sutton and Howard 1962) and the volume in them has been shown to be of the order of 5% of the total volume of the solid. Hence, if it be assumed that the entrances to some of these cracks are closed to helium atoms by cross-linked areas or disordered carbon, the existence of the closed porosity is explained, at least in part (cf. Section IIG).

The heat-treatment process with soft carbons produces a reduction in closed porosity and an increase in open porosity (Table II) which is consistent with the "straightening out" of layer planes and the removal of some of the "blockages" between near-parallel crystallites, although the fact that some closed porosity remains and the evidence from surface area measurements show that this process does not occur completely.

TABLE II

Variation of Open and Closed Pore Volumes with Temperature†

Starting material	Open pore volume (V_0) and closed pore volume (V_c) in cm^3/g for carbons prepared at:							
	700°C	1500°C	2000°C		2700°C		3000°C	
	V_0	V_c	V_0	V_c	V_0	V_c	V_0	V_c
Polyvinyl chloride	0.05_5	0.09_6	0.07_9	0.02_3	0.10_0	0.01_0	0.14_6	0.00_0
Polyvinyl acetate	0.03_4	0.03_8	0.02_1	0.06_5	0.03_7	0.01_8	—	—
Poly-acenaphthylene	0.03_8	0.04_3	0.04_4	0.02_1	$\left.\begin{array}{c}0.04_6\\0.06_5\end{array}\right.$	$\left.\begin{array}{c}0.02_7\\0.00_8\end{array}\right\}$	—	—
Dibenzanthrone	0.09_6	—	0.04_3	0.02_5	0.05_0	0.00_6	—	—

† After Kipling et al. (1964b).

Detailed studies of the microporosity of graphites by the method of small angle X-ray scattering used initially by Franklin (1950) and more recently developed by Schiller et al. (1967) confirms that the micropores are lenticular and bounded by crystallite basal planes.

3. Surface Area

The surface area (in m^2/g) of the bounding basal faces of a graphite crystallite must be

$$\frac{\pi L_a^2 \times 10^{-20}}{2Mx} \times \frac{N}{12} \simeq \frac{\pi L_a^2 \times 10^3}{4Mx} \tag{13}$$

where M is the number of layer planes in a packet, x the number of carbon atoms in a plane, L_a the plane area in Å, and N the Avogadro number.

If there are k benzene rings per plane and S (Å^2) is the area of a ring

$$\frac{\pi L_a^2}{4} \doteqdot kS. \tag{14}$$

For a large plane $x \simeq 2k$

$$\frac{\pi L_a^2}{x} = 2S \qquad (15)$$

so that surface area of packet

$$= \frac{S \times 10^3}{2M}.$$

Now $S \simeq 5 \cdot 2$ Å^2 so that the area for a single plane is 2600 m^2/g.

This figure for a single plane is in good agreement with the experimental value of 820–1200 m^2/g obtained by Boehm *et al.* (1963) for macromolecules consisting of aggregates of 2–3 layers (as estimated by X-ray) which they prepared by reduction of graphitic oxide.

For a large crystal M is about 100 according to the X-ray measurements of L_c, so that

plane surface area of packet $\simeq 25$m^2/g.

For a crystal of this size the edge area is of the same order as the plane area so that the total area is about 50 m^2/g. This is about two orders of magnitude greater than the figures recorded by Kipling *et al.* (1964b) for powdered PVC cokes heat treated to *ca* 2700°C (using krypton at 77°K as absorbate) and a BET method for estimating surface area. Also, well-established figures for commercial graphites are in the range 0·25–0·5 m^2/g. Hence, it follows that the thickness of the layer plane packet which is relevant to adsorption is much greater than that of the "crystallite" which is observed by X-ray line broadening. This is consistent with the model described above where near-parallel crystallites are separated by oriented closed micropores.

4. *Grinding Experiments*

May and Warner (1960) ground U.K. reactor-grade graphite by a combination of jaw-crushing, pin-mill grinding and ball milling for times up to 100 hr and, after leaching with nitric acid to remove contamination from the steel balls, obtained powders with surface areas (measured by BET nitrogen adsorption) of up to 11·2 m^2/g. At that point the surface area had ceased to increase. Surface area calculated from size distribution of particles measured by a micromerograph was only 0·4 m^2/g, that is substantially unchanged from the starting material.

Gregg and Hickman (1966) ground graphite powder of unstated provenance in a steel ball mill for periods up to 1300 hr. They did not attempt to leach their product to remove contamination dust from the steel balls. They found curves initially similar to those of May and Warner but after about 150 hr grinding the apparent surface area increased suddenly and reached an apparent steady state of about 500 m^2/g after about 800 hr. On the assumption that the BET method measures the plane area of the crystallites and that the gas evolved on vacuum degassing to 1000°C measures the crystallite edge area they deduced that their product consisted of crystallites with $L_a \simeq L_c \simeq 50$ Å. Since their area measurements were not checked by an independent method and since the possibility exists that the recorded areas were affected by metallic wear dust, this interpretation of their results should perhaps be treated with some reserve.

K. ELECTRONIC PROPERTIES

In the study of the structural evolution of soft carbons, their electronic properties have not been overlooked. Resistivity measurements on compacted powders are complicated by pressure dependence and wall effects, as are measurements of magnetic resistance and Hall effect. Magnetic measurements require careful purification from inorganic impurities and the unexpected discovery of paramagnetic resonance effects and their dependence on adsorbed oxygen in the mid-1950's (Ingram 1959) provided another considerable complication for a time. The position for all the electronic properties was well reviewed in 1960 by Pacault *et al.*, and Chapter III provides an up-to-date discussion. For present purposes magnetic susceptibility seems to be the most useful property and this section will be confined to it.

1. *Magnetic Susceptibility*

The primary work of the Northern Coke Research Association in the U.K. (Wynne-Jones *et al.* 1952; Adamson and Blayden 1958) and Mrozowski's school in the U.S. (Pinnick 1954, 1956; Kiive and Mrozowski 1959) showed that magnetic susceptibility is closely related to carbonization temperature, the form of the curve depending on the chemical nature of the raw material

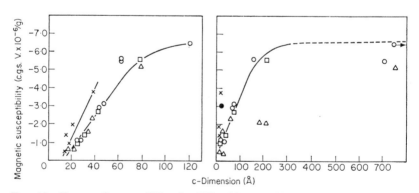

FIG. 19. Change of susceptibility (at 20°) with crystallite size. △, Dibenzanthrone carbons; □, benzene carbons; ○, butane carbons; ×, cellulose carbons; ●, polymer carbons. (a) Average layer size L_a, (b) average size of layer group L_c. (After Adamson and Blayden 1958.)

being carbonized. For soft carbons, the diamagnetic susceptibility measured at 20°C correlated well with the L_a and L_c dimensions as determined by X-ray methods, as shown in Fig. 19 from Adamson and Blayden (1958).

A more recent study (Pacault et al. 1960) of the effect on magnetic susceptibility of heat treatment of a pitch coke provides a large number of measurements which define the curve closely.

Comparison with X-ray measurements indicates that the development of the three-dimensional structure, as indicated by the appearance of (101) modifications begins, for any heat-treatment temperature, just after the susceptibility curve reaches its maximum. In terms of the Maire–Méring graphitization factor, this corresponds to $g = 0.3$.

2. Use of Magnetic Susceptibility Measurements for Kinetic Studies

A wealth of interesting kinetic information has been derived from this type of measurement (Mazza et al. 1962; Mazza 1964). Experiments were continued for 20 days at 1520°C and for shorter times at progressively higher temperatures, the experimental material being a carefully standardized pitch coke. For temperatures below 2000°C periods of five days were required for a steady value to be reached and at higher temperatures the magnetic susceptibility rose rapidly to a maximum and then declined slightly. This is attributed to growth of the layer planes at the higher temperatures at a faster rate than the three-dimensional ordering process can meet; ordering presumably becoming more difficult with larger planes.

Pacault and Gasparoux (1967) treated these measured mean susceptibilities as a simultaneous function of time and temperature in the same way as they treated L_a (cf. Section IIE), and again obtained a unique curve (Fig. 20). k_i is related to temperature of heat treatment by an Arrhenius-type plot with slope equivalent to an activation energy of 164 kcal/mol.

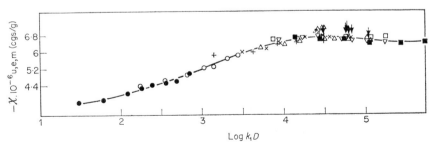

FIG. 20. Rationalized curve of mean magnetic susceptibility against "equivalent time". HTT (°C), ●, 1800; ○, 1900; +, 2000; ×, 2040; △, 2080; ▽, 2120; □, 2160; ■, 2200. (After Pacault and Gasparoux 1967.)

L. LIQUID PHASE OXIDATION STUDIES

It has long been known (Blayden and Riley 1935; Riley 1938) that well-crystallized carbons react more rapidly than poorly graphitized materials with liquid–phase oxidants. In recent years the Simon reagent (silver chromate dissolved in concentrated sulphuric acid) has been used (Oberlin and Méring 1961, 1964) as a solvent for carbons and the rate constant of solution has been found to be a powerful diagnostic tool for exploring structural differences. Oberlin and Méring found (1964), at 80°C, rate constants of about 10^{-1} min^{-1} for natural or artificial graphite, and 6×10^{-4} min^{-1} for ungraphitized soft carbon (pitch coke heat treated to 1000°C). During the transformation from the non-graphitized state to the graphitized state they found evidence for an intermediate state with rate constant 2×10^{-3} min^{-1}. Finally, the value for fully heat-treated material giving the fast reaction was found to be compounded of two separate rate constants.

Oberlin and Méring associated these states with four situations of the layer planes in decreasing order of rate constant, as follows:

(i) Distorted layer planes, as in turbostratic carbons (weakly diamagnetic).
(ii) Distorted layer planes, as in turbostratic carbons (but strongly diamagnetic).
(iii) Layer planes, free of interstitials (distortions) on one face.
(iv) Layer planes, free of interstitials (distortions) on both faces.

They found the proportions of these four types in partly graphitized soft carbons (that is the same pitch coke heat treated to different temperatures) to be in excellent agreement with the degree of graphitization as measured by X-ray line-broadening methods and with magnetic susceptibility measurements of other workers (Pacault *et al.* 1960) on the same materials. The technique has also been applied with apparent success, to irradiated graphites (Oberlin *et al.* 1964), metallurgical cokes (Rappeneau *et al.* 1964), and carbon blacks (Rappeneau *et al.* 1966).

M. LAMELLAR COMPOUND FORMATION

The formation of lamellar compounds between graphite and various electron donors or acceptors (for example potassium, oxygen, halogens) has been known for many years and the subject is discussed very fully by Ubbelohde and Lewis (1960) in their book. It is known that non-graphitic carbons ("soft" and "hard" alike) fail to form such compounds with oxygen or potassium (Maire 1951). Considerable importance therefore has been attached to the observation (Maire and Méring 1959) that bromine does not form a lamellar compound with a graphitizing carbon when the latter is in its ungraphitized state, although it does so readily after graphitizing. Since after graphitizing the *d*-spacing is smaller, this is taken by the authors to indicate some fundamental difference between the layer plane in the graphitized and ungraphitized states, the latter being in this sense analogous to the non-graphitizing carbons in which the entry of bromine is inhibited by cross-links. It is difficult to accept the idea of cross-links in a graphitizing carbon but the possibility of holes, leading to out of plane atoms, or of isolated aliphatic groups, within holes, is perhaps less difficult to imagine.

N. CHEMICAL RELATIONSHIPS

1. *Nature of the Layer Plane in Carbons*

Organic molecules consisting wholly or partly of condensed benzene nuclei are well known and bear an obvious resemblance to the layer planes of the classical model of the graphite crystal. Detailed study of such condensed structures confirms the similarities with graphite. Thus, in such structures the mean C—C bond length has for all practical purposes reached that of graphite for molecules containing more than fifty atoms (Bradburn *et al.* 1948) and the resonance energy changes with increasing size as expected theoretically (Pullman 1959). Such compounds show semi-conducting properties (Akamatu and Inokuchi 1950; Eley *et al.* 1953, 1955); although the electrical conductivity is much lower than the in-plane conductivity of the graphite crystal (Coulson *et al.* 1959) it increases as the size increases, the resistivity changing from 10^{19} ohm cm for anthranthrone to 10^{10} ohm cm for isoviolanthrone.

2. *Breakdown of Lamellar Compounds*

The layer plane has been "isolated" from graphite by Boehm *et al.* (1963) who prepared graphite oxide from a graphite of unstated origin, dispersed it as a very dilute suspension in caustic soda, and subsequently reduced it with hydrazine to form what were believed to be macromolecules consisting of a very few graphitic layers. Electron microscopy indicated the presence of wrinkles in these layers while X-ray analysis indicated an apparent "layer diameter", which in this case was clearly an average distance between wrinkles, of 150 Å, much less than the electron micrographically observed layer dimension. The graphite oxide layers before reduction were hydro-aromatic rather than aromatic, and some carbon atoms had hydroxyl and (probably chelated) ether groups as well as enol and keto groups. Neither the oxidation nor the reduction process involved any loss of carbon, so that the reduced product and, presumably, the original graphite layer, were taken to consist entirely of carbon atoms.

3. *Aromatic Hydrocarbons Forming Soft Carbons*

The condensed polyaromatic layer is already present as a constituent of the progenitors of many soft carbons. For example, coal tar pitch is believed (Wood and Phillips 1955) to contain a range of molecules with from about seven benzene rings in the lighter fractions (light petroleum extracts) to perhaps three groups of 10–15 joined by other structures such as coumarone rings or aliphatic bridges in the heavy (quinoline soluble) fractions. It seems that in these groups the arrangement of the rings is neither linear nor completely compact, so that a typical structure might have an L_a dimension corresponding on average to about four rings, that is about 11 Å.

Walker and Weinstein (1967) have demonstrated that the carbons formed from charring anthracene or phenanthrene (or their mixtures) in sealed bombs at 550°C yield "soft" carbons as judged by the standard criteria of surface area, density, magnetic susceptibility and crystal parameter changes on heat treatment.

Ubbelohde and Lewis (1960) noted that the separation of pairs of parallel fused ring molecules in the hydrocarbon molecular crystals decreases from 3·52–3·45 Å on passing from pyrene (four fused rings) to Ovalene (ten fused rings) and that such pairs are tilted with respect to neighbouring pairs at angles varying from 40–60° (see also Stadler and Thomson 1958). The existence of such tilts is of considerable interest in relation to the discussion in Section IIF. These authors also note the possibility of the presence of "holes" in carbon hexagon networks corresponding to broken bonds or missing carbon atoms and these have also been postulated for coal vitrains (Diamond and Hirsch 1958). The model proposed by the latter authors is shown in Fig. 21. A scheme for the synthesis of such networks containing holes has been proposed by Ruland (1965). Again the reference is clear to the discrepancies between the crystallographic parameter L_a and other estimates of plane diameter.

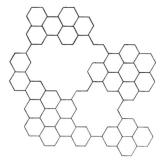

FIG. 21. Perfect molecules containing holes. (After Diamond and Hirsch 1958.)

4. *Polyvinyl Chloride*

Polyvinyl chloride has been extensively studied (Winslow *et al.* 1956; Gilbert and Kipling 1962b) as a comparatively simple known molecule which can be carbonized. The initial stages of this process involve the evolution of HCl and the formation of a residue with a conjugated polyene links, a natural precursor of an aromatic structure. In fact infrared spectroscopy (Gilbert and Kipling 1962b) indicates the development of aromatic links below 450°C and differential thermal analysis shows a clear exotherm beginning near 350°C which is attributed (Kipling *et al.* 1966c) to cyclization.

5. *The Vitrains*

The coal tar pitches are derived from (Volkmann and Russell 1962; Chistyakov 1965), and bear a close physical and chemical resemblance to, bituminous coal, the structure of which is therefore relevant. In these materials the condensed ring structure has been established by chemical (Van Krevelen and Chermin 1954) and crystallographic (Diamond and Hirsch 1958) studies. Similar structures predominate in the heavy petroleum residues used for the manufacture of petroleum coke.

III. HARD CARBONS

A. CRYSTALLOGRAPHY

1. *d-Spacing and Crystal Height*

These materials, after heat-treatment to about 1000°C, show d-spacings about 3·7 Å. The changes in crystal height on heat treatment are in general small (but see below). A stack height of two to three layers at HTT = 1000°C is typical for polyvinylidene chloride char (Franklin 1950; Greenhalgh *et al.* 1966) or cellulose carbon (Davidson and Losty 1966; Losty and Blakelock 1966) and on heat treatment up to 3000°C this does not grow beyond about 10 layers (Franklin 1951a).

However, it has been found (Yokokawa *et al.* 1967) that typical "hard" carbons (for example cross-linked polystyrene/divinyl benzene copolymers carbonized at 800°C) when heat treated in the presence of up to 20% copper (as copper oxide) develop sharp 002 lines in the X-ray diffractogram very quickly at temperatures *ca* 1500°C. The line position and width indicate a d-spacing of *ca* 3·37 Å and a c-dimension of 400–1000 Å. The amount of such material increased at a measurable rate as heat treatment was continued for periods up to 3 hr at the fixed temperature, and was followed by measurements of the intensity of the (002) lines in comparison with those obtained under similar experimental conditions with coal tar pitch. Rate measurements showed apparently first-order kinetics in relation to copper concentration. It was assumed that the copper oxide was able to break the aliphatic cross-linking bonds separating the small aromatic clusters and permit them to order. A similar explanation has been proposed (Noda and Inagaki 1962, 1964; Noda *et al.* 1965) for the apparent accelerating effect on crystal growth of oxygen and carbon dioxide in the atmosphere during graphitization.

The development of sharp (002) lines is reminiscent of Franklin's observation (1951b) of small amounts of very perfect graphitic structure in a heat-treated non-graphitizing carbon which she attributed to the effect of internal stress on those few clusters which might be freed by normal thermal processes.

2. *Layer Plane Diameter*

For hard carbons this value is also small. For hexachlorobenzene carbon it was found that the L_a diameter remained constant at about 10 Å (Gibson *et al.* 1956; Blayden *et al.* 1945; Franklin 1951a) for all heat-treatment temperatures between 500°C and 1200°C. Gibson *et al.* (1956) in fact believed this carbon to have a structure outside the normal classification, although the evidence has not found general acceptance. For cellulose carbon the layer plane diameter saturated at about 32 Å and 1200°C.

Franklin's measurements (1951b) were continued to heat-treatment temperatures of 3000°C for "hard" carbons (polyvinylidene chloride, sugar charcoal hexachlorobenzene and low rank coals), none of which reached an L_a of more than about 50 Å, which size had already been exceeded at 1720°C, with no sign of saturation, for the "soft" carbons, polyvinyl chloride char and petroleum coke.

3. *Orientation of Crystallites*

The X-ray photographs of hard carbons also indicate that the layer-plane stacks are normally randomly oriented within the body. However, for carbons derived from cellulose fibres comparison of the X-ray diffraction pattern of the original cellulose with that of the residue after heat-treatment to 2800°C, consideration of the shrinkage of the fibres on heat treatment, and electron micrography of the heat-treated fibre suggest (Bacon and Tang 1964) a direct relation between the morphology of the original fibre and that of the resultant layer plane system.

B. CHEMISTRY OF CRYSTALLITE FORMATION

The comparison of the pyrolysis behaviour of polyvinylidene chloride $[(CH_2—CCl_2—)_n]$, which gives a "hard" carbon, and polyvinyl chloride $[(—CH_2—CHCl—)_n]$, which gives a "soft" carbon, has been of great value in understanding the structural differences between carbons. The former loses one molecule of HCl at about 250°C (Winslow *et al.* 1956) giving rise to olefinic linkages which are believed to cross-link to aromatic structures through a Diels–Alder reaction, thus giving a high yield of solid carbon. There results a disordered structure in which small condensed layer planes are rotated at various angles around aliphatic bonds. The cross-links therefore behave as a rigid skeleton, of which the members are separated by pores, across which layer planes cannot fuse. Thus Franklin found (1950) for poly-vinylidene chloride that "the graphite-like layers are contained in small groups or particles having a mean separation of about 26 Å. About 65% of the carbon from PVDC was in the form of layers 16 ± 1 Å in diameter; about 55% of these were in pairs of parallel layers and about 45% showed no mutual orientation". The char formed from cellulose may be regarded as a typical "hard" carbon. This material also carbonizes with the formation of aromatic structures as first demonstrated (Smith and Howard 1937) by oxidation of the char with alkaline permanganate and decarboxylation to give hydro-carbons, including recovered benzene, diphenyl and tarry residue.

Detailed studies by Tang and Bacon (1964) of the pyrolysis of cellulose fibres and films up to 500°C, and by Davidson and Losty (1966) on "slip-cast" suspensions of cellulose, have made use of weight and dimensional changes and analysis of the evolved gases and residue (the latter by infrared spectro-scopy, elemental analysis and X-ray diffraction). Degradation schemes are postulated in which the breaking of C—O and C—C bonds in the rings at 240–400°C leads to four-carbon chain residues from each cellulose ring. These polymerize at about 400°C upwards to polyaromatic planes which cross-link at 550°C.

Although, as noted above, polyvinyl chloride normally pyrolyses to give a "soft" carbon, its carbonization in presence of oxygen at 250°C gives a residue of which the infrared spectrum shows (Gilbert and Kipling 1962b) an absence of conjugated double bonds and the presence of carbonyl groups and other oxygen-containing structures, probably derived from intermediate peroxides (Gilbert and Kipling 1962a). Most of the oxygen is lost by 600°C but its effect remains since the residues at 700–900°C are greater in yield, and harder and denser than those prepared in the absence of oxygen. These appear to be highly cross-linked "chars".

C. PORE STRUCTURE MEASUREMENTS

1. *Density*

For a "hard" carbon densities would be expected to be lower than the crystal density of graphite. If the pyknometric fluid used for the density determination cannot penetrate into the spaces in the three-dimensional network, the density will correspond, to a first approximation, to the apparent density of a randomly-packed bed of spheres of real density $(3 \cdot 35/3 \cdot 44) \times 2 \cdot 26$. Such a bed will contain about 40% voids so that the density should be about $1 \cdot 3$ g/cm^3.

Experimental data (Dacey and Thomas 1954; Kipling *et al.* 1964b; Marsh and Wynne-Jones 1964; Greenhalgh *et al.* 1966; Kipling *et al.* 1966d) show, for a wide range of hard carbons, a fall in density followed by a rise. Figure 18 shows typical results from Kipling *et al.* (1964b) and a comparison with "soft" carbons. The rise is probably to be explained by the removal of blockages obstructing entry of helium to the pore system at the highest temperatures. The sharp distinction between the two classes of carbons is clear, confirming the earlier observation of Franklin (1951b) and the values found are in reasonable agreement with expectation.

2. Surface Area

Surface area estimates for "hard" carbons are not simply interpretable. The main reason is that wide variations in the experimental data, about two orders of magnitude, occur because of molecular sieve effects (see Section IIIC 3) between the values measured by different absorbates (Kipling and Wilson 1960; Marsh and Wynne-Jones 1964; Lamond and Marsh 1964; Atkins 1965; Badami *et al.* 1966). These differences, and the way they vary with heat-treatment temperature, are themselves strongly indicative of a rigid cross-linked structure relatively stable to heat treatment (Marsh and Wynne-Jones 1964). An estimate from the crystallographic data of Section A above gives a value of the general order of 1000 m^2/g. The maximum values obtained experimentally for heat-treatment temperatures of about 700°C are in the region of 500 m^2/g. As the heat-treatment temperature is increased to 3000°C these fall, often to about the same level as those for the "soft" carbons, but parallel density and adsorption (Dubinin 1962) measurements indicate that this is due to pore closure rather than to crystallite growth. The micropore structure of PVDC char, when studied by a combination of electron microscopy and adsorption techniques, has been shown (Bailey and Everett 1966) to trace the pattern of the decomposition of the original PVDC polymers at temperatures below its softening point. Activation by partial oxidation removes blockages from sucrose chars carbonized at 700°C as is shown (Balwant Rai Puri and Bansal 1964) by the disappearance of the difference between adsorption and small-angle X-ray scattering estimates of micropore volume.

3. Pore Diameters

The estimates of pore diameter for a 700°C PVDC char obtained by adsorption methods (Marsh and Wynne-Jones 1964; Dacey and Thomas 1954; Pierce *et al.* 1949) are about 10–20 Å, in agreement with the small-angle scattering measurements of Franklin (1950) which gave a value of 16 Å. More highly cross-linked polymers give chars with smaller pore sizes, as expected, and their use has been proposed as molecular sieves (Kipling and Wilson 1960; Walker *et al.* 1965; Dacey and Thomas 1954; Lamond *et al.* 1965) with pore sizes of about 5 Å.

IV. CARBON BLACKS

The preceding discussion has confined itself to the "soft" and "hard" carbons. There remain, however, the carbon blacks which are of special interest as they were some of the first materials to be studied, and because they are sometimes considered (Steward and Davidson 1958) to be intermediate in character between the "soft" and the "hard" carbons. Discussion of the crystallography of such materials is best preceded by a consideration of their preparation.

A. CHEMISTRY OF FORMATION

The early stages in the formation of carbon blacks have been studied in relation to the chemistry of flames (Parker and Wolfhard 1950) and in studies of the carbonization of benzene, naphthalene, anthracene and other members of the series at temperatures in the region of 500°C (Conroy *et al.* 1959; Kinney 1954, 1956; Kinney and Slysh 1960). Benzene appears to form diphenyl as a first step while bianthryl shows a similar kinetic behaviour to anthracene. The subsequent stages of growth involve thermal hydrogen transfer reactions (Kinney 1954), as has been demonstrated by differential thermal analysis and supporting chemical studies (Lewis and Edstrom 1962), and these have been followed in detail in the temperature range 200–1200°C by X-ray methods (Ruland 1965). At high temperatures (>1200°C) the reaction appears to proceed differently, through acetylene and acetylenyl radicals (Kinney and Slysh 1960; Carley-Macauly and Mackenzie 1962). The possible trapping of free radicles would explain the high paramagnetic activity found (Szwarc 1954; Matsen 1959) in low-temperature carbons.

With increasing size the molecules eventually reach the stage when they condense out into the liquid phase as droplets (Parker and Wolfhard 1950), the basal planes of the eventual carbon crystal being tangential to the surface of the sphere.

B. CRYSTALLOGRAPHY

The history of the material, as noted above, would suggest the initial presence of layer planes and the existence of a fluid state during carbonization so that one would expect the carbon to be "soft". Of many crystallographic studies (Biscoe and Warren 1942; Schaeffer *et al.* 1953; Kmetko 1956; Houska and Warren 1954; Warren 1956; Steward and Davidson 1958; Austin 1959) those giving the results of Table III from Warren (1956) are typical and indicate some inhibition of crystal growth.

The development of a graphitic structure has been demonstrated by electron microscopy (Kmetko 1956; Kaye 1965), Fig. 22 being an idealized sketch of the resulting structure. It is believed that crystal growth is limited by the initial size of the droplet since crystal size has been found not to grow beyond about one-third of the particle diameter for a range of particle sizes (Pinnick 1952; Steward and Davidson 1958). Confirmatory results were obtained by liquid phase oxidation (Rappenau *et al.* 1966).

TABLE III

Numerical Values for an (FT) Black Heated 2 hr
at Various Temperatures

T (°C)	L_c (Å)	P_1	L_a (Å)
2000	59	0·03	97
2300	72	0·25	129
2500	78	0·33	136
2700	88	0·35	132

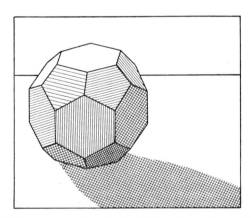

FIG. 22. A polyhedron representing the probable shape of graphitized carbon black particles.

C. SURFACE AREA

Surface areas have been measured by many workers; they vary considerably according to the type of black and values in the region of 300 m²/g are common. The quantities of oxygen (as CO, CO_2 or their sum) desorbed under vacuum heating are linearly related (Balwant Rai Puri and Bansal 1964) to the BET surface area (measured with nitrogen); different slopes are obtained for channel blacks, furnace blacks and colour blacks, but degassing even up to 1200°C does not remove all the hydrogen and the amount of hydrogen evolved does not correlate with the amounts of evolved oxygen.

Schaeffer *et al.* (1953) found, for a range of blacks with BET surface areas (measured with nitrogen) varying from 15–115 m²/g, a consistent drop of about 10% in area after heat treatment to 2700°C, which was attributed to a decrease in the surface roughness of the particle (as expected from the appearance of polyhedral formation as seen on the electron micrographs).

V. UNORGANIZED CARBON

This term will be used to describe carbon not incorporated in layer planes, but present in aliphatic linkages.

Carbons which have not been heat-treated above 1000°C may contain significant proportions of such material which can be detected in the X-ray diffractogram by analysis of the low angle scattering. Franklin (1950) found that 35% of the carbon atoms in a char prepared by carbonizing poly-vinylidene chloride for 2 hr in oxygen-free nitrogen at 1000°C were in this form. In a later piece of work (1951b) she used the low angle scattering technique to measure the proportion of unorganized carbon in chars prepared from sucrose, polyvinyl chloride, polyvinylidene chloride and hexachloro-benzene while at the same time determining the layer plane size (L_a) by analysis of the shape of the (11) band. Franklin found an inverse linear relationship between L_a and the proportion of unorganized carbon, the former increasing linearly from 13 to 22 Å while the latter fell from 42 to 8%. The results for polyvinyl chloride char were particularly significant since this material alone of those examined was carbonized at two different temperatures (1000°C and 2000°C) and both points fell close to the straight line. Hence, for this material at this stage of crystal development, material recorded by Franklin's technique as unorganized carbon was absorbed into the layer-planes as HTT was increased and had virtually disappeared when the planes had grown to 25 Å. Similar behaviour has been recorded for a commercial polymer carbon (Yamada *et al.* 1964).

Green (1960) has stressed Mrozowski's view (1956) of carbons as semi-crystalline polymers, in which polymeric chains may run through crystalline and amorphous regions. If chains containing more than one carbon atom (which would appear as unorganized carbon) link crystalline regions, profound effects are to be expected on mechanical and other properties.

VI. HETERO-ATOMS

It would be expected that small atoms from boron to oxygen in the Periodic Table and sulphur might be incorporated into layer planes by analogy with their existence in simple heterocyclic ring compounds. It is known that 1–2% of boron can be stably incorporated into graphite (Ubbelohde 1966). Baraniecki *et al.* (1958) have reviewed a large amount of work on hetero-atom carbon compounds containing oxygen, sulphur and nitrogen but as pointed out by Ubbelohde (1966) the literature is generally deficient in knowledge of the effects of high heat treatment temperatures which sometimes require analytical methods capable of dealing with hetero-atoms at the level of parts per million.

A. LOW-TEMPERATURE CARBONS

Carbons prepared at temperatures of 1000°C or less may contain several per cent of such foreign atoms, for example the incorporation of oxygen into a condensed ring structure has been suggested (Schmidt *et al.* 1959) in the model, shown in Fig. 23, for carbon suboxide polymer (the "red carbon" of Klemenc *et al.* 1934) and a similar model has been suggested for the carbon sulphide polymer $(C_2S_3)_n$. Smaller proportions of oxygen, similarly present as cross-links, may account for the fact that traces of oxygen in the atmosphere

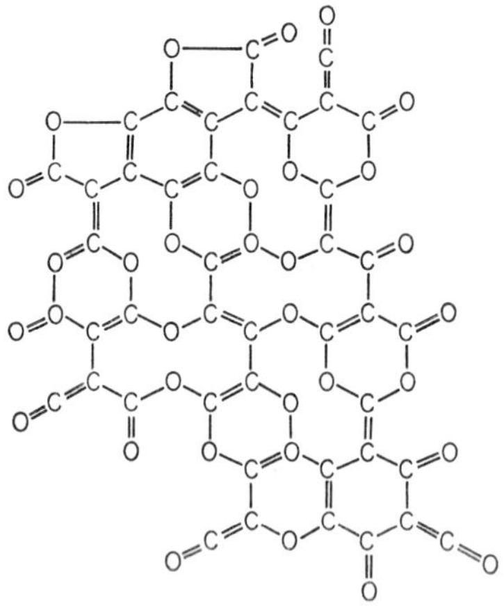

FIG. 23. Model of a layer formed by polymerization of 15 carbon suboxide molecules. (After Schmidt *et al.* 1959.)

of a baking furnace are reported (Lauer and Bonsted 1963) to increase the yield of coke from the binder and to increase the strength of small electrodes. The oxygen content of Japanese "glassy carbon" has been stated (Kakinoki 1965) to be 5–6% and it has been suggested that the oxygen atoms may provide links between tetrahedral and graphite zones in the structure. Similarly, polyacrylonitrile carbonizes to give a product containing heterocyclic nitrogen (Burlant and Parsons 1956) which, at HTT 700°C, contains 18·4% nitrogen (Gilbert et al. 1962c). Uncalcined pitch and petroleum cokes (HTT ≃ 450°C) contain hydrogen, oxygen, nitrogen and sulphur at the level of a few per cent by weight.

B. EFFECT OF HEAT TREATMENT

Gilbert et al. (1962c) noted that the nitrogen from their carbonized poly-acrylonitrile was only slowly lost as HTT was raised to 1500°C. Detailed studies have been made by French workers (Millet et al. 1963) of the loss of hydrogen, oxygen, nitrogen and sulphur from various cokes on heat treatment. Hydrogen is normally reduced to less than 0·1% by the time HTT reaches 1500°C, although more sensitive techniques (Mason and Owen 1966) give hydrogen contents of 40–50 ppm in commercial nuclear graphite (heat-treatment temperature about 2700°C). The other elements are normally retained to higher temperatures, sulphur in particular being present at about the 0·1% level up to heat treatment temperatures of about 2000°C, and still present at the level of 200 ppm (Julietti and Riley 1966) in commercial graphite.

The sulphur found in commercial cokes and the manner of its release are of considerable technical importance because its evolution at temperatures above 1500°C leads to the swelling and cracking of carbon blocks during graphitizing ("puffing").

It has been noted (Millet et al. 1963) that the temperature at which the hetero-atom concentration drops to low levels (<0·1%) is close to that at which three-dimensional ordering begins in many carbons and other properties of the carbon change rapidly. It has therefore been suggested (Millet et al. 1963; Burland and Parsons 1956) that the loss of hetero-atoms, with resultant generation of free valencies and consequent interaction between neighbouring layer planes or crystallites, plays a significant role in the evolution of the structure. The reported dependence (Hutcheon and Jenkins 1966) of the strongly structure-sensitive property, thermal expansion coefficient, on hetero-atom content of the coke source material points in the same direction.

The graphitizability of PVC/sulphur mixtures has been studied as a function of the amount of added sulphur (Kipling et al. 1966c). Up to 2·5% addition, the carbonization residue remains graphitic, as judged by measurement of the X-ray parameters after heating to 2700°C, by density measurements and by polarized light microscopy. For high sulphur additions the carbonized product becomes progressively less readily graphitized, and for a starting mixture containing 9% sulphur has the typical characteristics of a non-graphitizing carbon. The measurements are interpreted as due to the formation, below 250°C, of cross-links through sulphur atoms from the free radicles formed by dehydrochlorination, the effective temperature for this latter process being lowered by a separate catalytic effect of sulphur. The cross-links thus inhibit the formation of large aromatic residues and also, by increasing the viscosity of the material, the re-orientation process which otherwise leads eventually to graphite-like crystallites.

VII. SUMMARY

This review suggests that, important as the crystallographic approach has been in the development of the subject, the complementary evidence from other lines of research is essential to a complete understanding of the structure of carbons. It seems to be well established that, in one respect, namely the layer diameter of the crystallites in graphitizing carbons, the X-ray evidence has been definitely misleading. To the evidence from microscopy, surface studies and other directions, must be added the recent estimate of 2000 Å for layer diameter in artificial graphites by Taylor, Gilchrist and Poston (1968), from thermal conductivity measurements. All these estimates yield values several times higher than the X-ray determination and lend support, at least in general terms, to Maire and Méring's hypothesis (1960) that as far as the layer planes are concerned, the process of graphitization is one of smoothing out asperities in a wrinkled plane rather than two-dimensional polymerization.

Similarly, in the c-axis direction the evidence suggests that we must think of mosaic limits several times thicker than the 60 or so planes suggested by the crystallographic measurements, the crystallographic packets being marked off by imperfections where small amounts of unorganized carbon or foreign atoms seal off closed cavities.

Given mosaic packets of this size we can see the possibility that their dimensions are controlled by the gross geometry of the pore structure present in the carbonizing fluid phase in a kind of inversion of the situation with carbon black. While in the latter case it is the size of the droplet that limits crystal growth, in the true "soft" carbons it is perhaps the radius of the pore which provides the limitation. These considerations lead to a model for a typical "soft" carbon (in the fully heat-treated state) along the lines of Fig. 24(a). The conventional crystallographic model for carbon blacks is shown in Fig. 24(b), taken from Kmetko (1956), and this is to be compared with the model of a particle indicated by Fig. 22.

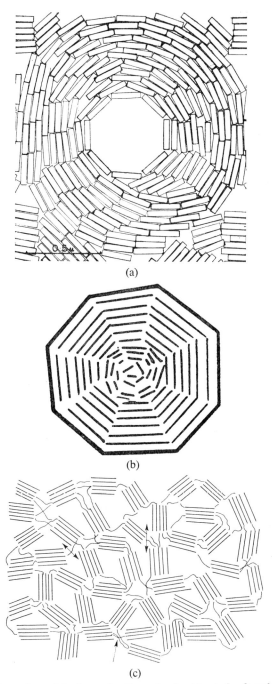

(a)

(b)

(c)

Fig. 24(a). Schematic model of a section through a heat-treated soft carbon. The mosaic blocks have approximate dimensions 4000 Å × 800 Å and the larger pores have diameters *ca* 10,000 Å. (b) Schematic arrangement of crystallites in a heat-treated thermal black body. (c) Schematic representation of the structure of a non-graphitizing carbon. (After Franklin 1951b).

In the hard carbons, also, as seen clearly by Franklin (1950) it is the porosity of dimensions of the order of 10–20 Å which limits crystal growth. In this case the porosity is created by the loss of volatile material, originally forming the "flesh" around the rigid three-dimensional cross-linked skeleton held together probably by aliphatic C—C bonds. The model broadly in keeping with the evidence is indicated in Fig. 24(c), due to Franklin (1951b).

Thus a full insight into the structure of the various types of polycrystalline carbon requires the best possible consideration of the starting materials, the nature of the chemical changes which they undergo, and the interaction of these chemical changes with the voids they produce to give a carbon skeleton. The subsequent changes on further heat treatment, which have been studied by such a wide range of physical techniques, then become relatively easy to understand.

As so often happens in technology, the scientific studies have nearly caught up with the empirical tradition. From the early days of his industry, the carbon manufacturer has recognized the importance of subtle variations in his raw materials as his primary weapon in controlling the properties of his products. This point will be developed in Chapter II.

REFERENCES

Adamson, A. F. and Blayden, H. E. (1958). *1st SCI*† 28.
Adamson, A. F. and Blayden, H. E. (1959). *3rd USC*† 147.
Akamatu, H. and Inokuchi, H. (1950). *J. chem. Phys.* **18**, 810.
Akamatu, H. and Kuroda, H. (1960). *4th USC* 355.
Akamatu, H., Inokuchi, H., Takahashi, H., Matsunaga, Y. (1956). *Bull. chem. Soc. Japan* **29**, 574.
Asher, R. C. (1961). *UKAEA Report AERE M/946.*
Atkins, J. H. (1965). *Carbon* **3**, 299.
Austin, A. E. (1959). *3rd USC* 389.
Bacon, G. E. (1951). *Acta crystallogr.* **4**, 558.
Bacon, G. E. (1952). *Acta crystallogr.* **5**, 392.
Bacon, G. E. (1956). *J. appl. Chem.* **6**, 477.
Bacon, G. E. (1958a). *UKAEA Report AERE M/R2702.*
Bacon, G. E. (1958b). *1st SCI* 183.
Bacon, R. and Tang, M. M. (1964). *Carbon* **2**, 221.
Badami, D. V., Campbell, C., Davy, A. D. and Lindsay, M. J. (1966). *2nd SCI* 48.
Bailey, A. and Everett, D. H. (1966). *Nature, London* **211**, 1082.
Balwant Rai Puri and Bansal, R. C. (1964). *Carbon* **1**, 451.
Baraniecki, C., Riley, H. L. and Streeter, E. (1958). *1st SCI* 283.
Bernal, J. D. (1924). *Proc. R. Soc.* **A106**, 749.
Beutell, M., Fitzer, E., Gain, R. and Vohler, O. (1963). *5th USC*, **2**, 319.
Biscoe, J. and Warren, B. E. (1942). *J. appl. Phys.* **13**, 364.
Blayden, H. E. and Riley, H. L. (1935). *J. Soc. chem. Ind., Lond.* **54**, 159T.
Blayden, H. E., Gibson, J. and Riley, H. L. (1945). *Inst. Fuel, Wartime Bull.* 117.

† See note at end of References, p. 48.

Boehm, H. P., Clauss, A., Fischer, G. and Hofmann, U. (1962). *5th USC* **1**, 73.
Bouraoui, A. (1960). Quoted by Méring and Maire, 1960.
Bouraoui, A. and Méring, J. (1964). *Carbon* **1**, 465.
Bowman, J. C. (1956). *1st and 2nd USC* 59.
Bowman, J. C., Krumhansl, J. A. and Meers, J. T. (1958), *1st SCI* 52.
Bradburn, H., Coulson, C. A. and Rushbrooke, G. S. (1948). *Proc. R. Soc., Edin.,* **62**, 336.
Brooks, J. D. and Taylor, G. H. (1965). *Carbon* **3**, 185.
Burlant, W. J. and Parson, J. L. (1956). *J. Polym. Sci.* **22**, 249.
Carley-Macauly, K. M. and Mackenzie, M. (1963). *5th USC* **2**, 449.
Cerutti, M., Uebersfeld, J., Millet, J. and Parisot, J. (1960). *J. Chim. phys.* **57**, 907.
Chistyakov, A. N. (1965). *Coke Chem. U.S.S.R.* **6**, 55.
Conroy, J. S., Slysh, R. S., Murphy, D. B. and Kinney, C. R. (1959). *3rd USC* 395.
Coulson, C. A. (1960). *4th USC* 218.
Coulson, C. A., Schaad, L. J. and Burnelle, L. (1959). *3rd USC* 27.
Cullis, C. F., Presland, A. E. B., Read, I. A. and Trimm, D. L. (1966). *2nd SCI* 195.
Dacey, J. R. and Thomas, D. G. (1954). *Trans. Faraday Soc.* **50**, 740.
Davidson, H. W. and Losty, H. H. W. (1966). *2nd SCI* 20.
Dawson, I. M. and Follett, E. A. C. (1959). *Proc. R. Soc.* **A253**, 390.
Diamond, R. and Hirsch, P. B. (1958). *1st SCI* 197.
Digonskii, V. V. and Krylov, V. N. (1964). *J. appl. Chem. USSR* **33**, 725.
Dubinin, M. M. (1962). *5th USC* **1**, 81.
Eeles, W. T. and Wilson, A. J. C. (1965). *Nature, Lond.* **205**, 66.
Eley, D. D. and Parfitt, G. D. (1955). *Trans. Faraday Soc.* **51**, 1529.
Eley, D. D., Parfitt, G. D., Perry, M. J., Taysum, D. H. (1953). *Trans. Faraday Soc.* **49**, 79.
Ergun, S. (1968). *In* "Chemistry and Physics of Carbon" (P. L. Walker, Jr., ed.), Vol. 3, pp. 211–288. Arnold, London.
Everett, D. H. and Redman, E. (1963). *J. chem. Soc.* **91**.
Fair, F. V. and Collins, F. M. (1962). *5th USC* **1**, 503.
Fialkov, A. S., Gumilevskaya, G. P. and Ogareva, N. N. (1964a). *J. appl. Chem. USSR* **37**, 1976.
Fialkov, A. S., Gumilevskaya, G. P., Smirnov, B. N., Ogareva, N. N. and Petakhova, R. P. (1964b). *Zh. fiz. Khim.* **38**, 1325.
Fischbach, D. B. (1963). *Nature, Lond.* **200**, 1281.
Fitzer, E., Fritz, W. and Overhoff, D. (1966). *2nd SCI* 144.
Franklin, R. E. (1950). *Acta crystallogr.* **3**, 107.
Franklin, R. E. (1951a). *Acta crystallogr.* **4**, 253.
Franklin, R. E. (1951b). *Proc. R. Soc.* **A209**, 197.
Geller, I. and Walker, P. L., (1963). *5th USC* **2**, 471.
Gibson, J. Holohan, M. and Riley, H. L. (1956). *J. chem. Soc.* **456**.
Gilbert, J. B. and Kipling, J. J. (1962a). *Fuel* **41**, 249.
Gilbert, J. B. and Kipling, J. J. (1962b). *Fuel* **41**, 493.
Gilbert, J. B., Kipling, J. J., McEnaney, B. and Sherwood, J. N. (1962c). *Polymer* **3**, 1.
Green, (1960). *4th USC* 497.
Greenhalgh, E., Miles, B. J., Redman, E. and Sharman, S. A. (1966). *2nd SCI* 405.
Gregg, S. J. and Hickman, J. (1966). *2nd SCI* 424.
Grenall, A. and Sosin, A. (1960). *4th USC* 371.
Grossman, A. (1958). *1st SCI* 132.

Hennig, G. R. and Kanter, M. A. (1960). *4th USC* 141.
Hofmann, U. and Wilm, D. (1936). *Z. Elektrochem.* **42,** 504.
Hong, K. and Mrozowski, S. (1955). *Phys. Rev.* **98,** 1565.
Houska, C. R. and Warren, B. E. (1954). *J. appl. Phys.* **25,** 1503.
Hutcheon, J. M. and Beirne, T. (1956). *1st/2nd USC* 167.
Hutcheon, J. M. and Jenkins, M. J. (1966). *2nd SCI* 433.
Ihnatowicz, Maria, Chiche, P., Devuit, J., Pregermain, S. and Tournant, R. (1966). *Carbon* **4,** 41.
Ingram, D. J. E. (1959). *3rd USC* 93.
Julietti, R. J. and Riley, D. L. (1966). *2nd SCI* 86.
Kakinoki, J. (1965). *Acta crystallogr.* **18,** 578.
Kaye, G. (1965). *Carbon* **2,** 413.
Kiive, P. and Mrozowski, S. (1959). *3rd USC* 165.
Kinney, C. R. (1954). *In* "Chemistry of Hydrocarbons" (B. T. Brooks, ed.), Vol. 2, p. 113. Reinhold, New York.
Kinney, C. R. (1956). *1st/2nd USC* 83.
Kinney, C. R. and Slysh, R. S. (1960). *4th USC* 301.
Kipling, J. J. and Shooter, P. V. (1966a). *Carbon* **4,** 1.
Kipling, J. J. and Shooter, P. V. (1966b). *2nd SCI* 15.
Kipling, J. J. and Wilson, R. B. (1960). *Trans. Faraday Soc.,* **56,** 563.
Kipling, J. J., Sherwood, J. N., Shooter, P. V. and Thompson, N. R. (1964a). *Carbon* **1,** 315.
Kipling, J. J., Sherwood, J. N., Shooter, P. V. and Thompson, N. R. (1964b). *Carbon* **1,** 321.
Kipling, J. J., Shooter, P. V. and Young, R. N. (1966c). *Carbon* **4,** 333.
Kipling, J. J., Sherwood, J. N., Shooter, P. V., Thompson, N. R. and Young, R. N. (1966d). *Carbon* **4,** 5.
Klemenc, A., Wechsberg, R. and Wagner, G. (1934). *Z. Elektrochem.* **40,** 488.
Kmetko, E. A. (1956). *1st/2nd USC* 21.
Lamond, T. G. and Marsh, H. (1964). *Carbon* **1,** 281.
Lamond, T. G., Metcalfe, J. E. and Walker, P. L. (1965). *Carbon* **3,** 59.
Lauer, G. G. and Bonstedt, K. P. (1963). *Carbon* **1,** 165.
Lewis, I. C. and Edstrom, T. (1963). *5th USC* **2,** 413.
Lipson, H. and Stokes, A. R. (1942). *Proc. R. Soc.* **A181,** 101.
Losty, H. H. W. and Blakelock, H. D. (1966). *2nd SCI* 29.
Maire, J. (1951). *C.R. hebd. Seanc. Acad. Sci. Paris* **232,** 61.
Maire, J. and Méring, J. (1958). *1st SCI* 204.
Maire, J. and Méring, J. (1959). *3rd USC* 337.
Maire, J. and Méring, J. (1960). *4th USC* 345.
Marsh, H. and Wynne-Jones, W. F. K. (1964). *Carbon* **1,** 269.
Mason, A. C. and Owen, T. H. (1966). *2nd SCI* 69.
Mason, I. B., Kellett, E. A. and Richards, B. P. (1966). *2nd SCI* 159.
Matsen, F. A. (1959). *3rd USC* 21.
May, J. R. and Warner, R. K. (1960). *4th USC* 741.
Mazza, M. (1964). *J. Chim. phys.* **61,** 721.
Mazza, M., Marchand, A. and Pacault, A. (1962). *J. Chim. phys.* **59,** 657.
Méring, J. and Maire, J. (1960). *J. Chim. phys.* **57,** 803.
Millet, Jacques, Millet, Jeannine and Vivares, A. (1963). *J. Chim. phys.* **60,** 553.
Mizushima, S. (1960). *4th USC* 439.
Mrozowski, S. (1956). *1st/2nd USC* 31.

Mrozowski, S. (1958). *1st SCI* 15.
Noda, T. and Inagaki, M. (1962). *Nature, Lond.* **196**, 772.
Noda, T. and Inagaki, M. (1964). *Carbon* **2**, 127.
Noda, T. and Kato, H. (1965). *Carbon* **3**, 289.
Noda, T., Inagaki, M. and Sekiya, T. (1965). *Carbon* **3**, 175.
Oberlin, M. and Méring, J. (1961). *C.R. hebd. Seanc. Acad. Sci., Paris* **253**, 2720.
Oberlin, M. and Méring, J. (1964) *Carbon* **1**, 471.
Oberlin, M., Rappeneau, J. and Yvars, M. (1964). *Carbon* **1**, 481.
Okada, J. (1960). *4th USC* 547.
Okada, J., Sekiguchi, A. and Ishii, T. (1962). *5th USC* **1**, 497.
Pacault, A. and Gasparoux, H. (1967). *C.R. hebd. Seanc. Acad. Sci., Paris* **264**, 1160.
Pacault, A., Marchand, A., Bothorel, P., Zanchetta, J., Boy, F., Cherville, J. and Oberlin, M. (1960). *J. Chim. phys.* **57**, 892.
Pandic, B. (1966). *2nd SCI* 131.
Parker, W. G. and Wolfhard, H. G. (1950). *J. chem. Soc.* **2038**.
Pierce, C., Wiley, J. W., Smith, R. N. (1949). *J. Phys. Chem.* **53**, 669.
Pinnick, H. T. (1952). *J. chem. Phys.* **20**, 756.
Pinnick, H. T. (1954). *Phys. Rev.* **94**, 319.
Pinnick, H. T. (1956). *Phys. Rev.* **102**, 58.
Pratt, G. C. (1958). *1st SCI* 145.
Pullman, B. (1959). *3rd USC* 3.
Rappeneau, J., Fillatre, A. and Yvars, M. (1964). *Revue gén. Caoutch.* **41**, 395.
Rappeneau, J., Fillatre, A., Yvars, M., Méring, J. and Oberlin, M. (1966). *2nd SCI* 180.
Redmond, J. P. and Walker, P. L., (1960). *J. phys. Chem.* **64**, 1093.
Riley, H. L. (1938). *Trans. Faraday Soc.* **34**, 1011.
Riley, H. L. (1947). *Q. Rev. chem. Soc.* **1**, 59.
Ruland, W. (1965). *Carbon* **2**, 365.
Schaeffer, W. D., Smith, W. R. and Polley, M. H. (1953). *Ind. Engng Chem.* **45**, 1721.
Schiller, C., Méring, J., Cornuault, P. and Du Chaffaut, F. (1967). *C.R. hebd. Seanc. Acad. Sci., Paris* **264B**, 309.
Schmidt, L., Boehm, H. P. and Hofmann, U. (1959). *3rd USC* 235.
Short, M. A. and Walker, P. L., Jr. (1963). *Carbon* **1**, 3.
Simbeck, L. and Kronenwetter, R. (1963). *5th USC* **2**, 611.
Smith, R. C. and Howard, II. C. (1937). *J. Am. chem. Soc.* **59**, 234.
Stadler, H. P. (1960). *4th USC* 337.
Stadler, H. P. and Thomson, C. M. (1958). *1st SCI* 186.
Steward, E. G. and Cook, B. P. (1960). *Nature, Lond.* **186**, 797.
Steward, E. G. and Davidson, H. W. (1958). *1st SCI* 207.
Sutton, A. L. and Howard, V. C. (1962). *J. nucl. Mater.* **7**, 58.
Szwarc, M. (1954). *J. chem. Phys.* **22**, 1621.
Takahashi, H., Kuroda, H. and Akamatu, H. (1965). *Carbon* **2**, 432.
Tang, M. M. and Bacon, R. (1964). *Carbon* **2**, 211.
Taylor, R., Gilchrist, K. E. and Poston, L. J. (1968). *Carbon*, **6**, 537.
Ubbelohde, A. R. (1966). *2nd SCI* 3.
Ubbelohde, A. R. and Lewis, F. A. (1960). "Graphite and its Crystal Compounds". Clarendon Press, Oxford.
Van Krevelen, D. W. and Chermin, H. A. G. (1954). *Fuel* **33**, 79.
Volkmann, E. W. and Russell, C. C. (1962). *Fuel* **42**, 535.
Walker, P. L., Jr. and Weinstein, A. (1967). *Carbon* **5**, 13.

Walker, P. L., Rusinko, F., Rakszawski, J. F. and Liggett, L. M. (1959). *3rd USC* 643.

Walker, P. L., Gardner, R. P., Short, M. A. and Austin, L. G. (1963), *5th USC* **2**, 483.

Walker, P. L., Lamond, T. G. and Metcalfe, J. E. (1966). *2nd SCI* 7.

Warren, B. E. (1956). *1st/2nd USC* 49.

White, J. L., Guthrie, G. L. and Gardner, J. O. (1967). *Carbon* **5**, 517.

Williamson, G. K. (1960). *Proc. R. Soc.* **A257**, 457.

Winslow, F. H., Baker, W. O., Yager, W. A. (1956). *1st/2nd USC* 93.

Wood, L. J. and Phillips, G. (1955). *J. appl. Chem.* **5**, 326.

Wynne-Jones, W. F. K., Blayden, H. E. and Iley, R. (1952). *Brennst.-Chem.* **33**, 268.

Yamada, S., Sato, H. and Ishii, T. (1964). *Carbon* **2**, 253.

Yokokawa, C., Hosokawa, K. and Takegami, Y. (1967). *Carbon* **5**, 475.

"1st SCI" refers to the first conference on "Industrial Carbon and Graphite" organized by the Society of Chemical Industry; "2nd SCI" to the second conference.

Similarly "1st/2nd USC", "3rd USC", "4th USC" and "5th USC" refer to the conferences on carbon held under the auspices of the American Carbon Committee. The Fifth Conference was published in two volumes. The correct reference in these instances is represented by 5th USC 1 or 5th USC 2 respectively.

Chapter II

MANUFACTURING TECHNOLOGY OF BAKED AND GRAPHITIZED CARBON BODIES

J. M. HUTCHEON

United Kingdom Atomic Energy Authority, Warrington, England

I. INTRODUCTION

It is clear from Chapter I that a very wide range of organic materials, natural and synthetic, yield solid carbons on heat treatment to *ca* 1000°C and that many of these can be transformed to the graphitic structure by further heat treatment to 2500–3000°C. The normal product of such an operation however will be a highly porous lump or powder. Hence, for the manufacture of the bulk of the carbon and graphite articles used in industry, a carbonized product has to be reformed in some way into a massive article.

The processes of melting and casting normally used with metals are inapplicable to carbon, as will be seen from Fig. 1. This figure, which is the phase rule diagram for carbon according to Bundy (1963) indicates that the triple point of carbon is close to 4020°C and 125 atmospheres, so that it would be very difficult to formulate a large-scale manufacturing process based on the melting of carbon.

Accordingly, the bulk of the manufactured carbon and graphite articles are made by a process analogous to powder metallurgy.

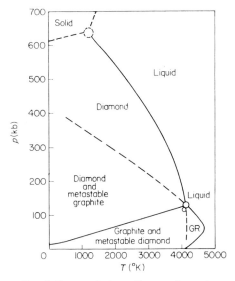

FIG. 1. Proposed phase diagram for carbon.

II. CONVENTIONAL PROCESS

Detailed accounts of the conventional processes employed have been published (Currie *et al.* 1956; Hader *et al.* 1954; Liggett 1964; Austin 1959); in particular the article by Liggett (1964) gives a great deal of information. In this chapter a general account only will be given with emphasis on the scientific basis of the procedures.

A. FLOW SHEET

Figure 2 shows a flow sheet for an experimental plant. A production plant follows the same general pattern with the addition of a final machining stage. It will be seen that the essential steps are:

Preparation of raw materials
Mixing
Forming mixture into "green" shapes
Baking
Impregnation
Graphitizing
Purification (if required)
Machining.

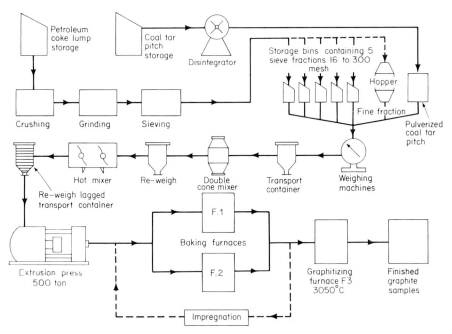

Fig. 2. Harwell experimental graphite plant flow sheet. (After Price and Yeats, 1958. Reproduced by courtesy of the Society of Chemical Industry.)

B. RAW MATERIALS

1. *The Filler*

The starting material is most commonly petroleum coke made by the delayed coking process (Abraham 1960; Scott 1967; Zrinscak and Payne 1967) and it is derived from a crude oil which is low in sulphur (Beuther *et al.* 1961). The feed to the coking still is the residue remaining after the various distillation processes have been carried out on crude oil as part of the normal petroleum refining operation. The resulting coke is available in adequate quantity. Metallurgical cokes, that is those derived from the carbonization of coal, and anthracites, are also used, but more for the production of lower quality and "amorphous carbon" (i.e. baked) electrodes because of the lower purity and higher electrical resistance which they confer on the product. Pitch coke is an acceptable raw material, but in most countries it is not in sufficiently secure supply to be used as the basis of a carbon industry. Cokes derived from shale oil, asphalts and bitumens are used in place of petroleum coke either where this is convenient from a supply point of view, or for special applications.

(a) *Calcining.* As delivered from the refinery the coke has been exposed to a temperature of 450–500°C and contains up to 15% volatile matter as normally determined. At this stage it is known as "green" coke. On further heating this volatile matter is lost together with further pyrolysis products, mainly as hydrogen and light hydrocarbons. Crystallite development occurs and there is a corresponding volume shrinkage producing a real density increase of the order of 30%. As will appear later, shrinkage during the subsequent stage of baking the artefact is a considerable embarrassment to the manufacturer. It is therefore common practice to pre-shrink the coke by calcining to a temperature in the range 1200–1300°C before treatment. Both from the point of view of economics, and because it gives a less porous, more isotropic product, (Hutcheon and Jenkins 1966) it would be preferable to avoid this step and patents exist (Bradwell and Harvey 1968; Great Lakes Carbon Corporation 1967) for so doing.

(b) *Grinding and Sizing.* The first stage in the manufacture is to crush the lumps of the starting material to remove the gross porosity, then to grind, sieve the product, and reconstitute a powder of the required size.

There are three main principles used for selecting the size distribution. The first is the reduction of voidage by packing small particles into the interstitials between larger particles (Andreasen 1939). The second, and opposing, principle is to provide enough porosity for the pyrolysis products to escape during the baking stage. The effect of this is to control the size ratios of particles from the point of view of the packing, but the absolute size of the coarsest particle is increased in proportion to the size of piece being fired. The third principle, for special applications (Bergognon *et al.* 1966), is to control the distribution of final porosity in the product, as well as its total amount. Typical distributions are shown in Fig. 3 where the Currie *et al.* (1956) and the Hader *et al.* (1954) distributions refer to products of about 10 in diameter.

In the manufacture of special nuclear grades and electrical brushes in particular (Price 1961), carbon black is introduced into the mix to increase

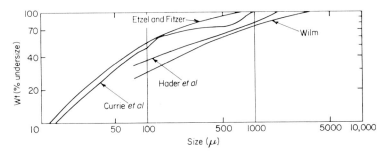

FIG. 3. Typical particle-size distribution of coke powder used in ordinary graphite manufacture. (After Bergognon *et al.* 1966.)

the density and strength, and hence wear life, of the brushes. The dependence of the properties of the material, and also of the ease of manufacture, on the proportions of components have been discussed by Fialkov (1958).

The shape of the particles, as well as their size, is significant. It has an effect on packing (Beirne and Hutcheon 1956; Amstein and Watson 1958) and also on the orientation of the particles by the forming process and hence on the degree of isotropy of some properties in the final product. Shape factors have been studied both by optical methods (Beirne and Hutcheon 1956) and by permeability measurements (Amstein and Watson 1958; Rusinko and Parker 1962) as functions of size, type of coke and type of grinder. Variations with size are found; in general the type of grinder is not important, but both conclusions are dependent on the type of coke, particularly its fissure structure.

2. *The Binder*

The function of this material is to plasticize the coke powder so that it can be formed into bodies of the required shape or size which have enough rigidity for handling in the later stages of the process. Subsequently, the material must carbonize in good yield in order to provide a strong dense body without harming any desirable properties induced by the choice of filler.

The preferred material is a coal tar pitch (Lowry 1963; Darney 1958) which softens at temperatures around 80°C and hardens again on cooling. The need for high carbon yield favours a pitch made from coke-oven tar, but the high yield must not be obtained predominantly (Darney 1958) by the presence (or addition) of "free carbon" since this does not wet the coke particles and contribute to the binding power. The pitch must be as dense as possible and give minimum shrinkage on baking in order to obtain the maximum density and strength in the product. These characteristics correlate (Charette and Bischofberger 1955; Dell 1959) with the aromaticity (carbon/hydrogen ratio) of the pitch and hence call for a high carbonizing temperature in the tar production, as is so with coke oven tars.

Furfuryl alcohol has also been examined (Riesz and Susman 1960) as a binder and claimed to give high density products with correspondingly low resistivity despite the poor graphitizability of this material. Additions to pitch, such as sulphur, or aromatic nitro-compounds, increase the carbon yield on baking (Moutard *et al.* 1963; Yamada 1963) in some cases at the expense of the degree of graphitization.

C. MIXING AND FORMING

Mixing is performed normally in kneader-type equipment heated (e.g. to about 120°C) to give sufficient fluidity to the mix. The proportion of binder is chosen so that at the next (forming) stage of manufacture the mass contains enough of this binder material to exclude air from the interstices between the particles. In calculating this amount allowance has to be made for the fact that the coke particles are still porous, so that some of the binder will penetrate within the particles themselves, and that in the forming stage the mass will be compacted, and will therefore require less binder than at the mixing stage. These requirements result in a typical formulation of one part of binder to three parts of coke, but variations around this, depending on the size distribution of the grist and other variables, will arise.

This mix is then formed either by direct moulding into blocks, or by extrusion. These operations are carried out at a temperature a little above the softening point of the pitch binder in order to reduce the press loadings needed. A typical temperature for electrode material is in the range 80–100°C.

Significant increases in density (0.03–0.5 g/cm^3) have been claimed by the application of a vacuum (Price and Yeats 1958) to remove trapped air during the tamping of the mix before extrusion. Apart from its direct effect, air removal at the mixing and forming stage will facilitate penetration of the coke particles by the binder. The experiments of Girolami (1963) suggest that the coke yield is higher under these circumstances.

D. BAKING

1. *Normal Process*

The moulded or extruded "green" blocks after cooling, for example by immersion in water, to harden the binder, can be stored for some time under normal conditions.

These "green" blocks are then fired, when the binder is pyrolysed. Typically, for every 100 lb of carbonized block, about 82 lb is derived from the coke particles and 18 lb from the binder, while 9 lb of volatile matter are distilled off during the firing process. This loss of volatile matter, combined with the shrinkage of the binder which takes place during the process (the coke particles being assumed to have been pre-shrunk) require that this firing process be carried out extremely carefully. It is normal to carry the process on up to a temperature of about 600°C with very slow heating rates, which may vary between 2°C per hr and 10°C per hr at different parts of the firing cycle.

The large sizes of the individual carbon pieces (commercially available from one supplier up to 77 in in length and 50 in in diameter, weighing about four tons each) with slow rates of heating lead to the use of very large firing installations. A common system is to have a series of pits sunk into the ground, into which the carbon articles are stacked; the intervening space is packed with coke powder, the pits being fired by the flue gases and their temperatures individually controlled by dampers. An idea of the type of furnace used can be obtained from Fig. 4. (Anglo Great Lakes Corporation, 1959).

FIG. 4. Baking furnace. (Reproduced by courtesy of Anglo Great Lakes Corporation Ltd.)

2. Pressure Baking

The application of pneumatic pressure during the baking operation (Price and Yeats 1958; Graham and Price 1966) has been found to result in a higher baked density, the increment resulting from the pressure increasing as the unfired density falls. For material of maximum unfired density pressurized baking resulted in a density of about $1 \cdot 70 \text{ g/cm}^3$, whereas non-pressurized baking gave a result of about $1 \cdot 60 \text{ g/cm}^3$. The pressures used in the pressure system were about 180 psig. Presumably the effect is to raise the boiling points of some of the constituents of the binder and thus to increase the relative extent of polymerization to distillation.

Mechanical constraint of the process material has also been used (Eatherly *et al.* 1958; Hedges 1958) to improve the baking operation.

E. IMPREGNATION

In order to reduce the porosity and increase the density, an impregnation stage is frequently inserted before the final graphitization. Commonly, blocks are sealed in an autoclave. This is first evacuated and then filled with molten pitch or similar material, which is then forced under pressure into the pores of the blocks. A subsequent carbonization step converts the impregnant to useful carbon thus giving a density increase of about $0 \cdot 15 \text{ g/cm}^3$ (Walker and Seeley 1959; Hutcheon and Price 1960) and improvement in other properties (see below). The process may, if necessary, be repeated, but with smaller gains at each repetition.

Impregnation with liquids which pyrolyse without fusion to hard carbon leaves a fine, predominantly closed, pore structure between the small cross-linked crystallites. This process is therefore particularly useful when the object is to reduce permeability rather than to increase density. Furfuryl alcohol (Graham *et al.* 1963; Ikeda *et al.* 1964; Graham and Price 1966), sugar (Boyland 1963; Rogers and Haines 1962) and divinyl benzene (Ikeda *et al.* 1964) have been used.

Although impregnation by the cracking of hydrocarbon gases within the pores of a structure is superficially attractive and has aroused much interest (Bickerdike and Brown 1961; Bickerdike *et al.* 1961; Blanchard *et al.* 1961), it is difficult to apply to large blocks because cracking occurs at the entry surface and hinders subsequent access of gas. To avoid this a steep rising temperature gradient from the entry face to the centre of the body is required so that cracking does not occur until the gas has penetrated to the interior. The most successful way of achieving this has been (Carley-Macauly and Mackenzie 1963) to build up the body from layers of cellulose material which can then be fired to give a low density mass of low thermal conductivity before impregnation.

F. GRAPHITIZING

The product from baking is a solid block, with dimensions somewhat less than the "green" body, but otherwise in its physical and chemical properties broadly similar to the carbon powder used as starting material. It normally has a density in the range $1 \cdot 5$–$1 \cdot 7$ g/cm^3 (that is a porosity of 25–35%), electrical resistivity of the order of 4×10^{-3} ohm cm, and is hard and abrasive.

For many applications, for example electrodes in steel melting furnaces, or nuclear reactor construction, it will now be subjected to graphitization. The process is carried out by heating the electrodes in absence of air to a temperature in the range 2500–3000°C. In industrial manufacture the process is carried out by stacking the electrodes one on top of another in "walls" which are separated and surrounded by coke powder. A view of a typical furnace is shown in Fig. 5.

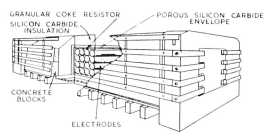

Fig. 5. Cut-away view of Acheson-type graphitizing furnace. (After Odening and Bowman 1958.)

The stacking is carried out on a base consisting of blocks of carborundum and the furnace is completed by fire-brick walls through which water-cooled graphite electrodes penetrate. These walls and the base form the permanent parts of the furnace. Sizes of furnaces vary, but a charge of material to be graphitized amounting to 20–50 tons is typical. An alternating current of up to 50,000 A at a voltage of 50–100 V is then passed through the furnace. The coke powder acts as a carbon resistor and the charge is then heated eventually by radiation from this resistor, since the resistivity of the blocks themselves as graphitization proceeds is relatively small. The furnace is brought up to temperature over a period of a few days, and is held at the maximum temperature for a few hours. The current is switched off, the furnace allowed to cool until its temperature has fallen to the point where the blocks may safely be exposed to the air, and the packing powder removed. The cooling time is the longest stage of the operation and is typically about seven days. Power consumption is typically 2–$2 \cdot 5$ kWh/lb of charge.

G. HOT WORKING

A "hot worked" material (Grade ZT) with density in the range $1 \cdot 80$–$2 \cdot 18$ g/cm^3 has been referred to in publications (Bushong and Neel 1962) without manufacturing details.

H. PURIFICATION

The graphitization step is a powerful means of removing metallic impurities since most oxides are reduced under these conditions and the resulting metals volatilized from the stock to the packing, where significant formation of, for example, carborundum occurs. The loss of impurities on graphitization is indicated in Table I.

TABLE I

Effect of Graphitization on Impurity Content

Element	Impurity content (ppm)	
	Baked block	Graphitized block
Ash	11,000	500
Sodium	2900	9
Silicon	490	93
Aluminium	250	8
Iron	225	34
Nickel	125	7
Calcium	110	85
Vanadium	87	52
Lead	40	0·4
Magnesium	40	0·2
Chromium	23	0·6
Boron	0·32	0·18

Results for the same six blocks before and after graphitizing (Owen 1968).

Two impurities which do not respond well to this process are vanadium and boron, both of which form refractory carbides. In addition boron is capable of substitution within the graphite lattice without appreciable instability. Both these elements are undesirable in graphite for nuclear applications because of their high capture cross-section for thermal neutrons, and the former, in particular, is specified not to exceed a few tenths of a part per million (Hutcheon and Thorne 1966). Special means are therefore adopted for the provision of such pure products. One method is to take particular note of the boron contents when selecting the raw materials, which is practicable for both the petroleum coke and the binder. The method requires great care in the avoidance of contamination which can be aided by using only high purity petroleum coke (Liggett 1964) as resistor packing in the graphitizing furnaces.

An alternative method which permits more freedom in the choice of the filler coke is to purify the graphite by a halogen treatment, either separately or during the graphitization process (Odening and Bowman 1958; Cornuault and des Rochettes 1958; Legendre *et al.* 1958). Although this process, which is based on one for the purification of spectrographic electrodes, was at one time carried out as a separate gas phase treatment, the currently more favoured method is to introduce sodium fluoride into the graphitizing furnace. Boron, and other impurities, are then volatilized out as fluorides.

I. GENERAL CONSIDERATIONS OF PROCESS

The process described above is slow, particularly because of the baking stage, and a period of four months normally elapses between the start of manufacture of a batch of material and its eventual preparation for dispatch. Hence, to the obvious cost components of materials, power for the graphitizing furnaces and other services and labour, must be added high inventory costs, the capital costs of very large items of fixed plant, such as baking furnaces and presses, and a considerable allowance for scrap, particularly when this occurs late in the process.

It follows that changes in the basic process are not easily made. The manufacturer's main possibilities of product control come in selection and pre-treatment of raw materials, although these call for careful preliminary tests to check processability, and in modifications of the impregnation step.

The process is clearly a challenge to the chemical engineer insofar as the baking step in particular could benfit from conversion to a faster continuous process. Such processes are described in the patent literature (Hedges 1958; Great Lakes Carbon Corporation 1964) and one such attempt has been described (Heitman 1967) as successful on a pilot plant scale in the manufacture of 2×2 in material.

III. POLYMER CARBONS

Liquid organic resins which can be cured at *ca* 100°C in a mould to give solid polymers, and subsequently pyrolysed to carbon, provide a fabrication route analogous to melting and casting. Since carbonization occurs in the solid phase the materials are strongly cross-linked, possibly partly through oxygen atoms (Kakinoki 1965). The product is therefore a "hard" low-density ($1\cdot4$ g/cm^3) carbon and its porosity is finely divided. Since these fine pores provide the only avenue of escape for the gaseous degradation products, and since the carbonization produces about 50% volume shrinkage (Yamada *et al.* 1964) slow and carefully controlled carbonization rates are required.

As expected, heat treatment does not result in significant crystal growth until temperatures of about 3000°C are reached (Yamada *et al.* 1964) but heat-treatment to 1600°C causes the fine porosity to close, thus producing an impermeable product.

A. VITREOUS AND GLASSY CARBONS

Phenol-formaldehyde resins of closely controlled composition (Lewis 1966) have been used in this way in the U.K. to manufacture a material known as "vitreous carbon" (Higgins and Antill 1966; Anon. 1963) for small crucible applications; a basically similar material, regarding which little fabrication information has been published, has aroused considerable interest in Japan under the name "glassy carbon" (Kakinoki 1965; Noda and Inagaki 1964a, b; Yamada and Sato 1962; Masuyama *et al.* 1964).

Table II gives published (Anon. 1963) properties of the material sold as "vitreous carbon".

TABLE II

Physical Properties of Vitreous Carbon†

Shear strength	$10,000 \simeq 30,000$ lb/in^2
Density	$1 \cdot 4$ g/ml
Coefficient of linear expansion (in the range 0–100°C)	$2 \cdot 9 \times 10^{-6}$ per °C
Thermal conductivity	$0 \cdot 01$ cal/cm sec °C
Electrical resistivity	$0 \cdot 001$ ohm cm
Working temperature	Up to 1800°C

† After Anon (1963).

B. CELLULOSE CARBON

A dilute suspension of cellulose fibres of controlled length can be substituted for the liquid phase monomer to yield, after processing, a product known as "cellulose carbon" (Davidson 1961; Davidson and Losty 1963, 1966; Losty and Blakelock 1966; Losty 1966). In one variant of the process the first step in the manufacture is the preparation of a very fine dispersion of cellulose in water by standard paper-making techniques. For the manufacture of tubes the excess water may be removed by centrifuging the suspension using a porous bucket ("centrifugal casting") so that a cellulose tube of reasonable mechanical strength is left. The remaining water is then removed in an air oven at about 200°C. The dried tubes are then machined and carbonized to 800°C, initially under nitrogen at a pressure of 2000 psi. Again very considerable shrinkage occurs at this stage and the tube has to be supported on a mandril during the carbonization process. Final heat treatment is normally taken to about 1500°C to give an impermeable product of density $1 \cdot 5$ g/cm^3 but further small changes in physical properties can be obtained if required by continuing the heat treatment to normal graphitizing temperatures.

IV. PYROLYTIC CARBON AND GRAPHITE

A method of manufacture which is simple and direct in principle, although not very adaptable to tonnage production, is the direct cracking of hydrocarbon gases onto a hot surface to produce solid carbon. The gas used is normally a low molecular weight hydrocarbon such as methane, and the carbon atoms produced by the cracking process, provided that the conditions are correctly chosen, build up well-formed crystals of carbon on the substrate. In early applications of this method the graphite so formed was highly oriented with basal planes parallel to the substrate surface. Later developments however have shown that there is a considerable amount of flexibility in the process, and that both the orientation and the size of the crystals can be varied by suitable choice of substrate temperature (and hence deposition rate), gas composition and pressure. The method has found considerable application in relation to specialist carbon products, particularly in connection with space vehicles, and in the United States such material is now in quantity production. If such material is subjected to a second heat treatment process at temperatures up to about 3000°C further crystal growth occurs and the product so obtained is the most nearly perfect graphite available from the crystallographic point of view. For scientific purposes it is used as a substitute for single crystal graphite.

V. CONTROL OF TECHNICAL PROPERTIES

Polycrystalline carbon and graphite were exploited in the metallurgical, electrical and electro-chemical industries in the first place because of their refractory nature, electrical and thermal conductivity, and resistance to aqueous corrosion. In these industries, as well as in its nuclear applications, mechanical properties and thermal expansion coefficients are also of importance.

It is a constant aim of the carbon technologist to relate these properties ultimately to the variables over which he has control, such as choice of starting material and manufacturing conditions. One type of relation may be direct and more or less empirical (that is, in its extreme form a manufacturing recipe). Alternatively, in principle such a link could proceed through a complete knowledge of all the relevant structural features of carbons, relating this in the one direction to the technical properties and in the other to the manufacturing variables. The practical approach is at present a compromise between these two. Some empirical relations are well known in the industry over a limited range of variables. The structural approach, on the other hand, can be used qualitatively as a guide but in general is insufficiently well understood to permit quantitative prediction.

For such a structural approach, one would need to start from a detailed knowledge of the following:

(i) the characteristics of the individual crystals;
(ii) the linkages between the boundaries of crystals, in particular the extent to which these involved aliphatic carbon chains;
(iii) a distribution function describing the mutual orientation of the crystals;
(iv) the size, shape orientation and spatial distribution of the porosity in the body.

Previous sections have described the wide variations, at all structural levels, which are possible between different forms of these materials, and give a general review of the information available under (i) and (ii) of the above headings. Before individual properties are discussed it will be helpful to review generally the contributions of orientation and porosity in the multiphase body.

A. ORIENTATION

The ultimate source of anisotropy lies in the nature of the carbon crystal itself, indicated for example by recorded ratios varying from 200 to 10^4 (Ubbelohde 1962) between the a- and c-direction electrical resistivities. This property derives from the different bonding energies in different directions in the crystal, which are reflected in the aggregation of the atoms into relatively distant parallel sheets. In the same way the layer plane packets will themselves form oriented structures, but these will be disturbed to a more or less degree by thermal randomization and the randomizing effects of gas evolution while the material is in a plastic state. Hence in its gross properties a carbon body will be considerably more isotropic than the crystals of which it is composed; anisotropy can be controlled in principle by comminution and reconstitution of the more highly anisotropic fragments in a controlled manner. In practice, since the long dimensions of the layer plane packets vary in size from tens of angstroms to thousands of angstroms, this is only practicable where the conditions of carbonization particularly favour the growth of large continuous, or semi-continuous, layer planes as in some petroleum cokes or anthracites (Chapter I) and even then requires careful control of grinding conditions. There remains, however, as noted in Chapter I, a preferred orientation in soft carbon particles which is reflected in anisometry of these particles and hence in a preferred orientation of the moulded or extruded product (Ali et al. 1958; White 1960). Thus most hard carbons are virtually isotropic while the multiphase soft carbon-based artefacts such as commercial electrode graphite show anisotropy ratios of most physical properties in the range 1·5–3. Even when the anisotropy of physical properties can be directly compared with the local crystal orientation (determined by X-ray methods) the agreement is only qualitative (Ali *et al.* 1958; Walker *et al.* 1959) because of the effect on the physical properties of oriented porosity.

B. POROSITY IN POLYMER CARBONS

Carbons such as glassy or cellulose carbons of the "hard" type contain pores as a result of the loss of material during the carbonizing stage. The structure is unable to shrink into this porosity on heat-treatment because the anisotropic carbon crystals are randomly oriented or cross-linked through strong tetrahedral linkages. As discussed in Chapter I these pores have dimensions of the same order as those of the crystallites and are generally closed when the material has been heat treated in the range 1500–2500°C. Such porosity is an inherent part of the structure and its effect on the physical properties of a body is included in measurements made on small specimens. Thus, in the absence of cracks, porous hard carbons may generally be regarded as homogeneous and isotropic.

An exception to this has been noted for some forms of vitreous carbon in which the porosity has been shown to exist (Nelson 1966) as well separated pores with diameters up to 0·2 mm. It is likely that these pores originate in the volatization of metallic impurities during the high-temperature treatment process.

C. POROSITY IN MULTI-PHASE CARBONS

1. *Distribution of Porosity*

For multi-phase carbons each phase initially contributes its own internal porosity, which changes during heat treatment (see Chapter I). Hence the pore size distribution of the body is influenced directly by the previous heat treatment history of the filler (Fialkov *et al.* 1964), so that the proportion of micropores (<40 Å) decreases with previous heat treatment temperature of the filler, these being at a minimum for pregraphitized coke, as a result of crystal growth and the elimination of bridges between crystallites.

In addition there are interactions between the components. Penetration of the coke particles by the binder during mixing and extrusion has been mentioned in Section IIC and similar effects occur with the impregnant. This interaction is also influenced by the temperature history of the filler before incorporation into the mix. Calcined coke particles undergo small volume changes on baking while the binder coke shrinks considerably, as noted above. The resulting stresses lead to the formation of microcracks which appear as porosity in the size range of a few microns (Fialkov *et al.* 1964). Uncalcined cokes or similar poorly crystalline carbons may shrink on baking at a rate closer to that of the binder coke (Graham and Price 1966), so that this porosity is much less.

But the bulk of the porosity arises from spaces between the filler particles (Walker and Rusinko 1959). These pores therefore have dimensions appropriate to the particle, rather than the crystal, and their total volume and distribution depends largely on the size distribution of the filler (Martens and Kotlensky 1963; Bergognon *et al.* 1966).

The integrated result of all these processes is usually a pore size distribution curve which has at least two peaks (Rappeneau *et al.* 1963; Clinton and Kaye 1965). Figure 6 shows a typical example. Such curves are normally obtained by mercury porosimetry but the major peak is confirmed by optical microscopy of polished sections (Clinton and Kaye 1965).

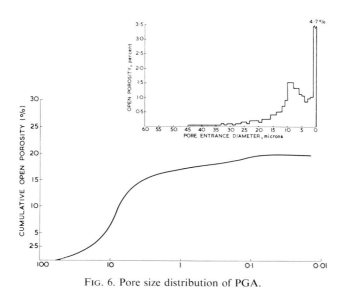

FIG. 6. Pore size distribution of PGA.

2. *Orientation of Porosity*

As has been noted above, the combination of a directional forming process, anisometric filler particles and some preferred orientation within these, leads normally to some anisotropy of those properties of the artefact which derive from the crystal structure.

The first two of these effects lead also to a spatially non-random distribution of the binder which appears, in the final product, as an orientation of the macroporosity. This has been directly demonstrated by stereo-radiography of sulphur-impregnated specimens (Broadbent *et al.* 1966) and its effects are shown in orientation of fluid transport properties such as diffusion and permeability.

3. *Effect of Heat Treatment on Porosity*

Once the major shrinkage process is complete (that is by approximately the conclusion of the baking stage) the external dimensions of the body and its gross structure change little with further heat treatment. Hence further changes in the macroporosity are small, although changes in the microporosity of the individual components continue as a result of crystal growth. The main effect expected (see Table II, Chapter I) is a small increase in the open porosity and consequent increase of a few per cent in helium density. These effects have been found for anthracite-based carbons (Geller and Walker 1963) although both the binder coke and a petroleum coke filler seemed to be behaving anomalously in these experiments.

4. *Effect of Impregnation on Porosity*

This has been studied by a number of authors (Martens and Kotlensky 1963; Walker and Rusinko 1959; Hutcheon and Price 1960; Rappeneau *et al.* 1963). As expected the total porosity is reduced. The shape of the cumulative pore size distribution curves changes little with impregnation but closer examination of the distributions shows that the macropores are partially filled by the impregnant while some of the micropores are blocked off so that the proportion of closed porosity increases (Walker and Rusinko 1959; Hutcheon and Price 1960), as shown in Table III.

By virtue of the fact that it leads to a "hard", closed-pore type of carbon, furfuryl alcohol is more effective than pitch in giving such a "blocking off" effect (Watt and Brown 1961).

TABLE III

Pore Closure by Impregnation†

Number of impregnations	Porosity (%) Total	Open	Closed	Ratio closed/total
0	28·3	27·0	1·3	0·05
1	21·7	18·0	3·7	0·17
2	19·0	14·5	4·5	0·29
3	17·4	12·2	5·2	0·30

†After Hutcheon and Price (1960).

5. *Effect of Gross Porosity on Mechanical and Structural Properties*

For many physical and chemical properties, it is the relatively coarse porosity, which includes most of the volume of the pores, that is dominant.

The gross mechanical properties and the transport of heat and electricity through the body clearly depend on the cross-sectional areas in the structure which carry the load or provide the conducting path. Hence there is a general dependence of these properties on density. Viewed as an engineering structure, however, a polycrystalline carbon body, particularly a multi-phase body, contains many redundant elements. The dependence on density is therefore not simple and the properties depend in a complicated way on the distribution of cross-sectional areas and hence on the distribution of porosity, rather than on the total amount.

Mrozowski has analysed (1956) the properties of such structures primarily in terms of "binder coke bridges". In a two-phase carbon he first imagined the binder distributed over the surface of the filler coke particles and calculated the thickness of the film. He then considered the numbers and areas of the "columns" at the points of contact of the particles after the baking process and proceeded to predict, to some degree, the mechanical and electrical properties of such a system from those of the separate components.

The equations he derived are as follows:

for electrical resistivity ρ:

$$\frac{1}{\rho} = \frac{1}{B} d_0^x (d-d_0)^{\frac{1}{4}} \tag{1}$$

for mechanical strength S:

$$S = S_0 d_0^y (d-d_0) \tag{2}$$

for elastic modulus E:

$$E = E_0 d_0^z (d-d_0) \tag{3}$$

where

$$x = z+0\cdot 5; \quad y > z. \tag{4}$$

In these equations d is the apparent density, d_0 the filler density (ratio of mass of filler coke to external volume of the body) and hence $(d-d_0)$ is the binder coke density (ratio of mass of binder coke to external volume of body).

These equations permit in particular a prediction of how the properties specified should vary with binder content (related to $(d-d_0)$). All properties show (Okada and Takeuchi 1960) an optimum value at about the same binder content. Although this depends on the size distribution of the filler, it is generally close to 22% by weight of binder to filler. Since this optimum also corresponds, not unnaturally, to an optimum practical condition for extrusion and much of the output of the carbon industry is made in this way, binder content is not practically an important variable. This reduces the value of the equation from the point of view of producing given variations of properties.

The binder coke density term can include, however, coke derived from impregnation: it can also be affected, with comparatively minor changes in the d_0 term, by thermal oxidation. In these areas the equations give guidance in the "tailor-making" of carbons. Greater scope for variation also exists, of course, with moulded products.

6. Interaction Effects

It has already been noted that penetration of filler particles by binder or impregnant modifies the pore size distribution in an artefact and that this penetration is controlled by the internal structure of the filler particles and hence by their thermal history. It has also been found that the crystallite growth of the individual phases is modified by this penetration. Mason *et al.* (1966) found that crystallite growth of a petroleum coke proceeded more slowly and to a less extent (as judged by L_c and L_a measurements) when incorporated with a coal tar pitch binder than when treated alone. Cornuault *et al.* (1966) studied the effect for mixture of a crystallographically wide range of components; they used liquid phase oxidation and microscopical measurements as well as physical property measurements and X-ray diffraction to characterize the products. Their results normally showed a clear positive influence of the graphitizing material on the non-graphitizing material, that is the "hard" carbon phase behaved more like "soft" carbons in the presence of another soft carbon phase.

D. CONTROL OF SPECIFIC PROPERTIES

The remainder of this chapter will be devoted to a brief review of methods which have been used to control specific technically important properties in manufactured carbons and graphites.

1. Mechanical Properties

The characteristic mechanical properties of commercial synthetic graphites by comparison with most structural materials are well known as:

(i) a comparatively low tensile strength (of the order of 2000 psi) and Young's Modulus (ca 10^6psi);

(ii) a low elastic strain to fracture (of the order of 0·15%);

(iii) the absence of any significant creep ductility for measurement temperatures below 1500°C;

(iv) an increase in strength as the measurement temperature is increased up to about 2500°C;

(v) a preferred orientation such that the tensile strength is highest in the direction in which the crystal basal planes predominantly lie;

(vi) for materials of constant crystallite arrangement but varying macropore structure, strength varies linearly with modulus (Losty and Orchard 1962).

Of these (iii) and (iv) are of considerable scientific and technological interest, and are discussed fully in Chapter V.

In this section we are concerned mainly with the manner in which the room temperature properties can be varied by control of manufacturing conditions and the available evidence can be stated very briefly.

(a) *Effects of raw materials.* Walker *et al.* (1959) measured the mechanical properties of plates formed from a range of twelve different raw materials, which were characterized crystallographically by the intensity of the (002) reflections when the specimens were mounted in a standard manner. They concluded, in line with observations in the Author's laboratory, that the strength of the artefact increased with increasing degree of crystallographic disorder in the cokes. Since this disorder corresponds presumably to the presence of cross-links in the cokes, this is the expected result. The relatively high values reported for the strength of vitreous carbon (Table II of this chapter) points in the same direction.

Andrew *et al.* (1960) used two filler materials and two binder materials to gave four combinations (soft filler/soft binder, soft filler/hard binder, hard filler/soft binder, hard filler/hard binder) and measured for each combination the variation of Young's Modulus with temperature. The hard binder always gave a higher modulus than the soft by about 30% (Fig. 7); the moduli for the hard-filler mixes were about the same as for the soft at HTT *ca* 1000°C but fell off much less steeply with increasing HTT up to 2500°C. Andrew and Distante (1963) continued the same experimental programme with graphitized fillers and found that these gave lower moduli than the corresponding ungraphitized fillers at all relevant HTT. This they ascribed to differences in interaction between the filler and binder particles (cf. Fialkov *et al.* 1964). Incorporation

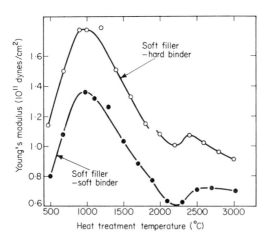

FIG. 7. Young's Modulus *versus* heat-treatment temperature for carbon bodies made from different starting materials. (After Andrew *et al.* 1960).

of carbon black into a coke/pitch mix gives a significant increase in strength (Bergognon *et al.* 1966).

The dependence of Young's Modulus on binder content for baked and graphitized petroleum coke/coal tar pitch mixes has been reported by Okada and Takeuchi (1960) whose results are shown in Fig. 8. For the region of the curve beyond 21 parts binder per 100 parts coke they are in fair agreement with the Mrozowski equation (3).

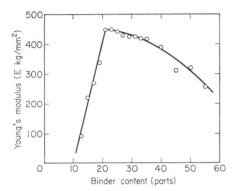

FIG. 8. Young's modulus *versus* binder content. (After Okada and Takeuchi 1960.)

(b) *Effect of impregnation.* In line with the Mrozowski equation (2) the strength of polycrystalline graphite bodies has been found to be increased by impregnation with pitch (Hutcheon and Price 1960; Martens and Kotlensky 1963), resins (Graham *et al.* 1962) or sugar solutions (Losty and Orchard 1962), and unstated materials (Seldin 1959). With practical numbers of impregnation steps, increases in tensile or bend strength by at least 50% are readily obtainable.

In one set of experiments this improvement was found to persist for test temperatures up to 2750°C. In the higher end of this range, from 2320–2750°C impregnation also significantly improved the elongation to fracture.

(c) *Effect of heat-treatment temperature.* The change of Young's Modulus with heat-treatment temperature has already been discussed in Section D 1(a) and Fig. 7 gives the results obtained by Andrew *et al.* (1960). Several other workers (Davidson and Losty 1960; Losty and Orchard 1962; Andrew and Distante 1963; Mason and Knibbs 1967) have obtained curves of the same general form. Over a similar heat-treatment temperature range (900–3000°C) the share scleroscope hardness falls from about 50 to about 22 and the

Rockwell hardness from about 90 to about 15 (Simbeck and Kronenwetter 1963).

2. Thermal Expansion Coefficient

The definitive measurements of the thermal expansion coefficient of the layer plane packet were made by Nelson and Riley (1945) by the use of X-ray measurements to follow the changes in the a and c lattice spacings of a natural graphite specimen as it was heated from 146 to 800°C. The strong valency links within the layer planes result in a small or negative coefficient within the plane, but in the c-direction the weak van der Waals' forces permit the mean interlayer distance to increase readily as the temperature is raised. Nelson and Riley found that the expansion was represented by the equation

$$d = 3\cdot352 + 90\cdot54 \times 10^{-6}t + 6\cdot33 \times 10^{-9}t^2$$

where d is the interlayer spacing (Å) at temperature t°C.

This equation was essentially confirmed by later workers (Walker et al. 1953; Matsuyama 1959; Steward and Cook 1959; Steward et al. 1960; Yang 1962) for temperatures up to 2600°C. For non-graphitic carbons with higher initial d-spacings, the d-spacing/temperature curve was found to be parallel to that for natural graphite, to a very close approximation, so that cross-links and frozen-in stresses apparently have little effect on the forces between the parallel layers in an individual packet.

It follows from this equation, and the very low a-direction expansion, that the statistical mean linear expansion coefficient of an assemblage of carbon crystals in any direction in the temperature range 0–100°C should be of the order of 8×10^{-6} °C^{-1} if the assemblage completely follows the behaviour of the crystals of which it is composed. The values obtained for typical commercial graphites (Roberts et al. 1961) are in the range $1\cdot7 \times 10^{-6}$ °C^{-1} in the a-direction and $4\cdot3 \times 10^{-6}$ °C^{-1} in the c-direction, corresponding to a mean of about 2–3×10^{-6} °C^{-1}.

The low values and the low anisotropy (compared with the crystal) correspond to some compensation of high c-axis coefficients by low a-axis coefficients. This results from randomizing of the orientation in a polycrystalline body and to some absorption of c-axis growth in internal voids in the polycrystalline body.

Simmons (1959) has derived thermodynamically the equation

$$\alpha_x = A_x\alpha_0 + (1 - A_x)\alpha_c$$

for the thermal expansion coefficient in the direction x of a polycrystalline body where α_c and α_a are the c-direction and a-direction coefficients for the crystal and A_x is a directionally dependent "accommodation coefficient" which combines the two structural properties of orientation and voidage.

This is essentially the same equation as that given earlier by Mrozowski (1956) who proposed models for the edge-linking of mutually oriented crystallites and attributed the internal voidage to basal-plane microcracks produced during the anisotropic shrinkage of the carbon crystals on cooling after the graphitizing stage. Sutton and Howard (1962) explained the shape of the expansion curves for various graphites on the basis of such a model and demonstrated the existence of the Mrozowski cracks by electron micrography. They also attempted, as did Cornuault *et al.* (1966), to separate the orientation and voidage components of the accommodation factor A_x by X-ray orientation measurements; a step which was improved by Morgan (1967). Equations formally similar to the above equation also relate irradiation-induced dimensional changes (Simmons 1959) of a polycrystalline graphite to that of the single crystals and apply to the dimensional changes produced by the intercalation of (for example) bromine between layer planes (Brocklehurst and Weeks 1963; Brocklehurst and Bishop 1964).

Hence the thermal expansion of a carbon, for a fixed temperature range and direction of measurement (in relation to the direction of application of pressure in forming) should depend on the preferred orientation of the carbon and on one or more voidage parameters. In experimental terms, for multi-phase carbons it has been studied in relation to type of filler, type of binder, size distribution of filler, proportion of binder and impregnant and heat-treatment temperature.

Since the filler particles are held tightly together in multi-phase carbons as a result of binder coke shrinkage during baking, and the thickness of the binder coke bridges between the coke particles is generally small in relation to coke particle diameter, it would be expected that the filler coke would dominate the thermal expansion behaviour and that the binder would exert only small effect. This has been confirmed experimentally, particularly for fully graphitized materials (Okada 1960a, b).

The experimentally found dependence on filler structure follows the general behaviour expected on the above model, although the explanations given below may be something of an over-simplification (Collins 1959) of a complex interaction of variables. Hard carbons are generally more isotropic (Collins 1959; Hutcheon and Jenkins 1966) in their thermal expansion behaviour and give volume coefficients of expansion, which are (Collins 1956) substantially independent of heat-treatment temperature of the coke because the rigid cross-linked structure is fixed at a temperature of 2–300°C. As the microporosity of these materials increases the thermal expansion coefficients of the artefacts made from them falls, as expected from the increase of accommodation provided (Loch and Austin 1956).

Bodies made from "soft" fillers are much more anisotropic (Roberts *et al.* 1961), the highest value being that measured in the direction perpendicular to the preferred orientation of the layer planes in the filler crystallites. This value, however, is only about one-third of that of the single crystal, as noted above, which is partly because of some contribution from basal planes (arising from imperfect orientation) but also due to the oriented micro-porosity (Mrozowski cracks). Hence, any modification of the crack structure modifies the expansion coefficient. Thus it increases with temperature of measurement (Sutton and Howard 1962) or with neutron irradiation (Simmons 1959) because under both conditions the cracks are closed by expansion of the crystallites. If uncalcined coke is mixed with binder the development of the oriented mosaic structure of the soft carbon is hindered by the presence of some cross-linking material. Accordingly the thermal expansion coefficient rises as the pre-calcination temperature falls from 1300 to 500°C (Fialkov et al. 1964; Collins 1956; Okada 1960a; Darney 1958; Great Lakes Carbon Corporation 1967; Hutcheon and Jenkins 1966). As the precalcination temperature is increased from 1300–2500°C the coefficient rises again slightly in keeping with the observation that the microporosity of the coke is decreased by this treatment (Asher 1961).

There is also a dependence on binder proportion, the expansion coefficient being at its maximum value at about the binder level normally used in commercial extruded products (Okada 1960a), and also on fineness of the filler coke material (Okada 1960a; Martens and Kotlensky 1963), because of the more complete penetration of the fine particles.

Similarly, impregnation of a baked artefact with hydrocarbon impregnants (but apparently not with sugar solution (Losty 1960) causes a small increase in the c-direction coefficient (Okada 1960a; Hutcheon and Price 1960; Graham et al. 1963) which is now associated with an *increase* in closed pore volume because open porosity is being closed by sealing (Hutcheon and Price 1960).

The introduction of cross-linking on an atomic scale by the use of raw materials containing heteroatoms is suggested as the cause of the unusually high degree of isotropy and high volume expansion coefficient (Walker et al. 1959; Hutcheon and Jenkins 1966) shown by some "soft" carbons.

3. *Transport of Heat and Electricity through the Solids*

For multi-phase carbons and graphites these properties generally follow the behaviour expected from the constituent materials (in particular a semi-empirical relation has been found between electrical resistivity and the reciprocal of the mean crystallographic layer plane diameter (Bowman et al. 1958)), modified by the pore structure imposed by the manufacturing route. Qualitatively at least, the Mrozowski equations quoted in Section C,5 have been shown to give an adequate account of electrical resistivity (Hutcheon and Price 1960; Seldin 1959) although numerous other more empirical relations are used industrially.

4. *Transport of Fluids through the Pores*

For a general discussion of the permeability of porous carbons, and in particular the theoretical aspects, the reader is referred to the chapter by Grove in the book edited by Bond (1967). The main technical interest attached to this property in commercial graphites concerns its extraordinary wide range.

The order of magnitude of permeability for a normal electrode or nuclear grade material is such that under a differential pressure of 1 atm the rate of flow of air across a cylindrical disc of area $1 \, cm^2$ and thickness 1 cm is about 2 cc/sec (measured at a pressure of 0·5 atm).

From the "porous carbons" manufactured with filler particles of uniform size, so as to give an open structure and used for chemical engineering plant applications to the quasi-impermeable graphites such as HX10 or similar materials (Price 1961) which are also made commercially, the variation in permeability coefficient covers about six orders of magnitude. Even so the quasi-impermeable graphites by no means reach the attainable limits; single phase carbons such as cellulose carbon have the same order of impermeability to gases as glass.

Major control is achieved by choice of raw materials in relation to whether or not they produce closed pore structures—in practice by the choice of materials giving "soft" or "hard" carbons. The latter can be used alone in the single-phase materials or as binder or impregnant in conjunction with "soft" carbon fillers. In the latter method the highest permeabilities will not be achieved because of cracks produced by differential shrinkage of the "phases". Nonetheless, factors of improvement of the order of 1000 compared with the unimpregnated materials have been readily achieved for special nuclear reactor applications (Graham *et al.* 1962). With "soft" carbon impregnants 5–10 fold reductions are obtained (Hutcheon and Price 1960), and it has been noted (Graham and Price 1966) that pressure baking produces the same reduction in permeability as one coke pitch impregnation. Since choice of particle size and packing density obviously affect pore size distribution, some control is achievable also by this route (Hutcheon *et al.* 1963) but it is of relatively minor degree.

The orientation of the flow paths within the structure of a conventional industrial graphite (see Section C.2) leads to an anisotropy of permeability such that the flow is highest in the direction parallel to the long axes of the coke particles, the value for the anisotropy ratio being normally about two (Hutcheon and Price 1960). Similar effects are found for the diffusion coefficient for gases (Walker *et al.* 1955; Walker and Rusinko 1959).

5. *Chemical Reactivity*

The reactivity of carbons towards oxidizing gases is technically the most important chemical reaction of these materials. Walker and Rusinko (1959) explored the effect of impregnation and also of filler type on this property. Although by impregnation seven times they were able to reduce the surface area from 0·31 to 0·13 m^2/g the reaction rate towards carbon dioxide at 900°C was unaffected and at higher temperatures the impregnated specimens reacted more rapidly, an effect attributed to the higher specific reactivity of the impregnant compared with the base material. In a further paper (Walker *et al.* 1959) they explored the effect of varying the nature of the filler coke and reached the conclusion that the most important method of control was to choose a coke of such a form that it exposed the minimum edge area and the maximum basal plane area to the attacking gas. In practice this amounts to a choice of an isotropic coke which can be recognized crystallographically, or by the relative isotropy of a property such as thermal expansion in the artefact.

From this point of view the structural and pore properties of an artefact are often dominated by the catalytic effects of trace impurities, particularly as graphitization may disseminate impurity particles present in the initial materials and thus increase their effect (Geller and Walker 1963).

Such effects are absent from the radiolytic reaction between graphite and carbon dioxide, which needs to be controlled in the U.K. types of nuclear power reactor. The rate of this reaction depends on the rate at which active species are generated by radiolysis of the carbon dioxide in the pores of the graphite and on the possibility of competing reactions for these before they reach the pore walls. Hence the reaction rate for given gas and radiation conditions should depend, to a first approximation, on the total open porosity of the graphite and a more precise description will take account additionally of the distribution of pore diameters. These predictions have been exactly borne out in practice (Hutcheon *et al.* 1963; Standring and Ashton 1965; Labaton *et al.* 1965).

VI. CONCLUSION

It has been shown that the conventional multi-phase graphite thus represents a practical optimum between many conflicting requirements. The technology of its manufacture and application rests on a broad field of basic knowledge available to the manufacturers and their customers, and also to a mass of accumulated empirical information. The manufacturing process has only limited flexibility which militates against the ability of the manufacturer to satisfy different demands from different customers. Moreover, the batch sizes of the various unit operations require a minimum of at least 50 tons of material in order to test a variant of the process adequately; at current prices this represents an expenditure of tens of thousands of pounds.

However, by taking maximum advantage of small-scale and pilot-scale tests, the manufacturer is able to remove many of the uncertainties connected with a new variant before risking it to the full plant scale, and thus to take advantage of many features of the process which contribute to flexibility of the product. These may be listed as:

1. Choice of raw materials, particularly grist.
2. Variation of heat-treatment conditions, particularly the inclusion or omission of the graphitizing stage.
3. Some variation on size distribution of the grist.
4. Variation of the number of impregnations and type of impregnant.

Of these, the first is the most powerful, but also requires the most careful introduction into the process, in order to avoid heavy scrap losses.

For very special applications special grades exist, made by a variety of unconventional processes, of which some stages at least involve special plant. Such materials frequently find their development hindered because of the difficulty of capitalizing the speculative manufacturing operations on a scale sufficient to launch them into commercial use.

REFERENCES

Abraham, H. (1960). "Asphalts and Allied Substances", 5 Vols. Van Nostrand, New York.
Ali, D., Fitzer, E. and Ragoss, A. (1958). *1st SCI*† 135.
Amstein, E. H. and Watson, C. (1958). *1st SCI* 125.
Andreasen, A. H. M. (1939). "Fineness of Solids", Vol. 3. Ingeniorvidensk Skrif, Denmark.
Andrew, J. F. and Distante, J. M. (1963). *5th USC*† **2**, 585.
Andrew, J. F., Okada, J. and Wobschall, D. C. (1960). *4th USC* 559.
Anglo Great Lakes Corporation, Ltd. (1959). *Nucl. Engng, Lond.* **4**, 175.
Anon. (1963). *Engineer, Lond.* **215**, 316.
Asher, R. C. (1961). *UKAEA Report AERE M/946.*
Austin, A. E. (1959). *3rd USC* 389.
Beirne, T. and Hutcheon, J. M. (1956). *1st/2nd USC* 167.
Bergognon, P., Bentolila, J., Cornuault, P., Price, M. S. T. (1966). *2nd SCI* 456.
Beuther, H., McKinley, J. B. and Flinn, R. A. (1961). *In* "Chemical Engineering Progress Symposium Series", No. 34. Vol. 57, p. 20. A.I.Chem.E., New York.
Bickerdike, R. L. and Brown, A. R. G. (1961). *In* "Nuclear Graphite", p. 109. Organization for European Economic Cooperation. European Nuclear Energy Agency, Paris.
Bickerdike, R. L., Hughes, G., Ranson, H., Clark, D. and Eastabrook, J. N. (1961). *In* "Nuclear Graphite", p. 91. Organization for European Economic Co-operation. European Nuclear Energy Agency, Paris.

† See note at end of References, p. 78.

Blanchard, R., Bochirol, L., Moreau, C. and Philippot, J. (1961). *C.R. hebd. Seanc. Acad. Sci., Paris* **252**, 3989.
Bond, R. L. (Ed.) (1967). "Porous Carbon Solids". Academic Press, London.
Bowman, J. C., Krumhansl, J. A. and Meers, J. T. (1958). *1st SCI* 52.
Boyland, D. A. (1963). *British Patent* 915062.
Bradwell, K. V. and Harvey, J. T. (1968). *British Patent* 1,098,882.
Broadbent, A. K., Dollimore, D. and Dollimore, J. (1966). *2nd SCI* 390.
Brocklehurst, J. E. and Bishop, R. A. (1964). *Carbon* **2**, 27.
Brocklehurst, J. E. and Weeks, J. C. (1963). *J. nucl. Mater.* **9**, 197.
Bundy, F. P. (1963). *J. chem. Phys.* **38**, 631.
Bushong, R. M. and Neel, E. A. (1962). *5th USC* **1**, 595.
Carley-Macauly, K. M. and Mackenzie, M. (1963). *In* "Special Ceramics, 1962", p. 151. Academic Press, London.
Charette, L. P. and Bischofberger, G. T. (1955). *Ind. Engng Chem.* **47**, 1412.
Clinton, D. and Kaye, G. (1965). *Carbon* **2**, 341.
Collins, F. M. (1956). *1st/2nd USC* 177.
Collins, F. M. (1959). *3rd USC* 659.
Cornuault, P. and des Rochettes, H. (1958). *1st SCI* 527.
Cornuault, P., du Chaffault, F., Rappeneau, J. Yvars, M. and Fillatre, A. (1966). *Carbon* **4**, 411.
Currie, L. M., Hamister, V. C. and McPherson, H. G. (1956). *In* "Progress in Nuclear Energy", Series IV, Vol. 1, p. 65. Pergamon Press, Oxford.
Darney, A. (1958). *1st SCI* 152.
Davidson, H. W. (1961). *British Patent* 860,342
Davidson, H. W. and Losty, H. H. W. (1960). *4th USC* 585.
Davidson, H. W. and Losty, H. H. W. (1963). *G.E.C. Jl* **30**, 22.
Davidson, H. W. and Losty, H. H. W. (1966). *2nd SCI* 20.
Dell, M. B. (1959). *Fuel* **38**, 183.
Eatherly, W. P., Janes, M., Mansfield, R. L., Bourdeau, R. A. and Meyer, R. A. (1958). *In* "Proceedings of 2nd United Nations Inter. Conf. on Peaceful Uses of Atomic Energy", Vol. 7, p. 389. United Nations, Geneva.
Fialkov, A. S. (1958). *1st SCI* 101.
Fialkov, A. S., Gumilevskaya, G. P. and Ogareva, N. N. (1964). *J. appl. Chem. USSR* **37**, 1976.
Geller, I. and Walker, P. L., Jr. (1963). *5th USC* **2**, 471.
Girolami, L. (1963). *Fuel* **42**, 2292.
Graham, L. W. and Price, M. S. T. (1966). *2nd SCI* 446.
Graham, L. W., Perels, D. R. and Greenwood, W. J. (1962). *5th USC* **1**, 567.
Graham, L. W., Watt, W., Johnson, W., Arragon, P. A. P. and Price, M. S. T. (1963). *5th USC* **2**, 387.
Great Lakes Carbon Corporation (1964). *British Patent* 1,047,137.
Great Lakes Carbon Corporation (1967). *British Patent* 1,054,961.
Hader, R. N., Gamson, B. W. and Bailey, B. L. (1954). *Ind. Engng Chem.* **46**, 2.
Hedges, J. D. (1958). *British Patent* 794,989.
Heitman, J. B. (1967). *Electrochem. Tech.* **5**, 307.
Higgins, J. K. and Antill, J. E. (1966). *2nd SCI* 269.
Hutcheon, J. M. and Jenkins, M. J. (1966). *2nd SCI* 433.
Hutcheon, J. M. and Price, M. S. T. (1960). *4th USC* 645.
Hutcheon, J. M. and Thorne, R. P. (1966). *2nd SCI* 441.
Hutcheon, J. M., Cowen, H. C. and Godwin, N. F. (1963). *5th USC* **2**, 379.

Ikeda, K., Kawasoe, K. and Fukuda, Y. (1964). *In* "Symposium on Carbon", Paper No. VII—2. Carbon Society of Japan, Tokyo.
Kakinoki, J. (1965). *Acta crystallogr.* **18**, 578.
Labaton, V. Y., Ashton, B. W., Lind, R. and Tait, J. N. (1969). *Carbon*, **7**, 59; *Carbon*, **2**, 59.
Legendre, A., Gueron, J. and Hering, H. (1959). *In* "Proceedings of 2nd United Nations Inter. Conf. on Peaceful Uses of Atomic Energy", 1958, Vol. 4, p. 243. United Nations, Geneva.
Lewis, J. C. (1966). *2nd SCI* 258.
Liggett, L. M. (1964). *In* "Kirk-Othmer Encyclopaedia of Chemical Technology", Vol. 4, p. 158. Interscience, New York.
Loch, L. D. and Austin, A. E. (1956). *1st/2nd USC* 65.
Losty, H. H. W. (1960). *4th USC* 671.
Losty, H. H. W. (1966). *British Patent* 1,033,207.
Losty, H. H. W. and Blakelock, H. D. (1966). *2nd SCI* 29.
Losty, H. H. W. and Orchard, J. S. (1962). *5th USC* **1**, 519.
Lowry, H. H. (1963). "Chemistry of Coal Utilization", Vol. 3. Wiley, New York.
Martens, H. E. and Kotlensky, W. V. (1963). *5th USC* **2**, 617.
Mason, I. B. and Knibbs, R. H. (1967). *Carbon* **5**, 493.
Mason, I. B., Kellett, E. A. and Richards, B. P. (1966). *2nd SCI* 159.
Masuyama, T., Teranishi, H. and Ishikawa, T. (1964). *In* "Symposium on Carbon", Paper No. III—13. Carbon Society of Japan, Tokyo.
Matsuyama, E. (1959). *Nature, Lond.* **184**, 544.
Morgan, W. C. (1967). *J. nucl. Mater.* **21**, 232.
Moutard, G., Millet, J. and Parisot, J. (1962). *5th USC*, **1**, 509.
Mrozowski, S. (1956). *1st/2nd USC* 31.
Nelson, J. B. (1966). *2nd SCI* 90.
Nelson, J. B. and Riley, D. P. (1945). *Proc. R. Soc.* **57**, 477.
Noda, T. and Inagaki, M. (1964a). *Bull. chem. Soc. Japan* **37**, 1534.
Noda, T. and Inagaki, M. (1964b). *In* "Symposium on Carbon", Paper No. III—10. Carbon Society of Japan, Tokyo.
Odening, C. A. and Bowman, J. C. (1958). *1st SCI* 537.
Okada, J. (1960a). *4th USC* 547.
Okada, J. (1960b). *4th USC* 553.
Okada, J. and Takeuchi, Y. (1960). *4th USC* 657.
Owen, T. H. (1968). Private communication.
Price, M. S. T. (1961). *In* "Nuclear Graphite", p. 43. Organization for European Economic Cooperation. European Nuclear Energy Agency, Paris.
Price, M. S. T. and Yeats, F. W. (1958). *2nd SCI* 111.
Rappeneau, J., Bocquet, M., Fillatre, A. and Trutt, J. C. (1963). *5th USC* **1**, 335.
Riesz, C. H. and Susman, S. (1960). *4th USC* 609.
Roberts, F., Mason, I. B., Price, M. S. T. and Bromley, J. (1961). *In* "Progress in Nuclear Energy", Series IV, Vol. 4, 3–1, p. 117. Pergamon Press, Oxford.
Rogers, N. W. and Haines, E. M. (1962). *Ind. Chem.* **38**, 397.
Rusinko, F. and Parker, W. E. (1962). *Fuel* **41**, 275.
Scott, C. B. (1967). *Chemy. Ind.* **1124**.
Seldin, E. J. (1959). *3rd USC* 675.
Simbeck, L. and Kronenwetter, R. (1963). *5th USC* **2**, 611.
Simmons, J. H. W. (1959). *3rd USC* 559.
Standring, J. and Ashton, B. W. (1965). *Carbon* **3**, 157.

Steward, E. G. and Cook, B. P. (1959). *Nature, Lond.* **185,** 78.

Steward, E. G., Cook, B. P. and Kellett, E. A. (1960). *Nature, Lond.* **187,** 1015.

Sutton, A. L. and Howard, V. C. (1962). *J. nucl. Mater.* **7,** 58.

Ubbelohde, A. R. (1962). *5th USC* **1,** 1.

Walker, P. L., Jr. and Rusinko, F. (1959). *3rd USC* 633.

Walker, P. L., Jr. and Seeley, S. B. (1959). *3rd USC* 481.

Walker, P. L., Jr., McKinstry, H. A. and Wright, C. C. (1953). *Ind. Engng Chem.* **45,** 1711.

Walker, P. L., Jr., Rusinko, F. and Raats, E. (1955). *Nature, Lond.* **176,** 1167.

Walker, P. L., Jr., Rusinko, F., Jr., Rakszawski, J. F. and Liggett, L. M. (1959). *3rd USC* 643.

Watt, W. and Brown, A. R. G. (1961). *In* "Nuclear Graphite", p. 237. Organization for European Economic Cooperation. European Nuclear Energy Agency, Paris.

White, E. S. (1960). *4th USC* 675.

Yamada, S. (1963). *5th USC* **2,** 431.

Yamada, S. and Sato, H. (1962). *Nature, Lond.* **193,** 261.

Yamada, S., Sato, H. and Ishii, T. (1964). *Carbon* **2,** 253.

Yang, K. T. (1962). *5th USC* **1,** 492.

Zrinscak, F. S. and Payne, G. L. (1967). *U.S. Patent* 3,338,817.

"1st SCI" refers to the first conference on "Industrial Carbon and Graphite" organized by the Society of Chemical Industry; "2nd SCI" to the second conference.

Similarly "1st/2nd USC", "3rd USC", "4th USC" and "5th USC" refer to the conferences on Carbon held under the auspices of the American Carbon Committee. The Fifth Conference was published in two volumes. The correct reference in these instances is represented by 5th USC 1 or 5th USC 2 respectively.

Chapter III

ELECTRON TRANSPORT IN GRAPHITES AND CARBONS

G. A. SAUNDERS

Department of Applied Physics,
The University, Durham, England

I. INTRODUCTION

Graphite is a semimetal. The valence and conduction bands overlap slightly (about 0·03 eV), so that always, regardless of the temperature, a few holes and electrons are available to carry current. In pure graphite the electron and hole densities are small and equal, and the carrier-effective masses are low. These features dominate the electron transport properties.

79

In one sense, graphite can be considered as intermediate between covalent semiconductors and metals: resembling a degenerate semiconductor on one hand and a metal with a small Fermi volume on the other.

The electrical properties of graphite, in relation to the energy band structure and to divergence from lattice perfection, are the present concern. But, while defectiveness is to be considered, emphasis will be placed on transport properties in graphites rather than on those grossly defective carbons where boundary and defect scattering so predominate that application of the band theory is minimized. As a yardstick we could take the uncertainty principle in the form

$$\Delta E \simeq \hbar/\Delta t.$$

When the mobile electrons are scattered within distances of rather less than 100 Å, the energy uncertainty of the electron states becomes greater than 0·1 eV, and band theory cannot hold.

At least so far as single crystals are concerned, the electron transport properties can be correlated satisfactorily with energy band theory. Recently, the Fermi surface of graphite has been detailed in a most sophisticated manner and, before an insight into electron transport can be gained, some attention at an elementary level must be paid to this work (see Section II). Already a classic is the review article available on this topic (Haering and Mrozowski 1960), and while including details necessary to a complete picture, we shall aim at concerning ourselves with more recent developments. Wherever possible, the solid state physics terminology used will be explained briefly to accommodate non-experts in band theory, where this is necessary and helpful.

Graphite shows extreme anisotropy of transport properties. For instance, c-axis to a-axis resistivity ratios as large as 10^4 are reported. We shall find in Section III that a-axis electrical transport properties can be well understood in terms of band theory, although the effect of defects is an added complication. Defect properties are difficult to deal with but new light has been shed by systematic studies of transport properties and defect structure of pyrolytic graphites. In the case of grossly defective material the concept of graphite as the limit of the homologous series of fused ring aromatic hydrocarbons is useful. Description of the electrical properties of polycrystalline graphite, of great technological import, fits naturally into the discussion of a-axis properties. Here the comparatively high electrical resistivity (about 10^{-3} ohm cm at room temperature) and the negative temperature coefficient of resistivity attest a somewhat different band structure than that of more near-ideal graphites. Fine details of band structure are to no purpose: in these materials, which have a grain size of about 10^{-6} cm, grain boundary, impurity and defect scattering now dominate electron transport. While anisotropy is of less importance, it must still be taken into consideration particularly in those polycrystalline graphites manufactured by processes tending to produce some crystallite orientation.

Further aspects of the anisotropy will be deduced in the discussion in Section IV of the c-axis electron transport properties. Details of the band structure are of less use in characterization of the c-axis properties. Certainly defects play a predominant role; a-axis paths along dislocations and through defective areas could dominate the experimental results. Controversy as to the mechanism of carrier transport still rumbles; within the bounds of possibility is conduction by a hopping process such as that occurring between aromatic molecules; however, here we are beyond the limit defined by the uncertainty principle. But evidence is mounting in support of the band process.

Plasma physics is a rapidly expanding field. In conjunction with magneto-hydrodynamics there are possible industrial applications such as direct conversion of thermal energy to electrical energy and, even more important, is the controlled thermonuclear process which is an enormous challenge to technology. Gas plasmas prove somewhat flighty, so solids, more tractable, are often used to study predicted plasma phenomena. Briefly, the existence and behaviour of the collective excitations known as plasma waves may be described as follows. Electrons moving to screen a charge disturbance tend to overshoot their mark, they are attracted back to the centre once more to overshoot, and oscillations are set up as the electrons fluctuate collectively about the centre. Semimetals behave as two-component plasmas; graphite is no exception. Certainly one region for future development is graphite in its aspect of a compensated, two-dimensional plasma. Preliminary work on this topic will be surveyed in Section V.

This chapter will be concluded with a brief discussion of recent developments in the understanding of transport properties in intercalation compounds and doped graphite.

During the last decade many new and interesting transport phenomena have been discussed in graphite and the other semimetals which may well lead to important technological developments. In order to describe as simply as possible the physical principles underlying these often rather complex phenomena it will be necessary to begin with a survey of the band theory and Fermi surface of graphite.

II. THE BAND STRUCTURE OF GRAPHITE

In the hexagonal modification of graphite, shown in Fig. 1, the carbon atoms are arranged in layer planes with in-plane bond distances a_0 (the a-axis spacing) of 1·42 Å. Each plane may be considered as an extended aromatic system. Stacking of the layer planes as ABABAB... and, as a result, the

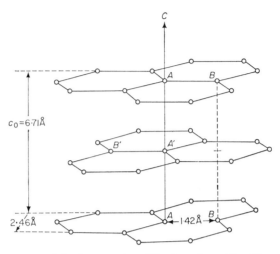

FIG. 1. The structure of the hexagonal modification of graphite. The c-axis spacing c_0 is twice the interplanar distance. Two types of atomic site occur: atoms on A sites have neighbours in adjacent layers while atoms on B sites do not.

crystallographic c-axis spacing c_0 is twice the interlayer spacing (3·354 Å). Such a large distance indicates weak, van der Waals' type, interlayer bonding; indeed, the estimated interaction turns out to be about one hundred times smaller than the tight binding interaction between in-plane neighbours. By setting aside the interlayer interactions, graphite may be treated to a first approximation as a two-dimensional lattice. It is useful to commence a description of the results of the energy band calculations from this viewpoint.

A. THE BAND STRUCTURE OF THE CARBON HEXAGON LAYER

Each carbon layer is to be regarded as a large aromatic molecule. The valence electrons of carbon are $2s^2 2p^2$. As in aromatic molecules, in graphite three of the four valence electrons occupy trigonal sp^2 hybrid orbitals directed at 120° to each other and which lie in the basal plane. These sp^2 hybrids overlap with those on adjacent carbon atoms to form tight, localized sp^2 σ-bonds. The remaining occupied orbital is the $2p_z$ state directed at right angles to the nodal carbon plane. Linear combination of the $2p_z$ orbitals produces a delocalized, π-type molecular orbital extending over either side of the lattice plane. A π-orbital is antisymmetric on reflection in the layer while σ-orbitals are symmetric; there are no non-zero matrix elements between σ and π Bloch functions: the electron eigenstates are rigorously separated into σ- and π-states and can be computed separately. This considerably simplifies calculations.

The major objective of energy band calculations is the characterization of those surfaces of constant energy in k-space near the Fermi level. Only electrons in these states on or near the Fermi surface are involved in ordinary transport processes in a conductor. Before we can examine the energy surfaces, we must construct the Brillouin zone for the two-dimensional model of graphite.

The unit cell of a graphite layer, $WXYZ$ in Fig. 2, contains two atoms, A and B. The lattice translation vectors $\mathbf{a}_1$ and $\mathbf{a}_2$ have a magnitude a of

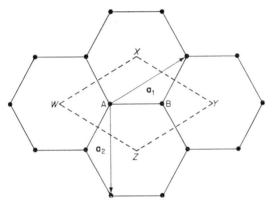

FIG. 2. The unit cell $WXYZ$ of a single layer contains two atoms A and B. The direct lattice translation vectors are $\mathbf{a}_1$ and $\mathbf{a}_2$.

$1{\cdot}42\sqrt{3}$ Å or $2{\cdot}46$ Å. Therefore, the reciprocal lattice vectors $\mathbf{b}_1$ and $\mathbf{b}_2$ defined by

$$\mathbf{b}_i \cdot \mathbf{a}_j = 2\pi . \delta_{ij}; \qquad \delta_{ij} = 0 \quad \text{when} \quad i \neq j$$

$$= 1 \quad \text{when} \quad i = j$$

$$i, j = 1 \ or \ 2 \tag{1}$$

will be directed at $60°$ to each other in reciprocal space and be of magnitude $4\pi\sqrt{3}a_0$. In consequence the reciprocal lattice is hexagonal in structure with a spacing $4\pi/\sqrt{3}a_0$. To build up the Brillouin zone we must construct in the usual way the perpendicular bisectors of the reciprocal lattice vectors. The result is a hexagon with sides of length $4\pi/3a_0$, turned through $90°$ with respect to the direct lattice hexagons, of area $8\pi/\sqrt{3}a_0^2$, that is 4π times the reciprocal of the area of the direct lattice unit cell.

There have been several energy band calculations for the two-dimensional model. Chemical considerations, based on the principles evolved for aromatic

molecules, suggest that, in order of increasing energy, the energy bands are
$\sigma, \sigma, \sigma, \pi$ (all bonding), $\pi^*, \sigma^*, \sigma^*, \sigma^*$ (all antibonding). In each unit cell
both carbon atoms provide four valence electrons. Now the number of
allowed electron k-states per energy band is equal to the number of unit cells
in the lattice. Therefore, for a layer of N atoms, there are $N/2$ unit cells and
consequently $N/2$ allowed k-states in each band. Allowing for spin, each band
can contain N electrons and the lowest four bands should be filled. On this
basis the π-band must be the valence band while the π^*-band is the conduction
band. Although the σ-electrons are collected in bands, these bands are full
and can play no part in the transport properties of graphite. As a result of
the Pauli exclusion principle, in a filled band every allowed k-state contains
two electrons of opposite spin. To conduct a current electrons must be
accelerated by the applied field and move through different momentum
states; in a filled band such transitions cannot take place.

Wallace (1947) first determined the π-band structure of the two-
dimensional layer using the tight-binding approximation, which is the
molecular orbital method applied to a solid. Only nearest-neighbour interactions were taken into account. In this single electron approximation linear
combination of $2p_z$ atomic orbitals produces electron eigenfunctions, corresponding to molecular orbitals, which can be written as Bloch wave functions:

$$\psi_{n,k}(\mathbf{r}) = \exp(i\mathbf{k}.\mathbf{r}).u_{n,k}(\mathbf{r}). \tag{2}$$

Here n identifies the band, the reduced wave propagation vector $\mathbf{k}$ can be
considered as a quantum number identifying a particular molecular orbital
and $u_{n,k}(\mathbf{r})$, which has the same translational symmetry as the lattice,
modulates the plane wave component $\exp(i\mathbf{k}.\mathbf{r})$. Each of these Bloch waves
describes an electronic state of motion in the periodic field of the lattice. This
is not the place in which to detail the calculations and we will now proceed
to examine the calculated shapes of the energy surfaces in the π-bands near
the Fermi level.

All calculations are at one as to the main features of the band structure
of the two-dimensional layer. The two π-bands touch at the six Brillouin zone
coerners U (Fig. 3). At any temperature above $0°K$ there are then a few
thermally excited electrons in the conduction band and an equal number of
holes in the valence band. Wallace (1947) found the energy dependence on
the wave-vector $\mathbf{k}$ to be

$$E(\mathbf{k}) = E_u \pm \frac{\sqrt{3}}{2} \gamma_0 ak + \text{function}(k^2). \tag{3}$$

where E_u is the energy at the zone corner U, and a is the length of the translation vector $\mathbf{a}_i$. The parameter γ_0 is equivalent to the resonance integral of
molecular orbital theory considering nearest-neighbour interactions only.
In aromatic compounds γ_0 is found from optical spectroscopy to be about

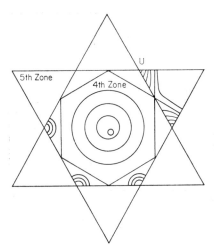

FIG. 3. A sketch for the two-dimensional model of the surfaces of constant energy for the lower π-band in the fourth zone and the upper π-band in the fifth zone. At 0°K the fourth zone is completely full while the fifth zone is completely empty.

3 eV (Pullman and Pullman 1952). Recent experimental data (McClure 1960; Inoue 1962; Dresselhaus and Mavroides 1964) indicates 2·8 eV for γ_0 in graphite in agreement with the value of 3 eV calculated by Lomer (1955) using the tight-binding method. The energy of allowed k-states in the upper and lower π-bands corresponds to use of the plus or minus sign respectively in eqn (3). For most purposes a linear approximation to this relationship is adequate

$$E = E_0 \pm \tfrac{3}{2}\gamma_0 ak. \tag{4}$$

In the vicinity of the Brillouin zone corners, that is for small values of k, the surfaces of constant energy are circular both for the lower π-band in the fourth zone and for the upper π-band in the fifth zone. A sketch of the energy surfaces in both π-bands is shown in Fig. 3. The energy dependence upon the wave vector **k** along the line from the centre 0 to a corner U of the Brillouin zone using the reduced zone scheme is shown in Fig. 4. A similar curve is obtained by plotting the energy against wave vector diagram along the zone edge starting at the centre of the edge and proceeding to a corner. Combination of these two diagrams shows that to a first order in k the energy surfaces consist of two circular cones whose apexes touch at the Brillouin zone corner. Group theoretical analysis (Slonczewski and Weiss 1958) establishes the origin of this result in the symmetry of the carbon hexagon layer.

So far as transport processes are concerned, the density of states $N(E)$, defined by writing $N(E)dE$ as the number of allowed electron states in the

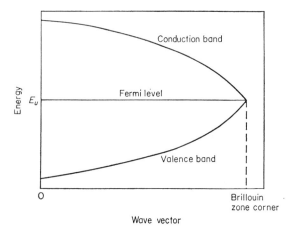

FIG. 4. The energy dependence in the valence and conduction bands upon the wave vector along the line from the centre 0 to the corner U of the Brillouin zone. The energies of the two bands are identical at the Brillouin zone corners: the bands touch here.

energy range between E and $(E+dE)$, is a most important parameter because ultimately it determines the number of carriers. For the two-dimensional model it can be readily shown from eqn (4) that near the Brillouin zone corners the density of states in both the valence and conduction bands is

$$N(E) = \frac{2(E-E_0)}{3\pi\gamma_0^2 a^2}. \tag{5}$$

Evidently the density of states is very sensitive to the resonance integral γ_0; a numerical value of $N(E)$ as a function of k is plotted in Fig. 5 using a value of 2·8 eV for γ_0. Although crude, the two-dimensional model leads to many of the important features of the band structure of graphite. The effective number of carriers is small and, in the absence of defects and impurities, there are equal densities of holes and electrons.

The assumption of Wallace (1947) and Coulson and Taylor (1952) among others that only the π-bands need be considered in a detailed treatment of transport properties of graphite has been justified by Corbato (1959) with a very extensive, rigorous, tight-binding calculation, including the effects of neighbours out to the ninth order starting, from the $1s$, $2s$, $2p_x$, $2p_y$ and $2p_z$ Hartree–Foch atomic orbitals of carbon to form the Bloch wave states in all the σ- and π-bands. His findings demonstrate that the π-bands do touch at the Brillouin zone corners and that this point of degeneracy in the π-bands is enclosed by a large energy gap (about 5 eV) between the highest bonding σ-band and the lowest antibonding σ^*-band. As illustrated in Fig. 5, the Fermi level is situated at the point where the π-bands touch: the electron transport

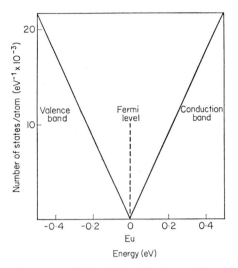

FIG. 5. The density of states near the band edges for the two-dimensional model assuming 2·8 eV for γ_0.

properties of graphite are determined by π-electrons in states in the near vicinity of the Brillouin zone corners. The σ- and π-bands do cross at points deep within the Brillouin zone where σ–π interactions have a negligible effect on the states near the Fermi level.

Although the two-dimensional model does show some of the essential features of the band structure of graphite, some of its implications are deceptive. Graphite would appear to be a semiconductor with a zero energy gap, whereas experiment shows it to be a semimetal. The valence and conduction bands overlap slightly, and even at very low temperatures the electrical and magnetic properties can only be explained on the basis of a comparatively high density of both electrons and holes. As might be expected, the two-dimensional model gives too low a carrier density even at room temperature; an on-the-cuff calculation taking γ_0 as 2·8 eV and using the result for the carrier density derived by Wallace (1947)

$$2 \int_0^\infty \frac{N(E)}{N_a} . f(E) . dE = \frac{\pi}{6\sqrt{3}} \left(\frac{kT}{\gamma_0} \right)^2 \tag{6}$$

where N_a is number of atoms in the lattice and $f(E)$ is the Fermi distribution function, gives a total carrier density of $2·3 \times 10^{18}$ carriers/cm^3 at room temperature in contrast to experimental values of the order of 10^{19} carriers/cm^3 both for single crystal graphite (Soule 1958) and pyrolytic graphite

(Blackman *et al.* 1961a; Klein and Straub 1961). Again in contradiction to experiment, the two-dimensional model predicts equal hole and electron effective masses. Study of the band structure in three dimensions resolves these difficulties.

B. THE BAND STRUCTURE OF THREE-DIMENSIONAL GRAPHITE

The inference that the π-band electrons only are responsible for transport properties must also be valid for three-dimensional graphite: insertion of the weak interlayer interaction modifies the energy by at most 0·5 eV as compared to the total band width of the order of 10 eV. However, these small variations are, so far as transport properties go, salient: now the π-bands overlap in the vicinity of the vertical zone edges defined by HKH in Fig. 6. These con-

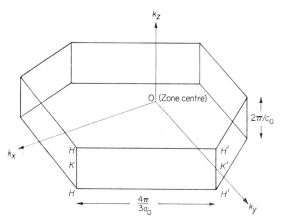

Fig. 6. The three-dimensional Brillouin zone.

siderations and the high symmetry at the zone corners led Slonczewski and Weiss (1958) to complete a group theoretical study of the electron energy surfaces close to the zone edges. As their formulation proves readily adaptable to comparison with experiment, we shall now concern ourselves with its essentials after a brief description of the way in which the three-dimensional graphite structure determines the geometry of the Brillouin zone.

In the Bernal structure of graphite, illustrated in Fig. 1, the displaced arrangement of the alternate layers results in two types of atomic sites having different environments. Atoms at points denoted by A in the diagram have neighbours directly above and below in adjacent planes while those at points such as B are next to empty hexagon centres. The unit cell, now associated with two layers, contains four atoms A, A^1, B and B^1 and has a height c_0 of 6·74 Å.

To construct the three-dimensional Brillouin zone we follow the usual procedure. The (002) planes are responsible for Bragg reflection of electrons moving along the c-axis: the Brillouin zone boundaries in the direction of the k_z are parallel to the hexagon planes. Therefore, the first Brillouin zone is the hexagonal prism illustrated in Fig. 6. As a result of the $180°$ screw axis perpendicular to the basal plane in the Bernal structure, Bragg reflections from adjacent planes spaced $c_0/2$ apart are π out of phase and add destructively. In other words the structure factor is zero for the planes $k_z = \pm 2\pi/c_0$. There is no energy discontinuity at such planes and thus the zone boundaries are the planes $k_z = \pm \pi/c_0$.

Only a synopsis of the band structure calculation of Slonczewski and Weiss (1958) need be given here. In the basal plane the Hamiltonian is expanded in terms of distances k_x and k_y from the zone edge; the zero-order wave functions are taken as being those at the Brillouin zone corner, and the dependence of energy upon wave vector at points inside the zone close to the edges and corners are calculated by $\mathbf{k.p}$ perturbation theory. Since the interlayer binding is so weak, the energy dependence along the k_z direction HKH can be determined in the tight-binding approximation.

The results of the calculations and their extension by McClure (1957, 1960) are expressed in terms of six parameters, having the dimensions of energy, used in forming the Hamiltonian and arising as matrix elements of momentum. These parameters relate to various kinds of interaction and, loosely speaking, correspond to integrals in the tight binding approximation: they represent orbital overlap. We have already considered the most important as the in-plane, resonance integral γ_0 in the two-dimensional calculation. The other parameters affect the energy band structure extensively, and appear as constants in the equations expressing the energy dependence on wave number for states near the zone edges. As these parameters have a formative influence on electron transport properties, it is pertinent to consider their physical origin and magnitude.

Overlap of orbitals centred on nearest neighbour atoms in adjacent layers, that is the atoms sited in A and A^1 in Fig. 1, is expressed by the nearest neighbour interaction integral γ_1, and leads to splitting of the energy bands. As would be expected, γ_1 turns out to be the largest of the interlayer interaction integrals. Discrepancies occur between the various experimental values; McClure's analysis (1960) of diamagnetism in graphite gives γ_1 as $0\cdot27$ eV while magnetoreflection work (Dresselhaus and Mavroides 1964) indicates $0\cdot4$ eV.

Overlap of orbitals on B site atoms on next nearest layers is represented by an integral γ_2 of higher order and much smaller than γ_1. So far as transport properties are concerned, γ_2 is a most important parameter, being responsible for overlap between the valence and conduction bands at the edge of the

Brillouin zone: thus, pure graphite contains both electrons and holes at all temperatures. The band overlap, $2\gamma_2$, shown diagrammatically in Fig. 7, estimated between 0·03 eV and 0·04 eV, is

$$2\gamma_2 = E_f^e + E_f^h \tag{7}$$

where E_f^e and E_f^h are the partial Fermi energies for electrons and holes respectively.

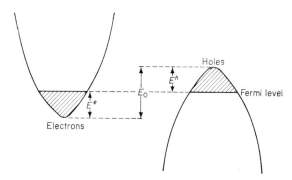

FIG. 7. A simple representation of the overlap between the valence and conduction bands. Energy is plotted along the ordinate and wave vector along the abscissa. The band overlap E_0 is equal to $2\gamma_2$.

The matrix elements of the transverse component of momentum between orbitals in nearest-neighbour layers are expressed as approximately equal γ_3 and γ_4. The latter specifies departure from mirror symmetry for magnetic energy levels in the valence and conduction bands. Although γ_3 has little effect on the cross-sectional area of the Fermi surface, it produces trigonal warping, and in consequence the Fermi surface shows threefold symmetry about the zone edge. The significance of this is detailed below. Finally, the parameter Δ, a result of the potential energy differences between orbitals on the A and B sites, lifts some degeneracy from the zone corner. Recent values of the parameters are given in Table I.

In principal, once the six parameters are known, the electronic band structure of graphite is described. The role played by some of these parameters can readily be seen from the energy dependence of the π-bands on the wave vector shown in three dimensions in Fig. 8. For three-dimensional graphite there are now four π-bands, separated by less than 1 eV; the variation along k_z of the energy at which two bands, degenerate along k_z, touch is represented by the doubly degenerate level E_3. The portions of the figure which jut out represent the energy dependence of the π-bands in a direction perpendicular to k_z along a line through a corner of the zone. As a result of the symmetry of graphite, the π-bands represented by E_1 and E_2 become

TABLE I

Band Parameters for Graphite

Parameter	Value
γ_0	2·9
γ_1	0·27 to 0·4
γ_2	0·016
γ_3	0·14
γ_4	−0·2
Δ	−0·02 to −0·10
E_F	0·019

For further details see Dresselhaus and Mavroides (1964).

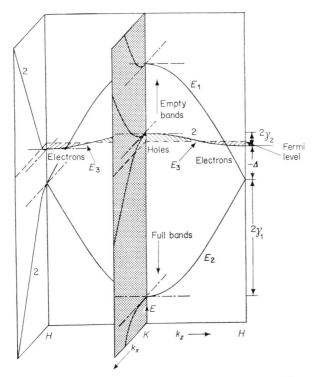

FIG. 8. The dependence of band energy upon the wave vector **k**. Energy is plotted vertically, k_z is horizontal (HKH are the same as in Fig. 6) while k_z is perpendicular to plane of the paper. Doubly degenerate levels are shown by the number 2. The horizontal dashed line indicates the position of the Fermi level in pure graphite. (After McClure 1960.)

degenerate at the Brillouin zone corner, where σ–π mixing is still not allowed, and so at the corner only two levels, both doubly degenerate as represented by the number 2 on the curves, need be drawn, as shown. Elsewhere E_1 and E_2 are not degenerate. At some points along k_z the lowest valley of the conduction band is below the Fermi level while at others this is true for the highest valley of the conduction band: pockets of holes and electrons are located along the Brillouin zone edge HKH. The maximum cross-sectional area of the hole pocket is at the point K. Both hole and electron pockets are essentially formed by the two bands whose locus of degeneracy is represented by E_3 in Fig. 8.

C. THE FERMI SURFACE OF GRAPHITE

From these band structure calculations the general nature of the Fermi surface of graphite is discernible, and is illustrated in Fig. 9. In the repeated zone scheme the electron and hole ellipsoid-like pockets are found strung like long, thin beads along the vertical triad Brillouin zone edges HKH

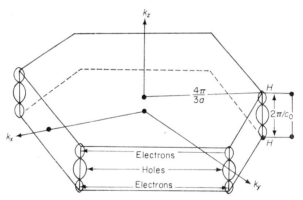

FIG. 9. The positions of the electron and hole pockets in the Brillouin zone. The sizes of pockets are much magnified in the $k_x k_y$ plane. Recent results indicate that the electron pockets extend beyond the zone corners at H.

parallel to the k_z direction. Along an edge there are one hole and two electron pockets, each belonging to three zones: the zone contains a total of four electron and two hole closed surfaces. These surfaces extend only about 1% of the distance into the zone and the carrier density is small.

Recently, the topology of the Fermi surface of graphite has been detailed in a most thorough way by experimental techniques combined with the Slonczewski and Weiss formalism. In essence, the band parameters, determined experimentally, are inserted into the theory to delineate a comprehensive picture of the Fermi surface. Much earlier supposition is consolidated and new, subtle details are exposed. It is worthwhile to touch upon the physical principles underlying the experiments before reviewing the detailed features of the Fermi surface.

Magnetoreflection experiments on pyrolytic graphite (Dresselhaus and Mavroides 1964) allow quantitative evaluation of most of the band parameters. An almost normally incident light beam is reflected from the predominantly c-plane cleavage face and an oscillatory magnetic field dependence arising from interband transitions between the quantized magnetic energy levels is observed, each π-band being split by the magnetic field into a series of levels like those in the quantized harmonic oscillator. From the dependence of the oscillations upon both magnetic field and the incident photon energy the band parameters γ_0, γ_1, γ_2, γ_4 and Δ can be estimated. Results are shown in Table I. It seems that the overlap parameters and the band structure of well-annealed pyrolytic graphite closely resemble those of the single crystal form. Previously, this was a subject of some controversy.

Further new details of the Fermi surfaces are forthcoming from the de Haas–van Alphen studies of Williamson et al. (1965). The de Haas–van Alphen effect, an oscillation of magnetic susceptibility as magnetic field changes, arises from variations in the electron density of states at the Fermi level as Landau levels, produced by quantization of the electron energy levels in a magnetic field, are swept through the Fermi surface. When a Landau level is coincident with the Fermi surface, the Onsager–Lifschitz quantization relationship holds between the period $P(1/H)$ of the oscillations in the inverse magnetic field and the maximum cross-sectional area A_M of the Fermi surface perpendicular to the magnetic field.

$$P(1/H) = \frac{2\pi e}{\hbar c A_M}. \tag{8}$$

As a method for detailing the Fermi surface, the de Haas–van Alphen effect is powerful: the cross-sectional area of the Fermi surface normal to the direction of the magnetic field can be determined from the period of the oscillations in the magnetic susceptibility. If measurements are made as a function of crystal orientation in the field, the whole Fermi surface can, at least in principal, be charted. A disadvantage of the technique lies in the difficulty of estimating the shape of Fermi surface from a measured area, and care must be taken to ensure that not too much reliance is put on structures ascertained for complex Fermi surfaces. Over the years the method has been applied extensively to the study of graphite, culminating in the work of Williamson et al. (1965) using the de Haas–van Alphen effect itself on both single crystal and pyrolytic graphite and that of Soule, McClure and Smith (1964) on single crystals. The latter workers employed the closely allied de Haas–Shubnikov effect based on the principle that the periodic fluctuations of the electron density on the Fermi surface produce oscillations in the magnetic field dependence of electrical resistivity. Both studies have been made over the whole Fermi surface by extending measurements to maximize coverage of the angles between the c-axis and the magnetic field. Results confirm that both the electron and hole surfaces are closed, as might be expected from the earlier observations that in the high field limit the transverse magnetoresistance does not saturate.

The probable topology of the Fermi Surface estimated from these recent experiments is shown in Fig. 10. Both hole and electron Fermi surfaces are extremely anisotropic, the major-to-minor axis ratio being about 17 to 1 and 12 to 1 respectively. Considerable trigonal warping of the Fermi surfaces arises from the influence of γ_3. The hole surface, somewhat "diamond shaped", has considerable trigonal anisotropy on the plane $k_z = 0$, constructed through the point K on the Brillouin zone edge, on which the hole pocket is at its maximum cross-sectional area and has an almost triangular cross-section. Outwards from K, along the zone edge HKH, the warping of the hole surface becomes more pronounced until, at a point about two-fifths out from K of the distance to the zone corner H, it breaks into four parts. The three satellites, shown in the figure, diminish until finally inexistent, and three somewhat similar pieces of electron Fermi surface take their place. At rather less than halfway out to the corner, the central portion of the hole surface vanishes, and the equivalent portion of the electron surface is extant. About seven-tenths of the distance out from H to K the electron Fermi surface is at its maximum cross-sectional area with an equivalent radius of $1 \cdot 2 \times 10^6$ cm^{-1}, rather less than that of the hole surface. The electron surface shows less deviation from rotational symmetry than the hole surface.

1. *Minority Carriers in Graphite*

As we have seen, the total height of the Brillouin zone is $2\pi/c_0$ or $93 \cdot 6 \times 10^6$ cm^{-1}. Now the length of each electron surface along k_z is about 30×10^6 cm^{-1} while that of the hole surface is about 50×10^6 cm^{-1}. As described, the hole and electron surfaces overlap but even so the total length of the electron-hole-electron "string" is greater than the height of the Brillouin zone: the electron surfaces extend about 7×10^6 cm^{-1} beyond the edge of the zone at H (Soule *et al.* 1964). In the extended zone scheme electron pockets overlap near the zone corners, as illustrated in Fig. 11(a), and a minority carrier pocket is formed (Fig. 11b) which is separated off from the Fermi surface of the majority carriers by the spin–orbit coupling interaction. Due to structural differences, finer details of the Fermi surface might be expected to vary between single crystal and even the best available pyrolytic graphite. This is so. Evidence exists (Williamson *et al.* 1965) for

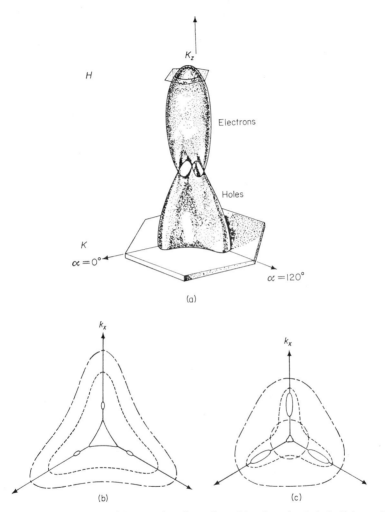

FIG. 10. (a) The topology of the Fermi surface of graphite along k_z. Only half the surface is drawn; the electron surface extends beyond H. (b) The shape of the hole surface in the $k_x k_y$ plane at various positions along k_z. ——, 0·4 HK; - - -, 0·28 HK; – – – –, K. (c) Electron surface cross-sections perpendicular to k_z. ——, 0·45 KH; - - -, 0·5 KH; – – – –, 0·7 KH; – – –, H. The electron and hole surfaces split into smaller portions near 0·4 $\overrightarrow{KH}$. (The numbers represent the distance along $\overrightarrow{HK}$ at which each cross-section is made.) (After Dresselhaus and Mavroides 1964.)

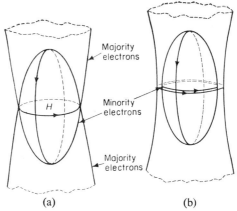

FIG. 11. The electron Fermi surface near the Brillouin zone corner H in an extended zone scheme. (a) The ends of the electron pockets from adjacent zones overlap to form a minority carrier pocket. (b) Spin–orbit coupling separates the minority carrier pocket off from the majority electron Fermi surface and two non-degenerate extremal areas are extant in the k_z plane through the zone corner H. (After Williamson et al. 1965.)

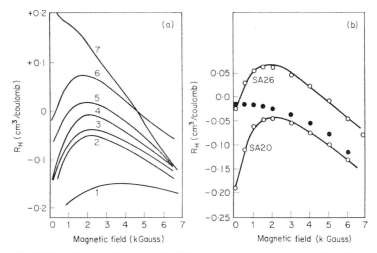

FIG. 12. (a) The Hall coefficient at 77·5°K as a function of magnetic field for a representative series of basal plane samples including hot-pressed pyrolytic graphites (Nos. 1–6) and (No. 7) single crystal EP 14 (Soule 1958). At low fields the behaviour of the two types of graphite is quite distinct: a result suggesting the presence of different minority carriers. (b) While the predictions of the two-carrier model (●) do not account for the Hall coefficient field dependence for hot-pressed pyrolytic graphite, the data can be fitted by a three-carrier model (○). For simple SA 20 the carrier densities and mobilities are:

Carrier	Density (cm^{-3})	Mobility (cm^2/V sec)
Minority electron	3·3 $\times$ 10^{16}	2·15 $\times$ 10^5
Majority electron	2·25 $\times$ 10^{18}	5·05 $\times$ 10^4
Majority hole	2·255 $\times$ 10^{18}	5·07 $\times$ 10^4

(After Spain et al. 1965.)

different effective masses of the minority carriers. For instance, the "a-axis" effective mass is $(4 \cdot 0 \pm 0 \cdot 4) \times 10^{-3} m_0$ for pyrolytic graphite while it is $2 \cdot 3 \times 10^{-3} m_0$ for single crystal graphite. The existence of minority carriers in single crystal graphite first came to light from the detailed analysis by McClure (1958) of Soule's low field Hall effect data (1958). Recently, "a-axis" Hall coefficient data has become available for pyrolytic graphite treated by a hot-pressing process, which appears to improve perfection (Spain et al. 1965). The magnetic field dependence of the Hall coefficient at $77 \cdot 5°$K, illustrated

TABLE II

Properties of the Current Carriers along the a-axis of Graphite. Note especially differences between the minority carriers in single crystal and pyrolytic graphite

Sample	Temperature		
	$4 \cdot 2°$K	$77°$K	$298°$K
Single Crystal Graphite (EP14)			
(McClure, 1958)			
Majority hole			
Density $\times 10^{-18}$ (cm^{-3})	2·9	2·2	7·0
Mobility $\times 10^{-14}$ (cm²/V sec)	104·0	7·3	1·0
Majority electron			
Density $\times 10^{-18}$ (cm^{-3})	2·9	2·2	7·0
Mobility $\times 10^{-4}$ (cm²/V sec)	83·9	6·4	1·1
Minority hole			
Density $\times 10^{-15}$ (cm^{-3})		3·3	
Mobility $\times 10^{-4}$ (cm²/V sec)		60·0	
Minority electron			
Density $\times 10^{-15}$ (cm^{-3})	200·0		0·5
Mobility $\times 10^{-4}$ (cm²/V sec)	0·7		39·0
Pyrolytic Graphite (hot pressed)			
(Spain et al., 1965)			
Majority holes (and electrons)			
Density $\times 10^{-18}$ (cm^{-3})		2·25	
Mobility $\times 10^{-4}$ (cm²/V sec)		5·0	
Minority electron			
Density $\times 10^{-15}$ (cm^{-3})		33·0	
Mobility $\times 10^{-4}$ (cm²/V sec)		21·5	
Pyrolytic Graphite			
(Williamson et al., 1965)			
Minority electron			
Density $\times 10^{-15}$ (cm^{-3})	7·5		
Single Crystal Graphite			
(Williamson et al., 1965)			
Minority electron			
Density $\times 10^{-15}$ (cm^{-3})	62·0		

in Fig. 12(a), can be accounted for quantitatively, see Fig. 12(b), in terms of a three-carrier model assuming the minority carriers to be electrons in agreement with the model in Fig. 11. The single crystal results of Soule imply that minority holes may also be present but the situation may well be obscured by substitutional doping with heteroatomic impurities (Spain *et al.* 1965). Plausibly, minority holes might arise in the satellite region of overlap between the electron and hole pockets. Carrier densities and mobility are shown in Table II to illustrate the relative importance of the minority carriers. At the bottom of this table the carrier densities of minority electrons estimated by Williamson *et al.* (1965) are given for both single crystal and pyrolytic graphite.

Another important parameter, so far as discussion of transport properties is concerned, is the carrier effective mass ($0.04m_0$ for electrons and $0.06m_0$ for holes). The effective mass can only be considered as a phenomenological parameter because it is dependent upon the part of the Fermi surface under observation as well as the impurity and defect concentration and consequent position of the Fermi level in the specimen.

The band theory of graphite proves invaluable to development of an understanding of the *a*-axis transport properties as we shall see in the next section. However, just how far it is valid for *c*-axis transport properties is not clearly established. We defer this problem until Section IV.

III. a-AXIS ELECTRON TRANSPORT PROPERTIES IN GRAPHITES

Both the electronic band structure and the mechanism of free carrier scattering determine the electrical transport properties of a solid. Thus, the considerable structural variations between the various materials designated as graphites lead to quite different electrical properties. We will assume the usual classification into single crystal, pyrolytic and polycrystalline graphites and partially graphitized carbons and, in the first instance, relate differences in electronic band structure to the transport properties. Over the last decade the development of an understanding of transport properties in single crystals has provided a useful foundation for description of transport processes in the more defective graphites.

A. ELECTRON TRANSPORT IN SINGLE-CRYSTAL GRAPHITE

Following Kinchin's pioneering study (1953) the most intensive work on transport properties of single crystal graphite is that of Soule (1958) analysed in terms of the multi-carrier band model by McClure (1958). This work is reviewed extensively by Haering and Mrozowski (1960). Ideally the transport properties can be related to the known details of the Fermi surface: in principle, if the scattering law is known, the Boltzmann equation in the form

$$\sigma_{xx} = -\frac{e^2}{4\pi^3} \int \tau v_x^2 \left(\frac{\partial f}{\partial E}\right) d^3k \tag{9}$$

allows calculation of the a-axis conductivity σ_{xx}. Here τ is the relaxation time, f is the Fermi–Dirac distribution function and k is the wave number. The electron velocity v_x at the Fermi surface is

$$v_x = \frac{1}{\hbar} \frac{\partial}{\partial k_x} E(k) \tag{10}$$

$E(k)$ being the surface of constant energy in k-space described as the Fermi surface. Assuming the three-dimensional band structure of graphite, while neglecting the trigonal warping parameter γ_3, McClure and Smith (1962) found agreement within 5% between the measured electrical resistivity of single crystals and their theoretical value. For the scattering law, they took a relaxation time inversely proportional to the product of the phonon density and the density of electron states (see Soule and McClure 1959). The magnetoresistivity, Hall coefficient and thermoelectric power are much more sensitive than the resistivity to details of the band structure and the scattering mechanism. At best the calculated values are only within about 50% of experimental data. Further calculations should improve matters.

B. ELECTRON TRANSPORT IN PYROLYTIC GRAPHITE

In the case of the defective graphites of technological importance such close correspondence with detailed theory can no longer be expected. In the limit of grossly defective carbons it is doubtful if the band theory holds at all. More recent studies of the effects of defects on transport properties include work on boron doped graphite (Soule 1962) and systematic investigations of the defect structure and properties of pyrolytic graphite (Blackman et al. 1961a; Klein 1961, 1964). In particular, such studies are prompted by the growing technological importance of pyrolytic graphite. By varying the deposition temperature, a series of pyrolytic graphites (type A) can be produced with structures covering a wide range of perfection. When the deposits are manufactured at temperatures above that at which self-diffusion onsets in graphite, that is about 2200°C, a critical change occurs in the structure. Deposits made below this temperature are grossly defective and show little preferred orientation while, on the other hand, preparation above this temperature leads to graphitic deposits. Crystal orientation improves progressively in specimens deposited up to 2600°C and recrystallization (to produce types AB and B graphites) further improves perfection. Electron transport properties in the most perfect pyrolytic graphites show a close resemblance to many of the properties of single crystal graphite. Further details of defects in pyrolytic graphites are forthcoming from studies of the effect of radiation damage (Blackman *et al.* 1961b; Ammar and Young 1964).

While the basal planes are more or less parallel to the deposition plane, pyrolytic graphite is polycrystalline, the *a*-axes are randomly orientated in the deposition plane and there is much general disorder including some turbostatic stacking. Both crystallite boundary and defect scattering of the carriers now play an important role. In consequence the complex model of the Fermi surface is an unrealistic basis for interpretation of transport properties, and the more convenient simple two-band model (Klein 1961; 1964) is, normally used. Cylindrical and parabolic energy surfaces are assumed for each π-band so that

$$E_e = \frac{\hbar^2 k^2}{2m_e^*}$$

$$E_h = E_0 - \frac{\hbar^2 k^2}{2m_h^*} \tag{11}$$

when subscripts e and h refer to the conduction and valence bands respectively. This model is depicted in Fig. 13(a) for well-graphitized pyrolytic

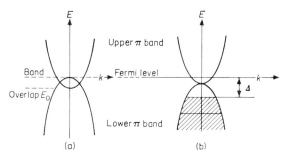

FIG. 13. The simple two-band model of the π-band model of (a) heat-treated pyrolytic graphite and (b) less perfect pyrolytic graphite. In this case the presence of electron traps depresses the Fermi level by Δ below the top of the valence band and the band overlap is much reduced or removed.

graphite in which, as for single crystal graphite, the interlayer interaction produces a band overlap E_0. Extensive studies show that defects in pyrolytic graphite as manufactured (Blackman *et al.* 1961a) or introduced subsequently by neutron irradiation damage (Blackman *et al.* 1961b) in general behave as electron traps. Hence in defective graphites the Fermi level is depressed (Δ), while at the same time the interlayer interaction is decreased, and the band overlap diminished, as shown in the energy band diagram in Fig. 13(b). Using the simple two-band model, analysis of the electron transport properties of pyrolytic graphites can be contrived.

C. TRANSPORT PROCESSES IN POLYCRYSTALLINE GRAPHITES AND CARBONS

Industrial polycrystalline graphite is so grossly defective that detailed description of transport properties in terms of a sophisticated band model would be futile. Mrozowski and his co-workers (1959) have made extensive studies on the effect of heat-treatment temperature on the graphitization of soft carbons. Transport processes can be explained by the simple band model for baked carbons suggested by Mrozowski (1952). When heated at temperatures below 700°C, the requisite organic compounds polymerize into a gamut of cross-linked aromatic molecules. The electrical resistivity ρ of these molecular solids is reasonably consistent (Kmetko 1951) with the linear log ρ *versus* $1/T$ law characteristic of an intrinsic semiconductor; the energy gap E_g, determined as $E_g/2k$ from the slope, decreases from 0·7 to 0·14 eV as the firing temperature is increased from 425 to 900°C. Thus, thermal activation of carriers dominates transport processes. Treatment at higher temperatures drives abundant hydrogen and hydrocarbons from the peripheries of the ring systems; small turbostatic crystals form, and crystallite size and perfection, and in consequence the electrical conductivity, improve with increasing heat-treatment temperature, until finally above 2500°C the product becomes industrial polycrystalline graphite. The results are summarized in Fig. 14. Evidence from the Hall effect, electrical resistivity and thermoelectric power shows that, on the basis of simple band theory, two processes occur: defects present tend to behave as electron traps, and the Fermi level is, as shown in Fig. 14(c), depressed below the top of the valence band. As perfection is

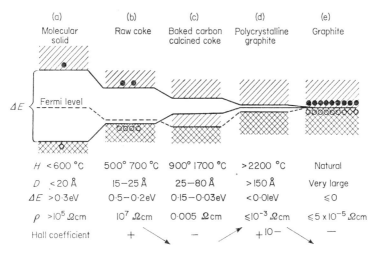

FIG. 14. The decrease in the energy gap (ΔE) for carbons after different heat treatments (H). As heat treatment temperature is increased the crystallite size (D) improves and the electrical resistivity (ρ) decreases rapidly. (After McMichael *et al.* 1954.)

improved and electron traps are annealed out, the Fermi level rises while the band gap decreases. In well-graphitized material the simple two-band model with a small band overlap, depicted in Fig. 14(d), is appropriate.

D. CARRIER MOBILITY IN NEAR-IDEAL GRAPHITES

A qualitative, phenomenological description of the transport processes in the various kinds of graphites can be developed from the band models which we have now outlined. However, it must not be overlooked that transport processes in materials at the grossly defective end of the scale are a function of microscopic variations throughout the structure. Exemplifying this is the observation of anomalous negative magnetoresistance. Before discussing this, we turn to survey carrier mobility and scattering processes in more ideal graphites.

1. Resistivity, Magnetoresistivity and Hall Coefficient

Measured values of the electrical resistivity of single crystals vary widely (see Table III) as a result of the difficulties of obtaining defect free specimens and of ensuring good electrode contact. The anisotropy ratio ρ_c/ρ_a emphasizes differences between assessments of ρ_c. Irregularities in Dutta's curves suggest contact troubles and, since the crystals were cleaved and cut, they may well have been mechanically damaged. Like Soule he copper-plated his crystals— a procedure criticized by Primak and Fuchs (1954) who point out that graphite swells during copper-plating probably due to interlamellar penetration by protons. In view of these detractions, the lower values about 4×10^{-5} ohm cm at room temperature would seem to be the true value of the a-axis resistivity.

The temperature coefficient of ρ_a is positive. Soule's results for crystal EP14 are plotted in Fig. 15 in comparison with some data for pyrolytic and

TABLE III

The Electrical Resistivity of Single Crystal Graphite at Room Temperature

Reference	a-Axis resistivity (ohm cm $\times 10^5$)	Temperature coefficient (°C^{-1})	c-Axis resistivity (ohm cm)	ρ_c/ρ_a (approximate)
Roberts (1913)	5	+0·001		
Washburn (1915)	5·6–8·0	+0·001	0·008–0·03	100
Kinchin (1953)	4–7	+0·0013		
Krishnan and Ganguli (1939)	10		2–3	10^4
Dutta (1953)	10	−0·001	1·0	10^4
Primak and Fuchs (1954)	3·8	+0·004	0·004–0·007	100–200
Soule (1958)	4	+0·0014		

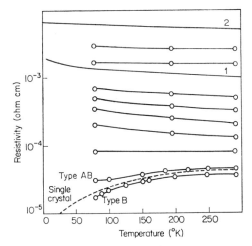

FIG. 15. The wide divergence between the electrical properties of graphite illustrated by the resistivity as a function of temperature for industrial pitch bonded polycrystalline graphites (Tyler and Wilson 1953), (1) being a coke base sample and (2) being a lampblack base sample. The dotted curve is the resistivity of a single crystal (Soule 1958) and the other curves are for a series of pyrolytic graphites deposited at temperatures between 1700°C and 2600°C. The highest conductivity sample is a type B, recrystallized pyrolytic graphite (Blackman *et al.* 1961a).

polycrystalline graphite. For a two-carrier conductor the conductivity σ is

$$\sigma = n|e|\mu_e + p|e|\mu_h \qquad (12)$$

where $|e|$ is the electronic charge, n and p are the carrier densities for electrons and holes respectively, and the carrier mobility μ_i is the drift velocity per unit field. Now the mobilities vary as $T^{-1\cdot2}$ while, over the temperature range 77–298°K, the carrier density increases about three times: the positive temperature coefficient of ρ_a of single crystals and more perfect pyrolytic graphites arises from the carrier mobility decrease with rising temperature.

From Matthiessen's rule it follows that the ratio of the electrical resistivities at room temperature and liquid helium temperature $\rho_{293°K}/\rho_{4\cdot2°K}$ is a sensitive parameter for assessment of relative defect and impurity content in crystals; metal physicists use this yardstick frequently. Unfortunately, Soule alone quotes this ratio (37 : 1 for EP14). Significantly, the best hot-pressed pyrolytic graphite give ratios which are only a little smaller (Spain *et al.* 1965).

An interesting feature is that there is a break at about 120°K in the temperature dependence of ρ_a for single crystals (Primak and Fuchs 1954; Soule 1958) and possibly also for pyrolytic graphite. The magnetoresistivity and Hall effect show carrier density increases at the average degeneracy temperature for holes and electrons, which corresponds to an energy of about half the band overlap, where kT becomes comparable to the Fermi level. Values of the approximate band overlap (0·02 eV) found by this method (McClure 1958) are rather less than those (0·03 eV) estimated by more conventional methods.

Carrier mobilities in graphites can be assessed approximately from the low field magnetoresistivity ($\Delta\rho/\rho_0$). Taking the ratio n/p of the carrier densities of electrons (n) and holes (p) as unity, Soule shows that an average mobility μ_{av} in cm²/V sec can be defined by

$$\mu_{av} = (\mu_e \mu_h)^{\frac{1}{2}} = \left(\frac{\Delta\rho}{\rho_0} \cdot \frac{1}{H^2}\right)^{\frac{1}{2}} \times 10^8 \tag{13}$$

H being the magnetic field in oersteds. Zero induction mobilities should be estimated because the magnetoresistivity does not obey a square law but is of the form illustrated in Fig. 16 for some pyrolytic graphites (Saunders 1962)

$$\left(\frac{\Delta\rho}{\rho_0}\right) = BH^x \tag{14}$$

where the exponent x varies from 1·8 at 77°K to 0·8 at liquid helium temperatures for single crystals (Soule 1958), from 1·5–1·9 for pyrolytic graphite (Blackman et al. 1961a), and is quoted as 1·77 for polycrystalline graphite (McClelland 1955). Some results for the temperature dependence of carrier

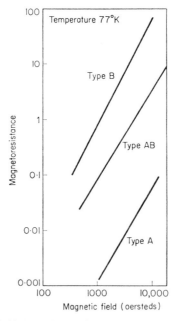

FIG. 16. The magnetic field dependence of the magnetoresistance of pyrolytic graphites at 77°K. (After Saunders 1962.)

mobility calculated from eqn (13) are plotted in Fig. 17. For near-ideal graphites the mobility turns out to be proportional to $T^{-1.3}$ above 25°K in agreement with acoustic mode, intravalley scattering of electrons. According to Soule and McClure (1959), the scattering power should be proportional to the product of the phonon density and the carrier density of states. Above 50°K the former factor is proportional to temperature while the second can be roughly represented by $T^{\frac{1}{2}}$. At low temperatures the mobility temperature dependence falls away as thermal scattering decreases in importance relative to boundary and residual defect scattering.

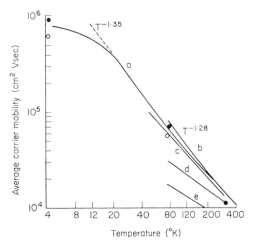

FIG. 17. The temperature dependence of the average carrier mobilities for single crystal (Soule 1958) and pyrolytic graphites: (a) heat treated at 3600°C (Klein *et al.* 1962), (b) Type B (Saunders 1962), (c) and (d) hot-pressed specimens (Spain *et al.* 1965), (e) untreated deposit (Saunders 1962). ●, Single crystal EP 14; ○, Single crystal EP 7.

The effect of variations in crystallite size and defect structure on the temperature dependence of the average carrier mobility is illustrated in Table IV by reference to a series of pyrolytic graphites (Saunders 1962). In more defective materials phonon scattering at boundaries and defects and electron–defect interactions are greater, and the electron–phonon scattering is much reduced. This crude picture explains the weak mobility temperature dependence in defective graphites. Assuming that carrier mean free paths are curtailed by boundary scattering L_B and phonon scattering L_p, Klein (1964) suggests that, from the free electron model, the average mobility (μ_{av}) is given by

$$\frac{1}{\mu_{av}} = \frac{m^* v}{e \times 10^7} \left(\frac{1}{L_p} + \frac{1}{L_B} \right). \qquad (15)$$

The temperature independent factor L_B ranges from 0·1–10 μ for specimens

TABLE IV

The Variation of the Temperature Dependence of Average Carrier
Mobility with Crystal Perfection Illustrated by Reference to a Series of
Pyrolytic Graphites (Saunders 1962)

Material	a-Axis resistivity at 20°C	Average carrier mobility μ_{av} at 20°C	Temperature dependence (77°–293°K) of μ_{av}
Single crystal (Soule, 1958)	3·6	90,000	$T^{-1\cdot2}$
Pyrolytic graphites			
Type B	3·6	81,500	$T^{-1\cdot28}$
Type B	4·5	45,200	$T^{-0\cdot98}$
Type AB	4·9	43,600	$T^{-0\cdot97}$
Type B	5·0	32,600	$T^{-0\cdot79}$
Type A	7·84	16,900	$T^{-0\cdot65}$
Type A	14·1	6,060	$T^{-0\cdot28}$
Type A	21·0	3,890	$T^{-0\cdot32}$
Type A	34·8	2,840	$T^{-0\cdot18}$

heat treated at 3500°C: crystallite sizes are of the order of microns. In agreement, Dresselhaus and Mavroides (1964) estimate a carrier mean free path of about one micron from line width measurements in magnetoreflection experiments in well-annealed pyrolytic graphites.

More rigorous calculations of carrier mobilities, applying magnetoconductivity tensor analys to the Hall coefficient and magnetoresistivity data, lead to mobility results similar to those calculated from the magnetoresistivity above, and at the same time total carrier densities $(n+p)$ can be estimated.

Some results for both single crystal and pyrolytic graphite are shown in Table V together with values for $(n+p)$ obtained from the magnetoresistivity and resistivity using the approximate relationship (Soule 1958)

$$(n+p) = \frac{1}{e\rho_0\left\{\dfrac{\Delta\rho}{\rho_0}\cdot\dfrac{1}{H^2}\right\}^{\frac{1}{2}}\times10^8}. \tag{16}$$

This assumes $n\mu_e$ equal to $p\mu_h$, a reasonable approximation for near-ideal graphite. Total carrier concentration varies only a modest amount, although room temperature resistivity, a measure of defectiveness, and carrier mobility vary by an order of magnitude. Plausibly, each electron trapping process produces a single positive hole.

In pyrolytic graphites the presence of equal numbers of free electrons and holes at very low temperatures is direct evidence of band overlap.

TABLE V

Total Carrier Densities $(n + p)$ and Average Mobilities in Near-ideal Graphites

Type of Graphite	a-Axis resistivity at 20°C (ohm cm)	Carrier density/cm³ $(n + p) \times 10^{-18}$			Average carrier mobility (cm²/V sec)		
		+20°C	−77°C	−196°C	+20°C	−77°C	−196°C
		(i) Calculated by magnetoconductivity analysis					
Single crystal (McClure, 1958)	$3{\cdot}6 \times 10^{-5}$	14·0		4·4			
Pyrolytic (Saunders, 1962)							
Type B	$3{\cdot}6 \times 10^{-5}$	12·2	10·0	2·8			
Type AB	$4{\cdot}5 \times 10^{-5}$	11·6	9·7	2·6			
Type A	$7{\cdot}8 \times 10^{-5}$	10·6					
Type A	$14{\cdot}1 \times 10^{-5}$	8·0					
		(ii) Calculated from eqns (13) and (16)					
Single crystal (Soule, 1958)	$3{\cdot}6 \times 10^{-5}$	9·9		3·3	16,000		90,000
Pyrolytic (Saunders, 1962)							
Type B	$3{\cdot}6 \times 10^{-5}$	11·6	9·4	2·9	15,000	22,000	81,500
Type AB	$4{\cdot}9 \times 10^{-5}$	10·7		3·5	12,000		44,000
Type AB	$8{\cdot}2 \times 10^{-5}$	9·4	8·9	4·1	8,100	10,000	18,000
Type A	$14{\cdot}1 \times 10^{-5}$	11·1		4·5	4,060		6,060
Type A	$21{\cdot}0 \times 10^{-5}$	11·9	8·2	4·3	2,500	2,900	3,850

2. *Thermoelectric Power*

The thermoelectric power is sensitive to the position of the Fermi level and to the shape of the Fermi surface, and can provide important details of carrier distribution near the top of the valence band and the bottom of the conduction band. For the two-band model the thermoelectric power α is in terms of the partial conductivities σ_e and σ_h (Chandrasekhar 1959)

$$\alpha_i = \frac{(\sigma_e)_i S_e + (\sigma_h)_i S_h}{(\sigma_e)_i + (\sigma_h)_i} \tag{17}$$

where i may be either parallel or perpendicular to the hexagonal axis. In a semimetal in which the electron and hole densities are equal we can write eqn (17) as

$$\alpha_i = \frac{b_i S_e + S_h}{1 + b_i} \tag{18}$$

where b_i is the mobility ratio (μ_e/μ_h). The partial Seebeck coefficients S_e and S_h of electrons and holes respectively are defined by

$$S_e = -\frac{k}{|e|} \left\{ \frac{(5/2+s)F_{3/2+s}(\xi_e)}{(3/2+s)F_{1/2+s}(\xi_e)} - \xi_e \right\} \tag{19}$$

$$S_h = \frac{k}{|e|} \left\{ \frac{(5/2+s)F_{3/2+s}(\xi_h)}{(3/2+s)F_{1/2+s}(\xi_h)} - \xi_h \right\} \tag{20}$$

The Fermi integrals

$$F_j(\xi) = \int_0^\infty \frac{x^j}{e^{(x-\xi)}+1} \, dx \tag{21}$$

are obtainable from Tables (Madelung 1957) and the reduced Fermi energies are

$$\xi_e = E_F^e/kT \tag{22}$$

$$\xi_h = E_F^h/kT = -(E_0 + E_F^e)/kT \tag{23}$$

if E_0 is the band overlap and E_F^e and E_F^h are the Fermi energies of electrons and holes measured from the respective band edges. The mobility data suggest intravalley, acoustic mode, lattice scattering for graphite above 20°K, corresponding to s equal to $-\frac{1}{2}$. This assumption holds for bismuth (Gallo et al. 1963) and possibly for antimony and arsenic (Saunders et al. 1965). Like graphite, these semimetals have two-carrier, multivalley band structures. Equations (19) and (20) now become

$$S_e = -\frac{k}{|e|} \left\{ \frac{2F_1(\xi_e)}{F_0(\xi_e)} - \xi_e \right\} \tag{24}$$

$$S_h = \frac{k}{|e|} \left\{ \frac{2F_1(\xi_h)}{F_0(\xi_h)} - \xi_h \right\}. \tag{25}$$

If we use the single crystal values 0·022 eV for E_F^e and 0·008 eV for E_F^h, and take for well-annealed pyrolytic graphite $\alpha_\perp$ at room temperature as $12\,\mu V/^\circ K$ (Blackman *et al.* 1961a) then from the foregoing argument the mobility ratio $b(=\mu_e/\mu_h)$ turns out to be 1·05. This is in good agreement with the value (1·10) found by Soule (1958) for single crystal graphite from galvano-magnetic measurements. On this evidence the scattering law and the model for the thermoelectric power hold at room temperature.

At low temperatures the thermoelectric power of both pyrolytic (Blackman *et al.* 1961a) and polycrystalline graphite (Tyler and Wilson 1953; Hove 1956) is characterized by a pronounced minimum around 90°K or below. Some results for pyrolytic graphite are shown in Fig. 18. One explanation (Blackman

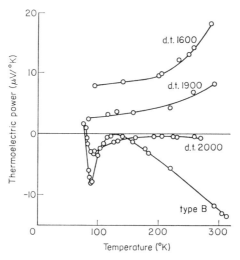

FIG. 18. The thermoelectric power of pyrolytic carbons as a function of temperatures. (After Blackman *et al.* 1961a.)

et al. 1961a) of the minimum is that it results from the phonon drag effect. A phonon current flows down a temperature gradient, and normal phonon scattering of electrons is not random but impels more current carriers towards the cold end than in the opposite direction. This phonon drag component having the same sign as the "diffusion" contribution enhances the thermoelectric power. At high temperatures phonon drag diminishes as phonon–phonon and phonon–defect scattering predominate and the thermo-electric power arises from diffusion only. Neither does the effect occur in defective materials.

Following the discovery of minority carriers in pyrolytic graphite (Spain *et al.* 1965), comes the possibility that these mobile carriers may dominate the thermoelectric power at low temperatures and be the cause of the low temperature anomalies. Certainly more extensive studies are required to elucidate the phenomenon.

Much attention is being paid to the possible application of thermoelectric and thermomagnetic effects in refrigeration. Below room temperature the most effective thermoelectric cooling is produced by the bismuth–antimony alloys (Smith and Wolfe 1962). Graphite is inefficacious. At one time pyrolytic graphite appeared a useful prospect for Ettinghausen cooling at low temperatures (Wright 1963). The Ettinghausen effect P is related to the Nernst effect Q by $Q = PK/T$, where K is the thermal conductivity. Measurements (Mills *et al.* 1965) showed Q to be only about 10 cm^2 deg^{-1} sec^{-1} at 80°K in near-ideal pyrolytic graphite: useful Ettinghausen cooling with this material must be counted out.

E. CARRIER TRANSPORT IN GROSSLY DEFECTIVE GRAPHITES

Defective polycrystalline and pyrolytic graphites and irradiation-damaged material, in which trapping of electrons at lattice defects leads to a preponderance of positive holes, are single carrier, p-type conductors. Transport properties confirm the simple picture of a narrow gap between the bands with the Fermi level depressed into the valence band. The thermoelectric power of a single carrier conductor (cf. Mott and Jones 1936)

$$S = \frac{\pi^2 k^2 T x}{3 e E_F} \tag{26}$$

indicates that, if the carrier density is relatively insensitive to temperature, then the thermoelectric power should be proportional to the absolute temperature. This is so. If the deposition temperature of pyrolytic graphite or the heat-treatment temperature of polycrystalline graphite is increased, the Fermi level rises towards the top of the valence band.

Hall effect data confirms and extends these results on defective graphites. The Hall coefficients R are positive (in agreement with the sign of the thermoelectric power), and field independent (characteristic behaviour of single-carrier, p-type conductors). Carrier mobilities μ can be calculated from

$$\mu \rho = cR \tag{27}$$

where c is the velocity of light; some results, together with carrier densities p calculated from

$$p = \frac{3\pi}{8 R c e} \tag{28}$$

are shown in Table VI. Too much reliance must not be placed on these numbers because, among other effects, the anomalous magnetoresistances observed in defective graphites show that macroscopic inhomogeneity plays a dominant role in determining transport properties in these materials.

TABLE VI

Hall Mobilities and Carrier Densities in Grossly Defective Pyrolytic Graphites
(estimated from Blackman *et al.*, 1961a)

Deposition temperature (°C)	Temperature (°C)	Resistivity (ohm cm × 10³)	Hall coefficient (cm³/C)	Mobility (cm²/V sec)	Carrier density per cm⁻³ (× 10¹⁹)
1800	20	2·83	+0·135	40·3	5·48
	−77	2·94	+0·168	47·0	4·40
	−196	3·08	+0·209	57·4	3·54
1900	20	2·61	+0·218	70·9	3·39
	−77	2·77	+0·290	88·7	2·55
	−196	2·93	+0·412	119·3	1·80
1950	20	1·60	+0·186	98·7	3·98
	−77	1·70	+0·337	168·3	2·20
	−196	1·81	+1·15	539·4	0·63
2000	20	1·20	+0·145	100·9	5·10
2050	20	1·22	+0·156	108·0	4·74
	−77	1·38	+0·315	193·0	2·35
	−196	1·50	+1·01	567·0	0·74

1. *Negative Magnetoresistance: the Effects of Inhomogeneity*

Negative magnetoresistance, an anomalous decrease of resistance on application of a magnetic field, arises in poorly graphitized, p-type, polycrystalline carbon (Mrozowski and Chaberski 1954) and in those defective pyrolytic carbons deposited below the critical graphitization temperature (Blackman *et al.* 1961a). The effect can be interpreted (Saunders 1964) on the basis of the work of Bate and his colleagues (1961) on inhomogeneous crystals of InSb. Measurement by the four probe method in inhomogeneous specimens, wherein competition occurs between Hall fields in neighbouring regions doped at different levels, produces negative magnetoresistance. For a first approximation the simple function model shown in Fig. 19 is used for mathematical analysis of the problem and the effective magnetoresistance is given by Bate and Beer (1961)

$$\left(\frac{\Delta\rho}{\rho_0}\right)_{EFF} = \left(\frac{\Delta\rho}{\rho_0}\right) + \frac{(d_2 R_2 - d_1 R_1)}{(d_2 \rho_2^0 + d_1 \rho_1^0)} \cdot \frac{(R_2 - R_1)}{(\rho_1 + \rho_2)} \cdot H^2 \qquad (29)$$

where ρ_1^0 and ρ_2^0 denote the two zero induction resistivities in the two regions, R_1 and R_2 are the respective Hall coefficients, d_1 and d_2 represent distances of the potential probes from the inhomogeneity, and H is the magnetic field. On the right-hand side the first term is a weighted average of the material magnetoresistance in the two regions, while the second term results from the

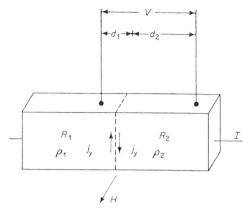

FIG. 19. Model of a sample with an abrupt boundary between two regions of different doping level used to calculate the magnetoresistance of inhomogeneous specimens. (After Bate *et al.* 1961.)

inhomogeneity. If this latter term becomes so large and negative that it outweighs the former, then the resultant magnetoresistance is negative. Of course, the model is a much simplified version of the practical structural situation, but it is valid qualitatively for those defective graphites containing regions of differing crystallite size, orientation and carrier concentration. Indeed boundaries between such regions can be observed under the microscope in pyrolytic graphites (Blackman *et al.* 1961a).

In agreement with this hypothesis is the direct correlation between Hall coefficients and magnetoresistance of defective graphites: polycrystalline (Mrozowski and Chaberski 1954) and pyrolytic graphites (Blackman *et al.* 1961a) with the largest positive Hall coefficients show the largest negative magnetoresistances.

Differences throughout the specimens between the galvanomagnetic-effect temperature-dependences lead to the possibility of a change of sign of the magnetoresistance as temperature is increased: as the Hall coefficients decrease with rising temperature so the difference $(R_2 - R_1)$ diminishes to reduce the size of the second term on the right-hand side in eqn (29). This effect is observed (Saunders 1964) and is illustrated in Fig. 20. Regional Hall coefficients in these defective graphites are field independent, and so the negative magnetoresistance, as might be expected from eqn (29), is proportional to H^x with the exponent lying between 1·5 and 2·0.

Should the second term in the governing equation become so negative that the total magnetoresistance can fall below -1, then the potential difference across the voltage probes can change sign on application of a sufficiently large magnetic field: an effect, with interesting possibilities for

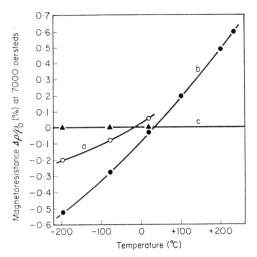

FIG. 20. The temperature dependence of the magnetoresistance of pyrolytic carbons showing the change of sign of magnetoresistance near room temperature. (After Saunders 1964.) (a) $\rho 20°C = 2.2 \times 10^{-3}$ ohm cm, (b) $\rho 20°C = 1.62 \times 10^{-3}$ ohm cm, (c) $\rho 20°C = 1.22 \times 10^{-3}$ ohm cm.

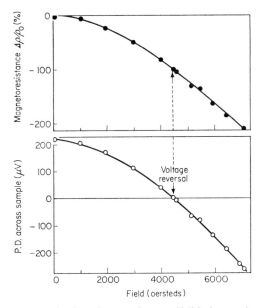

FIG. 21. Voltage reversal in C_{2700} Br sample at $-196°C$ due to decrease of magneto-resistance below -100%. (After Saunders 1964.)

device application, which is observed (Saunders 1964) in certain very dilute bromine–pyrolytic graphite residue compounds. This behaviour, illustrated in Fig. 21, is probably associated with the uneven bromination of different crystallites inferred from studies of the mechanism of bromination of pyrolytic graphite (Saunders *et al*. 1963a) and the effect of pressure on bromination (Saunders *et al*. 1963b).

To conclude, although the *a*-axis transport properties can be related to the band model for near-ideal graphites, in less perfect materials the effects depend upon macroscopic structural defects and correlation with band structure is of secondary importance. We turn now to discuss the *c*-axis transport properties.

IV. ELECTRON TRANSPORT ALONG THE c-AXIS

The outstanding feature of graphite is the marked anisotropy of the physical properties. Electron transport along the layer planes is typically semimetallic and can, as we have seen, be described quantitatively. Along the *c*-axis this is not so. In the first place, those interlayer interactions, which should determine the *c*-axis phenomena, are only considered in the three-dimensional band theory as weak, second-order effects. How variations in stacking order, certainly a predominate feature in graphites, effect the interlayer forces is unknown. Theoretical calculations of ρ_c/ρ_a vary from 10^2 (Wallace 1947) to 10^5 (Haering and Wallace 1957). At the other end of the scale from the band theoretical approach is the possibility of treatment of graphite as a packed, layer structure of infinitely large, aromatic molecules across which *c*-axis conduction takes place by an interlayer hopping mechanism.

Furthermore, the effect of defects will be much magnified along the *c*-axis direction. Screw dislocations with Burger's vectors along the hexagonal axis unite the planes into a connected helicoid to produce *a*-axis conduction paths. In general any divergence from perfect planar alignment will increase the contribution of *a*-axis current flow, and there is no doubt that the ratio $n_a\bar{\mu}_a/n_c\bar{\mu}_c$ is so large that a modestly small *a*-axis component could swamp true *c*-axis effects. Defect-free natural crystals are unobtainable and even in the best pyrolytic graphites the *c*-axis misorientation of individual crystallites can be more than $1°$. Cracks, grain boundaries and impurity layers parallel to the layer planes will decrease carrier mobilities.

Experimental measurements on single crystals are particularly difficult along the *c*-axis direction owing to the thinness and fragility of specimens and to contact problems. Differences between the published data, see Table III, are not surprising. The magnitude of ρ_c remains uncertain; two ranges of possible values occur: a low region of about 10^{-2} ohm cm to give a resistivity ratio ρ_c/ρ_a of the order of 100, and a higher range with ρ_c about 1 ohm cm and a ratio ρ_c/ρ_a about 10^4. The most careful and intensive experiments are those of Primak and Fuchs (1954) and Primak (1956), in which the high a-axis conductivity evidences specimen perfection. In agreement with the low resistivity results is an estimate of σ_c as $3 \cdot 2 \times 10^2$ (ohm cm)$^{-1}$ by Wagoner (1960) from the line shape in electron spin resonance experiments.

Pyrolytic graphite presents a similar problem. Type A samples deposited at high temperatures have c-axis resistivities in the range $0 \cdot 1$–$0 \cdot 4$ ohm cm while carefully selected specimens of recrystallized graphites (types B and AB) show significantly smaller values between $0 \cdot 01$ and $0 \cdot 05$ ohm cm (Blackman et al. 1961a). The more defective graphites prepared below the critical region of graphitization are, like industrial polycrystalline graphites, much less anisotropic.

There is a maximum in the temperature-dependence curve of the c-axis electrical resistivity of single crystal graphite (Primak and Fuchs 1954), recrystallized pyrolytic graphite (Saunders 1962) and hot-pressed pyrolytic graphite (Spain et al. 1965). Some results for various graphites are given in Fig. 22. This must be a manifestation of a change either in carrier concentration at the degeneracy temperature or in scattering mechanism. Significantly, the temperature dependence of the c-axis resistivity in these specimens bears no relation to that along the a-axis whereas it should if a sizeable contribution were made by a-axis paths.

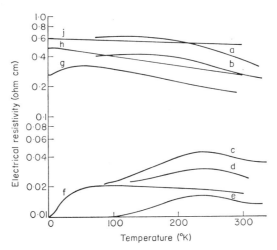

FIG. 22. The temperature dependence of the c-axis resistivity of near-ideal graphites. Curves (a)–(e) are for type B pyrolytic graphite (Saunders 1962), (f) for natural single crystal (Primak 1956), (g) for hot-pressed pyrolytic graphite (Spain et al. 1965), (h) for pyrolytic graphite heat treated at 3600°C (Klein 1962) and (j) for a deposited type A pyrolytic graphite (Klein 1962). Two distinct ranges of result occur.

Much detailed information can be obtained from the thermoelectric power but no measurements have been made on single crystals. However, data are available for pyrolytic graphite (Blackman *et al.* 1961a) and, with the usual proviso about defects and *a*-axis paths, lead to some interesting conclusions. Selected data (Saunders 1962) are presented in Table VII. Values lie between $+5 \cdot 0 \simeq +9 \cdot 0 \, \mu V/^{\circ}K$ for deposits prepared below the critical graphitization temperature, and are not representative of the *c*-axis. Unannealed high temperature type A deposits have thermoelectric powers in the region of

TABLE VII

c-Axis Resistivity and Thermoelectric Power of Pyrolytic Graphites at Room Temperature

a-Axis resistivity (ohm cm)	*c*-Axis resistivity (ohm cm)	Temperature coefficient of *c*-axis resistivity	Thermoelectric power (*c*-axis) ($\mu V/^{\circ}K$)
Type A			
$3 \cdot 5 \times 10^{-4}$	0·38	$-2 \cdot 2 \times 10^{-3}$	$+5 \cdot 7$
$1 \cdot 5 \times 10^{-4}$	0·53	$-2 \cdot 2 \times 10^{-3}$	$+5 \cdot 6$
Type AB			
$8 \cdot 2 \times 10^{-5}$	0·24	$-4 \cdot 4 \times 10^{-3}$	$+1 \cdot 84$
$5 \cdot 5 \times 10^{-5}$	0·02	$-6 \cdot 1 \times 10^{-4}$	$-0 \cdot 07$
$4 \cdot 9 \times 10^{-5}$	0·027	$-3 \cdot 7 \times 10^{-3}$	$-0 \cdot 56$
Type B			
$3 \cdot 9 \times 10^{-5}$	0·044	$-2 \cdot 0 \times 10^{-3}$	$-0 \cdot 84$

$+3 \, \mu V/^{\circ}K$. Once again, as for the resistivity, the behaviour of carefully selected specimens from the innermost layers of recrystallized graphite is quite different from that of less perfect material. Small, negative thermoelectric powers are found in agreement with the small negative Hall coefficient observed by Spain *et al.* (1965) for hot-pressed pyrolytic graphites.

The transverse *c*-axis magnetoresistance $(H \perp c \| j)$ is certainly small. Room temperature values for recrystallized, pyrolytic graphites at 7000 Oe are of the order of $0 \cdot 1 \%$ for specimens with a room temperature *c*-axis resistivity of about 0·3 ohm cm but again the high conductivity ($\sim 0 \cdot 02$ ohm cm), selected specimens from near the centre of the deposit are anomalous: the magnetoresistance is greater than $0 \cdot 1 \%$ at 7000 Oe (Saunders 1962). The *c*-axis magnetoresistance is proportional to $H^{1 \cdot 7}$. In hot-pressed graphite (Spain *et al.* 1965) values about $3 \times 10^{-3} \%$ are observed at 2000 Oe. Tentatively, using eqns (13) and (16) for magnetoresistance, these results indicate a carrier mobility of about 250–1000 cm^2/V sec and a carrier density between 4 and 6×10^{16}/cm^3 for the "*c*-axis" direction in the best pyrolytic graphites. On this basis, discussion of the c-axis transport properties in terms of band theory is justified.

However, it can be argued that the total carrier density $(n_e + n_h)$ should be the same $(\sim 10^{19}/cm^3)$ for both major crystallographic directions (Klein 1961) and

$$\frac{1}{\rho_c} = e(n_e + n_h)\bar{\mu}_c. \tag{30}$$

Taking ρ_c as 0·15 ohm cm at room temperature, Klein finds $\bar{\mu}_c$ to be about 3 cm^2/V sec—suggestive of the hopping mechanism; the carriers must first be raised into an excited state before they can tunnel across the barrier. But, if in fact the true c-axis resistivity is about 0·02 ohm cm, $\bar{\mu}_c$ will be an order of magnitude larger.

After irradiation damage (10^{17} neutrons/cm^2) the c-axis electrical conductivity of near-ideal pyrolytic graphites increases (see Fig. 23), the thermo-

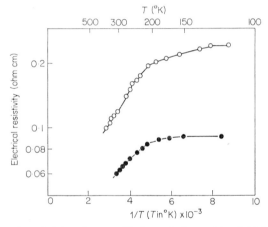

FIG. 23. The c-axis resistivity of a near-ideal pyrolytic graphite (initial a-axis resistivity 3·8 × 10^{-5} ohm cm) measured after neutron irradiation (●) and after subsequent mild annealing (○). (After Blackman et al. 1961b.)

electric power becomes large (about $+40$ μV/°K) and the magnetoresistance becomes immeasurable (Blackman et al. 1961b). Electron traps introduced lead to samples which are strongly p-type in both directions. The c-axis resistivity of boronated pyrolytic graphite also decreases markedly with increasing boron concentration while the thermoelectric power goes strongly positive ($+30$ μV/°K) at 300°K (Klein 1961). Here boron atoms substitute within the layers and cannot act as bridges across the layers as interstitial carbon atoms introduced during irradiation possibly could. These results both for boronation and irradiation recommend the band approach, implying, as they do, a depression of the Fermi level away from the Brillouin zone edges.

To conclude, the mechanism of c-axis conduction remains uncertain although, since both n- and p-type behaviour is observed in structures of different defective nature, the two-band mechanism is the most plausible. The carrier density is unknown; arguments can be made in support of equal carrier densities in both directions in contrast to suggestions of a ratio of carrier densities $(n_e + n_h)_{(a\text{-axis})}$ to $(n_e + n_h)_{(c\text{-axis})}$ of about 300 to 1. The mechanism of c-axis carrier scattering is undetermined. Hall coefficient measurements on the best pyrolytic graphite available should help to resolve these problems.

V. GRAPHITE AS A SOLID STATE PLASMA

A solid state plasma can be visualized as a gas of mobile carriers, either electrons or holes, with electrical neutrality maintained by the rigid lattice of positive ions. Such a plasma can support a variety of collective motions resembling sound waves in that phase velocities are determined by the carrier Fermi velocity V_F rather than by the speed of light. Longitudinal plasma waves consist of contractions and dilatations in the electron gas. Restoring forces are Coulombic. The resulting plasma frequency, ω_p, the natural mode of oscillation, is (see Pines 1963)

$$\omega_p = \left(\frac{4\pi N e^2}{m^* \varepsilon}\right)^{\frac{1}{2}} \tag{31}$$

where the symbols have their usual significance. The plasma oscillations resemble those of a harmonic oscillator; the energy Ep of the levels is given by

$$E_p = (n + \tfrac{1}{2})\hbar\omega_p \tag{32}$$

where n is a positive integer or zero. Each quantized plasma oscillation is called a plasmon. When n is zero, the plasma system is in the zero point energy state $\tfrac{1}{2}\hbar\omega_p$. The energy of excitation to the first level is $\hbar\omega_p$; usually $\hbar\omega_p$ is well beyond the Fermi level and the system is in the plasma ground state. At the high frequencies involved the complex refractive index N is given by

$$N^2 = 1 - \frac{\omega_p^2}{\omega^2}. \tag{33}$$

When an electromagnetic wave of frequency $\omega \gg \omega_p$ is applied, the refractive index becomes real. Metals and semimetals are transparent to frequencies beyond ω_p and behave as dielectrics.

Graphite is most interesting in that it behaves as a two-dimensional plasma. Peaks at about 7 eV and 25 eV due to plasma resonances have been observed in the optical absorption and reflectance experiments of several workers (see Taft and Phillip 1965 and Carter et al. 1965).

A. ALFVÉN WAVE PROPAGATION

The type of plasma wave propagated depends upon the band structure. In the semimetals, which are compensated, that is have equal electron and hole densities and have ellipsoid-like Fermi surfaces, allowing only closed carrier orbits, equal densities of positive and negative charge oscillate with equal amplitude in phase about the magnetic lines of force. While the effective Hall current is small, there is a net kinetic energy of mass motion in the Hall direction and magnetohydrodynamic or Alfvén waves are propagated. Alfvén waves have been observed in the compensated, degenerate semimetal bismuth (Williams and Smith 1964). A criterion for Alfvén wave propagation is that the plasma must be pure, strain-free and cold: pure single crystals at liquid helium temperature are prerequisite. Recently the phenomenon has been observed (Surma et al. 1964), see Fig. 24, using a 35 Gc/sec absorption cavity spectrometer at 4·2°K, in both annealed pyrolytic and single crystal graphite. Samples, with parallel c-plane faces, are mounted at the centre of

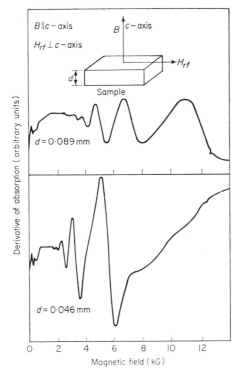

FIG. 24. Oscillations representing the Alfvén wave interference pattern for two pyrolytic graphite samples of different thickness. Cyclotron resonance peaks can be seen at the low-field end. (After Surma et al. 1964.)

the bottom of a cylindrical TE_{112} mode absorption cavity so that the c-axis is perpendicular to the cavity axis. Electromagnetic radiation is present at both sample faces and an interference condition occurs for an integral number of wavelengths N across the sample.

Theoretical treatment yields for the effective dielectric constant in a compensated material such as graphite (see Buchsbaum 1964).

$$\varepsilon_{\text{eff}} = \varepsilon_0 + \frac{4\pi c^2}{H^2} \cdot D(n, m^*) \qquad (34)$$

writing $D(n, m^*)$ as the carrier mass density function $(n_e m_e^* + n_h m_h^*)$. For such an anisotropic material as graphite $D(n, m^*)$ will be complicated but, neglecting trigonal warping, is found to be $3 \cdot 25 \times 10^{-10}$ g/cm. Taking $0 \cdot 057$ for m_h^* and $0 \cdot 039$ for m_e^*, n_e and n_h are approximately $3 \cdot 3 \times 10^{18}$ cm^3, in good agreement with the results of the other methods described in Sections 2 and 3.

Thus graphite, like other semimetals, behaves as a compensated, degenerate, solid state plasma. These materials are most useful as vehicles for the study of plasma physics as well as having in their own right great device potentiality.

B. THE KINK EFFECT IN GRAPHITE

While measuring the transverse magnetoresistance of bismuth at liquid helium temperatures Esaki (1962) observed, contrary to Ohm's law, a kink in the current-voltage characteristic. Goldsmid and Corsan (1964) have found this "kink" effect in pyrolytic graphite annealed at 3000°C. Although not a plasma effect, discussion of this phenomenon falls naturally into this section. Esaki (1962) showed that the kink occurs at a critical electric field E_k at which the transverse carrier velocity in the magnetic field H exceeds the sound velocity (u), so that

$$u = E_k/H. \qquad (35)$$

The effect may be considered as a decrease in the resistance of the semimetal at the critical field. Beyond the critical field an enhanced electron–phonon interaction takes place and the electrons give energy to the phonons. This effect may turn out to be of some technological importance: ultrasonic amplification should be possible in a pyrolytic graphite specimen in crossed electric and magnetic fields.

VI. ELECTRICAL PROPERTIES OF GRAPHITE COMPOUNDS

The electrical properties of graphite are very sensitive to the presence of impurities. Among those impurities affecting the carrier distribution in the bands are substitutional atoms, lattice defects, radiation damage and atoms intercalated between the layers. To detail the effects of defects in polycrystalline graphites, several workers have looked into the galvanomagnetic properties of the intercalation compounds (see for instance Hennig 1960). Only a brief review is pertinent here.

A. COMPOUND STRUCTURE AND TRANSPORT PROPERTIES

Two types of lamellar compounds occur. In the first group—which does not concern us—including graphite oxides and fluorides, bonding is covalent: the carbon atoms are tetrahedrally hybridized and the layer planes are puckered. The crystal compounds constitute the second group. Foreign species are intercalated between carbon hexagon layers retaining planar structure and aromaticity. These compounds decompose readily into the intercalate and a "residue" compound. Find further details of the chemical physics in comprehensive reviews by Ubbelohde and Lewis (1960) and Croft (1960). But before discussing transport processes mention must be made of the types of crystal compound and their preparation.

Crystal compounds are made either by direct combination or by electro-chemical oxidation. Graphite, in the presence of strong acids, can be oxidized by strong oxidizing agents or by anodic oxidation to graphite salts, and anions such as HSO_4^-, ClO_4^-, HF_2^- together with acid molecules are incorporated between the layer planes. In this process graphite shows certain properties in common with metals undergoing salt formation. Oxidation removes electrons from the valence band, producing positively charged carbon layers between which acid anions are held by Coulombic forces.

Compounds may be classified, following the practice of semiconductor physics, according to whether the reactant is a donor or an acceptor; included among the former type are the graphite-alkali metal compounds in which a small negative Hall coefficient witnesses an increased electron density. X-ray structural analysis (Rüdorff and Schulze 1954) of the saturated compounds C_8M, where M may be K, Cs or Rb, reveals alkali metal ions in every interplanar space. Carbon planes stack AAA..., the metal ions siting between the hexagon centres.

The aromatic macromolecules donate electrons to halogens intercalated between the layers: the Hall coefficient becomes more positive and the conductivity increases. The Fermi level sinks into the valence band (Hennig 1952; Hennig and McClelland 1955) to a region of higher density of states: the number of carriers increases. Magnetic susceptibility measurements leave no doubt that both donor and acceptor compounds are "more metallic" than graphite itself (McDonnell et al. 1951).

The anisotropy of the crystal compounds has been examined using well-aligned pyrolytic graphite as the starting material (Blackman, Matthews and Ubbelohde 1960a, b, c). Formation of the saturated compounds leads to a decrease of about ten times the "a-axis" resistivity (see Fig. 25). Con-

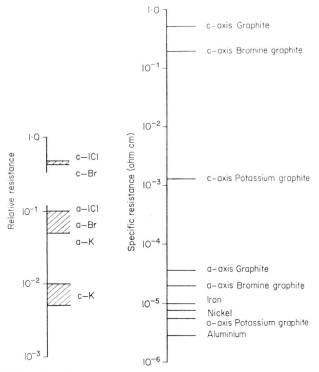

Fig. 25. (a) Relative change of resistance in the a- and c-axis directions forming the crystal compounds of graphite. (b) Comparison of resistivity of well-aligned graphite and its crystal compounds with that of some metals. (After Ubbelohde *et al.* 1959.)

ductivity in these compounds is metallic: the resistivity can be less than that of nickel and temperature coefficients of resistivity are positive for potassium-graphite for both crystallographic directions.

If the relaxation time is assumed independent of the depression of Fermi level Δ from the top of the valence band, then the two-dimensional band model of Wallace (1947) leads to

$$R_0/R = 2 \cosh (\Delta/2kT) \qquad (36)$$

for the ratio of resistances before (R_0) and after intercalation (R). On this basis Blackman *et al.* (1960a) find that for bromine-graphite the Fermi level is depressed far below the top of the lower π-band ($0{\cdot}4$ eV for $C_{32}Br$).

Along the "c-axis", a striking difference occurs between the effects of donor and acceptor intercalates. For electron acceptor species $(R/R_0)_c$ is only about one-half, whereas after total reaction with alkali metal the c-axis conductivity increases by at least two orders of magnitude: results are in agreement with the hypothesis of interlayer van der Waals bonding in acceptor compounds, in contrast to metallic bonding in the c-axis direction in alkali metal compounds.

At high potassium concentrations the thermoelectric power is almost identical (~ 20 μV/°K at room temperature) along both the a- and c-axis. The hole ellipsoid major-to-minor axis ratio decreases substantially as the Fermi surface is expanded well into the Brillouin zone by the donor action.

At present the picture of the band structure of the graphite compounds remains sketchy. Since the band overlap in ideal graphite depends on the interlayer interaction, stronger in the compounds, it seems likely that the overlap increases when compounds are formed. The density-of-states curves in compounds are shown in Fig. 26. Both types are metallic. Plausibly the ellipsoid volumes are much larger and the major-to-minor axes diminished with a consequent decrease in anisotropy. Carrier effective masses and densities are larger. Extensive galvanomagnetic measurements in pyrolytic graphite compounds would give substance to this model. But the rub lies in doubtful validity of a band approach in those compounds with gross departures from lattice regularity and variations in stoichiometry from crystallite to crystallite.

B. SUPERCONDUCTIVITY IN GRAPHITE COMPOUNDS

Superconductivity has been observed (Hannay *et al.* 1965) in pyrolytic graphite—alkali metal compounds of ideal formula C_8M (where M may be K, Rb or Cs). Transition temperatures are low, being 0·02–0·13°K for C_8Cs, 0·02–0·15°K for C_8Rb and up to 0·56°K for potassium-graphite, and sensitive to perfection of the starting material, although the width of the transition for a given sample is only of the order of millidegrees. Extreme anisotropy is manifested. The critical magnetic field H_{c2} depends strongly upon crystallographic orientation. For instance, for a compound C_8K made with excess potassium ($T_c = 0·55°K$)H_{c2} at 0·032°K was 160 Gs for $H \perp C$ while being 730 Gs for $H \parallel C$. For a stoichiometric C_8K compound ($T_c = 0·39°K$) these critical fields were 25 Gs and 250 Gs respectively.

Significantly, superconductivity is not found in $C_{16}K$ in which only every other available layer is occupied, there are carbon layers adjacent to each other, and van der Waals bonding plays a role along the c-axis direction. Superconductivity then is not a two-dimensional property in these compounds. It would be interesting to know if only graphite compounds in which every possible layer contains intercalate can be superconducting. Especially pertinent would be compounds of the type exemplified by aluminium chloride-graphite, in which the carbon layers apparently remain staggered even though every layer is filled. Not only would study of a variety of compounds shed further light on the materials themselves but also may prove useful, in view of the anisotropy, in augmenting the fundamental understanding of super-conductivity. While the Bardeen, Cooper and Schrieffer theory gives an acceptable explanation of the phenomenon (see Saunders 1966) the theory does not suggest which materials should be superconducting. It may well be that a study of the energy surfaces and bonding in relation to superconductivity in this unusual, extremely anisotropic group of compounds may provide the answer to this unresolved problem.

C. TRANSPORT PROPERTIES IN SUBSTITUTIONALLY-DOPED GRAPHITES

Electron transport properties in semimetals are very sensitive to small shifts of the Fermi level, and the effects of doping graphites with atoms close to carbon in the periodic table are of considerable interest. Boron with one less valence electron than carbon substitutes into the layer planes to produce "p-type" material. Boron facilitates graphitization and, in consequence, the effect of boron doping in polycrystalline graphite is well known (Grisdale et al. 1951; Albert and Parisot 1959): metallic properties, such as increased electrical conductivity and a positive temperature coefficient of resistance, result. However, only work on lightly boron doped, near-ideal graphites can be analysed quantitatively in terms of the band structure and carrier scattering (Soule 1962, 1964).

As the boron concentration is increased beyond about 10^{-4} boron atoms per carbon atom (B/C), to about $2 \cdot 5 \times 10^{-3}$ B/C, the magnetic susceptibility decreases sharply by an order of magnitude from the pure crystal value of $-22 \cdot 1 \times 10^{-6}$ emu/g to $-1 \cdot 9 \times 10^{-6}$ emu/g. This change, when the boron concentration matches the carrier concentration, is suggestive of close to 100% ionization efficiency of the boron; a quantitative estimate is 75% ionization efficiency. Increasing the boron concentration lowers the Fermi level as in Fig. 26(a) and the hole density increases. At a boron concentration

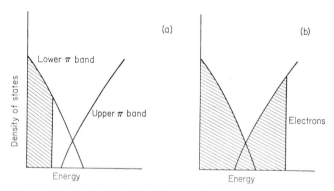

Fig. 26. The position in the Fermi level in graphite crystal compounds. (a) Acceptor intercalate, (b) donor intercalate.

of the order of 100 ppm the Fermi level lies below the bottom of the conduction band; for such a single carrier conductor the Hall coefficient is
described by eqn (28). The hole concentration is essentially independent of
temperature and two orders of magnitude larger than that in pure graphite;
a clear indication of metallic behaviour. The hole effective mass becomes
larger as the boron concentration is increased.

Further significant details of the band structure arise from studies of the
de Haas–van Alphen effect in graphite single crystals lightly doped with
boron (Soule 1964). Tentative identification between the major hole and
electron Fermi surfaces and the de Haas–van Alphen periods becomes
possible. As the boron concentration is increased, both the radius of the
electron Fermi surface and the dimension along k_z decrease; for instance the
anisotropy ratio falls from about 12 : 1 for pure graphite to 8 : 1 in a sample
doped with 13 ppm of boron. At the same time the hole surfaces are dilated.

Soule's work provides striking confirmation of the sensitivity of the
carrier mobility in graphite to the presence of scattering sites in the layer
planes. For a boron concentration larger than 10^{-3} B/C the hole mobility
becomes independent of temperature between 77°K and 298°K and the
mobility at 77°K decreases two orders of magnitude to less than 10^3 cm^2/
V sec. In this regime of boron, substitutional doping scattering from the
ionized impurities dominates that of lattice vibration scattering. Such
behaviour contrasts markedly with carrier scattering in graphite intercalation
compounds where a similar concentration of dopant between the layers has
little effect on the mechanism of carrier scattering.

REFERENCES

Albert, P. and Parisot, J. (1959). *In* "Proc. of the 3rd Carbon Conf", p. 467.
    Pergamon Press, Oxford.
Ammar, A. and Young, D. A. (1964). *Br. J. appl. Phys.* **15**, 131.
Bate, R. T. and Beer, A. C. (1961). *J. appl. Phys.* **32**, 800.
Bate, R. T., Bell, J. C. and Beer, A. C. (1961). *J. appl. Phys.* **32**, 806.
Blackman, L. C. F., Mathews, J. F. and Ubbelohde, A. R. (1960a), *Proc. R. Soc.
    Lond.* A**256**, 15.
Blackman, L. C. F., Mathews, J. F. and Ubbelohde, A. R. (1960b), *Proc. R. Soc.
    Lond.* A**258**, 329.
Blackman, L. C. F., Mathews, J. F. and Ubbelohde, A. R. (1960c), *Proc. R. Soc.
    Lond.* A**258**, 339.
Blackman, L. C. F., Saunders, G. A. and Ubbelohde, A. R. (1961a), *Proc. R. Soc.
    Lond.* A**264**, 19.
Blackman, L. C. F., Saunders, G. A. and Ubbelohde, A. R. (1961b). *Proc. phys. Soc.
    Lond.* **78**, 1048.
Buchsbaum, S. J. (1964). "7th International Conference on the Physics of Semi-
    conductors," vol. 2, p. 3. Academic Press, London.

Carter, J. G., Huebner, R. H., Hamm, R. N. and Birkhoff, R. D. (1965). *Phys. Rev.* **137**, A639.

Chandrasekhar, B. S. (1959). *Physics Chem. Solids* **11**, 268.

Corbato, F. J. (1959). *In* "Proc. of the 3rd Carbon Conf.", p. 173. Pergamon Press, Oxford.

Coulson, C. A. and Taylor, R. (1952). *Proc. Phys. Soc.* A**65**, 815.

Croft, R. C. (1960). *Q. Rev.* XIV, 1.

Dresselhaus, M. S. and Mavroides, J. G. (1964). *IBM Jl Res. Dev.* **8**, 262.

Dutta, A. K. (1953). *Phys. Rev.* **90**, 187.

Esaki, L. (1962). *Phys. Rev. Lett.* **8**, 4.

Gallo, C. F., Chandrasekhar, B. S. and Sutter, P. H. (1963). *J. appl. Phys.* **34**, 144.

Goldsmid, H. J. and Corsan, J. M. (1964). *Phys. Lett.* **8**, 221.

Grisdale, R. O., Pfister, A. C. and van Roosbroeck, W. (1951). *Bell Syst. tech. J.* **30**, 271.

Haering, R. R. and Mrozowski, S. (1960). "Progress in Semiconductors" (A. F. Gibson, ed.), Vol. 5, pp. 273–316.

Haering, R. R. and Wallace, P. R. (1957). *Physics Chem. Solids* **3**, 253.

Hannay, N. B., Geballe, T. H., Matthias, B. T., Andres, K., Schmidt, P. and MacNair, D. (1965). *Phys. Rev. Lett.* **14**, 225.

Hennig, G. R. (1952). *J. Chem. Phys.* **23**, 1443.

Hennig, G. R. (1960). *In* "Proc. of the 4th Carbon Conf.", p. 221. Pergamon Press, Oxford.

Hennig, G. R. and McClelland, J. D. (1955). *J. Chem. Phys.* **23**, 1431.

Hove, J. E. (1956). *In* "Proc. of the 3rd Carbon Conf.", p. 125. Pergamon Press, Oxford.

Inoue, M. (1962). *J. phys. Soc., Japan* **17**, 808.

Kinchin, G. H. (1953). *Proc. R. Soc. Lond.* A**217**, 9.

Klein, C. A. (1961). *J. appl. Phys.* **33**, 3338.

Klein, C. A. (1962). *Rev. mod. Phys.* **34**, 56.

Klein, C. A. (1964). *J. appl. Phys.* **35**, 2947.

Klein, C. A. and Straub, W. D. (1961). *Phys. Rev.* **123**, 1581.

Klein, C. A., Straub, W. D. and Diefendorf, R. J. (1962). *Phys. Rev.* **125**, 468.

Kmetko, E. A. (1951). *Phys. Rev.* **82**, 456.

Krishnan, K. S. and Ganguli, N. (1939). *Nature, Lond.* **144**, 667.

Lomer, W. M. (1955). *Proc. R. Soc. Lond.* A**227**, 330.

Madelung, O. (1957). "Handbuch der Physik", Vol. 20, p. 58. Springer Verlag, Berlin.

McClelland, J. D. (1955). *Phys. Rev.* **100**, 1807.

McClure, J. W. (1957). *Phys. Rev.* **108**, 612.

McClure, J. W. (1958). *Phys. Rev.* **112**, 715.

McClure, J. W. (1960). *Phys. Rev.* **119**, 606.

McClure, J. W. and Smith, L. B. (1962). *In* "Proc. of the 5th Carbon Conf.", p. 3. Pergamon Press, Oxford.

McDonnell, F. R. M., Pink, R. C. and Ubbelohde, A. R. (1951). *J. chem. Soc.* **191**.

McMichael, B. D., Kmetko, E. A. and Mrozowski, S. (1954). *J. opt. Soc. Am.* **44**, 26.

Mills, J. J., Morant, R. A. and Wright, D. A. (1965). *Br. J. appl. Phys.* **16**, 479.

Mott, N. F. and Jones, H. (1936). "The Theory of the Properties of Metals and Alloys", p. 311. University Press, Oxford.

Mrozowski, S. (1952). *Phys. Rev.* **85**, 609.

Mrozowski, S. and Chaberski, A. (1954). *Phys. Rev.* **104**, 74.
Mrozowski, S., Chaberski, A., Loebner, E. E. and Pinnick, H. T. (1959). *In* "Proc. of the 3rd Carbon Conf.", p. 211. Pergamon Press, Oxford.
Pines, D. (1963). "Elementary Excitations in Solids", p. 180. W. A. Benjamin, New York.
Primak, W. (1956). *Phys. Rev.* **103**, 544.
Primak, W. and Fuchs, L. H. (1954). *Phys. Rev.* **95**, 22.
Pullman, B. and Pullman, A. (1952). "Théorie Electronique de la Chemie Organique", p. 493. Masson et Cie, Paris.
Roberts, D. E. (1913). *Ann. Phys.* **40**, 453.
Rüdorff, W. and Schulze, E. (1954). *Z. anorg. allg. Chem.* **277**, 156.
Saunders, G. A. (1962). Ph.D. Thesis, London University.
Saunders, G. A. (1964). *Appl. Phys. Lett.* **4**, 138.
Saunders, G. A. (1966). *Contemp. Phys.* **7**, 192.
Saunders, G. A., Ubbelohde, A. R. and Young, D. A. (1963a). *Proc. R. Soc. Lond.* **A271**, 499.
Saunders, G. A., Ubbelohde, A. R. and Young, D. A. (1963b). *Proc. R. Soc. Lond.* **A271**, 512.
Saunders, G. A., Miziumski, C., Cooper, G. A. and Lawson, A. W. (1965). *Physics Chem. Solids* **26**, 1299.
Slonczewski, J. C. and Weiss, P. R. (1958). *Phys. Rev.* **109**, 272.
Smith, G. E. and Wolfe, R. (1962). *J. appl. Phys.* **33**, 841.
Soule, D. E. (1958). *Phys. Rev.* **112**, 698.
Soule, D. E. (1962). *In* "Proc. of the 5th Carbon Conf.", p. 13. Pergamon Press, Oxford.
Soule, D. E. (1964). *IBM Jl Res. Dev.* **8**, 268.
Soule, D. E. and McClure, J. W. (1959). *Physics Chem. Solids* **8**, 29.
Soule, D. E., McClure, J. W. and Smith, L. B. (1964). *Phy. Rev.* **134**, A453.
Spain, I. L., Ubbelohde, A. R. and Young, D. A. (1965). *In* "Proc. 2nd Ind. Carbon and Graphite Conf." p. 123. Society of Chemical Industry (1966).
Surma, M., Furdyna, J. K. and Praddaude, H. C. (1964). *Phys. Rev. Lett.* **13**, 710.
Taft, E. A. and Philipp, H. R. (1965). *Phys. Rev.* **138**, A197.
Tyler, W. W. and Wilson, A. C. (1953). *Phys. Rev.* **89**, 870.
Ubbelohde, A. R. and Lewis, F. A. (1960). "Graphite and its Crystal Compounds", Oxford University Press, London.
Ubbelohde, A. R., Blackman, L. C. F. and Mathews, J. F. (1959). *Nature, Lond.* **183**, 454.
Wagoner, G. (1960). *In* "Proc. of the 4th Carbon Conf.", p. 197. Pergamon Press, Oxford.
Wallace, P. R. (1947). *Phys. Rev.* **71**, 622.
Washburn, G. E. (1915). *Ann. Phys.* **48**, 236.
Williams, G. A. and Smith, G. E. (1964). *IBM Jl Res. Dev.* **8**, 353.
Williamson, S. J., Foner, S. and Dresselhaus, M. S. (1965). *Phys. Rev.* **140**, A1429.
Wright, D. A. (1963). *Br. J. appl. Phys.* **14**, 329.

Since this chapter was written, a detailed and important contribution to the understanding of electron transport in pyrolytic graphites has been published by I. L. Spain, A. R. Ubbelohde and D. A. Young in *Phil. Trans. Roy. Soc.* **262**, 345 (1967).

Chapter IV

THERMAL GAS REACTIONS OF GRAPHITE

J. B. Lewis

Chemical Engineering Division,
A.E.R.E., Harwell, England

I. INTRODUCTION

Apart from their technological importance, the gasification reactions of carbon are of considerable scientific interest as they are the only common type of gas–solid reactions where the product is entirely gaseous. In addition the stable crystalline form of carbon, graphite, is peculiarly anisotropic in structure. These reactions have been studied for many years but substantial progress in understanding them has only come in the last 20 years or so. Much of the earlier work suffered because the structure and porosity of the carbons used were not properly characterized and because the purity of the carbons and the gases were not known. Much still remains unexplained and the output of published papers continues to increase. The "state of the art" has been reviewed frequently, among the more recent reviews are those of Wicke (1954), Walker *et al.* (1959a), Culver and Watts (1960), Lewis (1963), Clarke *et al.* (1962) and more recently the complementary reviews by Duval (1965), Bonnetain and Hoynant (1965) and Guérin and Bastick (1965) in "Les Carbones", a new French compendium on carbon. These last authors discussed respectively, (a) the reactions of carbons above 1000°C, (b) the reactions of graphite below 1000°C, and (c) the gasification of non-graphitic carbons.

The whole field of carbon gasification cannot be adequately condensed into a single chapter and this review is principally concerned with the thermal gas reaction of relatively pure graphite, in particular, together with recent developments in this field. Earlier work is included only where necessary for the sake of completeness or comprehension.

II. CRYSTALLOGRAPHIC AND PHYSICAL STRUCTURE OF CARBON

A. CRYSTALLOGRAPHY

Carbon exists in nature in two crystallographic forms, diamond and graphite. Diamond is metastable at pressures below about 20,000 atm so that it can readily be converted into graphite, for example by heat. Very little work has been carried out on the gasification reactions of diamond. One of the few recently published papers is that by Evans and Phaal (1961) who studied the oxidation of diamond at temperatures between 650 and 1350°C in oxygen at pressures ranging from 0·5–0·05 torr. They found that a graphitic layer was produced on the diamond surface and that this played an important role in the overall kinetics of the reaction.

The heat of combustion of diamond is slightly greater than that of graphite and the difference is important because it gives the energy of transformation between the two structures. The best value of the heat of transition from diamond to graphite is (Hawtin *et al.* 1966)

$$-\Delta H^{\circ}_{298·16} = 447·3 \pm 17·6 \text{ cal/mole.}$$

Graphite is peculiarly anisotropic, consisting as it does of layers of hexagonally arranged carbon atoms held together by weak van der Waals' forces. The atoms in the layer planes, or basal plane, are held together by strong covalent bonds of sp^2 type. It can be seen from Fig. 1 that there are two types of edges $\{10\bar{1}l\}$ and $\{11\bar{2}l\}$; these have been termed the "zig-zag" and the "armchair" face respectively. As would be expected from their

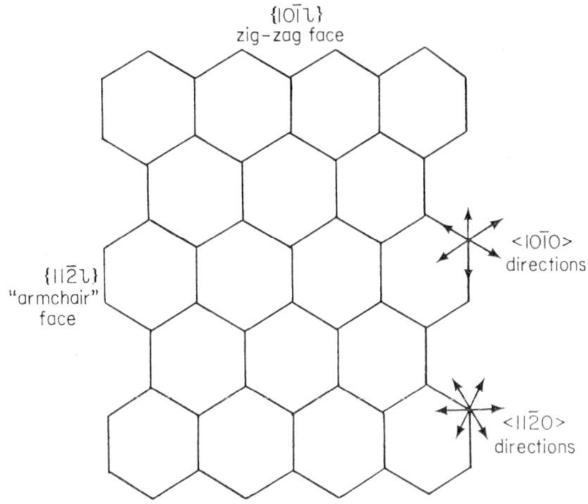

FIG. 1. Graphite crystal lattice.

different electronic environment the edge atoms are much more reactive than those in the basal plane. Hennig (1965b) estimated the difference to be a factor of at least 10^{12}. However, the basal plane invariably contains a multitude of defects, many of which expose reactive edge atoms, so that the geometric edge of a single crystal does not react very much faster than the apparent basal plane. Thomas and Roscoe have reviewed the properties of such defects (Thomas and Roscoe 1968; Roscoe 1968). They were able to reveal that single crystals were made up of a mosaic of crystallites by the use of catalysts, such as boric and molybdic acids, which oxidized preferentially at lattice defects.

Graphite is found in some abundance in nature (Tron 1964) as microcrystalline flakes mixed with clay and other impurities. This natural graphite is used extensively in the manufacture of crucibles and as a component of electrode graphite. Small deposits of "single crystal" flakes also occur embedded in calcite or pyroxene rocks, those of Ticonderoga, New York State, being especially well known. These deposits have no commercial value but are of considerable scientific importance since the crystals, although only about 1 or 2 mm in size, are large enough for the properties of the different crystal faces to be studied.

By far the largest amount of graphite used in industry, however, is synthetic, or electrode, graphite manufactured from petroleum coke and a coal tar pitch binder. The coke is mixed with the warm pitch and the mix extruded or moulded to shape. This is then baked at a temperature of about 900°C to carbonize the pitch and the baked "carbon" converted to crystalline graphite.

by being heated to a temperature of about 2800°C in an Acheson-type electric resistance furnace. The product is very porous and to reduce the porosity the carbon may be impregnated with more pitch or a suitable polymer before graphitization. Natural graphite, electrode graphite or carbon black may also be added to the initial mix to give a product of suitable physical properties. The graphite produced this way is made up of microcrystallites whose sizes range from some tens to hundreds of Angstrom units in dimension. These microcrystallites are orientated in all directions but there is a preferred orientation which depends on the direction of extrusion or moulding of the original mix. The crystallites are rigidly bound together and enclose a proportion of poorly crystalline material. If a non-graphitizable carbon black or polymer is present the proportion of non-graphitic material may be high.

There is also a substantial use of baked but ungraphitized carbons which are sometimes made up of coal coke or anthracite instead of petroleum coke. These carbons, and the metallurgical coke used in large quantities in industry, are non-graphitic, being very hard and relatively poor conductors of heat and electricity. The structure of these carbons is not completely amorphous since very small layer planes are present, stacked one above the other but in random orientation. This is described as a turbostratic structure. These "pseudo crystallites" are surrounded by more truly amorphous material and there may also be some cross-linking between the layer planes. Then, provided this is not too strong, on heating the carbon above, say 2200°C, the layer planes begin to grow at the expense of the amorphous material and orientate themselves correctly. In some materials, such as the carbons produced from cellulose and from some polymers, there is cross-linking that strongly resists reorientation of the layer planes. Such carbons are very glass-like in appearance and properties and are termed vitreous carbons.

Carbons produced by the pyrolysis of hydrocarbon gases and vapours, such as carbon blacks and pyrolytic carbons have their layer planes arranged preferentially parallel to the external surfaces. Very large near-perfect single crystals of graphite have been produced by heating a suitable pyrolytic carbon under stress.

Carbons which have not been heated to graphitizing temperatures normally contain a higher proportion of impurities than electrode graphites. In particular, coal-based cokes may contain several per cent of impurities while nuclear grade graphites manufactured from selected petroleum cokes and coal tar pitches may contain as little as 100 ppm. Treatment of the latter material which fluorides during or after manufacture may reduce this level to 10 ppm or so. The impurity content of carbon is commonly and wrongly described as ash. Ash is the oxide residue left after combustion whereas, at least in nuclear graphite, the original impurities are best thought of as carbides. Hydrogen is usually present in a high proportion in low-temperature treated carbons but its concentration in nuclear graphite is very low (Hawtin *et al.* 1966).

If the difference in reactivity between an ungraphitized and a graphitized carbon is being examined as a function of crystal structure then it is essential to ensure that both have a similar, and low, impurity content because of the catalytic effect of many common impurities. The mineral content of cokes has been reduced by treatment with chlorine at elevated temperatures but it is difficult to remove all the hydrogen and significant amounts of chlorine may be retained (Stacy *et al.* 1966). Heating to a much higher temperature will of course change the crystal structure.

B. PHYSICAL STRUCTURE

Natural graphite flakes have a low porosity but cokes, carbons and synthetic graphite are highly porous with a spectrum of pore sizes ranging from about ten Angstrom units up to several microns in diameter. This porosity is due to the evolution of gas during carbonization. The pore structure may be deliberately increased by gasification with steam or CO_2 if a very high surface area carbon, or "activated carbon", is needed for gas adsorption purposes. The porosity of most electrode graphites is about 20–25% with, perhaps, a quarter of the pores closed and inaccessible to gases. The accessible surface area, as measured by low-temperature adsorption of nitrogen or krypton using the BET equation, may lie between 0.1 and 1.0 m^2/g. The porosity and surface areas of cokes are greater than this and the surface area of activated carbons may be some hundred times greater. This is similar to the surface area of charcoal. The closed pores become progressively accessible as the carbon or graphite is gasified and the surface area consequently increases. A graphite of initial area 0.2 m^2/g may give a maximum area of 4 m^2/g or more during oxidation. This surface area can alternatively be produced by grinding the material finely so as to break open the pores mechanically (Bond *et al.* 1961).

Transport of oxidizing gas to the interior surfaces of the pores is normally by molecular diffusion but if a total gas pressure gradient exists then there may also be a substantial bulk flow of gas along the larger pores. At a high enough temperature the rate of gasification of the internal surface will be controlled by in-pore gas transport while at very high temperatures all the gas is used up at the external surface of the body and no significant reaction takes place in the pores. Under these last conditions the rate of gasification becomes controlled by transport of gas through the gas boundary layer outside the body.

These factors are discussed more fully in Section VI below.

III. THERMAL GAS REACTIONS AT TEMPERATURES
BELOW 1000°C

A. GENERAL

Until comparatively recently many, if not most, of the carbons used in gasification experiments (for example, electrode and natural graphite, sugar chars, coal and petroleum cokes, carbon blacks and wood charcoal) were of doubtful purity. The graphites generally contained considerably more than 100 ppm of impurities, while the cokes and charcoals usually contained several per cent of inorganic matter. On the other hand, the sugar chars and carbon blacks, although substantially free from metallic impurities, were usually prepared at temperatures too low to remove all the hydrogen. The sugar chars usually contained oxygen also. Low temperature carbons are non-graphitic and confusion has arisen because some of the differences in their reactivities, compared to graphite, which were in fact due to their different impurity contents, were wrongly ascribed to their non-graphitic nature. In these early studies the gases used were generally "dried" but significant amounts of water vapour, say 100 ppm, were often present.

In recent years experimentalists have taken much more care about the purity of the carbons used and the dryness of the gas. Both natural and synthetic electrode graphites have been purified to better than 5 ppm total impurities either by chemical treatment or by heating to temperatures in excess of 3000°C. "Spectroscopic grade" graphite of this purity is also available commercially. Non-graphitizing cross-linked carbons have also been used after being heat treated to 3000°C. Improved gas drying techniques have enabled the moisture level to be reduced to less than 2 vpm. The results obtained are more reproducible and have enabled the effects of impurities and moisture to be better understood.

Recently, also, the use of optical and electron microscopy to study the oxidation of single crystals of pure natural graphite, and of individual crystallites in electrode graphite, have shown how complicated the kinetic processes are on this scale. The different crystallographic directions in the basal plane are attacked at different rates and the basal plane itself is found to contain a multitude of crystal defects which become the sites of localized attack. Minute amounts of foreign atoms can have an enormous effect on the local rates of oxidation. Indeed, if taken in isolation these experiments would suggest that no simple pattern could possibly emerge from a study of the gasification of microscopic amounts of multicrystalline graphite or carbon.

Fortunately, although the overall kinetics are complicated, the behaviour of purified multicrystalline graphite is simpler than might be expected provided that the gases used are really dry and the gasification rates are expressed in terms of the accessible area of the material, as measured by low temperature gas adsorption. Different results can be obtained if the gas contains water vapour or if the graphite is "dirty". The behaviour of industrial cokes depends very much on their origin. Such information as is obtained is of course of considerable practical importance but often of limited scientific interest in that extrapolation of the results to other related materials is not possible.

If reactions are carried out at temperatures much in excess of 1000°C then it is found that new kinetic factors operate. The gasification rate normally reaches a maximum at some temperature near 2000°C and, if the temperature is further increased, the rate then falls off. Eventually at a sufficiently high temperature the rate begins to rise again. At temperatures above 3500°C carbon volatilization begins to become a significant factor in the gasification rate. Care must of course be taken in interpreting results obtained at high temperatures to ensure that gas diffusion in the pores or to the external surface does not limit the overall rate. It is convenient therefore to discuss the kinetics of high-temperature gasification separately from those of reactions taking place at temperatures below 1000°C.

B. REACTIONS WITH OXYGEN

1. *Experimental Techniques*

As already indicated the majority of experiments carried out to measure the reactivity of cokes and "dirty" carbons to air, while of considerable practical importance, are of little help in interpreting the mechanism of the reaction. The oxidation rates are markedly catalysed by the high and variable amounts of impurities present, and at the higher temperatures they are often controlled by in-pore diffusion. A wide range of reactivities is obtained for apparently similar materials. Attempts have however been made, notably by Guérin and his collaborators, to investigate the factors controlling the observed rates, especially the importance of the pore structure (Guérin and Bastick 1965; Guérin and Rebaudières 1965; Grillet *et al.* 1967; Grillet and Guérin 1969).

In order to understand the kinetics of the carbon–oxygen reaction it is necessary to examine the results obtained with "pure" graphite, that is material containing less than 5 ppm impurities, in very dry oxygen or air. The effect of impurities can then be investigated by comparing these results with those obtained with pure graphites contaminated by specific impurities. It is then possible to explain in part the behaviour of nuclear grade graphite containing perhaps 100 ppm of impurities. The behaviour of carbons containing some per cent of impurities may, however, be so complicated that the results, while of practical utility, may be difficult to relate to those obtained with purer material. Because of wide differences in the accessible surface areas of graphites, and so on, it is essential to express all rates as specific reactivities in terms of these areas.

Most experiments have been carried out at a total pressure of 1 atm with the specimen suspended from a suitable balance inside a silica furnace tube through which a stream of air, oxygen or O_2/N_2 mixture flows. The specimen is weighed continuously and the overall rate of carbon gasification obtained from the rate of weight loss. In many cases the exit gases are analysed continuously for CO and CO_2, usually by infrared gas analysers, so that the individual rates of formation of these two gases can be obtained.

In some experiments the specimen is oxidized in a static system under a low pressure of oxygen. The rate of reaction is then obtained by following the change in gas pressure and composition. A mass spectrometer is sometimes used for analysing the product, and this enables very low pressures to be employed and, in particular, isotopic O^{18}.

In one laboratory the heat evolved during oxidation has been measured directly in order to investigate possible transient effects due to gas diffusion, adsorption or desorption at the start of oxidation (Cowen et al. 1960; Lewis et al. 1967b).

As already mentioned, the surface area of the graphite is now generally measured before and after oxidation so as to obtain a specific rate expressed in terms of the accessible surface. In some experiments the change in surface area during oxidation has also been measured so that effects unrelated to the surface area can be investigated. Although the validity of the premises on which the BET equation is based has often been challenged, the results obtained are reproducible and reasonably consistent. There is reason to believe that at any time only a small fraction, perhaps 5%, of the BET area is actually involved in the reaction, but the fraction is reasonably constant, at least for electrode graphite, so that use of the BET area merely brings in a proportionality constant.

The pore structure of graphite has been examined by several workers in order to understand better the changes in reactivity during oxidation. By measuring the apparent density and the density in a wetting liquid or, better, helium gas, and comparing the results with the X-ray crystal density of graphite it is possible to calculate the relative proportion of open and closed pores. The spectrum of open pores is determined by two techniques, that of the smallest pores, of say 20–300 Å in radius, is calculated from the hysteresis loop obtained from a nitrogen adsorption–desorption isotherm using the Kelvin equation, while the large pore spectrum is measured by means of high-pressure mercury porosimetry. Non-wetting mercury enters finer and finer pores, or pore openings, as the pressure is increased. This latter technique is destructive and can only be used once on any specimen. It may therefore be necessary to use a number of control specimens in parallel. Spencer (1967) has recently received the use of gases and wetting liquids in the characterization of porous carbons, and Scholten (1967) has similarly discussed the use of mercury porosimetry.

A variation of mercury porosimetry has been used where the specimen is impregnated with liquid bismuth (Hewitt 1963, 1967) or silver (Lang *et al.* 1961b; Lang and Magnier 1967) after oxidation, and the pore structure determined directly by X-ray photography or by ashing away the unburnt graphite. Cine X-ray pictures of pores being successively impregnated with mercury have also been taken (Hewitt 1962, 1967).

The experimental information obtained during oxidation consists of (a) the total rate of oxidation, and the individual rates of formation of CO and CO_2 when these have been sought, (b) the temperature coefficient of these rates, that is the apparent activation energies, (c) the order of reaction with respect to oxygen pressure, and (d) the changes in these values during progressive oxidation.

An additional factor often examined is the stoichiometry of the reaction since some oxygen is chemisorbed during oxidation. It is in this connection that O^{18} has proved to be valuable since by changing the isotopic composition of the oxygen it is possible to detect when oxygen chemisorbed at an early stage of the reaction is subsequently desorbed as CO and CO_2. This technique is also useful in studying the effect produced by outgassing the specimen immediately before oxidation.

The effect of impurities in the graphite can be examined both by adding specific impurities and also by following changes in the kinetics during the extended oxidation of initially clean graphite. Even if the initial impurity level is, say, less than 5 ppm there will be a gradual increase in the surface impurity concentration during oxidation as the non-volatile impurities are left; after, say, 75% burn-off the surface concentration may be as high as 0·5%. The effect of water vapour is obtained by the controlled addition of moisture to a dry gas. The amount of water adsorbed on the surface can be examined by the use of radioactive tritiated water. One difficulty encountered in comparing the results obtained with clean graphite and those with carbons of high impurity level, is that the reactivity of clean graphite is so much less than the reactivity of, say, coke that experiments with the former are usually carried out at much higher temperatures than the latter in order to obtain measurable concentration of CO and CO_2 in the exit gases. It is therefore necessary to apply a correction to bring the rates to a common temperature for comparison.

2. *Experimental Results*

No theoretical equations analogous to those proposed for the C—CO_2 and C—H_2O reactions have been suggested for the C—O_2 system but it is customary and convenient to express the overall and individual rates in the form

$$\text{rate} = A \exp(-E/RT)(p0_2)^n \tag{1}$$

where A is the pre-exponential factor, E the apparent activation energy, PO_2 the partial pressure of oxygen and n the order of reaction.

An equation of a different form has been proposed by Gulbransen and Andrew (1952a), viz.

$$\text{rate} = A' + Bp0_2.$$

However, Bonnetain and Hoynant (1965) have pointed out that this equation does not hold at low pressures and in fact the experimental results can be represented quite well by eqn (1) if $n = 0.5$.

The order of reaction is obtained by measuring the rate of oxidation at different oxygen pressures, or, more commonly, in a series of O_2/N_2 mixtures of different oxygen concentration. Values ranging from zero to unity have been reported at various times, but most recent workers, for example Lewis et al. (1964a, 1965), Rebaudières and Guérin (1965), Amariglio and Duval (1967), have found that for pure and low impurity content electrode graphites a value of between 0·5 and 0·6 applies at temperatures up to 600°C when the total pressure is 1 atm. Hennig (1961b) obtained a similar order for single crystals whose purity was not certain. A half order has also been obtained for graphites containing substantial amounts of impurities (Gulbransen and Andrew 1952a; Effron and Hoelscher 1964) and for vitreous carbon (Otterbein and Bonnetain 1968).

More recently Essenhigh and Froberg (1967) oxidized $\frac{1}{2}$ in diameter graphite spheres in both air and oxygen and reported a zero order of reaction. The temperature of the sphere was measured directly by embedded thermocouples. These authors have criticized the techniques used by other workers, who measured furnace or gas temperatures, and attribute the finite orders found by these to a rise in temperature produced by the heat of reaction and secondary oxidation of CO. This criticism is not valid for experiments carried out at relatively low temperature where no CO is formed with a wide range of O_2/N_2 mixtures (Lewis et al. 1964a, 1965).

No reliable estimate for the individual orders for the CO and CO_2 reactions have been obtained but they appear to be different for pure graphite since Amariglio and Duval (1967) found the CO/CO_2 ratio to increase with diminishing O_2 pressure. At 571°C the ratio is 0·5 at 1 atm and 1·3 at 50 torr. On the other hand, they and Lewis et al. (1964a, 1965) obtained a pressure independent ratio with impure graphites.

Experiments carried out by Lang and Magnier (1964a) on the oxidation of purified electrode graphite in air at 500°C and at a range of pressures up to 18 atm show that the order of reaction falls off at pressures above 3 atm and may even become negative. The effect depends on the pore structure of the graphite and is explained as being due to the accumulation of product gases in the fine pores. It will be shown in Section VI that above a certain temperature the reaction becomes controlled by diffusion of the reactant gas through the pores of the material. Both the effective order of reaction and the activation energy are thereby reduced.

A quite different behaviour is obtained at temperatures much in excess of 1000°C, see Section IV.

The energy of activation is obtained from the usual Arrhenius-type plots of the log-rate against $1/T$. It is necessary to carry out the experiments over a very small total weight loss because reaction rates generally change significantly with different degrees of burn-off, largely because of changes in the BET area. This has not always been done in the past and some of the earlier activation energies, especially those measured on very reactive materials, are therefore of doubtful value. A wide range of activation energies has been found by different workers. Carbons containing a high concentration of impurities normally yield values of about 35 kcal/mole while graphites containing less than 5 ppm impurities give values of 60 kcal/mole. Blyholder and Eyring (1957, 1959b) claim that the true value for clean graphite is 80 kcal/mole, any lower value being due to in-pore diffusion. This view is not supported by other workers and there is now general agreement that for graphites containing less than 5 ppm impurities the overall activation energy for oxidation in a dry gas is between 60 and 62 kcal/mole (Lewis 1963; Lewis et al. 1967a; Bonnetain and Hoynant 1965; Heuchamps et al. 1965a; Heuchamps and Duval 1966; Amariglio and Duval 1966; Lang et al. 1965a). Few measurements have been made of the individual activation energies for the two products but the results obtained suggest that for pure graphite they are similar, possibly 60–62 for CO and 58–60 for CO_2 (Lang et al. 1961b; Lewis et al. 1967a). With contaminated graphites the CO_2 value is significantly lower than the CO. For example, with a nuclear grade graphite containing about 150 ppm of impurities the overall activation energy lies between 40 and 45, the CO value being about 48 and the CO_2 41 (Lewis et al. 1967a). As the proportion of CO_2 is now greater than with clean graphite the overall value depends more on the CO_2 than on the CO figure.

It has been proposed by Heuchamps and Duval (1966) that these varying results can be explained by assuming that two parallel reactions take place on the surface of graphite. One, with an activation energy of some 60 kcal/mole, takes place on a clean graphite surface, the other with an activation energy of between 35 and 38 kcal/mole, takes place on the contaminated surface. The more contaminated the graphite the lower is the energy of activation and also the lower the ratio of CO to CO_2 in the product. These authors made systematic studies of the relationship between E and the CO/CO_2 ratio, r, for graphites of different degrees of contamination. In the

140   J. B. LEWIS

majority of experiments clean graphites were oxidized up to 90% burn-up
and the parallel changes in E and r caused by the accumulation of ash on the
surface measured. In other experiments clean graphites were contaminated
by varying amounts of sodium and potassium oxides, such as may be produced
by glass blowing. Graphites of different initial impurity were also examined.
It was found that when the oxidation was carried out in dry air a simple
relation existed between E and r (Fig. 2). This held for all temperatures
between 520° and about 700°C and for graphites of such diverse origin as

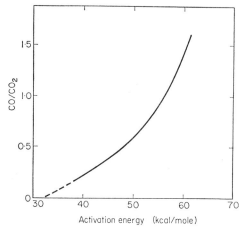

FIG. 2. Oxidation of graphite in air at 630°C, showing the relation between CO/CO_2
ratio and activation energy. (Based on Heuchamps and Duval 1966.)

electrode graphite, natural graphite and graphite obtained from the decomposition of silicon carbide. The relationship was explained in terms of the
coexistence of the two reactions referred to above. No such simple relation
was, however, found when the oxidations were carried out in moist air.

It has already been noted by various authors that although the rate of
oxidation increases progressively with the degree of contamination it does
not increase as much as would be expected from the corresponding fall in the
energy of activation, that is eqn (1) does not hold. This effect is very noticeable
in the work of Heuchamps and Duval (1966). For example, the rate of oxidation of an initially clean graphite remained substantially constant over the
oxidation range 6·5–65% weight loss despite a marked fall in E and, again, a
reduction of E by about 12 kcal/mole caused by the addition of alkali oxides
was associated with only a twofold increase in rate instead of the factor of
several hundred as would be expected from eqn (1). Clearly, changes in E are
largely compensated by corresponding changes in the pre-exponential factor A.

An equation of the form

$$E/RT = \ln A + \text{constant} \qquad (2)$$

used in conjunction with eqn (1) was found to represent the variation of rate with activation energy, see Fig. 3. This relationship did not, however, hold when the reaction rate was inhibited by the addition of phosphorous pentoxide. If sufficient of this was added to reduce the rate to a quarter of the original value then E remained constant even though the CO/CO_2 ratio changed.

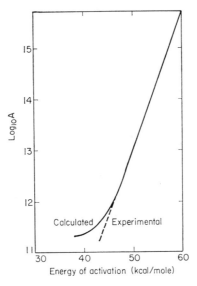

FIG. 3. Relation between A and activation energy. (Based on Heuchamps and Duval 1966.)

Any oxidation mechanism which has been derived from experiments where E was significantly less than 60 kcal/mole applies to a reaction which is predominantly catalytic in nature. This mechanism will almost certainly be invalid for the oxidation of pure graphite and, indeed, because of the selective nature of catalysts, may not apply even to other catalysed reactions where the impurities are different. Unfortunately, until quite recently, most of the mechanisms published were based on results from experiments where E was between 35 and 45 kcal/mole. The results of Gulbransen et al. (1952a, 1963), Effron and Hoelscher (1964), Horton (1961), Gregg and Tyson (1965) and Mar'yasin and Tesner (1965), amongst others, are in this category and will not therefore be discussed here.

The effect of water vapour on the rate of oxidation depends on the purity of the carbon and also on its structure. Most authors report that moisture inhibits the oxidation of pure graphite, the biggest decrease in rate occurring when the moisture level is raised from about 10 to 200 vpm. Hoynant et al. (1958), for example, found that at 671°C the rate of oxidation of spectroscopic graphite in air fell by an overall factor of four as the water concentration of the air was increased from 10^{-7} to 10^{-3} mole fraction. The individual rates of formation of CO and CO_2 were reduced by different amounts, the former by a factor of six and the latter by a factor of three. When a molar concentration of 5×10^{-6} of water vapour was added to the oxidizing air the overall rate fell to 40% of the original value over a period of 6 min. If the inhibition was due to the adsorption of the added water then during the period when a new steady state was being set up sufficient water molecules were added to cover only about 0·2% of the surface of the graphite. Two extreme conditions can be postulated, that every surface carbon atom is reactive, in which case each water molecule inhibits about 200 carbon atoms, or else that each water molecule inhibits only one carbon atom, in which case only about 0·5% of the surface is reactive.

Heuchamps et al. (1965b) found that the inhibiting action of water on pure graphite was less marked at lower temperatures. Below 500°C there was no effect. When the graphite was contaminated by alkali impurities water had a catalytic effect. For example, a spectroscopic graphite to which 23 ppm of sodium, 27 ppm of potassium and 3·5 ppm of boron were added as oxides reacted four times as rapidly in air at 637°C as before. When 3×10^{-4} mole fractions of moisture were introduced, the rate was further increased by a factor of 1·6. This concentration of moisture would have reduced the oxidation rate of the clean graphite by a factor of 1·8. The inhibitory action of water on the original graphite diminished after extensive burn-off, due presumably to the gradual accumulation of ash on the surface. After 70% burn-off the inhibition changed to catalysis. The change in effect was accompanied by a corresponding fall in the activation energy.

Hennig and Lang found that water vapour had a catalytic effect on the oxidation of single crystals of graphite (Hennig 1961a; Lang 1962; Lang and Magnier 1964c; Lang et al. 1963). The energy of activation in Hennig's experiment was low, some 43 kcal/mole. Lang did not quote an activation energy but pre-heated all specimens to 3000°C to purify them. In earlier experiments Lang used pyrolytic carbon flakes and found that if a stack of 80 or so flakes was made up then water had an inhibitory effect on the oxidation of the stack just as it had with purified electrode graphite (Lang et al. 1961b). Lang and his co-workers have used the technique of silver impregnation to examine the pore structure of the oxidized material (Lang et al. 1965c). They found that when purified electrode graphite was oxidized in dry air at 620°C all the pores were attacked, whereas in moist air only the large pores were attacked. Further, the changes produced in the BET area and pore structure after a given burn-off were the same if the oxidation was at 510° or 620°C provided the air was dry. If, however, the oxidation had been carried out in moist air the effects were quite different. Moisture appeared to act as a catalyst at temperatures below 530°C and as an inhibitor at higher temperatures. The results could be explained on the hypothesis that the whole of the BET area is available for reaction only if moisture is absent. Moisture inhibits the oxidation in fine pores at the higher temperature, hence the effect produced by making a type of porous body by stacking many flakes one on top of the other.

In a study on the oxidation of purified nuclear graphite Lang *et al.* (1967) concluded that the larger pores were lined with micropores of less than 100 Å diameter and that closed pores were also adjacent to the surface of the large pores. In dry air, oxidation removed carbon uniformly but in moist air the oxidation was inhibited in the micropores. Thus, for a given weight loss, relatively more carbon would be removed from the macropore wall in moist air and there would be a greater measure of pore opening.

Lang and Magnier (1968) in a comprehensive review of all their earlier work tentatively suggested that water reacts in two different ways, firstly by forming reactive intermediary COOH groups on the surface which give CO_2, and secondly by chemisorbing to form a complex which breaks down above 600°C to give CO and H_2. The latter may become trapped in fine pores due to slow diffusion and therefore inhibit the reaction in such pores. Any hydrogen present in the carbon should exhibit a similar effect. The overall effect becomes very complicated if the carbon is dirty.

Lavrov (1964) has proposed a mechanism for the catalytic action of moisture on the oxidation of carbon blacks which is based on dissociation of water into hydrogen and oxygen atoms and hydroxyl radicals at the surface. This interferes with the normal reaction which involves dissociation of O_2 molecules at the surface. Such a mechanism does not account, however, for the inhibitory action of moisture on clean graphites.

Lang *et al.* (1966) recently demonstrated that a different type of etch pattern is produced by oxidizing single crystals in air at 620°C depending on whether the air is dry or moist. Hennig had earlier shown how the profile of steps on the basal plane is changed by the presence of moisture (1961a).

Hennig also showed that chlorine altered the oxidation pattern. Chlorine is known to be an inhibitor for the oxidation of pure electrode graphite (Bridger and Appleton 1948; Day *et al.* 1957; Dahl 1961; Asher and Kirstein 1968). The most likely explanation for this is that it adsorbs on "reactive sites" and protects them from attack. This explanation is supported by the fact that both CCl_4 (Bridger and Appleton 1948; Asher and Kirstein 1968) and CCl_2F_2 (Pallmer 1966) are good inhibitors for the oxidation of graphite while $CClF_3$ is not. The first two compounds would be expected to decompose more easily to give Cl_2 than the last. However, the argument is not completely proven. A catalytic action can be produced by any of these compounds if the graphite is dirty due presumably to the formation of catalytic metal chlorides from impurities present on the surface. It is interesting to note that Robson et al. (1968) found that halogens destroyed e.s.r. signals on amorphous carbons. Another effective inhibitor is $POCl_3$ (Arthur 1951; Beattie et al. 1964; Lewis et al. 1967c). The inhibition produced by this compound persists for some time after its addition has stopped, probably due to a phosphate coating having been formed on the graphite surface. However, the degree of inhibition falls off markedly with increasing moisture content (Lewis et al. 1967c). Inorganic phosphates are good inhibitors (Earp and Hill 1957).

These inhibitors have also been shown by Hedden et al. (1959) to be effective in the CO_2 reaction. They also inhibit the secondary oxidation of CO to CO_2 and have been added to the gas stream in attempts to show how much secondary oxidation takes place. Because of the effect of inhibitors on the primary reaction the results obtained from such experiments are difficult to interpret (Arthur 1951; Bridger and Appleton 1948).

The effect of specific inorganic impurities has been investigated by many workers but no simple theory has been proposed that will account for all the observed results. When oxidizing very contaminated, and therefore very reactive, carbons it is difficult to avoid in-pore diffusion effects. Most of the work has been reviewed by Walker et al. (1959a, 1968a) and only a few of the more recent and relevant experiments will be discussed here.

It was at one time believed that catalysts acted by forming intermediates which then oxidized neighbouring carbon atoms with the catalyst returning to its original state. Some fifteen years ago, however, Long and Sykes (1950, 1952) proposed that catalysis in the steam and CO_2 reaction was due to electron transfer between C—C bonds and the catalyst, if the latter was a transitional metal, or else by the formation of a covalent bond with the catalyst if this was an alkali metal. This mechanism was thought to be essentially the same for all gasification reactions. Attempts have therefore been made to correlate the catalytic effectiveness of various elements in terms of such properties as their ionization energies.

Rakszawski and Parker (1964) examined the effect of adding 0·1 mole per cent of group IIIA–VIA elements and their oxides to graphite. The graphite and the additive were mixed as powders and compacted into cylindrical specimens which were then oxidized in air at 700°C and 800°C. In a later and similar series of experiments at 600°C and 700°C Heintz and Parker (1966) used transition metals and inner transition metal oxides as catalysts. In both cases it was concluded that in general the results were in accord with the mechanism proposed by Long and Sykes. There was, however, no correlation between the activation energies and the lattice energies for the third row transition metals. It was suggested that this might be due to these metals taking part in the oxidation mechanism in a valency state other than the divalent one. Some very low activation energies were obtained, for example, in the first series of experiments; Bi, Pb, Sb and Se gave values of zero, 1, 4 and 8 kcal/mole respectively, while in the second series Ag, Zn and Mn gave 11, 16 and 20. On the other hand, Pd, Pt and Au gave abnormally high values of 125, 90 and 85. It is very difficult to explain these high values which are at variance with those found by other workers. In particular, very few workers have reported activation energies in excess of 63 for catalysed reactions; the values of 11 for silver, which is stated to be an inhibitor, is also unexpected. A weakness of the technique used by these workers is that the oxidation rates were calculated in terms of the mass of the specimen and not its accessible surface area. Although oxidations were carried out at 5 to 20% burn-off there would still be surface area changes and these could well be different depending on the additive. That changes did occur is instanced by the fact that the cylinders expanded 20% in length during oxidation. It is also clear from the authors' remarks that at 800°C there was uncertainty in measuring the temperature accurately. Again, although boundary layer diffusion was absent in-pore diffusion seems to have been taking place. It should be noted, however, that Fryer (1968) also obtained an activation energy of 125 kcal/mole for the Pd catalysed reaction.

L'Homme *et al.* (1967) found that platinum catalysed the oxidation of carbon black in argon/oxygen mixtures in the temperature range 350–500°C. At 370° the order of reaction was unity for the uncatalysed reaction but zero in the presence of platinum. There was not much change in the activation energy, for example, an increase from about 34·5–36 at an O_2 partial pressure of 0·1. These workers suggest that oxygen dissociates on the platinum surface and the atoms produced migrate over the surface to the carbon.

Alternative explanations to the Long and Sykes mechanism have been proposed. Harker (1959) and Gallagher and Harker (1964), for example, compared the catalytic effect of the alkali metals on the one hand and the transition metals, iron, cobalt and nickel, on the other, on both the air oxidation and CO_2 gasification reaction. The alkali metals behaved differently in the two types of reaction and differently again from iron, cobalt and nickel. A systematic investigation of the catalytic action of various elements on the oxidation of very pure graphite in air at 430°C was made by Amariglio and Duval (1966). The elements were added generally as nitrates in solution, the solution evaporated and the nitrate decomposed to the metal to give a final concentration of 120 ppm. It was found that the following elements catalysed the reaction by the factors shown in brackets after the symbols: Ba (100), Cd (90), Na (130), Au (240), Cu (500), Mn (86,000) and Pb (470,000). Despite the large variation in catalytic efficiencies the energies of activation were all similar, being between 35 and 40 kcal/mole, and the CO/CO_2 ratios were all about 0·1. Increasing the amounts of impurity increased the effect but with the two most effective catalysts, manganese and lead, the maximum effectiveness, defined as catalytic factor per unit of added material, was reached when the amount added was sufficient to cover between 3 and 10% of the BET surface. Amariglio and Duval also found that platinum and palladium, while not catalysts for the reaction proper, catalysed the secondary oxidation of CO so that the product consisted entirely of CO_2. Elements such as Ca, Mg, Sr, Be and Al exhibited either no effect or such a weak one that it might be explained by the presence of lead as an impurity in the material added. These results were interpreted in terms of the formation of an intermediate oxide and not by the electron transfer theory. It was considered relevant that all the metals exhibiting a catalytic effect could form such oxides whereas those that were inactive, or feebly active, could not. The enormous effect produced by manganese and lead were attributed to a mechanism postulated by Kobozev (1946) where the surface is considered to consist of a mosaic of zones inside, and between, which the catalytic element can migrate freely. Each zone becomes catalysed when it contains a definite number of catalyst atoms.

A very large catalytic effect, of 10^5, coupled with a low activation energy, of 28 kcal/mole, was found with lead by Wendel (1966) who impregnated spectroscopic graphite with an aqueous solution of $PbCl_2$. NaCl was much less effective and Wendel explains this in terms of the higher "surface concentration" expressed in terms of solubility and molecular weight of the $PbCl_2$.

The location of the impurity atoms in the material may be important, catalytic impurities added to the graphite after manufacture may produce a different type of oxidation pattern from that produced by the presence of the same impurities in the original mix. Migration of impurities from coke to pitch carbon may occur during the high temperature graphitization process so that the "pitch carbon" regions of the artefact may become the most reactive (Walker et al. 1961). Quite large pits are often produced where there are high local concentrations of impurities. Analytical techniques, such as auto-radiographs following neutron irradiation, can often show the nature of the local impurities in the pits (Héring et al. 1959; Lang et al. 1961a). Catalysts sometimes exhibit cooperative effects so that the behaviour of a graphite contaminated by a mixture of impurities may be difficult to predict (Lewis et al. 1964b).

In an attempt to understand better the cause of catalysis the behaviour of impurities on single crystals and on microcrystallites of electrode graphite have been studied using both electron microscopy and optical microscopy. The results have not simplified the position, on the contrary they have shown that catalytic effects are extremely complicated and often highly specific. For example, Hennig (1962a, b) showed that colloidal particles of the noble metals could act as extremely efficient catalysts, a result at variance with all previous theories.

It has been found by several workers that catalytic particles may move over the surface, usually in preferred crystallographic directions, gouging out shallow channels as they do so; on the other hand, a catalyst particle may remain more or less stationary and cause the formation of a pit. In addition, some particles may first exhibit a period of near random or Brownian movement over the surface. The various types of behaviour are very well demonstrated in a motion picture taken by Thomas and Walker (1965) of the behaviour of colloidal particles of Fe, Ni, Co, Mn, Ta, Ti, Ag, Mo and B on the basal plane of a single crystal of graphite when this was exposed first to nitrogen and then oxygen at temperatures between 650° and 850°C. This work has been summarized by Thomas (1966). Iron was initially a good catalyst giving rise to localized edge pits, but as oxidation proceeded it lost its effectiveness presumably due to oxidation since FeO, Fe_2O_3 and Fe_3O_4 were all found to be inactive in a separate experiment. The catalytic activity of the iron could be regenerated by heating the crystal in a stream of CO. Nickel was also a good catalyst and formed pits but unlike iron it retained its effectiveness. Cobalt particles remained stationary in nitrogen but when oxygen was introduced they moved vigorously over the surface leaving behind a pattern of stepped and corrugated channels. Eventually cobalt, like iron, became de-activated and the migration ceased, although the particles continued to rotate about a fixed position. If the cobalt particles were deliberately oxidized by introducing CO_2 then on reintroducing oxygen, although the particles were now made mobile again, no channels were obtained and the particles eventually all agglomerated. Manganese was a very effective catalyst forming both channels and pits. The direction of these channels suggest that if Hennig's theory of reaction anisotropy is correct (1962a, b), viz that channels are formed perpendicular to the direction of fastest oxidation rate, then the maximum catalytic activity is in the $\langle 11\bar{2}0 \rangle$ direction rather than the $\langle 10\bar{1}0 \rangle$ direction. Like iron and cobalt it tends to become de-activated with time. Tantalum is inactive as a catalyst, although the particles again move freely over the surface. Titanium rapidly produced deep etch pits, in some cases by spiral channelling of the particles. Silver proved to be an extremely powerful catalyst, interpretation of the pattern produced indicated that the two crystallographic directions, $\langle 11\bar{2}0 \rangle$ and $\langle 10\bar{1}0 \rangle$, were equally catalysed. A rather different sequence of effects was displayed by molybdenum in that molten MoO_3 appeared to be formed. Both the $\langle 11\bar{2}0 \rangle$ and the $\langle 10\bar{1}0 \rangle$ directions were affected but, strangely enough, one would be preferred at one instant and the other during the next phase, Thomas and

Walker (1964) have discussed the possibility that catalytic particles are mobile because they move over a chemisorbed gas layer on the surface of the graphite. They become fixed when in contact with carbon atoms proper.

Thomas and Roscoe (1965) have shown that boron forms boric oxide which is an inhibitor in perfectly dry oxygen but a catalyst if moisture is present. These authors have used this property of boric oxide to "decorate" lattice imperfections on single crystals and to show that these are active centres (Roscoe and Thomas 1967; Roscoe 1968).

Other workers have used electron microscopy to obtain information on catalytic effects. Dawson and Follett (1963) examined the behaviour of micro-crystallites of nuclear graphite during oxidation and found that the catalytic impurities present were only active if located at the edges of the basal plane. If, however, the graphite had been previously exposed to neutron irradiation then the catalytic impurities were active in the basal plane also. This work was extended by Follett (1964) who showed that although colloidal ferric hydroxide was adsorbed on both the edges and basal plane it only catalysed the latter if the graphite had been irradiated beforehand. It was concluded that the irradiation produced vacancies in the basal plane which were catalysed by ferric hydroxide. The results are complementary to the observation made by Hennig (1957) that catalysts capable of producing pits and channels on single crystals were much more effective if the graphite had previously been irradiated. Hughes and Thomas in collaboration with Marsh and Reed (1964) used electron microscopy to show that etch pits are produced in purified single crystals and concluded that these are due to existing vacancy loops and screw dislocation. Presland and Hedley (1963) investigated the oxidation of flakes of purified natural graphite in oxygen at low pressures, 10^{-4}–10^{-3} torr, and at temperatures between 600° and 1000°C. Attack took place at the edges, at cleavage steps and, occasionally, on the basal plane. In the last case hexagonal pits with sides parallel to the $\langle 11\bar{2}0 \rangle$ directions were obtained.

When platinum particles of approximately 100 Å in diameter were present these migrated randomly over the surface but showed no catalytic action unless, and until, they were trapped at an edge, at a cleavage step or some surface imperfection. When they had been captured they initiated channels across the surface of the flakes. Each channel was about the same depth as the particle and originally of the same width. However, as each particle moved along, the sides of the channel were gradually oxidized away so that the channels became somewhat tapered. New secondary channels originated from the first one, these were usually parallel to the $\langle 11\bar{2}0 \rangle$ direction. Some particles were, however, trapped firmly on the surface and produced deep pits. This occurred particularly if the graphite had been irradiated previously. The authors were unable to relate the mode of attack, either catalysed or un-catalysed, with specific crystal imperfections.

In a later series of investigations Hennig (1966) showed that the orientation of channels differed if moisture was present, the sides had an $\langle 10\bar{1}0 \rangle$ orientation in wet gas and $\langle 11\bar{2}0 \rangle$ in dry.

3. *Theories of Graphite Oxidation*

As already mentioned no satisfactory mechanism exists for the reaction between carbon and oxygen although several have been suggested. Indeed, until comparatively recently there was wide disagreement concerning the overall activation energy of the process, the order of reaction, the effect of crystal structure, the relative amounts of CO and CO_2 formed, the effect of water and the behaviour of catalysts. Even now, although most of the major workers in the field agree on common values for E and n (eqn 1) and for the CO/CO_2 ratio for pure graphite, values not in line with these continue to be published. Recently, Ong (1964) examined the overall kinetics, that is the formation of CO, CO_2 and the various secondary reactions, in terms of the thermodynamic properties of the gases postulating the existence of one type of reaction site only. The model, however, does little to clarify the actual gas–solid reaction. Two major lines of research are currently being used in attempts to understand the basic mechanism of the reaction. The first, the examination of the behaviour of single crystals, has already been mentioned, the other is the use of isotopic tracers, such as O^{18}, to examine the structure and stability of the surface oxide complexes which may be formed as intermediates in the reaction.

The use of optical microscopy to study the oxidation of single crystal of graphite was pioneered by G. R. Hennig at the Argonne National Laboratories. In particular, Hennig investigated the effect of lattice defects on the rate and showed how these could be influenced by gases or solid impurities (Hennig 1957, 1959; Hennig and Kanter 1959, 1960). More recently, he developed a technique whereby individual lattice vacancies could be revealed by "decoration" with gold and their reactivities determined directly (1965b). Most of his latest work has been summarized in a review published posthumously (1966). This technique has also been used by his former co-worker Montet to examine the kinetics of the graphite water vapour reaction (Montet and Myers 1967). The decoration technique was earlier adopted and developed by Thomas and his co-workers at Bangor. Their work and the related investigations of Hennig, Lang and others were reviewed by Thomas (1966). Earlier work in this field has also been discussed by Bonnetain and Hoynant (1965).

The edges of crystals, flakes and microcrystallites are observed to oxidize away more rapidly than the surface, which consists of basal planes. Examination of the latter shows that oxidation is due to the recession of surface steps and to the formation of hexagonal etch pits. The crystallographic orientation of both steps and pits can be established in single crystals by reference to the twin lines which are always present. Measurements of the rate of recession of the steps and expansion of the pits enable the rate of oxidation in the two crystallographic directions in the basal plane, i.e. $\langle 10\bar{1}0 \rangle$ and $\langle 11\bar{2}0 \rangle$, to be measured. It was found by Thomas and Hughes (1964) that at temperatures between 812° and 872°C the rate in the $\langle 10\bar{1}0 \rangle$ direction is about 15% greater than that in the $\langle 11\bar{2}0 \rangle$ direction; the respective activation energies are about 65 and 62 kcal/mole and the orders of reaction 0·3 and 0·2. These results are consistent with the fact that the exposed sides of the pits are always the armchair or $\{11\bar{2}l\}$ faces at temperatures below 900°C, that is the $\{10\bar{1}l\}$ face is more readily oxidized. At temperatures above 1000°C, however, the pits are differently orientated and consist of the zig-zag or $\{10\bar{1}l\}$ faces. These pits have been shown to arise from lattice defects, such as spiral dislocations and vacancies, often coupled with the presence of impurity atoms (Roscoe and Thomas 1967; Thomas and Evans 1967; Roscoe 1968). The rate of oxidation of the atoms in the basal plane of a crystallographically perfect lattice is negligible.

A number of authors have measured the rates of oxidation perpendicular and parallel to the surface of both flakes of natural graphite and also pyrolytic graphite. A recent review is given by Volkov (1969). The rate of oxidation of the edges is usually between 4 and 100 times faster than the oxidation rate perpendicular to the surface. Lang *et al.* (1962, 1963) have pointed out that the surface, or cleavage planes, contain very many steps which expose edge-type atoms while, however, the geometrical edges of the specimen contain a high proportion of cleavage planes, see Fig. 4. Indeed, if the "roughness" of the

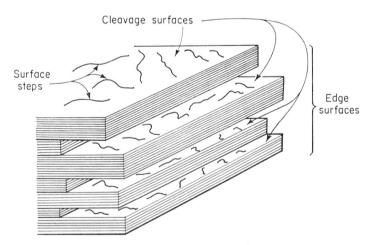

Fig. 4. Schematic representation of the "cleavage" and "edge" surfaces of graphite. (Reproduced with permission from Bonnetain and Hoynant 1965.)

edge is high, as much as 98% of the exposed edge surface may consist of cleavage planes. Thus, since these cleavage planes contain the same proportion of steps as the main surface cleavage planes, the proportion of edge atoms proper may not be so very much greater at the geometrical edge of the specimen than on the flat surface. There is therefore little relation between the overall rate of removal of surface or edge atoms and the true rates in these crystallographic directions. This argument is supported by recent work of Hennig who found that about 10% of the basal plane consisted of edge atoms (1966). By using his decoration technique Hennig was also able to show that the edge atoms are actually at least 10^{12} times as reactive as those in the basal plane (1965b). As already mentioned, different results have been produced by carrying out the oxidations in moist air. Lang's suggestion that these can be explained by assuming that moisture causes the narrow edge cracks to become blocked is not universally accepted.

J. C. Lewis (1965) examined the pits produced during oxidation of vitreous carbon in air and concluded that these were associated with local impurity centres. Blackman (1967) has, however, pointed out that the extension of such pits cannot be readily explained by catalytic oxidation alone; neither can it be explained by a release of strain energy. It is interesting to note that Lewis found the activation energy for the oxidation of non-porous vitreous carbons and pyrolytic graphites to fall from about 43–36 kcal/mole when moisture was added to the initially dry air.

Until recently, it was generally assumed that the oxidation rates of ungraphitized carbon were inherently greater than those of well-graphitized materials. However, much of the earlier work was done with rather "dirty" carbons of high surface area. Due allowance was not made for the catalytic action of impurities nor for the higher surface area of the carbons. Measurements carried out by Lang and his colleagues on pure carbons before and after graphitization show that the specific reactivities are unchanged (Lang 1962; Lang *et al.* 1962).

It can be seen from the above brief summary that it is extremely difficult to predict "*a priori*" the reactivity of a graphite, or ungraphitized carbon, of given crystallographic structure. Fortunately, the proportion of edge to basal plane atoms appears to be much the same in all electrode graphites made from petroleum coke and a coal tar pitch binder. Similar specific reactivities are usually obtained for purified electrode graphite (Bonnetain and Hoynant 1965) and these remain constant during the larger part of the burn-off (Hoynant *et al.* 1964).

The other major area of experimental investigations into the mechanism of the oxidation reactions of carbon is concerned with the role played by chemisorbed oxygen, that is the so-called surface oxide. All manufactured carbons such as carbon blacks, charcoal and electrode graphite are covered with a layer of chemisorbed oxygen and hydrogen atoms derived from adsorption of moisture during manufacture.

It is necessary to heat graphites *in vacuo* to temperatures in excess of 2000°C to remove all the chemisorbed water. Some water vapour and CO_2 are evolved at temperatures below about 450° but most of the adsorbate is evolved as CO and H_2 at temperatures above 1000°C (Asher 1960; Redmond and Walker 1960; Overholser and Blakely 1961).

Lang and Magnier (1963b, 1964b) have shown that gases continue to be given off even at 2500°C and conclude that this gas was trapped during manufacture in pores that subsequently closed as the temperature fell. This theory is supported by the fact that Asher (1960) showed that argon is evolved from graphites heat-treated in an argon atmosphere. If graphite, which has been initially outgassed at a high temperature, is subsequently exposed to moisture then the adsorbed gas is evolved completely at a temperature of 1000°C. Such material can therefore be used in chemisorption experiments provided that it has been rigorously outgassed. Non-porous natural graphite need only be evacuated at 1000°C (Lang and Goenvec 1966; Lang *et al.* 1965b).

Napier and Spencer (1965, 1968) have measured the open pore volumes of a number of electrode graphites at temperatures of 25°, 480° and 740°C. There is a small but significant increase with temperature.

Investigations into the nature of the chemisorbed layer on materials of high surface area such as carbon blacks and charcoals indicate that carboxylic, phenolic and quinoid groups may be present. Such experiments are difficult to carry out on graphite because of its low surface area. Recent studies on the nature of surface groups have been reviewed by Boehm (1966); earlier work was reviewed by Smith (1959) and by Culver and Watts (1960).

Several workers have studied the kinetics of adsorption of oxygen on carbon but again much of the early work was carried out with contaminated material. Only a small fraction of the BET area appeared to be reactive. The early work has been reviewed by Walker *et al.* (1959a). More recently, adsorption studies have been carried out on pure graphite by Bonnetain (1961), Bonnetain *et al.* (1957), Héring *et al.* (1964), le Bail (1963) and by Walker and his co-workers whose work will be discussed in more detail below. The rate of adsorption was found to follow the usual Elovich law up to a maximum coverage of about 5% of the BET area. All oxygen chemisorbed could be removed, as CO, by outgassing the graphite at 950°C.

Graphites of high surface areas, up to 380 m^2/g, have been produced by various Russian workers by grinding purified natural graphite in steel and glass vibro-mills (Federov *et al.* 1961, 1963; Zarif'yants *et al.* 1962, 1963, 1967; Démidovitch *et al.* 1968). Oxygen adsorbed rapidly at first and then more slowly on this material. A maximum coverage of 10% of the BET area was obtained. The activation energy for adsorption increased with coverage and the heat of adsorption fell. The surface oxides were irreversibly hydrated when the graphite powder was exposed to water vapour giving carboxylic and tertiary hydroxyl groups. Most of the chemisorbed oxygen could not be accounted for and it was suggested that neutral or basic groups might be present and possibly interstitial oxygen also. Some molecular oxygen was evolved on outgassing at 200°C. It was stated that the powder from the steel mill contained 0·5% of iron and had different adsorption characteristics from that prepared in the glass mill. This latter material would undoubtedly be contaminated with alkalis so that any interpretation of the nature of chemisorbed species would be open to criticism. For example, as little as 30 μg of iron present as Fe_2O_3 absorbs as much oxygen as 1 g of graphite. Again, Overholser and Blakely (1961) found a direct correlation between the volume of gas desorbed from nuclear grade graphites and the impurity content, while Sato and Akamatu (1954) and Harker (1959) have suggested that alkali metals increase the fraction of surface able to adsorb oxygen. Kiselev and Nikitina (1966) have also shown that the active centres are the atoms on the prismatic faces. However, free radicals appear to be absent and the reactivity is attributed to the unusual bond structure which is due to crystal deformation.

Most of the recent investigations into the role played by the surface oxide in controlling the carbon–oxygen reactions have been made by Walker and his colleagues (Laine et al. 1961, 1963; Lussow et al. 1967; Vastola et al. 1964, 1965; Walker et al. 1966, 1967, 1968b). Isotopic O^{18} has been used extensively in these experiments and has enabled the fate of oxygen chemisorbed on the surface before and during oxidation to be followed. It has also shown conclusively that secondary oxidation of CO to CO_2 is unimportant. Graphon, a graphitized carbon black has been used in most cases. The material has polyhedral surfaces which consist essentially of basal planes. During oxidation the edges are preferentially burnt away and the ratio of edge to plane atoms increases markedly, see Fig. 5.

The technique used depends on the fact that oxygen adsorbed at temperatures of 300°C and above can be removed quantitatively by a subsequent vacuum degassing at 950°C. Walker was the first to propose that a distinction should be drawn between the total BET area and the small fraction which is "active" and takes part in the reaction. The latter has been termed the active surface area or ASA. As the studies with single crystals have shown the reaction is confined solely to exposed edge-type atoms so that the ASA is a measure of the amount of these. It is assumed that this same area adsorbs oxygen so that the ASA can be determined from the amount of oxygen chemisorbed at 300°C, a temperature at which the oxidation rate of pure graphite is negligible.

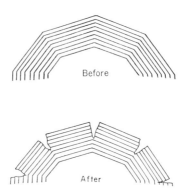

FIG. 5. Graphon surface before and after oxidation—schematic cross-section.

As would be expected from its geometry the ASA of Graphon increases markedly while the BET area only changes slightly. For example, for a burnoff of 14·4% the BET area increases from 76–98 m^2/g while the ASA increases tenfold from 0·2–2·2 m^2/g. The rate of oxidation increases in proportion to the ASA so that if the specific rate were based on the BET area it would appear to increase nearly tenfold.

It has been concluded by Vastola *et al.* (1965) and Walker *et al.* (1967) that the first stage in the carbon–oxygen reaction is the formation of a transient complex of adsorbed oxygen $C(O_2)_t$ which then reacts with a second atom to form an intermediate complex $C(O)_i$. The complex either breaks down immediately to form CO and CO_2, leaving a "free site" C_f on the surface

$$2C(O)_i \rightarrow CO_2 + C_f \tag{3}$$

$$C(O)_i \rightarrow CO \tag{4}$$

or changes to a relatively stable complex $C(O)_s$

$$C(O)_i \rightarrow C(O)_s. \tag{5}$$

It is this latter complex which is normally present on graphite. At temperatures below 500°C the stable complex acts only in blocking off part of the ASA so that the rate is given by

$$\text{rate} = kp_{O_2}(1-\theta) \text{ ASA}$$

where θ is the proportion of the ASA covered by $C(O)_s$. At temperatures above 500°C some exchange between $C(O)_s$ and $C(O)_i$ takes place, that is reaction (5) becomes reversible. The reverse reaction is slow at 500°C but rapid at temperatures above 650°C. The experiments of Hart *et al.* (1967) and Lussow *et al.* (1967) indicated that at least two types of active sites were present. The number of sites was increased by repeated adsorption and desorption. More recently, Walker *et al.* (1968b) have shown that no less than five different types of sites can be identified if the chemisorption of oxygen on Graphon is studied from the pressure range 0·7 m torr to 1 atm. These sites are probably located at the different zig-zag and armchair positions on the edges. Water vapour will adsorb on this chemisorbed oxygen.

Somewhat similar studies have been carried out on Graphon by Tucker and Mulcahy (1969). They found that a labile C atom was removed for each O atom chemisorbed. Two distinct processes seemed to occur during uncatalysed oxidation and only one of these produced stable oxide. They suggest that this reaction takes place at the {112l} edge of the carbon lattice.

Lang and Noblet (1967) also found that active sites were created by adsorption, at 25°C, followed by desorption at 900°C. The presence of moisture diminished the effect.

Such experiments as these are more difficult to carry out on graphite than on Graphon because of the very much lower surface area of the former. There are indications that the ASA and BET areas increase roughly in proportion during oxidation so that no great error is introduced if the specific rate is based on the BET area. This conclusion might be expected from the fact, as already mentioned, that the specific rates of oxidation of a wide range of purified carbons are very similar.

Recently a new technique, the measurement of the thermo-electric power, has been used by Walker et al. (1965) to follow oxygen chemisorption on graphite. This technique has also been reviewed in some detail by the authors (Walker et al. 1966). Another technique, low-temperature activated adsorption of nitrogen, has been used by W. J. Thomas (1966) and Griffiths et al. (1964) to follow the changes in the "active" areas of carbon blacks and nuclear graphite during thermal oxidation. As would be expected the proportion of such active areas in the carbon blacks increase markedly during burn-off whereas only a slight effect is observed with graphite.

Bonnetain (1959a, b) and Bonnetain et al. (1959) have investigated the outgassing behaviour of clean graphite at temperatures below 950°C and have shown that the CO/CO_2 ratio in the desorbate changes as the oxygen is removed. At first little CO is formed, then the CO/CO_2 ratio is the same as that produced by oxidation at the same temperature; finally a very high CO/CO_2 ratio is obtained. These results have been interpreted in terms of secondary oxidation of CO by active sites or impurities during the first two stages. These authors also showed, as have Hennig (1961a,b), Lang et al. (1964) and others, that the reactivity of graphite is increased by outgassing but that this increase rapidly passes off after about 1/10th of the superficial area has been oxidized away. The effect is most marked if the outgassing is carried out at 950°C when up to a twenty-five fold increase is obtained, but a significant increase can be produced by outgassing at the oxidizing temperature. The explanation given is that outgassing removes stable surface oxide which comes off as CO leaving two free valencies in the lattice, see Fig. 6. These subsequently adsorb oxygen very readily but the surface oxide now produced is unstable and decomposes readily. The effect, however, does not persist. It is noteworthy that dirty carbons do not exhibit this effect to anything like the same extent, a 30% increase only being obtained with graphite obtained by decomposing silicon carbide.

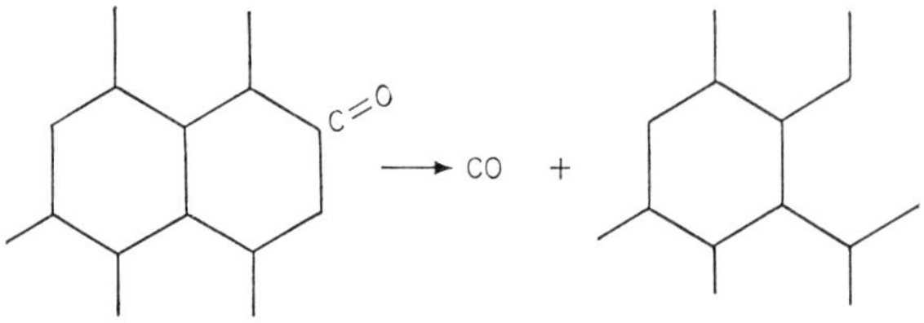

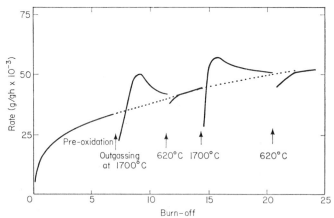

Fig. 6. Effect of removal of stable surface oxide.

The effect of degassing on the rate of reaction has been studied at some length by Lang *et al.* (1964). These workers oxidized purified nuclear graphite in oxygen at a temperature of 620°C, the specimen being degassed at intervals *in situ* at temperatures of 620°, 1000°, 1300° and 1700°C. It was found that after outgassing at 620°C or 1000°C the rates of reaction in both dry and wet oxygen were slightly diminished but returned to the original values after a short burn-off. A similar state of affairs was obtained after outgassing at 1300° and 1700°C when wet oxygen was used, but when the gas was dry the initially low rate rapidly increased to about 50% above the original value and then fell slowly back to the original rate, see Fig. 7. The initial fall in rate was

Fig. 7. Oxidation in dry oxygen at 620°C effect of outgassing. (Based on Lang *et al.* 1964.)

interpreted as being due to the partial closing of micropores when the graphite was heated *in vacuo*. The enhancement of the rate in dry oxygen when the specimen was outgassed at temperatures above 1000°C was considered to be due to the desorption of gases from micropores where these gases had previously blocked reactive sites. Since the acceleration was not obtained with moist oxygen it was assumed that moisture "poisons" the new sites exposed by outgassing. This is in accord with the observations of Lang and Noblet (1967) referred to above. Lang and Magnier (1963b, 1964b) have shown elsewhere how outgassing above 1000°C removes gases trapped in pores which are closed at low temperatures. They have also shown (1963a) that pores of diameter less than 50 Å are closed when the graphite is heated above a temperature of 1000°C *in vacuo* but open on oxidation. These results are in accord with the observations of Héring *et al.* (1964) that chemisorbed oxygen is all removed by outgassing at 950°C, so that gases desorbed at temperatures above this must have been trapped in some way and are not normal "surface oxides".

However, this hypothesis of Lang does not satisfactorily explain the results obtained by Hennig (1961b) who examined the increase in reactivity produced by outgassing single crystals of graphite. Hennig explained his results as being due to the presence of two types of surface oxides, one $>C_2O$ and the other $>CO$, the former being less stable than the latter. On degassing the stable $>C_2O$ group evolves carbon monoxide and leaves a singly-bonded carbon atom which is very reactive.

More recently Shelef and Walker (1967) obtained very high transient rates after degassing when oxidizing graphite in CO_2. These experiments were concerned with examining the inhibitory effect of traces of hydrogen. The results obtained are tentatively interpreted as being due to a mechanism somewhat similar to that outlined by Hennig.

4. *Discussion*

It is clear from the results obtained with near perfect crystals and from the use of O^{18} studies that the mechanism of oxidation is complicated even at the atomic level and in the absence of impurities. At first sight, therefore, it would seem to be extremely difficult, if not impossible, to relate the observed reactivity of a manufactured graphite or carbon, with any measurable property. Fortunately this is not quite the case. It has been well demonstrated that with pure multicrystalline graphite the oxidation rate in dry air is proportional to the BET area. Such a proportionality sometimes exists with such less pure graphite as nuclear graphite (Blake 1964; Blake *et al.* 1964) and sometimes does not (Lewis *et al.* 1967a). Again, Lang and others have shown that although the admission of very low concentrations of water vapour has a large effect on the observed rate the effect saturates and consistent, if somewhat different, kinetics are thereafter obtained.

The role played by impurities has been shown to be complicated on an atomic scale but here again the effects saturate and reasonably consistent, if low, activation energies are obtained. Moreover, as Duval has pointed out, low activation energies are associated with low exponential factors so that the increase in rate, although large, is not catastrophic. Further, Duval's work has enabled at least a qualitative understanding to be obtained of the variation in the CO and CO_2 ratio of the product.

Empirical experiments are still needed if the reactivity of a carbon of industrial importance has to be known but the results obtained can now be far better explained and compared with those of other carbons. The reactivities of industrial cokes of high impurity content have been studied at considerable length by Guérin and his colleagues; these authors have shown how the pore structure can influence the properties of such reactive materials. Their work has been recently summarized and reviewed by Guérin and Bastick (1965) and compared with the results obtained by other workers. Most of the investigations of this team have, however, been concerned with the CO_2–carbon reaction since this is the principal reaction of industrial importance with these carbons.

C. REACTION WITH CARBON DIOXIDE (THE BOUDOUARD REACTION)

The CO_2–carbon reaction is reversible and the product, carbon monoxide, inhibits the forward reaction. Most authors have found that the rate of gasification of carbon can be represented by an equation of the form

$$\text{rate} = \frac{k_1 \, pCO_2}{1 + k_2 \, pCO + k_3 \, pCO_2} \tag{6}$$

but some have suggested that this equation requires modification under certain experimental conditions. It is clear from the form of eqn (6) that no simple order of reaction nor activation energy can exist, but conditions occur when the equation can be simplified. For example, at low pressures of CO_2, if no CO is added, the rate is approximately equal to $k_1 pCO_2$ and the reaction is of the first order; on the other hand at high CO_2 pressures, if pCO is kept small, the rate then becomes equal to k_1/k_3 and the reaction should be of zero order.

The first step in the reaction is the formation of a surface oxide, C(O), on an active free site, C_f, on the surface

$$CO_2 + C_f \rightarrow C(O) + CO_g.$$

An equimolar amount of carbon monoxide is produced. This reaction takes place with pure graphite at temperatures as low as 350°C.

The second step is the breakdown of the surface oxide to form gaseous CO leaving a new active site behind:

$$C(O) \rightarrow CO_g + C_f.$$

This step only occurs with pure graphite at temperatures above 600°C.

Two mechanisms have been proposed to account for the inhibiting action of carbon monoxide. In the first, CO is assumed to adsorb reversibly on the active sites forming an inactive complex C(CO) which thus blocks off these sites and so reduces the rate of reaction. In the second mechanism, adsorption of CO is assumed to be negligible and the inhibition is considered to be due to the first step being reversible. Thus

$$CO_2 + C_f \rightarrow C(O) + CO_g \qquad (7)$$

and

$$C(O) \rightarrow CO_g + C_f. \qquad (8)$$

Both mechanisms can lead to eqn (6) and in the past there has been much debate as to which was correct. In recent years the consensus of opinion has been in favour of the second, but there is still some doubt because even when using pure graphite under conditions where in-pore diffusion is absent quite different values of the rate constants and activation energies have been obtained by different authors. The earlier work in this field has been extensively reviewed by Walker et al. (1959a).

Two of the strongest arguments against the first mechanism are firstly that Reif (1952) showed chemisorption of carbon monoxide to be negligible and secondly that Ergun (1956) obtained an equilibrium constant for reaction (7) which was independent of the purity and surface area of the three very different carbons used.

There has been much debate as to whether reaction (8) is always the rate-controlling step or whether, under some conditions, the forward step of reaction (7) may be the slowest. Ergun (1956) and Bonner and Turkevich (1951) favoured the former view while Hedden et al. (1959) and Freundlich (1962) favoured the latter. Recently, however, Mentser and Ergun (1967) were able to show, by the use of C^{14}, that an equilibrium was established in reaction (7) much more rapidly than the decomposition reaction (8).

Various degrees of surface coverage by the oxide have been reported. Gulbransen and Andrew (1952b) using spectroscopic graphite in 0·1 atm of pure CO_2 obtained values of about 5, 20 and 30 % at 500°, 600° and 700°, but zero above 900°C. Tonge (1959) found a 4 % coverage on nuclear graphite at 450°C, and a 20 % coverage at 550°C. However, Lang et al. (1965d) using three different techniques concluded that the coverage on purified nuclear graphite was less than 0·5 % in the same temperature range. Sykes and Thomas (1961) were unable to detect any adsorbed oxygen on the surface of graphite at temperatures between 750° and 900°C. More recently, Grabke

(1966) has shown that the amount of oxygen adsorbed on graphite at temperatures between 900° and 1100°C is independent of the total pressure, from 1–760 torr, but is critically dependent on the CO_2/CO ratio of the gas.

Although, as already stated, there are no unique values for the overall order of reaction and activation energy it is convenient for many purposes to measure effective values for these, especially for CO_2, at a pressure of 1 atm. As with the oxygen reaction, a wide range of activation energies has been reported. In part this is due to the use of "dirty" carbons; in some instances in-pore diffusion effects were also present. Most recent authors have obtained activation energies between 80 and 90 kcal/mole in the temperature range 850–1100°C under pressures ranging from 0·1–1·0 atm.

Wicke et al. (1961) gasified purified carbon black, activated carbon and spectroscopic grade graphite in CO_2 at a pressure of 1 atm and temperatures between 850° and 1100°C. They obtained an overall activation energy of about 86 kcal/mole in each case. There was no evident relation between the reactivity and the degree of graphitization or crystallite size of the material. However, X-ray diffraction measurements on the spectroscopic graphite showed that the non-graphitic fraction of the carbon reacted in preference to the truly graphitic material. These authors have reviewed the work of others and concluded that where lower activation energies have been reported for pure carbons it is likely that in-pore diffusion was responsible. Lang and co-workers (Lang 1962; Lang et al. 1961b, 1962) showed that the activation energies for the gasification of a range of pure carbons of such diverse origin as charcoal, nuclear graphite and natural graphite were all about 87 kcal/mole in CO_2 at a pressure of 1 atm provided that the temperature was below that at which in-pore diffusion commenced. This depended on the pore structure of the material and varied from 750–1000°C. The specific reactivities were all similar, that is the reactivities were proportional to the BET areas. Moisture had only a slight effect on the rate. It was found that nuclear graphites gave the same activation energy even though their reactivities were greater.

Gulbransen et al. (1965a) studied the gasification of pure graphite at a pressure of 19 torr and at temperatures between 1000° and 1600°C. They found that the reaction had an activation energy of 88 kcal/mole up to 1350°C; at higher temperatures the rate was influenced by external diffusion. The rate was only 1/12th of that calculated from the collision frequency of the gas and it was concluded that only about 3·4% of the BET surface area was active.

Bregazzi et al. (1965) reacted two high-temperature treated polymer carbons with CO_2 at pressures between 1 and 12 torr and temperatures from 750–850°C. One carbon, from polyvinyl chloride, was graphitic, the other, from polyvinylidene chloride, was not. Both carbons gave the same activation energy but this depended on whether the specimen had been well outgassed beforehand or not. Outgassed carbons gave an activation energy of 85 kcal/mole, while non-outgassed or highly oxidized carbons gave a figure of only 69. These workers could not account for the pressure dependency of the rates in terms of the usual mechanism for the carbon–CO_2 reaction and instead proposed a new mechanism involving complex reactions at two kinds of sites. The low activation energies obtained with non-outgassed specimens were explained as being due to the intercalation of oxygen, moisture of CO_2 in the carbon which thus weakened surface bonds.

As with the oxygen reaction, many workers have used carbons of unknown purity and obtained low activation energies in consequence. In some cases also, there are indications that in-pore diffusion was influencing the rate. Thus, the reaction mechanisms suggested by these workers are of doubtful value. Long and Sykes (1950) used purified charcoal but the activation energy was only 66 kcal/mole. In earlier work in the same laboratory Gadsby et al. (1948) obtained still lower values, 38 for charcoal and 59 for coke. A similar value of 59 kcal/mole has been reported by Orning and Sterling (1954) for graphite and by Ergun (1956) for both graphite and coke. Mar'yasin and Tesner (1965) calculated a value of 62 for carbon black, although the same material gave a low value for the oxygen reaction.

Various authors have shown, as would be expected from eqn (6), that the overall order of reaction is markedly influenced by the presence of a high partial pressure of CO in the CO_2. If the carbon is gasified in a recirculating system there is a marked difference if the CO is continuously removed (for example by oxidation to CO_2 over a bed of hot copper oxide) or not. Heuchamps (1965) showed recently that when cokes were oxidized at 1000°C in a CO/CO_2 mixture at a total pressure of 1 atm the rate was almost independent of the partial pressure of CO_2, unless this was less than 0·75 bar, but was strongly dependent on the CO/CO_2 ratio. At low partial pressures of CO_2 the reaction was of the first order in CO_2. Lang and Magnier (1964a) examined the dependence of the rate of gasification of purified graphites with CO_2 at pressures from 1–20 atm. The order of reaction was almost zero. A similar result was obtained by Board (1965) who gasified nuclear grade graphite in CO_2 at temperatures from 700–800°C under CO_2 pressure of 5–15 atm. Board found that when CO was added the rate was reduced and became proportional to the CO_2/CO pressure ratio. In pure CO_2 the activation energy was 55 kcal/mole but when 0·7% of CO was added the activation energy increased to 90 kcal/mole. Moisture at a level of 600 vpm reduced the rate; this result is in contrast to Lang et al.'s observations (1961b) where water was found to act as a catalyst.

As already mentioned some authors have concluded that eqn (6) need not always apply. Long and Sykes (1950) reacted purified charcoal with both

CO_2 and steam at temperatures between $700°$ and $884°C$ and pressures from 10–760 torr. They found a discrepancy between their experimental results with CO_2 and eqn (6) and a bigger discrepancy between the steam results and the corresponding equation—eqn (13), Section D. The explanation proposed was that the active sites on the surface exhibited a range of reactivities to the different stages of the overall reaction. As stated above the activation energy obtained was low—66 kcal/mole. However, this explanation has been supported by Temkin and his co-workers (for example Cherednik et al. 1967; Temkin et al. 1968). The Russian workers claim that the overall rate of reaction with CO_2 can be expressed by the equation

$$\text{rate} = K \left(\frac{pCO_2}{1 + k'pCO} \right)^{\frac{1}{2}}$$

a somewhat similar equation which applies to the reaction with steam.

In contrast to this equation Blackwood (1962a) found that when nuclear grade graphite was gasified in CO_2 at temperatures between $650°$ and $870°C$ and pressures from 1–30 atm the results could be represented by the equation

$$\text{rate} = \frac{k_1 pCO_2}{1 + k_2 pCO}.$$

The rate was related to the geometric surface area and independent of the pore structure. Graphite behaved quite differently from low temperature chars which when gasified under similar conditions gave a very high rate. For these an equation of the type

$$\text{rate} = \frac{k_1 pCO_2 + k_4 (pCO_2)^2}{1 + k_2 pCO + k_3 pCO_2}$$

was suggested (Blackwood and Ingeme 1960).

In contrast to this work at moderate or high CO_2 pressures many experiments have been carried out to study the gasification of graphite in helium which contains very low partial pressures of CO_2 and steam. The interest in this stems from the use of helium at pressures of about 50 atm as a coolant in some types of graphite moderated nuclear reactors. Any traces of carbon dioxide and steam present in the helium will cause the graphite moderator to become slowly corroded by thermal gasification. The CO_2 may be present as a direct impurity or be formed by secondary reactions from CO produced by the steam–carbon reaction. Steam is the more likely contaminant as it may leak into the primary circuit from the heat exchangers. The concentrations will be very low in practice, possibly less than 1 vpm, and it is necessary to carry out experimental work at higher concentrations in order to obtain measurable rates. Blakely and Overholser (1965) and Overholser and Blakely (1965), for instance, used CO_2 concentrations of 550 and 1100 vpm in helium at a pressure of 1 atm. They measured activation energies of 55 and 60 kcal/

mole for the gasification of two nuclear graphites of different purities in the temperature range 875–1025°C and 775–925°C respectively. The orders of reaction, as measured in the CO_2 concentration ranges 60–1000 vpm, were about 0·7 with both graphites. Both CO and hydrogen were found to have a marked inhibiting action on the reaction.

Somewhat similar experiments were carried out by Antill and Peakall (1960) and by Bourke et al. (1966) but at even lower concentrations of CO_2. These two groups found lower activation energies and again found that CO strongly retarded the rate. However, the retardation reached a constant and limiting value as the partial pressure of CO was increased and was not therefore in accord with eqn (6).

Hedden and Löwe (1964, 1966, 1967) gasified nuclear graphite in CO_2 at a partial pressure of 0·1–1·0 atm with CO added up to a maximum of 0·7 atm. It was found that eqn (6) only held when the CO/CO_2 ratio was greater than 0·5; otherwise the results were fitted better by the equation

$$\text{rate} = \frac{k_1\, pCO_2}{1 + k_2 \sqrt{pCO} + k_3\, pCO_2}.$$

In contrast to these results Yamauchi and Mukaibo (1968) more recently obtained results, under somewhat similar conditions, which confirmed eqn (6).

Some light may be thrown on the reason why different results have been obtained by different workers as a result of recent experiments in Walker's laboratory. Somewhat similar techniques were used in these investigations as in connection with the carbon–oxygen reaction. Two different types of carbon were used, Graphon and SP1 graphite. The former material has already been referred to; the latter is a highly purified natural graphite powder which is compacted into a solid, but somewhat porous, body before use. As with oxygen, it was found that only a small fraction of the BET area was active.

Experiments were carried out by Strange (1964) in the CO_2 pressure range 10–100 torr at temperatures between 900° and 1000°C and by Biederman (1965) at the much lower pressures of 10–100 mtorr and at temperatures between 960° and 1120°C. Both experimentalists obtained similar activation energies, of about 100 kcal/mole, for k_1, eqn (6), but the pre-exponential factor was $1·9 \times 10^{17}$ in Strange's experiments and $1·1 \times 10^{19}$ in Biederman's.

It was subsequently found that the CO_2 contained traces of hydrogen and that this gas could significantly reduce the reaction rate when present at partial pressures as low as 3 mtorr. The experiments were repeated by Shelef and Walker (1967) using hydrogen-free CO_2. At a pressure of 40 torr it was found that a high initial transient rate was obtained when the temperature was 940°C or above, but no transient was observed at 916°C. The transient lasted for about an hour or so and the rate then fell to give ultimately a steady value about fifty times lower than the transient. This final rate was similar to that obtained in the previous experiments with non-purified CO_2. The activation energies for the transient and steady state conditions were 76 and 87 kcal/mole respectively. During the transient the BET area changed more rapidly for the same burn-off than during the final steady state and there appeared to be a much higher proportion of basal plane attack, by pitting, than during the final period. Addition of CO or H_2 accelerated the decay of the transient, the latter being particularly effective; a pressure as low as 42 mtorr reduced the rate in a matter of minutes. The explanation proposed was that two surface oxide complexes could exist, one much more reactive than the other. Initially the former was produced preferentially. This then disappeared, by gasification to CO and also, possibly, by conversion to the more stable and less reactive form as a result of interaction with CO_2. Thus, the initially high transient was due to the decomposition of the more reactive complex. The inhibiting effect of hydrogen arose from it poisoning, selectively, the sites which gave reactive complexes. This explanation was supported by the fact that graphite specimens inhibited by hydrogen evolved much less oxygen compounds on outgassing than did specimens which had not been in contact with hydrogen.

The rate constants measured in low pressure hydrogen-free CO_2 were still not the same as those measured in the hydrogen-free intermediate pressure experiment so that hydrogen inhibition did not seem to be entirely the cause. Further work, by Walker and Miles (1966), showed that there appeared to be pick-up of impurities by the active surface of SP1 at 950°C, even in a vacuum as low as 2×10^{-9} torr which resulted in a fall-off of reactivity. The reactivity was renewed by outgassing at 1100°C. When such clean graphite was gasified at 1050°C the activation energy of k_1 during the initial part of the experiment was only 17 kcal/mole indicating that a new type of carbon surface had been exposed during the outgassing. Somewhat complicated kinetics were obtained when the gasification was carried out at lower temperatures, the reaction order being sometimes greater and sometimes less than unity.

These results suggest that under normal conditions only the more stable type of surface oxide takes part in the reactions. It is thus still possible to examine, and indeed explain, the observed kinetics even if the hydrogen content of the CO_2, or of the graphite, is significant.

It is well known that halogen compounds such as CCl_4 and $POCl_3$ act as inhibitors for the gasification of impure carbons by CO_2. The effect of these substances on the gasification of pure graphite is, however, more complicated. All are catalysts at low concentrations, but at concentrations over about 1% the last two compounds act as inhibitors. Hedden and his co-workers (Hedden and Wicke 1957; Hedden et al. 1959) have examined this behaviour in some detail and conclude that the inhibiting action of halogens and their compounds on impure carbons is due to the removal of catalytic impurities.

The inhibition of pure graphites, on the other hand, is attributed to dielectric polarization of the crystal lattice by the adsorbed vapour. This effect, which is similar to the inhibiting effect of CO, is most marked on graphites containing large crystallites.

Yamauchi and his co-workers have studied the effect of halogens on the reaction. They showed that iodine acts as a catalyst for pure graphite but as an inhibitor for impure graphite. This effect was claimed as being due to the removal of vanadium which otherwise acts as a catalyst. The gasification of pure graphite was also catalysed by bromine and, at low concentrations, by chlorine. At concentrations over 6 % chlorine acted as an inhibitor (Yamauchi et al. 1967, 1968).

The reaction of CO_2 with carbon is strongly influenced by the same catalysts as is the carbon oxygen reaction, although there is some evidence that the mechanism may not be the same. Most of the systematic investigations into the behaviour of catalysts for this reaction have been concerned with the effect of iron. Sykes and Thomas (1961) showed that iron added as ferric oxide powder catalysed the reaction of CO_2 with both graphite and diamond. As π- bonds are absent from diamond the electronic theory of catalysis, as previously applied to graphite, needs to be changed if the catalysis of diamond is also due to an electronic mechanism. There is a slight possibility, however, that gasification of diamond proceeds through a graphitic layer, as in the oxygen reaction; but such a layer was not detected. These experiments were carried out in CO_2 at pressures of about 10^{-2} torr at temperatures of 900°C for the graphite and about 800°C for the diamond. The iron content was about 1 part in 580 by weight. The rates of reaction were increased by factors of about 300 and 100 for graphite and diamond, respectively. More recently, Rakszawski et al. (1961) examined the catalytic action of iron powder, ferric oxide and ferric oxalate on spectroscopic graphite in a pressure 1 atm of CO_2 in the temperature range 900–1200°C. All these forms of iron catalysed the reaction but the catalytic effect was reduced if the contaminated graphites were heat treated to 1400° or above before the reaction started. The catalysis was, however, restored if the specimen was heated in a reducing atmosphere of hydrogen or CO. Anderson (1964), working in the same laboratory, used a magnetic susceptibility technique in an attempt to identify the valency state of the iron species most active when carbonyl iron powder was added to spectroscopic graphite. This was not identified but it was found that if the iron was oxidized to magnetite the catalytic activity ceased. Reduction by H_2O or CO regenerated the catalyst. In earlier studies, Gulbransen and Andrew (1952b) concluded that the catalytic action of iron necessitated this being present either as the reduced metal or as the carbide.

The catalytic effect of iron, nickel and cobalt on cellulose char has been studied by Gallagher and Harker (1964) who compared the behaviour of compounds of these metals, especially the oxides and oxalates, on the reaction of the char with both air and CO_2. It was found that the catalysts behaved differently in the two reactions and the authors concluded that two different mechanisms apply. In the reaction with air, the catalytic action appears to be due to chemisorption of oxygen, which then combines with the carbon, whereas in the CO_2 reaction the effect is due to the formation of free metal which then becomes incorporated in the carbon lattice. The char used was prepared at 1000°C and contained 2·4% oxygen and 0·4% hydrogen in addition to 0·19% ash. Its behaviour therefore could well be different from that of graphite. More recently, Marsh et al. (1967) extended these investigations to an examination of the catalytic effect of silver, sodium, iron and nickel on the gasification of carbons derived from polyfurfuryl alcohol and cracked methane. No significant change in the e.s.r. signal was observed during oxidation. Carbon monoxide retarded the reaction except when catalysed by Fe or Ni. The reason for this is not clear.

Most industrial carbons contain a high proportion of impurity atoms and partly because of this and partly because of in-pore diffusion their behaviour is often different from that of pure graphite. Kini (1963) has shown that, unlike pure graphites, the reactivities of cokes obtained from demineralized coals are not proportional to their BET areas. Because of the possibility that activated diffusion in fine pores might affect adsorption measurements carried out at the usual liquid nitrogen temperature, Kini used adsorption of Xenon at 0°C instead. Jacquet and Guérin (1962) also found a non-linear dependency of the rate on the BET area in their studies on the reactivities of nuclear graphites containing varying amounts of impurities. Vastola and Walker (1961) oxidized graphite "wear dust", obtained by grinding electrode graphite, in O_2 and CO_2 at low pressures. The rate of reaction was of the first order with respect to the CO_2 pressure in the temperature range 400–700°C and there was a small but significant chemisorption of CO. However, the graphite was highly contaminated with iron introduced by the grinding process and this almost certainly must have influenced the kinetics of the reaction. The behaviour of cokes and non-graphitic carbons has been studied at length by Guérin and his collaborators, especially M. Bastick. Most of this work has been summarized recently by Guérin and Bastick (1965) and compared with that of other workers. Some results obtained with anthracites by Jozefczak-Ihler and Guérin (1966) have been published subsequently. Anthracites behave somewhat differently from cokes and this has been attributed to being due to their greater proportion of micropores. Another worker who has carried out much work with industrial carbons is Ergun. He has recently reviewed much of this work and, in particular, discussed the relationship between the CO_2 and steam reactions of carbon (Ergun and Mentser 1966).

In recent years graphite has been used more and more as a high temperature structural material, sometimes under conditions where corrosion or gasification might occur. There is therefore a need to know how its mechanical and physical properties change during gasification. This is particularly important in the design of modern gas-cooled graphite-moderated nuclear power stations where a small but significant amount of gasification might take place as a result of radiolytic or thermal attack. With most reactors the coolant is CO_2 and radiolytic attack by this is the important process. Because it is much easier to carry out investigations into thermal corrosion than into radiolytic attack, thermal gasification in CO_2 has been used to obtain useful data on the relation between strength, etc., and carbon weight loss. Collins *et al.* (1965) showed that the compressive strength of nuclear graphite diminished with burn-off in an identical manner irrespective of whether the reaction took place in air at 700°C or in CO_2 in the temperature range 750–960°C. Board and Squires (1965) found the fall-off in both strength and moduli for the same material to be linear with burn-off up to 7% weight loss, when the gasification took place in CO_2 at 20 psig and temperatures between 750° and 950°C. This was interpreted as meaning that the graphite failed at constant strain. In unoxidized specimens, fracture took place as a result of pores linking up by cracks through the large grist grains; but in highly oxidized specimens cracks tended to propagate either through the binder coke grains or else along the grain boundaries. Somewhat similar results were obtained by Rounthwaite *et al.* (1965) who examined the changes in strength, permeability and coefficient of friction of nuclear graphites gasified in CO_2 at atmospheric pressure up to 40% weight loss. In all these experiments it was found that graphite lost between one-third and one-half of its strength during the first 5% weight loss. Hawkins (1965), however, showed that graphite gasified in a reactor exhibited a different strength burn-off relationship. In general, for the same amount of weight loss, radiolytically attacked graphites were significantly stronger than thermally gasified material.

The reverse reaction, or "back reaction",

$$2CO \rightarrow C + CO_2 \tag{9}$$

is of considerable importance in industrial processes where gases containing CO are used, as for example in town gas manufacture and chemical processes involving CO. The equilibrium conditions for carbon deposition have been summarized by Walker *et al.* (1959a). At about 700°C and a pressure of 1 atm the concentrations of CO and CO_2 are approximately equal. The proportion of CO increases with temperature.

The rate of reaction is strongly dependent on the nature of the surface on which the carbon deposits. In the absence of a catalytic surface little reaction takes place below 700°C but over a suitable catalyst the reaction will proceed rapidly at 500°C. The reaction has been studied by many workers. Earlier work has been summarized by Donald (1956). More recent work has been carried out by Henry (1963), Taylor (1956), Ruston *et al.* (1966), amongst others. Most investigations have been concerned with the catalytic activity of ferrous metals because of their industrial importance. The consensus of opinion is that metallic iron is the true catalyst but some authors reject this and claim that the Hägg carbide is the active species.

Recently, Pursley *et al.* (1966) measured the rate of reaction in Vycor vessels at temperatures between 740° and 860°C. The reaction was very slow, of zero order, and had an activation energy of 35 kcal/mole. Pressures of 25–945 torr were used.

Walker and his co-workers (1959b) have investigated the effect of hydrogen on the iron catalysed reaction and have shown that as the hydrogen content of the gas increases the temperature at which the maximum rate of carbon deposition occurs also increases. The iron surface is gradually converted to cementite which is inactive but the activity can be restored by reduction with hydrogen. These workers also conclude that iron, on which CO chemisorbs, is the active catalyst.

The extensive programme of experiments carried out to study the corrosion of graphite by traces of CO_2 and moisture, present as impurities in the helium coolant of the O.E.C.D. reactor experiment "Dragon", has recently been summarized by Everett *et al.* (1968). The effect of impurities and the conditions under which the back reaction occurs are also described.

D. REACTION WITH STEAM

The reaction between steam and carbon is of considerable technical importance in water–gas manufacture, for instance, and, more recently, in nuclear technology. Consequently many empirical investigations have been carried out on this system. The primary reaction resembles the corresponding CO_2 reaction:

$$C + H_2O \rightleftharpoons CO + H_2 \tag{10}$$

but the products may then react further and the final composition of the product depends on the experimental conditions. The secondary reactions are (a) the water–gas shift reaction:

$$CO + H_2O \rightleftharpoons CO_2 + H_2, \tag{11}$$

(b) the Boudouard reaction, which might go in either direction but probably under the conditions of the experiment in the "reverse" direction:

$$2CO \rightleftharpoons C + CO_2 \tag{9}$$

and (c) the methane formation reaction:

$$C + 2H_2 \rightleftharpoons CH_4. \tag{12}$$

The various equilibria can be calculated; Walker *et al.* (1959a) have given a convenient summary of the equilibrium constants which, although based on 1949 data, are quite satisfactory for most purposes. More recently Majewski and Spurrier (1962) have calculated the effect of high pressures on the equilibria. Usually conditions are far removed from equilibrium and the composition of the product depends on the relative rates of the various steps, especially if these are catalysed. Under most experimental conditions reaction (12) is unimportant; it will be considered in detail in the next section. Some workers, however, have shown that hydrogen has a marked inhibiting action on the overall reaction. Unlike CO in the analogous CO_2 reaction, hydrogen is strongly adsorbed (Strickland-Constable 1950; Redmond and Walker 1960b). Ergun (1962) claims that carbon monoxide also inhibits the reaction whereas in earlier experiments Gadsby *et al.* (1946) found CO to have no effect.

The steam–carbon reaction has not received the same amount of basic study as the CO_2–carbon reaction but a mechanism, or rather two mechanisms, analogous to those proposed for the CO_2 reaction have been suggested by several workers, for example Long and Sykes (1952), Gadsby *et al.* (1946), Johnstone *et al.* (1952), Blyholder and Eyring (1959a), Derman (1960), Derman *et al.* (1960) and, earlier, by Key (quoted by Strickland-Constable 1950). No clear-cut conclusion as to which is the correct mechanism has been reached but most workers have found that an equation analogous to that used for the CO_2 reaction will correlate the data. Thus

$$\text{rate} = \frac{k_1 \, pH_2O}{1 + k_2 \, pH_2 + k_3 \, pH_2O}. \tag{13}$$

An order of reaction varying from zero to unity can therefore be obtained and indeed such a range of values has been found. A wide range of activation energies has also been reported. Many of these have been influenced by catalytic effects and in-pore diffusion. Most recent workers have obtained values in the range 65–75 kcal/mole (Walker *et al.* 1959a; Bonnetain and Hoynant 1965).

As in the case of the analogous CO_2 reaction, the possibility that the active sites are not uniformly reactive to the various steps has been discussed (Long and Sykes 1950; Cherednik *et al.* 1967; Temkin *et al.* 1968). If this were the case then eqn (13) would not hold. In fact Long and Sykes (1950) noted a discrepancy between their results and eqn (13) while the Russian authors were better able to represent their results by the equation

$$\text{rate} = K \left(\frac{pH_2O}{pH_2} \right)^{\frac{1}{2}}.$$

The majority of experiments have been carried out at atmospheric pressure or at low pressures but Blackwood and McGrory (1958) used steam pressures up to 50 atm. They showed that in the temperature range 750–830°C methane is formed in substantial quantities and the overall rate equation was

$$\text{rate} = \frac{k_1 \, pH_2O + k_4 \, pH_2 \, pH_2O + k_5(pH_2O)^2}{1 + k_2 \, pH_2 + k_3 \, pH_2O}.$$

As already mentioned there is considerable interest in the reaction of nuclear grade graphite with trace amounts of steam in helium because of the use of helium as a coolant for graphite moderated reactors operating at temperatures of about 1000°C. Blakely and Overholser (1965) and Overholser and Blakely (1965) have examined the gasification rates of two grades of nuclear graphite in both steam and CO_2 at steam concentrations of 20–760 vpm in the temperature range 775–1025°C. One graphite contained less than 20 ppm ash and the other more than 1000 ppm. The activation energy of the latter was about 50 kcal/mole between 775° and 925°C while the former graphite showed a value of 60 at 875°C and 40 at 1025°C. An order of reaction of about 0·7 was obtained with both graphites except at 20 vpm H_2O when a unit order was found. The reaction was faster with steam than with a comparable amount of CO_2 and the effect was greater with the clean graphite. Both hydrogen and CO inhibited the rate. With clean graphite, hydrogen inhibited the rate more strongly than the CO but with dirty graphite both were equally effective.

It is interesting to note than Hedden and Löwe (1967) found that both H_2 and CO inhibited the reaction more strongly at low concentrations than would be expected from results obtained at high partial pressures. Steam reacted seventeen times faster than CO_2 at 1000°C.

Giberson and Walker (1966) have investigated the reaction at steam pressures of 0·1–10 torr, with hydrogen at pressures from 0·08–8·0 torr. They used graphite containing less than 8 ppm ash and found that eqn (13) would not fit their results. Instead they proposed

$$\text{rate} = \frac{k_1 \, pH_2O}{1 + k_2\sqrt{pH_2} + k_3 \, pH_2O}.$$

The effect of hydrogen was considered to be due to dissociative adsorption. This equation appeared to fit the data of other workers better than the accepted eqn (13) but at hydrogen pressures of about 1 torr the difference in fit was small and either equation could be used. It may be noted that this equation is similar to that proposed by Hedden for the CO_2 reaction at low pressures.

The steam reaction is catalysed by essentially the same elements as are the CO_2 and O_2 reaction. Iron, nickel, cobalt and vanadium, for instance, have all been shown to be strong catalysts. The behaviour of highly impure cokes in steam has been reviewed by Guérin and Bastick (1965). As in the corresponding reaction with CO_2, in-pore effects are extremely important because the cokes are so reactive. Ergun and Mentser (1966) have also discussed the reaction of cokes, etc., with steam, in particular they have calculated the effect of having a reacting mixture of both CO_2 and steam.

The role played by coal ash in catalysing reaction (11), (12) and (13) has been examined by Fedoseev (1967).

E. REACTION WITH HYDROGEN

The reaction of carbon with hydrogen has been investigated by a number of workers. It is, or was, of industrial importance in the manufacture of methane by hydrogenation of coal. Under most conditions methane is the sole product

$$C + 2H_2 \rightleftharpoons CH_4. \tag{12}$$

At atmospheric pressure and a temperature of about 800°C, the concentration of methane at equilibrium is somewhat less than 5% while at 1000°C the concentration is less than 1%. The amount of methane, of course, increases with the total pressure. At temperatures significantly above 1500°C methyl and other radicals are obtained. Equilibrium data up to 6000°K have been published by Kroepelin and Winter (1959), and up to 2600°K and 45 atm pressure by Ievleva (1964).

The kinetics of the carbon hydrogen reaction have not been as extensively studied as the other gasification reactions and, unfortunately, the carbons used in many experiments were poorly characterized low temperature chars. The subject has been reviewed by Walker *et al.* (1959a), Blackwood (1962b) and Clarke *et al.* (1962).

Attempts have been made to relate the reactivity of a carbon to the degree of chemisorption of hydrogen. Palmer (1967) found that hydrogen, unlike oxygen, is not adsorbed on the new sites produced by grinding graphite in an inert atmosphere.

Zielke and Gorin (1955) studied the rate of hydrogenation of a low-temperature char in hydrogen at pressures up to 30 atm. They found that in the temperature range 810–928°C their results could be expressed as

$$\text{rate} = \frac{k_1(pH_2)^2}{1 + k_2\, pH_2}$$

methane had no retarding effect on the rate.

Blackwood (1959, 1962a, b) carried out an extensive series of measurements with nuclear graphite and charcoal. He found that at pressures up to 40 atm and temperatures between 650° and 870°C, if the methane concentration was low, the rate of reaction was given by

$$\text{rate} = \frac{k_1(pH_2)^2}{1 + k_2\, pH_2 + k_3(pH_2)^2}.$$

At pressures below 10 atm this simplified to

$$\text{rate} = k' p\text{H}_2$$

an activation energy of 43 kcal/mole then being obtained.

Methane, if present at pressures up to 20 atm, inhibited the rate and a more complicated expression was then needed:

$$\text{rate} = \frac{k_1(p\text{H}_2)^2 - k_2 \, p\text{CH}_4}{1 + k_3 \, p\text{H}_2 + k_4(p\text{H}_2)^2 + k_5 \, p\text{CH}_4}.$$

With coal chars the reactivity was a function of the carbonization temperature (Blackwood *et al.* 1967). The higher the latter the lower the reactivity. There was a linear relation between the reactivity and the active surface areas as calculated by the amount of hydrogen chemisorbed.

Hedden (1961, 1962) studied the reaction of electrode carbon at pressures up to 100 atm in the temperature range 1000–1250°C. The rate of the forward reaction was proportional to the hydrogen pressure while the rate of methane decomposition was proportional to the methane pressure and inversely proportional to the hydrogen pressure. An overall activation energy of 85·5 kcal/mole was obtained. Under similar conditions CO_2 reacted 230 times as fast. Very different activation energies and rates were obtained with charcoal and with soot.

Breisacher and Marx (1963) examined the reaction between pure graphite containing less than 10 ppm ash and very pure hydrogen at temperatures between 360 and 800°C. They found a zero order reaction below 580°C for hydrogen pressures between 90 and 180 atm. There were two distinct activation energies, 70 kcal/mole at low temperatures changing to 12 kcal/mole at temperatures above 515°C. At temperatures above 800°C an order of reaction of 0·6 was observed while there were indications that an order of unity might be obtained at 1000°C. Rogers and Sesonski (1962) used a pressure of 10 atm and a temperature of 1600°K. They obtained a zero order in the forward direction and a half order in the reverse direction. The corresponding activation energies were 38 and 78 kcal/mole.

Gulbransen *et al.* (1965b) studied the reaction between very pure graphite and hydrogen at a pressure of 19 torr in the temperature range 1200–1650°C. No methane was detected although the carbon lost weight at a rate of 6×10^7 atoms carbon/cm^2 sec at 1650°C. The activation energy for carbon removal was 72 kcal/mole. It was assumed that carbon hydrogen compounds decomposed immediately after reacting. Subsequently Gulbransen and Hickam (1967) were able to quench the products rapidly enough to show the presence of benzene, acetylene, methylene and methane in the product.

Baddour and Iwasyk (1962) rapidly quenched the product obtained by contacting hydrogen with carbon vapour from an electric arc at temperatures above 2800°K. Acetylene was the main product. This was consistent with the hypothesis that C_2H radicals exist at high concentrations in the reaction mixture. More recently Spangler et al. (1967) exploded graphite rods in various gases, and they concluded that methylene radicals, CH_2, were obtained in hydrogen. Clarke and Fox (1967) reacted hydrogen with graphite filaments at temperatures between 2000 and 3400°K and at pressures ranging from 0·01 to 1·0 atm. At the lower temperatures and high pressures the rate was proportional to the hydrogen pressure and to the square root of its dissociation constant. At the highest temperature and lowest pressures the rate was proportional to the rate of sublimation of the graphite. In a subsequent investigation (1968) they showed that at temperatures below 3600°K most of the reaction energy is dissipated while at temperatures above 3700°K the energy is used up subliming the graphite and in the formation of acetylene.

There is little information on the effect of catalysts on the hydrogenation of carbon. Deitz and McFarlane (1964) showed that hydrogen reacted rapidly with a mixed carbon–nickel evaporated film at temperatures as low as 28–300°C. The rate of methane production was directly proportional to the amount of hydrogen chemisorbed.

Hedden and Mienkina (1965) have examined the reaction of steam–hydrogen–argon mixtures at steam pressures of 5, 12·5 and 25 atm and hydrogen pressures between zero and 50 atm (the total pressure being always 50 atm) in the temperature range 950–1150°C. The rate of formation of methane could be represented by the complicated expression

$$\text{rate} = \frac{k_1 pH_2}{1 + k_2 pH_2O} + \frac{k_3 pH_2O}{1 + k_4 pH_2} + k_5 pH_2 pH_2O.$$

F. COMPARISON OF REACTION RATES

Various authors have compared the relative rates of reaction of carbon with oxidizing gases in an attempt to find common factors in the reaction mechanisms. Walker et al. (1959a) showed that at 800°C and a pressure of 0·1 atm the relative rates of the reactions with O_2, CO_2, H_2O and H_2 are 1×10^5, 1, 3 and 3×10^{-3} while Bonnetain and Hoynant (1965) have similarly shown that while O_2, CO_2 and H_2O the rates at 1000°C and at a pressure of 1 atm are 56×10^4, 21 and 100, expressed as mg carbon/m²h. The reaction rates could be expressed as

$$C\text{—}O_2 \qquad 112 \times 10^{14} \exp(-60,000/RT)$$
$$C\text{—}CO_2 \qquad 118 \times 10^{14} \exp(-86,000/RT)$$
$$C\text{—}H_2O \qquad 65 \times 10^{11} \exp(-63,000/RT).$$

These latter authors have discussed possible related mechanisms and have come to the following conclusions.

(1) A hypothesis that CO_2 and H_2O react following thermal dissociation to O_2 molecules in the gaseous phase allows for the inhibiting action of CO and H_2 while the calculated rates are not incompatible with the observed rates;

(2) if it is assumed that molecular oxygen reacts *via* the intermediary of atomic oxygen then the observed rates are too small even though both the calculated order of reaction and the activation energy are reasonable;

(3) the hypothesis that CO_2 and H_2O react *via* O atoms again allows for the inhibiting action of CO and H_2 and the calculated values are not incompatible with the observed rates.

No clear-cut answer can be reached regarding these three hypotheses.

Earlier, Rossberg (1956) proposed that dissociation of the molecules in the adsorbed state was the rate controlling process. He showed that the activation energies of the three reactions lay in the same order as the enthalpy of formation of O atoms in the gase phase—data are not available for these values in the adsorbed phase. However, Walker *et al.* (1959a) have criticized this argument and pointed out that the effective enthalpy of formation of O from O_2 is double the value proposed by Rossberg so that all the dissociation energies become substantially the same, which is not true of the activation energies of the reactions.

Bonnetain and Hoynant (1965) have discussed at length the various mechanisms proposed for the simplest of the three reactions, that with CO_2, and have criticized two hypotheses in particular: firstly that all surface atoms are equally active and secondly that there are no interactions between neighbouring atoms. They concluded that no complete interpretation of this reaction is yet available. This criticism applies in greater measure to the other gasification reactions.

Lavrov and Khaustovich (1965) have proposed a mechanism for the reaction between carbon and both oxygen and CO_2 at temperatures above $1000°K$ in which the rate is dependent on the concentration of oxygen atoms produced by thermal dissociation. This theory has been developed further by Kozlov and Kozlova (1967) who claim that the reactions of carbon with O_2, CO_2 and H_2O are all controlled by the rate of reaction of atomic O with the surface. The primary product is CO which then undergoes secondary reactions.

IV. REACTIONS AT HIGH TEMPERATURES

Care must be taken in interpreting experimental results obtained at temperatures much in excess of $1000°C$ because of the difficulty of avoiding in-pore and boundary layer diffusion. In the past workers such as Meyer (1938, 1950), Strickland-Constable (1944, 1947), Duval (1950, 1955) and

Boulanger *et al.* (1957) avoided these difficulties by working at very low pressure using carbon in the form of electrically-heated filaments. More recently, Strickland-Constable and his co-workers (Nagle and Strickland-Constable 1961; Walls and Strickland-Constable 1964; J. C. Lewis *et al.* 1967) have shown that diffusion effects can be overcome by using pyrolytic and other graphites exposed to a very high velocity gas flow. It is satisfying to note that very similar results have been produced by these two very different techniques.

The extremely important result found by all workers is that the specific reactivity passes through a maximum for O_2 and CO_2, sometimes for steam, and then falls off to a minimum value whereupon the rate increases once again, see Fig. 8. With pyrolytic or nuclear graphite in oxygen at 0·2 atm

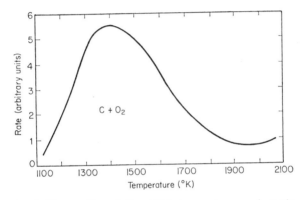

FIG. 8. Charge of reactivity at high temperatures—schematic.

pressure the maximum occurs at about 1800°C whereas with carbon filaments at 10^{-5} or 10^{-6} atm the maximum is at about 1200°C. The reactions with CO_2 at 8·5 mtorr and steam at 3 mtorr give maxima at about 1300° and 1400°C respectively. A similar behaviour has been observed in the reaction between carbon and sulphur (Wehrer and Duval 1967).

Another related phenomenon, observed by Duval (1955, 1965), is that a hysteresis effect is produced on changing the temperature of the graphite. For example, if the temperature in the O_2 reaction is suddenly changed from, say, 900 to 1400°C, two temperatures where under steady state conditions the reactions are the same, then there is an initially very high rate which drops off quickly to the usual value. On the other hand, if the temperature is dropped suddenly from 1400 to 900°C the initial rate is slow but increases to the customary value, see Fig. 9. The reaction is dependent on oxygen pressure in a complicated manner. Below 900°C and above 1500°C there is little effect but between these the rate passes through a maximum at about 1200°C.

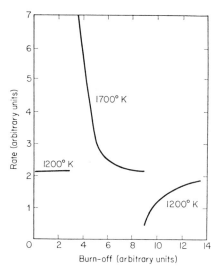

FIG. 9. Hysterisis after temperature changes—reaction of carbon with O_2 at 0·7 torr. (Based on Duval 1965.)

There is also a hysteresis effect associated with pressure. If for example at 1300°C the pressure of oxygen is suddenly increased from 0·3 to 0·5 torr the new rate takes some time to become established. This effect is absent in the regime where the rate is independent of pressure.

Both Duval (1965) and Strickland-Constable (1965) have recently discussed the implication of these observations. Both agree that the effect is due to surface changes on an atomic scale. Duval proposes that the phenomena can be explained by assuming that active carbon sites are produced by O_2 attack. These sites can then either react with another molecule or oxygen or else be "deactivated" by some process of surface migration whereupon they pass into a more stable lattice site. The two important factors are then the time between two separate collisions by O_2 molecules and the lifetime of the active species. These two are independent of each other; the first is a function of gas pressure the second of temperature. Between them they determine the stationary concentration of active sites at any temperature and pressure. At temperatures below about 900°C the rate of deactivation is very low and the reactivity of the surface is therefore independent of the pressure and temperature. At temperatures above 1600°C, on the other hand, the rate of deactivation considerably exceeds the reaction rate so that the reaction takes place on that part of the surface which was originally active, for example edge atoms. In the intermediate temperature range the lifetime of the active species is comparable with the collision frequency. Thus, if the temperature is dropped the many active sites produced at the higher temperature anneal only slowly and there is a temporary acceleration of rate until these are all used up. On the other hand, if the temperature is increased the fewer sites produced at the low temperatures are quickly annealed and the rate remains low until more active sites are produced.

The effect of pressure is explained in that, at a high pressure, the stationary concentration of reactive atoms is large because of the increased collision frequency. A higher temperature is therefore needed to reduce this by thermal deactivation. Consequently the maximum rate is displaced to a high temperature.

Duval postulates that the deactivation process is a thermal closure of fissures produced in the graphite lattice which is in accord with the fact that heating the specimen in a vacuum also reduces the reactivity temporarily. This process, being related only to the carbon, should thus be independent of the nature of the oxidizing gas and this explains why essentially the same effect is produced by CO_2 and steam. Similar hysteresis effects are in fact observed with these two gases although the quantitative results differ slightly from those obtained with oxygen.

Strickland-Constable (1965) interprets his results, and those of Duval and others, on the basis of the existence of two types of sites, reactive or A sites, and the much less reactive sites produced from A, by an "annealing" process, which are referred to as B sites. This mechanism is based on a concept originally proposed by Blyholder et al. (1958).

Both sites react with oxygen to give CO and the overall rate is given by

$$\text{rate} = \frac{k_A pO_2}{1 + k_z pO_2} x + k_B pO_2 (1 - x)$$

where k_A and k_B are the rate constants for A and B sites, k_z is the ratio of two constants, one concerning the adsorption of oxygen and the other the evaporation of the product, and x is the fraction of A sites on the surface.

Under the steady state conditions the rate of annealing is given by

$$k_T x = k_B pO_2 (1 - x)$$

where k_T is the annealing constant and

$$x = \frac{1}{1 + (k_T / k_B pO_2)}.$$

At low temperatures $x = 1$, although the reaction will still be complex unless $k_z pO_2$ is $\ll 1$. At high temperatures x is very small and the rate is equal to $k_B pO_2$. Strickland-Constable has derived values for these constants which have enabled him to predict with satisfactory agreement the experimental results obtained in the oxygen pressure range 10^{-6}–$0\cdot2$ atm and temperatures of 1000–2400°C. He has not, however, made any suggestion as to the nature of the two sites. (As previously mentioned when graphite is finely ground the fresh surface exposed appears to exhibit more than one type of site, in relation to chemisorption.) The activation energies for k_A, k_B, k_T and k_z are 30, 15, 97 and -41 kcal/mole respectively. Strickland-Constable's model has been extended further by his associate Egerton (1968).

Gray and Kimber (1967) studied the reaction between coal char and both CO_2 and steam at temperatures up to 2800°C. They found that at the highest temperature most of the reaction was due to dissociated O atoms and they suggest that this is the reason why there is a sharp increase in rate at the highest temperatures. As already mentioned, Clarke and Fox (1967) found the reaction with hydrogen to be dependent on its dissociation constant. They, and others, point out that ultimately the rate becomes dependent on the rate of sublimation of carbon.

A completely different explanation for the shape of the rate/temperature curve has been proposed by Khaustovich (1968). It is claimed that the observed results obtained with both O_2 and CO_2 can be explained on the basis that the accessible area diminishes with temperature. This is due to changes in pore structure as the reaction takes place nearer and nearer the surface which affects the BET area and the rate of in-pore diffusion. Khaustovich's theory does not adequately explain the minimum in the curve but his view that surface area changes are important should be given consideration.

Space research has aroused an interest in the reaction kinetics at temperatures where vaporization of graphite takes place. The kinetics are then complicated because the reaction zone may be some distance away from the carbon surface.

The effect of gas velocity on the kinetics of high temperature gasification is discussed in Section VI.

V. REACTIONS WITH ATOMIC GASES

A number of workers have studied the reaction between carbon and atomic gases in order to obtain a better understanding of the reaction with gas molecules. Streznewski and Turkevich (1957) found that evaporated carbon films and carbon black were oxidized readily by oxygen atoms, produced in a discharge tube, at room temperature. The rate was temperature independent and proportional to the oxygen atom concentration. Hydrogen atoms also reacted at room temperature but not ozone. Blackwood and McTaggart (1959a, b) oxidized diamond, natural graphite and a low-temperature wood char in oxygen atoms produced by an r.f. discharge. They found CO to be the primary product but some CO_2 was formed by secondary oxidation of CO at the carbon surface. The rates of reaction were lowest with diamond and highest with the wood char, but no surface areas were measured.

Vastola *et al.* (1963) found that the reaction between a spectroscopic grade graphite and atomic oxygen at room temperature was reduced, but not stopped, if the specimen was removed outside the actual discharge zone; in contrast the reaction with hydrogen atoms would only take place inside the discharge. Carbon monoxide was the principal product with oxygen atoms; a mixture of hydrocarbons was obtained with hydrogen atoms.

In a preliminary experiment Marsh *et al.* (1963) found that graphite would not react with oxygen at temperatures below 100°C unless located inside the discharge zone. Later work by these authors (1965a) in which amorphous carbons and electrode graphite were used showed that the reaction would take place at room temperature outside the zone but with an apparent activation energy of about 10 kcal/mole. This activation energy diminished at temperatures above 200°C becoming zero at 350°C. The actual reaction rates were approximately the same for all the carbons and proportional only to the concentration of atomic oxygen. It was concluded that above 300°C molecular oxygen reacted with the surface producing surface oxides which blocked off some of the available area. In a complementary study (1965b) the appearance of the surfaces of single crystals of graphite, pyrolytic carbons and two types of amorphous carbons were examined after oxidation. Both optical and electron microscopic techniques were used. It was found that oxygen atoms produced a general background of conical pits on the basal plane of the single crystals in addition to the usual etch pits. There was much less anisotropy than in the attack with molecular oxygen, atoms being removed from the basal plane proper. On the other hand, the edge atoms produced by such attacks seemed to have received some measure of protection subsequently, probably by the formation of surface oxides. No pits were seen on pyrolytic carbon which was considered to be due to the turbostatic nature of this material. In contrast, however, the amorphous carbons, which were produced from polyvinylidene chloride and polyfurfuryl alcohol did exhibit extensive pitting so that this simple explanation is not sufficient. The presence of iron on the single crystals promoted local recombination of atomic oxygen thereby decreasing the local rate of attack. Small hexagonal-sided hillocks were left at these iron-contaminated sites, the edges consisting of $\{10\bar{1}l\}$ or zig-zag planes. Because the mode of attack was quite different from that by molecular oxygen it was concluded that it is unlikely that the latter reaction takes place through a dissociation step followed by a free reaction by the oxygen atoms. Dissociation must take place only at "active" sites and the atoms formed must then either form a surface complex or gaseous CO.

In a further series of experiments Marsh and O'Hair (1967) examined the activation energy of oxidation and the amount of surface oxide produced on single crystals of Ticonderoga graphite and on polyvinylidene chloride carbon using oxygen containing no nitrogen whatsoever. Activation energies of 9 and 5 kcal/mole were obtained. The results were very similar to those obtained using oxygen containing traces of nitrogen and hence the suggestion, sometimes made, that NO affects the reaction is not valid.

Gleit *et al.* (1963) measured an activation energy of 6·5 in their study of the oxidation of spectroscopic grade graphite at temperatures between 215° and 300°C. In an earlier study, however, Hennig and Kanter (1959, 1960) reported that the activation energy for the oxidation of Ticonderoga graphite was zero. Hennig found that pitting attack took place preferentially at the centre of the layer planes. Otterbein and Bonnetain (1964b) showed that the activation energy for the reaction of spectroscopic graphite with atomic oxygen at a pressure of 0·15 torr is about 5 kcal/mole between room temperature and 100°C, 30 kcal/mole between 100° and 200°C and very low above 200°C. These values had been corrected for diffusional effects which it was assumed were present. The authors attributed these results to the reaction rate being controlled by the decomposition of surface oxide at temperatures below 100°C and by the rate of formation of oxygen atoms above 200°C. These workers had previously reported (1964a) that at room temperature the reaction was confined to the external geometric surface of the specimen. The efficiency of the reaction, based on the collision frequencies of atoms, was low, about 10^{-4}. It was found that if the specimens were outgassed at temperatures above 200°C then the rates of reaction were temporarily increased. More recently, Otterbein and Lespinasse (1968) found that the reaction rate was only decreased to a third when the specimen was placed outside the discharge. Since O atoms are absent in this region they concluded that other species, for example excited ions, must also take part in the reaction.

In a rather different type of experiment Rosner and Allendorf (1965) oxidized graphite in atomic oxygen ⸢at temperatures between 800° and 1700°C. They found that the probability of attack, based on collision frequency, was about unity and therefore greater by a factor of between 5 and 80 than in the corresponding reaction with molecular oxygen. The order of reaction was thus also unity. A maximum was found in the reaction rate but unlike the analogous maximum with molecular oxygen the position of this was independent of the pressure.

In all the experiments referred to above the oxygen atoms were produced by electric discharges. Lang *et al.* (1965a) have criticized this technique on the grounds that secondary products such as ions, excited molecules and free radicals which are also formed might react with the carbon and so give an erroneous picture. These workers therefore examined the reaction between very pure graphite and oxygen atoms produced by the thermal decomposition of ozone. The ozone was obtained from a solution in Freon and used as a 15% mixture at atmospheric pressure with the vapour of the latter. An activation energy of about 1·9 kcal/mole was observed over the temperature range 100–200°C; at a higher temperature the activation energy became negative. The order of reaction, expressed in terms of the ozone partial pressure, was unity. The rate of reaction was approximately the same as that obtained with air at 620°C, and remained constant over 2–15% weight loss. Examination of the specimens after oxidation showed that the reaction had taken place to some extent in the pores and not just on the external surface.

Lang's technique has been criticized in turn by Marsh (1965) on the grounds that halogens may well be present in the gas and that these would then act as inhibitors. Marsh pointed out that the oxidation rates obtained by Lang were comparable with those obtained by himself, and also by Otterbein and Bonnetain (1964b), at very much lower concentrations of oxygen atoms.

Hennig studied the oxidation of single crystals of graphite with ozone–oxygen mixtures containing 4% of ozone. In an early experiment (1959) he obtained an activation energy of 16 kcal/mole applicable at temperatures up to 270°C. Later (1965a) he examined the reaction in more detail and found that the attack in the parallel direction at edges was some 900 times faster than perpendicular to the basal plane. The corresponding activation energies were 16·7 and 20 kcal/mole respectively in the temperature regime 50° to 70°C. However, quite different values of the rates and activation energies were obtained in some experiments and it was found that the reaction was very susceptible to catalysis and inhibition by traces of contaminants. The appearance of the oxidized specimens suggested both localized catalytic attack and localized inhibition, due possibly to surface oxide protection, had taken place.

The reaction between atomic hydrogen and carbon has been examined by a number of workers. Blackwood and McTaggart (1959b) obtained methane from wood char at room temperature and a pressure of about 0·4 torr. Shahin (1962) used a similar gas pressure and obtained a mixture of methane, acetylene, ethylene and ethane from graphite at about 700°C, with the specimen located outside the discharge, but found no reaction at room temperature. King and Wise (1963) used pressures between 0·02 and 0·10 torr and obtained a mixture of methane and acetylene from carbon films at temperatures between 92° and 227°C. They found two distinct rates with energies of activation of 9 and 7 kcal/mole for films of different crystallinity. It was concluded that the predominating reaction was recombination of hydrogen atoms. The results of Vastola et al. (1963) have already been described.

The reaction between graphite and hydrogen inside a nuclear reactor has been examined by Corney and Thomas (1958) at temperatures of 500° and 600°C. Methane was produced and it was assumed that this was formed by the reaction of graphite with short-lived active species produced by the absorption of radiation in the hydrogen. In a complementary out-of-pile experiment, methane was shown to be formed exceedingly slowly at these temperatures. Over the temperature range 600–800°C the out-of-pile reaction had an activation energy of 65 kcal/mole.

Blackwood and McTaggart (1959b) and Vastola et al. (1963) have also examined the reactions of carbon in the product obtained from a microwave discharge in water vapour. The former workers used wood char and obtained a mixture of hydrogen, CO, CO_2 and oxygen. It was found that the gasification rate was less than that produced by a comparable partial pressure of oxygen alone, although the reduction in rate was not due to the presence of hydrogen. Vastola et al. used spectroscopically pure graphite located outside the discharge and obtained mainly hydrogen and carbon monoxide with some CO_2 and oxygen. The composition of the product depended on the distance of the specimen from the discharge. It was concluded that as the specimen was outside the discharge most of the hydrogen atoms formed would have combined to form H_2 leaving atoms to attack the graphite. Fu and Blaustein (1967) showed that when pure graphite and coal were exposed in a microwave discharge of water the former gave hydrogen and CO only whereas the latter gave acetylene, methane and CO_2 as well.

Because of the extensive use made of CO_2 as a coolant for graphite moderated reactors there is considerable interest in examining the nature of energy absorption in CO_2 and the nature of any subsequent attack between the irradiated CO_2 and graphite. Despite the considerable amount of work carried out, the reaction mechanism is still far from clearly understood. The extensive British work in this field has been summarized in three papers; the first, a composite paper, by Anderson et al. (1958) was presented at the 2nd U.N. International Conference on the Peaceful Uses of Atomic Energy, Geneva (1958) and the others, by Lind and Wright, were presented at a conference on Advanced Gas Reactors in London (1963) and at the 3rd U.N. Conference, Geneva (1964).

Because of the complexity of the reactions, techniques such as irradiation of CO_2 by ultraviolet light and by electrons have also been used. By using the first technique Feates and Sach (1965a, b) have been able to show that oxygen atoms produced by u.v. radiation gasify carbon with a zero energy of activation over the temperature range 25–300°C and that this rate is materially reduced by the addition of 0·1 volume per cent of methane. The mechanism of the inhibitory action is postulated as arising from the interaction of methyl and methylene radicals with the graphite surface. This technique has also been used in collaboration with electron microscopy studies by Adamson and Dawson (1966) to examine the nature of the attack on nuclear graphite and spectroscopically pure graphite. It was found that carbon was removed from the edges of microcrystallites and also from vacancy or impurity sites on the surface at temperatures of 25° and 350°C.

Claxton and Strickland-Constable (1964) activated CO_2 with low-voltage electrons in order to limit the number of excited species obtained and reacted the product with a carbon layer produced by burning naphthalene. It was concluded that the carbon was being attacked either by oxygen atoms produced from CO_2 at 5·5 eV or by CO_2 excited by 10 eV electrons. Zhitneva and Pshezhetskii (1967) found that CO_2 molecules excited to 8·4 eV also attacked carbon. Watanabe *et al.* (1965) examined the effect of an electric field on the X-ray-induced reaction between CO_2 and graphite. It was found that a negative voltage on the graphite increased the rate of production of CO some 2·5 times, but a positive voltage had no effect. It was suggested that the reaction was between negatively-charged carbon atoms and CO^+ ions. The latter has also been shown to play a significant role in the oxidation of graphite by X-radiolysed CO_2 (Brewer and Feates 1968).

As already referred to in Section IIIC, carbon may be present as an impurity in the helium used as a coolant in certain types of high-temperature gas-cooled graphite moderated nuclear reactors. In addition to the thermal CO_2–graphite reaction the reactions between irradiated CO_2 and graphite is also important. Valette and van Massenhove (1965) have shown that energy transfer from the helium greatly enhances the radiolysis of the CO_2. These experiments were carried out in the temperature range 500–900°C, with CO_2 present in 50–100 vpm, in helium at a pressure of 10 atm.

Blake (1964) and Blake *et al.* (1964) oxidized graphite in CO_2, and in oxygen, in the presence of a pure γ-flux principally to determine whether the graphite was thereby rendered more active to molecular oxygen. The oxidations were carried out at a temperature of 32°C and a gas pressure of 20 atm. It was found that graphite burnt off to a given weight loss in a γ-flux was more reactive to subsequent thermal oxidation in air at 500°C than a specimen burnt off to the same weight loss in air, or oxygen. The effect was more marked with oxidation in irradiated oxygen than irradiated CO_2.

The effect of radiolytic oxidation in CO_2 on the structure of graphite has been studied by a number of workers from the Culcheth Laboratories of the U.K. Atomic Energy Authority. Standring and Ashton (1965) extending the earlier work of Hutcheon *et al.* (1961) showed that up to 40% of the original closed pores in nuclear graphites were opened at 2% weight loss. The remaining pores, which were opened only slowly, were tentatively identified with cleavage cracks and plugged pores. It was possible to correlate the oxidation rate in the reactor with the open pore volume, except for heavily oxidized specimens. It was assumed that in these the gas was ineffectively radiolysed at the centre of large pores. Subsequently Ashton *et al.* (1965) showed that the BET surface area of Pile Grade A graphite increased only slightly to about 0·33 m²/g and thereafter remained constant up to 20% weight loss in contrast to thermal oxidation in which a steady increase in area was obtained.

These reactions were carried out at temperatures between 170° and 200°C at a CO_2 pressure of 50 atm. Changes in the mechanical and physical properties were also measured. These can be compared with the experiments of Board and Squires (1965) and Rounthwaite *et al.* (1965) on the effect of thermal oxidation in CO_2 on the strength of the same material.

VI. PHYSICAL FACTORS CONTROLLING GASIFICATION RATES

With few exceptions, such as pyrolytic graphite, carbons and graphites of industrial importance are porous with most of the accessible surface in the interior of the pores. The gasification reactions of carbons are therefore typical of heterogeneous gas–solid reactions where the solid is porous.

There are three major steps involved in a reaction of this type:

(a) transport of gas molecules to the external geometric surface of the solid from the bulk of the gas;
(b) transport of gas molecules from the external surface to reactive sites on the internal surface of pores;
(c) reaction at these sites.

A similar sequence of steps, but in the reverse order, takes place with any gaseous product.

Gas transport is normally by molecular diffusion; in step (a) across an external boundary layer and in step (b) through the pores. Mathematical relationships have been derived for such reactions by Thiele (1939), Frank-Kamenetskii (1947), Wheeler (1951), Weisz and Prater (1954), Walker *et al.* (1959a) and Khitrin and Golovina (1963). If the temperature is increased the rate controlling step changes from step (c) to step (b) and finally to step (a). Wicke (1954) and Rossberg and Wicke (1956) have shown that the temperature dependence of the rate can be idealized in the form of an Arrhenius-type plot of log rate against reciprocal temperature, see Fig. 10(a). The graph contains three linear portions, termed zones I, II and III, connected by two transition regions. The gas concentration profiles in the pores and at the carbon surface corresponding to these zones are shown in Fig. 10(b).

At the lowest temperature, zone I, the overall rate is controlled by the surface reaction, step (c), and the observed energy of activation E and reaction order n are those pertaining to this reaction. Because gas diffusivities are greater than the reaction rates the concentrations of reactant and products are substantially uniform in the pore structure and are equal to the values in the bulk gas.

If the temperature is increased the rate of reaction increases faster than the diffusivities so that the former approaches the value of the latter. There will

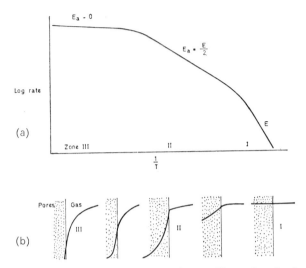

FIG. 10. Corresponding changes in concentration profiles and activation energy. (a) Idealized Arrhenius plot effect of diffusion, (b) corresponding reactant concentration profile in pores and free gas.

thus be a depletion of reactant molecules along the length of the pores, and a corresponding increase in the concentration of product. Eventually, a situation will arise when the concentration of reactant falls to zero at some point inside the specimen. Under this condition, zone II, all gas molecules entering the pores will react. There will also be a concentration gradient external to the specimen but if there is rapid flow of gas along the surface this will be of secondary importance and the rate controlling step is in-pore diffusion. Wheeler (1951) and Weisz and Prater (1954) have shown that under these conditions, provided that the total pressure remains constant, the observed energy of activation is $E/2$ and the reaction order $(n+1)/2$. A complication that may arise, however, is that the product gas may retard the observed rate, as for example CO in the reaction with CO_2. When this occurs the observed kinetics become more complicated (Petersen 1965).

This linear portion, zone II, only persists as long as the concentration gradient external to the specimen is small. With increasing temperature the depth to which molecules can penetrate before reacting becomes less and less and the reaction becomes confined to a thinner and thinner layer adjacent to the external surface. At the same time the concentration gradient external to the surface becomes more and more important until eventually this controls the rate, zone III. The rate-controlling step is then transport of gas molecules from the bulk of the gas to the surface of the specimen.

If the bulk gas is stagnant or in laminar flow past the surface the mechanism of gas transport in it is molecular diffusion. However, such an ideal situation is rarely obtained. Convective effects due to gas density differences are inevitably present while in many, if not most, industrial systems the gas velocities are sufficiently high for turbulence to be present. Gas transport will therefore be partly by the much more rapid eddy diffusivity. However, eddies will be damped at the surface of the carbon giving a boundary layer in which the flow is substantially laminar. Molecular diffusion across this layer will thus be the rate-controlling step in the transport of reactant to, and product away from, the surface. The thickness of this layer depends on the Reynolds number, that is for any gas at a given temperature, on the gas velocity and specimen geometry. At high velocities the boundary layer will be thin and zone II prolonged longer than if the velocity is low or absent. On the other hand, if the gas flow rate is very small or absent, the thickness of the boundary layer will be large and the external concentration gradient always comparable to the in-pore gradient. Under these conditions there may be no linear portion of the graph corresponding to zone II.

The various flow and diffusion conditions which determine whether the reaction is in zone I, II or III have been summarized and reviewed by Walker *et al.* (1959a). However, although several workers have interpreted their results in terms of a reaction changing from zone I to zone II and some have examined the change in pore structure after oxidation, only one group has actually measured in-pore diffusion effects directly. In this work carried out at the Atomic Energy Research Establishment, Harwell, Lewis *et al.* (1962), Hawtin and Gibson (1964a) and Hawtin *et al.* (1964) studied the oxidation characteristics of large tubular specimens of nuclear graphite exposed to air and to O_2/N_2 mixtures along the bore. Access to the pore structure in the walls was by in-pore diffusion. In some experiments a pressure difference was applied between the bore and the stagnant gas around the periphery of the tubes, so that bulk flow took place through the pores. Experiments were carried out in zone I, the first transition regime, and zone II. A mathematical model developed by Hawtin and Murdoch (1964) was found to explain the results and, indirectly, to give values of in-pore diffusivities in good agreement with those calculated from experimental data previously obtained at room temperature by Hewitt (1966). Subsequently, Hawtin and Roberts (1969) made diffusivity measurements at elevated temperatures and showed that these values were in excellent agreement with those calculated from room temperature data. Because the proportion of fine pores was small the contribution of Knudsen diffusion could be neglected in the graphite used. Hawtin and Gibson (1964b) showed that the mathematical model could be applied to the oxidation of a quite different type of carbon, an ungraphitized baked carbon some thirty times as reactive as nuclear graphite and more permeable. More recently, the model has been extended to apply to the oxidation of long graphite channels where depletion of oxygen takes place along the bore as well as through the pores. Preliminary experiments carried out with a 14 ft long stack of graphite with a 2 in internal bore indicate that the extended model agrees well with the observed values (Hawtin *et al.* 1968).

It is in a way somewhat surprising that the diffusivity relevant to in-pore diffusion control is that diffusivity which relates to gas flow through graphite. In the latter case it is the diffusion through "transport" pores connecting one external surface to the other that is important, whereas in the former case it is diffusion through the very many capillaries, where most of the area lies, that is the controlling factor. Nevertheless, the two diffusivities are very nearly the same. It could be, for example, that diffusion along the larger transport pores to the ends of the short capillaries that is important. Not all workers have found that a simple pore diffusion model fits their results; for example, Perrot (1965) was unable to correlate his observations on the gasification of cokes by CO_2 and steam in terms of Thiele's equations. Perrot concluded that the entrance to many pores was narrow and prevented molecules that had entered leaving before they had time to react. He proposed that it was not correct to use diffusivities to explain the results unless the pore openings were larger. Instead, he compared the gas transport conditions to effusion from a small pore in a thin wall.

The kinetics are very complicated if a temperature gradient exists in the specimen. Wicke (1963) has discussed the behaviour of a fine-grained nuclear graphite exposed to helium containing a low concentration of CO_2 under conditions where both a concentration gradient of CO_2 and a temperature gradient exist. More recent work has been reviewed by Everett *et al.* (1968).

Complicated kinetics also arise when the reactant can inhibit the reaction, as can for example CO in the CO_2 gasification reaction. Walker and Raats (1956) and Austin and Walker (1963) have shown that no clear-cut conclusion can be drawn from their studies of this system. In the latter investigation the rate was only 1% of that calculated using the Thiele model.

Calculations of the rate-controlling step in zone III are in general based on well-established semi-empirical relationships which enable the thickness of the boundary layer to be calculated under a variety of conditions. Both heat transfer and mass transfer experiments show that to a good approximation the boundary layer thickness is proportional to the half power of the gas Reynolds number. Thus, for a given system the gasification rate should be proportional to the square root of the gas velocity. Many workers have indeed found such a relationship to hold at atmospheric pressures. The results obtained up to 1959, including work in their own laboratories (Day *et al.* 1957), have been summarized by Walker *et al.* (1959a). Other more recent results confirm the results; for example, Golovina and Khaustovich

(1964) gasified carbon with CO_2 at temperatures between 1000° and 2900°C and obtained a half-power exponent on the Reynolds number while Levy and Wong (1964) obtained a 0·4 power on the gas velocity when oxidizing pyrolytic graphite in air at temperatures above 900°C. Because pyrolytic carbon is non-porous zone II is absent. Essenhigh et al. (1965) have claimed that boundary layer diffusion becomes progressively less important when the carbon is present as small particles. Essenhigh concludes that for particles less than 100 µ in diameter the rate controlling step is the chemical rate, step (c).

Gulbransen et al. (1963, 1964a) have shown how two very different carbons, pyrolytic carbon and spectroscopic graphite, oxidized at the same rate (expressed in terms of their geometric area) when the reaction was in zone III. The oxidations were carried out in a static atmosphere of oxygen at pressures between 2 and 38 torr and at temperatures up to 1500°C. Subsequently, experiments were carried out with the oxygen streaming past graphite the specimen so as to eliminate external diffusion effects. Spectroscopic graphite was used in one series of experiments (1964b) and nuclear graphite in another (1964c). Very high oxidation rates were obtained with collision efficiencies between 2 and 3%. These results were interpreted in terms of a reaction mechanism based on the mobile adsorption of oxygen as the rate-limiting step. The activation energy was 39 kcal/mole. The mechanism was based on that used by Gulbransen and Andrew (1952a) in their experiments carried out at temperatures between 425° and 575°C. As has already been pointed out the activation energy observed in this experiment was low being only 37 kcal/mole. A further criticism is that a significant amount of spalling took place in the high temperature, high velocity studies; indeed the authors refer to ablation and not oxidation. It is therefore difficult to judge the relevance of their kinetic mechanism.

In contrast to these results, Graham et al. (1957) had earlier found a marked difference between the rates of oxidation of rotating cylinders of graphite and pyrolytic carbon when these were exposed to the products of combustion of an oxy-acetylene flame at a temperature of 2430°C. The oxidation rates were dependent on the one-quarter to the one-third power of the velocity of rotation, and the reaction efficiency, based on the collision frequency, lay between 0·5 and 1·3%.

A number of authors have claimed that at high temperatures a blue glow can be seen around a carbon particle oxidizing in air. It has been proposed that this is due to secondary oxidation of CO to CO_2. More recently van der Held (1961) calculated that at temperatures above 1100°C oxygen never reaches the surface. The surface reaction is between CO_2 and carbon forming CO which is then oxidized back to CO_2 at a zone inside the laminar boundary layer. The temperature at this region is high, perhaps 2300°C, and supplies the necessary heat to sustain the endothermic reaction between CO_2 and carbon at the surface. This theory has been confirmed qualitatively both by de Graff (1965) and by Kisch (1967) by the use of a spectral line reversal technique to measure the local temperature in the reacting zone. Wicke and Wurzbacher (1962) had earlier studied the oxidation of spectroscopic graphite in very dry oxygen at temperatures between 1000° and 1230°C. They used a capillary suction probe to sample the gases at various depths of the boundary layer and so obtained the concentration profile of CO, O_2 and CO_2. They interpreted their results in terms of the $C+O_2$, $C+CO_2$, and $CO+O_2$ reactions. By adding water vapour, which is a catalyst for the last reaction, they were able to modify substantially the concentration profiles. In other experiments they added CCl_4 which effectively suppresses the oxidation of CO. Although they found that the oxygen concentration fell to a very low value near the graphite surface, they did not find a zero value in the boundary layer.

Another effect which has been claimed to come into play at high temperatures is self-diffusion of carbon. Khitrin and Golovina (1963) and Golovina and Kotova (1966a, b, 1968) have shown, for example, that when graphite reacts with CO_2 at temperatures above 2200°C there is a significant change in density in the interior of the specimen and they attributed this as being due to diffusion of carbon to the external surface. This interpretation of their results is not universally accepted, the effect could, for example, be due to a temperature gradient in the specimen.

The projected use of carbons as heat shields for the re-entry of rockets into the upper atmosphere has stimulated an interest in the very high temperature oxidation characteristics of carbon. Under these conditions, with ionized gases, temperatures, say, of 5000°C and supersonic velocities, the conditions are often far removed from those previously examined. The evaporation of carbon is significant and an appreciable amount of oxidation may take place away from the surface proper. In addition the carbon surface may spall. Ladd et al. (1967), for example, found spalling to take place at temperatures below 2000°C due to preferential oxidation of the binder carbon. Heat transfer away from the surface plays a key role in determining the temperature of the carbon and therefore its rate of oxidation. Scala (1964) has recently reviewed methods of calculating heat and mass transfer from a graphite surface exposed to hypersonic flow. Temperatures up to 5200°C are considered and the values compared, when possible, with existing experimental data. Plasma arc tests have been used by Haviland and Medford (1965) to calculate the oxidation and spalling rates of carbonaceous materials under re-entry conditions. Goldstein et al. (1966) have also used plasma arc tests in a study of the effect of titanium and zirconium carbides in reducing spalling. These carbides oxidize forming a viscous melt which protects the underlying graphite.

ACKNOWLEDGEMENT

The author wishes to thank Professor X. Duval, Dr F. M. Lang and Professor P. L. Walker Jr. for permission to quote from unpublished work. He also wishes to thank Pergamon Press and Masson et Cie for giving permission to include figures based on illustrations that have appeared in "Carbon" and "Les Carbones".

REFERENCES

Adamson, I. Y. R., Dawson, I. M., Feates, F. S. and Sach, R. S. (1966). *Carbon* **3**, 393.
Amariglio, H. and Duval, X. (1966). *Carbon* **4**, 323.
Amariglio, H. and Duval, X. (1967). *J. Chim. phys.* **64**, 916.
Anderson, A. R., Davidson, H. W., Lind, R., Stranks, D. R., Tyzack, C. and Wright, J. (1958). *In* "Proceedings of 2nd United Nations Intern. Conf. on Peaceful Uses of Atomic Energy", Vol. 7, 335. United Nations, Geneva. (Pub. 1959.)
Anderson, A. R. (1964). *Diss. Abstr.* **25**, 1801.
Antill, J. E. and Peakall, K. A. (1960). *J. nucl. Mater.* **2**, 31.
Arthur, J. R. (1951). *Trans. Faraday Soc.* **47**, 164.
Asher, R. C. (1960). *In* "Proceedings U.S./U.K. Meeting on Compatibility Problems of Gas-Cooled Reactors", Oak Ridge, U.S. At. Energy Comm. Report TID 7597, p. 504.
Asher, R. C. and Kirstein, T. B. A. (1968). *J. nucl. Mater.* **25**, 344.
Ashton, B. W., Wilson, P. D. and Labaton, V. Y. (1965). *In* "Proceedings of 2nd Ind. Carbon and Graphite Conf.", London, p. 350. (Pub. 1966.)
Austin, L. G. and Walker, P. L. (1963). *A.I.Ch.E.Jl* **9**, 303.
Baddour, R. F. and Iwasyk, J. M. (1962). *Ind. Engng Chem. Process Design Develop.* **1**, 169.
Beattie, J. R., Lewis, J. B. and Lind, R. (1964). *In* "Proceedings of 3rd United Nations Intern. Conf. on Peaceful Uses of Atomic Energy", Vol. 13, 138. United Nations, Geneva. (Pub. 1965.)
Biederman, D. L. (1965). *Diss. Abstr.* **26**, 2093.
Blackman, L. C. F. (1967). *Carbon* **5**, 196.
Blackwood, J. D. (1959). *Aust. J. Chem.* **12**, 14.
Blackwood, J. D. (1962a). *Aust. J. appl. Sci.* **13**, 199.
Blackwood, J. D. (1962b). *Aust. J. Chem.* **15**, 397.
Blackwood, J. D. and Ingeme, A. J. (1960). *Aust. J. Chem.* **13**, 194.
Blackwood, J. D. and McGrory, F. (1958). *Aust. J. Chem.* **11**, 16.
Blackwood, J. D. and McTaggart, F. K. (1959a). *Aust. J. Chem.* **12**, 114.
Blackwood, J. D. and McTaggart, F. K. (1959b). *Aust. J. Chem.* **12**, 533.
Blackwood, J. D., Cullis, B. D. and McCarthy, D. J. (1967). *Aust. J. Chem.* **20**, 1561, 2525.
Blake, A. R. (1964). *J. appl. Chem., Lond.* **14**, 382.
Blake, A. R., Hempstead, C. A. and Jennings, P. P. (1964). *J. appl. Chem., Lond.* **14**, 115.
Blakely, J. P. and Overholser, L. G. (1965). *Carbon* **3**, 269.
Blyholder, G. and Eyring, H. (1957). *J. phys. Chem.* **61**, 682.

Blyholder, G. and Eyring, H. (1959a). *J. phys. Chem.* **63**, 693.

Blyholder, G. and Eyring, H. (1959b). *J. phys. Chem.* **63**, 1004.

Blyholder, G., Binford, J. S. and Eyring, H. (1958). *J. phys. Chem.* **62**, 263.

Board, J. A. (1965). *In* "Proceedings of 2nd Ind. Carbon and Graphite Conf.", London. p. 277. (Pub. 1966.)

Board, J. A. and Squires, R. L. (1965). *In* "Proceedings of 2nd Ind. Carbon and Graphite Conf.", London. p. 289. (Pub. 1966.)

Boehm, H. P. (1966). *Adv. Catalysis* **16**, 179.

Bond, R. L., Spencer, D. H. T. and Tee, P. A. H. (1961). *In* "Proceedings U.S./U.K. Meeting on the Compatibility Problems of Gas-Cooled Reactors", p. 374. Oak Ridge. U.S. At. Energy Comm. Report TID 7597.

Bonner, F. and Turkevich, J. (1951). *J. Am. chem. Soc.* **73**, 561.

Bonnetain, L. (1959a). *J. Chim. phys.* **56**, 266.

Bonnetain, L. (1959b). *J. Chim. phys.* **56**, 486.

Bonnetain, L. (1961). *J. Chim. phys.* **58**, 34.

Bonnetain, L. and Hoynant, G. (1965). *In* "Les Carbones", (A. Pacault, ed.), Vol. 2, pp. 277–385. Masson et Cie, Paris.

Bonnetain, L., Duval, X. and Letort, M. (1957). *C.r. hebd. Seanc. Acad. Sci., Paris* **246**, 105.

Bonnetain, L., Duval, X. and Letort, M. (1959). *In* "Proceedings 4th Conf. Carbon", Buffalo, N.Y., p. 107. (Pub. 1960.)

Boulanger, F., Duval, X. and Letort, M. (1957). *In* "Proceedings 3rd Conf. Carbon", Buffalo, N.Y., p. 257. (Pub. 1959.)

Bourke, P. J., Gray, M. D. and Denton, W. H. (1966). *J. nucl. Energy Pt A/B* **20**, 441.

Bregazzi, M., Greenhalgh, E., Sutherland, J. W. and Tucker, D. J. (1965). *Carbon* **3**, 73.

Breisacher, P. and Marx, P. C. (1963). *J. Am. chem. Soc.* **85**, 3518.

Brewer, J. M. and Feates, F. S. (1968). U.K.A.E.A. report AERE-R 5907; also (1969). *Carbon*, **7**, 393.

Bridger, G. W. and Appleton, H. (1948). *J. Soc. chem. Ind., Lond.* **67**, 445.

Cherednik, E. M., Apel'baum, L. O. and Temkin, M. I. (1967). *Dokl. Akad. Nauk SSSR* **174**, 891.

Clarke, J. T. and Fox, B. R. (1967). *J. chem. Phys.* **46**, 827.

Clarke, J. T. and Fox, B. R. (1968). *Ind. Engng Chem., Fund.* **7**, 197.

Clark, T. J., Woodley, R. E. and de Halas, D. R. (1962). *In* "Nuclear Graphite" (R. E. Nightingale, ed.), pp. 387–444. Academic Press, New York.

Claxton, K. T. and Strickland-Constable, R. F. (1964). *Carbon* **1**, 495.

Collins, A. C., Masterson, H. G. and Jennings, P. P. (1965). *J. nucl. Mater.* **15**, 135.

Corney, N. and Thomas, R. B. (1958). *U.K. At. Energy Auth. Report AERE* R 2502.

Cowen, H. C., Lewis, J. B. and Sharratt, E. W. (1960). *In* "Proceedings U.S./U.K. Meeting on Compatibility Problems of Gas-Cooled Reactors", Oak Ridge, U.S. At. Energy Comm. Report TID 7597, p. 359.

Culver, R. V. and Watts, H. (1960). *Rev. Pure appl. Chem.* **10**, 95.

Dahl, R. E. (1961). *U.S. At. Energy Comm. Report* HW–67255.

Dawson, I. M. and Follett, E. A. C. (1963). *Proc. R. Soc.* **A274**, 386.

Day, R. J., Walker, P. L. and Wright, C. C. (1957). *In* "Proceedings Ind. Carbon and Graphite Conf.", London, p. 348. (Pub. 1958.)

de Graff, J. G. (1965). *Brennst.-Wärme-Kraft.* **17**, 227.

Deitz, V. R. and McFarlane, E. F. (1964). *Carbon* **1**, 117.

Démidovitch, G. B., Kiselev, V. F., Lejnev, N. N. and Nikitina, O. V. (1968). *J. Chim. phys.* **65**, 1072.

Derman, B. M. (1960). *Trudy Inst. goryuch. Iskop.* **13**, 27.

Derman, B. M., Rogaibin, M. I. and Farberov, I. L. (1960). *Trudy Inst. goryuch. Iskop.* **13**, 33.

Donald, H. J. (1956). "An Annotated Bibliography on the Decomposition of Carbon Monoxide". Mellon Institute, Pittsburgh, U.S.A.

Duval, X. (1950). *J. Chim. phys.* **47**, 339.

Duval, X. (1955). *Ann. Chim. Phys.* **10**, 903.

Duval, X. (1965). *In* "Les Carbones" (A. Pacault, ed.), Vol. 2, pp. 256–276. Masson et Cie, Paris.

Earp, F. K. and Hill, M. W. (1957). *In* "Proceedings Ind. Carbon and Graphite Conf.", London, p. 326. (Pub. 1958.)

Effron, E. and Hoelscher, H. E. (1964). *A.I.Ch.E.Jl* **10**, 388.

Egerton, J. R. (1968). Ph.D. Thesis, University of London.

Ergun, S. (1956). *J. phys. Chem.* **60**, 480.

Ergun, S. (1962). *Bull. U.S. Bur. Mines*, No. 598.

Ergun, S. and Mentser, M. (1966). *Chem. Phys. Carbon* **1**, 203.

Essenhigh, R. M. and Froberg, R. W. (1967). Paper presented at 8th Carbon Conference, Buffalo, N.Y.; abstract (1968) *Carbon* **6**, 222.

Essenhigh, R. M., Froberg, R. W. and Howard, J. B. (1965). *Ind. Engng Chem.* **57**, 33.

Evans, T. and Phaal, C. (1961). *In* "Proceedings 5th Conf. Carbon", Univ. Park Penna, Vol. 1, 147. (Pub. 1962.)

Everett, M. R., Kinsey, D. V. and Römberg, E. (1968). *Chem. Phys. Carbon* **3**, 289.

Feates, F. S. and Sach, R. S. (1965a). *Carbon* **3**, 261.

Feates, F. S. and Sach, R. S. (1965b). *In* "Proceedings 2nd Ind. Carbon and Graphite Conf.", London, p. 329. (Pub. 1966.)

Fedorov, G. G., Zarif'yants, Yu. A. and Kiselev, V. F. (1961). *Dokl. Akad. Nauk SSSR* **139**, 1166.

Fedorov, G. G., Zarif'yants, Yu. A. and Kiselev, V. F. (1963). *Zh. fiz. Khim.* **37**, 1619, 2344.

Fedoseev, S. D. (1967). *Zh. Prikl. Khim.* **40**, 1079.

Follett, E. A. C. (1964). *Carbon* **1**, 329.

Frank-Kamenetskii, D. A. (1947). "Diffusion and Heat Exchange in Chemical Kinetics" (trans. 1955 by N. Thon) Princeton University Press, Princeton, New Jersey.

Freundlich, J. (1962). *Z. Elektrochem.* **66**, 647.

Fryer, J. R. (1968). *Nature, Lond.* **220**, 1121.

Fu, Y. C. and Blaustein, B. D. (1967). *Chemy Ind.* 1257.

Gadsby, J., Hinshelwood, C. N. and Sykes, K. W. (1946). *Proc. R. Soc.* A**187**, 129.

Gadsby, J., Long, F. J., Sleightholm, P. and Sykes, K. W. (1948). *Proc. R. Soc.* A**193**, 357.

Gallagher, J. T. and Harker, H. (1964). *Carbon* **2**, 163.

Giberson, R. C. and Walker, J. P. (1966). *Carbon* **3**, 521.

Gleit, C. E., Holland, W. D. and Wrigley, R. C. (1963). *Nature, Lond.* **200**, 69.

Goldstein, E. M., Carter, E. W. and Kluz, S. (1966). *Carbon* **4**, 273.

Golovina, Ye. S. and Khaustovich, G. P. (1964). *Teplofiz. Vysokikh Temp. Akad. Nauk SSSR* **2**, 267 (see also *Inzh. Fiz. Zh.* **7**, 106).

Golovina, Ye. S. and Kotova, L. L. (1966a). *Teplofiz. Vysokikh Temperatur Akad. Nauk SSSR* **4**, 703; (1966) *High Temp.* **4**, 658.
Golovina, Ye. S. and Kotova, L. L. (1966b). *Dokl. Akad. Nauk SSSR* **169**, 807.
Golovina, Ye. S. and Kotova, L. L. (1968). *Carbon* **6**, 637.
Grabke, H. J. (1966). *Ber. Bunsen Ges. Phys. Chem.* **70**, 664.
Graham, J. A., Brown, A. R. G., Hall, A. R. and Watt, W. (1957). *In* "Proceedings Ind. Carbon and Graphite Conf.", London, p. 309. (Pub. 1958.)
Gray, M. D. and Kimber, G. M. (1967). *Nature, Lond.* **214**, 797.
Gregg, S. J. and Tyson, R. F. S. (1965). *Carbon* **3**, 39.
Griffiths, D. W. L., Thomas, W. J. and Walker, P. L. (1964). *Carbon* **1**, 515.
Grillet, Y. and Guérin, H. (1969). *C.r. hebd. Seanc. Acad. Sci.*, Paris **268**, 125.
Grillet, Y., Rebaudières, P. and Guérin, H. (1967). *Bull. Soc. chim. Fr.* 2423.
Guérin, H. and Bastick, M. (1965). *In* "Les Carbones" (A. Pacault, ed.), Vol. 2, pp. 386–455. Masson et Cie, Paris.
Guérin, H. and Rebaudières, P. (1965). *Bull. Soc. chim. Fr.* 2573.
Gulbransen, E. A. and Andrew, K. F. (1952a). *Ind. Engng Chem.* **44**, 1034–1047.
Gulbransen, E. A. and Andrew, K. F. (1952b). *Ind. Engng Chem.* **44**, 1048.
Gulbransen, E. A. and Hickam, W. M. (1967). *Electrochem. Tech.* **5**, 217.
Gulbransen, E. A., Andrew, K. F. and Brassart, F. A. (1963). *J. electrochem. Soc.* **110**, 476.
Gulbransen, E. A., Andrew, K. F. and Brassart, F. A. (1964a). *J. electrochem. Soc.* **111**, 626.
Gulbransen, E. A., Andrew, K. F. and Brassart, F. A. (1964b). *Carbon* **1**, 413.
Gulbransen, E. A., Andrew, K. F., Brassart, F. A. and Feild, A. L. (1964c). *J. nuci. Mater.* **13**, 40.
Gulbransen, E. A., Andrew, K. F. and Brassart, F. A. (1965a). *Carbon* **2**, 421.
Gulbransen, E. A., Andrew, K. F. and Brassart, F. A. (1965b). *J. electrochem. Soc.* **112**, 49.
Harker, H. (1959). *In* "Proceedings 4th Conf. Carbon", Buffalo, N.Y., p. 125. (Pub. 1960.)
Hart, P. J., Vastola, F. J. and Walker, P. L. (1967). *Carbon* **5**, 363.
Haviland, J. K. and Medford, J. E. (1965). *Carbon* **3**, 141.
Hawkins, N. (1965). *In* "Proceedings 2nd Ind. Carbon and Graphite Conf.", London, p. 355. (Pub. 1966.)
Hawtin, P. and Gibson, J. A. (1964a). *U.K. At. Energy Auth. Report A.E.R.E.* R 4450; (1966) *Carbon* **4**, 489.
Hawtin, P. and Gibson, J. A. (1964b). *U.K. At. Energy Auth. Report A.E.R.E.* R 4776; (1966) *Carbon* **4**, 501.
Hawtin, P. and Murdoch, R. (1964). *Chem. Engng Sci.* **19**, 819.
Hawtin, P. and Roberts, J. (1969). *Trans.I.Ch.E.* **47**, T109.
Hawtin, P., Gibson, J. A., Murdoch, R. and Lewis, J. B. (1964). *Carbon* **2**, 299.
Hawtin, P., Lewis, J. B., Moul, N. and Phillips, R. H. (1966). *Phil. Trans. R. Soc.* **A261**, 67.
Hawtin, P., Gibson, J. A. and Huber, R. (1968). *Carbon* **6**, 901.
Hedden, K. (1961). *In* "Proceedings 5th Conf. Carbon", Univ. Park, Pennsylvania, Vol. 1, p. 125. (Pub. 1962.)
Hedden, K. (1962). *Z. Elektrochem.* **66**, 652.
Hedden, K. and Löwe, A. (1964). *Chem. Ing. Tech.* **36**, 876.
Hedden, K. and Löwe, A. (1966). *Chem. Ing. Tech.* **38**, 846.
Hedden, K. and Löwe, A. (1967). *Carbon* **5**, 339.

Hedden, K. and Mienkina, G. (1965). *Brennst.-Chem.* **46**, 366.
Hedden, K. and Wicke, E. (1957). *In* "Proceedings 3rd Conf. Carbon", Buffalo, N.Y., p. 249. (Pub. 1959.)
Hedden, K., Kopper, H. H. and Schulze, V. (1959). *Z. Phys. Chem. Frankf. Ausg.* **22**, 23.
Heintz, E. A. and Parker, W. E. (1966). *Carbon.* **4**, 473.
Hennig, G. R. (1957). *In* "Proceedings 3rd Conf. Carbon", Buffalo, N.Y., p. 265. (Pub. 1959.)
Hennig, G. R. (1959). *In* "Proceedings 4th Conf. Carbon", Buffalo, N.Y., p. 145. (Pub. 1960.)
Hennig, G. R. (1961a). *J. Chim. phys.* **58**, 12.
Hennig, G. R. (1961b). *In* "Proceedings 5th Conf. Carbon", Univ. Park Pennsylvania, Vol. 1, p. 143. (Pub. 1962.)
Hennig, G. R. (1962a). *J. inorg. nucl. Chem.* **24**, 1129.
Hennig, G. R. (1962b). *Z. Elektrochem.* **66**, 629.
Hennig, G. R. (1965a). *Carbon* **3**, 107.
Hennig, G. R. (1965b). *In* "Proceedings 2nd Ind. Carbon and Graphite Conf.", London, p. 109. (Pub. 1966.)
Hennig, G. R. (1966). *Chem. Phys. Carbon* **2**, 1.
Hennig, G. R. and Kanter, M. A. (1959). *In* "Proceedings 4th Conf. Carbon", Buffalo, N.Y., p. 141. (Pub. 1960.)
Hennig, G. R. and Kanter, M. A. (1960). *In* "Proceedings 4th Intern. Symposium Reaction Solids", Amsterdam, p. 649.
Henry, J. F. (1963). *Bull. Soc. chim. Belg.* **72**, 740.
Héring, H., Keraudy, S., Lang, F. M. and May, S. (1959). *In* "Proceedings 4th Conf. Carbon", Buffalo, N.Y., p. 115. (Pub. 1960.)
Héring, H., le Bail, H., Sutton, J. and Vanderschmitt, A. (1964). *In* "Symposium on Carbon", Tokyo, Session 8, paper 9.
Heuchamps, C. (1965). *Bull. Soc. chim. Fr.* 2955.
Heuchamps, C. and Duval, X. (1966). *Carbon* **4**, 243.
Heuchamps, C., Duval, X. and Letort, M. (1965a). *C.r. hebd. Seanc. Acad. Sci., Paris* **260**, 1160.
Heuchamps, C., Duval, X. and Letort, M. (1965b). *C.r. hebd. Seanc. Acad. Sci., Paris* **260**, 1657.
Hewitt, G. F. (1962). Unpublished information.
Hewitt, G. F. (1963). *U.K. At. Energy Auth. Report A.E.R.E.* 4366.
Hewitt, G. F. (1966). *Chem. Phys. Carbon* **1**, 74.
Hewitt, G. F. (1967). *In* "Porous Carbon Solids" (R. L. Bond, ed.), pp. 203–224. Academic Press, London.
Horton, W. S. (1961). *In* "Proceedings 5th Conf. Carbon", Univ. Park, Pennsylvania, Vol. 2, p. 233. (Pub. 1963.)
Hoynant, G., Collart, F., Duval, X. and Letort, M. (1958). *C.r. hebd. Seanc. Acad. Sci., Paris* **246**, 2889.
Hoynant, G., Duval, X. and Letort, M. (1964). *C.r. hebd. Seanc. Acad. Sci., Paris* **259**, 2827.
Hughes, G., Thomas, J. M., Marsh, H. and Reed, R. (1964). *Carbon* **1**, 339.
Hutcheon, J. M., Cowen, H. C. and Godwin, N. F. (1961). *In* "Proceedings 5th Conf. Carbon", Univ. Park, Pennsylvania, Vol. 2, p. 379. (Pub. 1963.)
Jacquet, M. and Guérin, H. (1962). *Bull. Soc. chim. Fr.* 411.
Johnstone, H. F., Chen, C. Y. and Scott, D. S. (1952). *Ind. Engng Chem.* **44**, 1564.

Jozefczak-Ihler, M. and Guérin, H. (1966). *Bull. Soc. chim. Fr.* 2018.
Khaustovich, G. P. (1968). *Zh. fiz. Khim.* **42**, 1646, 1684.
Khitrin, L. N. and Golovina, Ye. S. (1963). In "Proceedings Intern. Symp. High Temp. Tech.", California, p. 485. (Pub. 1964.)
King, A. B. and Wise, H. (1963). *J. phys. Chem.* **67**, 1163.
Kini, K. A. (1963). *Fuel* **42**, 344.
Kisch, D. (1967). *Ber. Bunsen Ges. Phys. Chem.* **71**, 60.
Kiselev, V. F. and Nikitina (1966). *Dokl. Akad. Nauk SSSR* **171**, 374, O.V.
Kobozev, N. I. (1946). *Acta phys.-chim. URSS* **21**, 294.
Kozlov, G. I. and Kozlova, S. G. (1967). *Zh. fiz. Khim.* **41**, 1079.
Kroepelin, H. and Winter, E. (1959). In "Thermodynamics and Transport Properties of Gases", pp. 436–452. McGraw-Hill, New York.
Ladd, I. R., Wilson, H. W. and Walsh, P. N. (1967). *Carbon* **5**, 195.
Laine, N. R., Vastola, F. J. and Walker, P. L. (1961). In "Proceedings 5th Conf. Carbon", Univ. Park, Pennsylvania, Vol. 2, p. 211. (Pub. 1963.)
Laine, N. R., Vastola, F. J. and Walker, P. L. (1963). *J. phys. Chem.* **67**, 2030.
Lang, F. M. (1962). *C.r. hebd. Seanc. Acad. Sci., Paris* **255**, 1511.
Lang, F. M. and Goenvec, H. (1966). *C.r. hebd. Seanc. Acad. Sci., Paris* **262**, 1820.
Lang, F. M. and Magnier, P. (1963a). *J. Chim. phys.* **60**, 1251.
Lang, F. M. and Magnier, P. (1963b). *C.r. hebd. Seanc. Acad. Sci., Paris* **256**, 2372.
Lang, F. M. and Magnier, P. (1964a). *C.r. hebd. Seanc. Acad. Sci., Paris* **258**, 889.
Lang, F. M. and Magnier, P. (1964b). *Carbon* **2**, 7.
Lang, F. M. and Magnier, P. (1964c). In "Proceedings Symposium Carbon", Tokyo, Session 8, Paper 15.
Lang, F. M. and Magnier, P. (1967). In "Porous Carbon Solids" (R. L. Bond, ed.), pp. 251–271. Academic Press, New York.
Lang, F. M. and Magnier, P. (1968). *Chem. Phys. Carbon* **3**, 121.
Lang, F. M. and de Noblet, M. (1967). Paper presented at 8th Conf. Carbon, Buffalo, N.Y.; abstract (1968) *Carbon* **6**, 210.
Lang, F. M., Magnier, P., May, S. and Pinto, G. (1961a). *J. Chim. phys.* **58**, 47.
Lang, F. M., Magnier, P. and May, S. (1961b). In "Proceedings 5th Conf. Carbon", Univ. Park, Pennsylvania, Vol. 1, p. 171. (Pub. 1962.)
Lang, F. M., Magnier, P., Sella, C. and Trillat, J. J. (1962). *C.r. hebd. Seanc. Acad. Sci., Paris* **254**, 4114.
Lang, F. M., Magnier, P. and May, S. (1963). *Carbon* **1**, 33.
Lang, F. M., Koch, C. and Merle, A. (1964). *Carbon* **2**, 15.
Lang, F. M., Magnier, P. and Brie, M. (1965a). In "Proceedings 2nd Ind. Carbon and Graphite Conf.", London, p. 243. (Pub. 1966.)
Lang, F. M., Magnier, P., Vallé, C. and Cazard, J. (1965b). Paper presented at 7th Conf. Carbon, Pittsburgh; abstract (1965) *Carbon* **3**, 345.
Lang, F. M., Magnier, P., Gilles, P., Pollet, R. and Brie, M. (1965c). Paper presented at 7th Conf. Carbon, Pittsburgh; abstract (1965) *Carbon* **3**, 345.
Lang, F. M., May, S., Goenvec, M., de Noblet, M. and Chenion, J. (1965d). Paper presented at 7th Conf. Carbon, Pittsburgh; abstract (1965) in *Carbon* **3**, 346.
Lang, F. M., Gilles, P., Magnier, P. and Maire, P. (1966). *J. Chim. Phys.* **63**, 1084.
Lang, F. M., Blanchard, R. and Magnier, P. (1967). Paper presented at 8th Conf. Carbon, Buffalo, N.Y.; abstract (1968) *Carbon* **6**, 210; see also Lang, F. M., Blanchard, R. and Fessler, J. C. (1968). *Carbon* **6**, 827.
Lavrov, N. V. (1964). *Dokl. Akad. Nauk SSSR* **156**, 662.

Lavrov, N. V. and Khaustovich, G. P. (1965). *Dokl. Akad. Nauk SSSR* **165**, 1317.

le Bail, H. (1963). *J. Chim. phys.* **60**, 703.

l'Homme, G. A., Boudart, M. and d'Or, L. (1967). *Bull. Acad. R. Belg. Cl. Sci.* **52**, 1206, 1249.

Levy, M. and Wong, P. (1964). *J. electrochem. Soc.* **111**, 1088.

Lewis, J. B. (1963). *Prog. nucl. Energy*, Ser. 4, **5**, 145 (C. M. Nicholls, ed.), Pergamon, Oxford.

Lewis, J. B., Murdoch, R. and Hawtin, P. (1962). *In* "Proceedings Corrosion Reactor Mater. Conf.", Salzburg, Austria, Vol. 2, p. 469.

Lewis, J. B., Connor, P. and Murdoch, R. (1964a). *Carbon* **2**, 311.

Lewis, J. B., Hawtin, P. and Murdoch, R. (1964b). *J. Br. nucl. Energy Soc.* **3**, 95.

Lewis, J. B., Dix, J. and Murdoch, R. (1965). *Carbon* **3**, 321.

Lewis, J. B., Murdoch, R. and Dix, J. (1967a). Unpublished work.

Lewis, J. B., Murdoch, R., Stevens, J. A. and Klaschka, J. T. (1967b). To be published.

Lewis, J. B., Moul, A. N. and Murdoch, R. (1967c). *U.K. At. Energy Auth. Report A.E.R.E.* 5552.

Lewis, J. C. (1965). *In* "Proceedings 2nd Ind. Carbon and Graphite Conf.", London, p. 258. (Pub. 1966.)

Lewis, J. C., Floyd, I. J. and Cowland, F. C. (1967). Paper presented at 8th Conf. Carbon, Buffalo, N.Y.; abstract (1968) *Carbon* **6**, 223.

Lind, R. and Wright, J. (1963). *J. Br. nucl. Energy Soc.* **2**, 287.

Lind, R. and Wright, J. (1964). *In* "Proceedings 2nd U.N. Intern. Conf. Peaceful Uses At. Energy", Vol. 9, p. 541. (Pub. 1965.) United Nations, Geneva.

Long, F. J. and Sykes, K. W. (1950). *J. Chim. phys.* **47**, 361.

Long, F. J. and Sykes, K. W. (1952). *Proc. R. Soc.* **A215**, 100.

Lussow, R. O., Vastola, F. J. and Walker, P. L. (1967). *Carbon* **5**, 591.

Majewski, E. A. and Spurrier, P. L. (1962). *J. Inst. Fuel* **35**, 296.

Marsh, H. (1965). Contribution to discussion at 2nd Ind. Carbon and Graphite Conf., London, p. 247. (Pub. 1966.)

Marsh, H. and O'Hair, T. E. (1967). Paper presented at 8th Conf. Carbon, Buffalo, N.Y.; abstract (1968) *Carbon* **6**, 230.

Marsh, H., O'Hair, T. E., Reed, R. and Wynne-Jones, W. F. K. (1963). *Nature, Lond.* **198**, 1195.

Marsh, H., O'Hair, T. E. and Wynne-Jones, W. F. K. (1965a). *Trans. Faraday Soc.* **61**, 274.

Marsh, H., O'Hair, T. E. and Reed, R. (1965b). *Trans. Faraday Soc.* **61**, 285.

Marsh, H., Rand, B. and Robson, D. (1967). Paper presented at 8th Conf. Carbon, Buffalo, N.Y.; abstract (1968) *Carbon* **6**, 227.

Mar'yasin, I. L. and Tesner, P. A. (1965). *Dokl. Akad. Nauk SSSR* **163**, 1430.

Mentser, M. and Ergun, S. (1967). *Carbon* **5**, 331.

Meyer, L. (1938). *Trans. Faraday Soc.* **34**, 1056.

Meyer, L. (1950). *J. Chim. phys.* **47**, 328.

Montet, G. L. and Myers, G. E. (1967). Paper presented at 8th Conf. Carbon, Buffalo, N.Y.; see (1968) *Carbon* **6**, 627.

Mukaibo, T. and Yamauchi, S. (1965). *Carbon* **3**, 87.

Nagle, J. and Strickland-Constable, R. F. (1961). *In* "Proceedings 5th Conf. Carbon, Univ. Park, Pennsylvania, Vol. 1, 154. (Pub. 1962.)

Napier, B. A. and Spencer, D. H. T. (1965). *In* "Proceedings 2nd Ind. Carbon and Graphite Conf., London, p. 418. (Pub. 1966.)

Napier, B. A. and Spencer, D. H. T. (1968). *Nature, Lond.* **218**, 948.
Ong, J. N. (1964). *Carbon* **2**, 281.
Orning, A. A. and Sterling, E. (1954). *J. phys. Chem.* **58**, 1044.
Otterbein, M. and Bonnetain, L. (1964a). *C.r. hebd. Seanc. Acad. Sci., Paris* **258**, 2563.
Otterbein, M. and Bonnetain, L. (1964b). *C.r. hebd. Seanc. Acad. Sci., Paris* **259**, 791.
Otterbein, M. and Bonnetain, L. (1968). *Carbon* **6**, 877.
Otterbein, M. and Lespinasse, B. (1968). *C.r. hebd. Seanc. Acad. Sci., Paris* **267**, 1377.
Overholser, L. G. and Blakely, J. P. (1961). *In* "Proceedings 5th Conf. Carbon, Univ. Park, Pennsylvania, Vol. 1, p. 194. (Pub. 1962.)
Overholser, L. G. and Blakely, J. P. (1965). *Carbon* **2**, 385.
Pallmer, P. G. (1966). *Carbon* **4**, 145.
Palmer, D. J. (1967). *Nature, Lond.* **215**, 388.
Perrot, J. M. (1965). *Bull. Soc. chim. Fr.* 3198.
Petersen, E. E. (1965). *Chem. Engng Sci.* **20**, 587.
Presland, A. E. B. and Hedley, J. A. (1963). *J. nucl. Mater.* **10**, 99.
Pursley, S. A., Matula, R. A. and Witzell, O. W. (1966). *J. phys. Chem.* **70**, 3768.
Rakszawski, J. F. and Parker, W. E. (1964). *Carbon* **2**, 53.
Rakszawski, J. F., Rusinko, F. and Walker, P. L. (1961). *In* "Proceedings 5th Conf. Carbon, Univ. Park, Pennsylvania, Vol. 2, p. 243. (Pub. 1963.)
Rebaudières, P. and Guérin, H. (1965). *C.r. hebd. Seanc. Acad. Sci., Paris* **260**, 6864.
Redmond, J. P. and Walker, P. L. (1960a). *Nature, Lond.* **186**, 72.
Redmond, J. P. and Walker, P. L. (1960b). *J. phys. Chem.* **64**, 1093.
Reif, A. E. (1952). *J. phys. Chem.* **56**, 778, 785.
Robson, D., Harker, H. and Wynne-Jones, W. F. K. (1968). *Surf. Sci.* **9**, 246.
Rogers, J. D. and Sesonski, A. (1962). *U.S. At. Energy Comm. Report* LADC–5433.
Roscoe, C. (1968). *Carbon* **6**, 365.
Roscoe, C. and Thomas, J. M. (1967). *Proc. R. Soc.* A**297**, 397.
Rosner, D. E. and Allendorf, H. D. (1965). *Carbon* **3**, 153.
Rossberg, M. (1956). *Z. Elektrochem.* **60**, 952.
Rossberg, M. and Wicke, E. (1956). *Chem. Ing. Tech.* **28**, 181.
Rounthwaite, C., Lyons, G. A. and Snowdon, R. A. (1965). *In* "Proceedings 2nd Ind. Carbon and Graphite Conf.", London, p. 299. (Pub. 1966.)
Ruston, W. R., Warzee, M., Hennaut, J. and Waty, J. (1966). O.E.C.D. High Temperature Reactor Project, Dragon Report DR 394; (1969) *Carbon* **7**, 47.
Sato, H. and Akamatu, H. (1954). *Fuel* **33**, 195.
Scala, S. M. (1964). *In* "Developments in Heat Transfer", pp. 422–444 (W. M. Rohsenow, ed.). M.I.T. Press, Cambridge, Massachusetts.
Scholten, J. J. F. (1967). *In* "Porous Carbon Solids" (R. L. Bond, ed.), pp. 225–249. Academic Press, London.
Shahin, M. M. (1962). *Nature, Lond.* **195**, 992.
Shelef, M. and Walker, P. L. (1967). *Carbon* **5**, 93.
Smith, R. N. (1959). *Q. Rev. chem. Soc.* **13**, 287.
Spangler, C. W., Lott, S. K. and Joncich, M. J. (1967). *Electrochem. Tech.* **5**, 214.
Spencer, D. H. T. (1967). *In* "Porous Carbon Solids" (R. L. Bond, ed.), pp. 87–154. Academic Press, London.
Standring, J. and Ashton, B. W. (1965). *Carbon* **3**, 157.
Stacy, W. O., Imperial, G. R. and Walker, P. L. (1966). *Carbon* **4**, 343.

198 J. B. LEWIS

Strange, J. F. (1964). Ph.D. Thesis, Pennsylvania State University.
Streznewski, J. and Turkevich, J. (1957). *In* "Proceedings 3rd Conf. Carbon",
Buffalo, N.Y., p. 273. (Pub. 1959.)
Strickland-Constable, R. F. (1944). *Trans. Faraday Soc.* **40**, 333.
Strickland-Constable, R. F. (1947). *Trans. Faraday Soc.* **43**, 769.
Strickland-Constable, R. F. (1950). *J. Chim. phys.* **47**, 356.
Strickland-Constable, R. F. (1965). *In* "Proceedings 2nd Ind. Carbon and Graphite
Conf.", London, p. 235. (Pub. 1966.)
Sykes, K. W. and Thomas, J. M. (1961). *J. Chim. phys.* **58**, 70.
Taylor, J. (1956). *J. Iron Steel Inst.* **184**, 1.
Temkin, M. I., Cherednik, E. M. and Apel'baum, L. O. (1968). *Kinetika Katal.* **9**,
95, 824.
Thiele, E. W. (1939). *Ind. Engng Chem.* **31**, 916.
Thomas, J. M. (1966). *Chem. Phys. Carbon* **1**, 122.
Thomas, J. M. and Evans, E. L. (1967). *Nature, Lond.* **214**, 167.
Thomas, J. M. and Hughes, E. E. G. (1964). *Carbon* **1**, 209.
Thomas, J. M. and Roscoe, C. (1965). *In* "Proceedings 2nd Ind. Carbon and
Graphite Conf.", London, p. 249. (Pub. 1966.)
Thomas, J. M. and Roscoe, C. (1968). *Chem. Phys. Carbon* **3**, 1.
Thomas, J. M. and Walker, P. L. (1964). *J. chem. Phys.* **41**, 587.
Thomas, J. M. and Walker, P. L. (1965). *Carbon* **2**, 434.
Thomas, W. J. (1966). *Carbon* **3**, 435.
Tonge, B. L. (1959). *In* "Proceedings 4th Conf. Carbon", Buffalo, N.Y., p. 87.
(Publ 1960.)
Tron, A. R. (1964). "The Production and Uses of Natural Graphite", H.M.S.O.,
London.
Tucker, B. G. and Mulcahy, M. F. R. (1969). *Trans. Faraday Soc.* **65**, 274.
Valette, L. and van Massenhove, G. (1965). *In* "Proceedings 2nd Ind. Carbon and
Graphite Conf.", London, p. 337. (Pub. 1966.)
van der Held, E. F. M. (1961). *Chem. Engng Sci.* **14**, 300.
Vastola, F. J. and Walker, P. L. (1961). *J. Chim. phys.* **58**, 20.
Vastola, F. J., Walker, P. L. and Wightman, J. P. (1963). *Carbon* **1**, 11.
Vastola, F. J., Hart, P. J. and Walker, P. L. (1964). *Carbon* **2**, 65.
Vastola, F. J., Hart, P. J. and Walker, P. L. (1965). Paper presented at 7th Conf.
Carbon, Cleveland; abstract (1965) *Carbon* **3**, 350.
Volkov, G. M. (1969). *Teor. I. Eksp. Khim.* **5**, 66.
Walker, P. L. and Miles, A. J. (1966). Private communication.
Walker, P. L. and Raats, E. (1956). *J. phys. Chem.* **60**, 364, 370.
Walker, P. L., Rusinko, F. and Austin, L. G. (1959a). *Adv. Catalysis* **11**, 133.
Walker, P. L., Rakszawski, J. F. and Imperial, G. R. (1959b). *J. phys. Chem.* **63**,
133, 140.
Walker, P. L., Kinney, C. R. and Baumbach, D. O. (1961). *J. Chim. phys.* **58**, 86.
Walker, P. L., Austin, L. G. and Tietjen, J. J. (1965). *Carbon* **2**, 434.
Walker, P. L., Austin, L. G. and Tietjen, J. J. (1966). *Chem. Phys. Carbon* **1**, 328.
Walker, P. L., Vastola, F. J. and Hart, P. J. (1967). *In* "Fundamentals Gas–Surface
Interactions" (Symposium San Diego Calif. 1966, H. Saltburg, ed.), p. 307.
Academic Press, New York.
Walker, P. L., Shelef, M. and Anderson, A. R. (1968a). *Chem. Phys. Carbon* **4**, 287.
Walker, P. L., Bansal, R. C. and Vastola, F. J. (1968b). Paper presented at Carbon
and Graphite Symposium, Newcastle.

Walls, J. R. and Strickland-Constable, R. F. (1964). *Carbon* **1**, 333.
Watanabe, T., Matsumura, H., Washino, M. and Natori, M. (1965). *J. chem. Phys.* **42**, 2154.
Wehrer, P. and Duval, X. (1967). *C.r. hebd. Seanc. Acad. Sci., Paris* **265**, 432.
Weisz, P. B. and Prater, C. D. (1954). *Adv. Catalysis* **6**, 143.
Wendel, W. (1966). *Brennst.-Chem.* **47**, 321.
Wheeler, A. (1951). *Adv. Catalysis* **3**, 249.
Wicke, E. (1954). *In* "Proceedings 5th Symp. Combustion", Pittsburgh, p. 245. (Pub. 1955.)
Wicke, E. (1963). Paper presented at 6th Conf. Carbon, Pittsburgh; abstract (1964). *Carbon* **1**, 372.
Wicke, E. and Wurzbacher, G. (1962). *Int. J. Heat Mass Transfer* **5**, 277.
Wicke, E., Kopper, H. H. and Wurzbacher, G. (1961). *J. Chim. phys.* **58**, 25.
Yamauchi, S. and Mukaibo, T. (1968). *Bull. Soc. chem. Japan* **41**, 754.
Yamauchi, S., Mukaibo, T. and Hirano, M. (1967). *Carbon* **5**, 243.
Yamauchi, S., Mukaibo, T. and Ikeda, T. (1968). *Bull. chem. Soc. Japan* **41**, 755.
Zarif'yants, Yu. A. and Kiselev, V. F. (1962). *Dokl. Akad. Nauk SSSR* **143**, 1358; **144**, 151.
Zarif'yants, Yu. A., Kiselev, V. F. and Federov, G. G. (1963). *Zh. fiz. Khim.* **37**, 1846, 2344.
Zarif'yants, Yu. A., Kiselev, V. F., Lezhnev, N. N. and Nikitina, O. V. (1967). *Carbon* **5**, 127.
Zhitneva, G. P. and Pshezhetskii, S. Ya. (1967). *Zh. fiz. Khim.* **41**, 1707.
Zielke, C. W. and Gorin, E. (1955). *Ind. Engng Chem.* **47**, 820.

Chapter V

MECHANICAL PROPERTIES

H. H. W. LOSTY

The General Electric Company Ltd., Wembley, England

Polycrystalline graphite to the engineer is a weak brittle solid. Its tensile strength is usually less than 1 ton/in^2 although stronger grades up to about 4 ton/in^2 are available. Although its density is low (less than 2 g/cm^3), it has only a modest strength to weight ratio at room temperature compared with conventional engineering materials. However, its strength increases with increasing temperature and reaches about twice the room temperature strength between 2000 and 2500°C. At these temperatures, its strength to weight ratio is the highest of those materials that are at present manufactured in significant quantities throughout the world.

Its low thermal expansion and low Young's modulus coupled with its high thermal conductivity give it excellent thermal shock resistance. Unlike most materials that are thought of as brittle, it is remarkably insensitive to notches and the normal precautions against stress raisers, such as rounding off sharp internal corners, are unnecessary.

But if the engineer is to make wider use of these materials at high temperatures, he must have a better understanding of their properties. Equally, if the manufacturer is to attempt to improve the properties, he must understand the mechanism by which graphites fail under stress. This chapter attempts at least to rationalize these properties.

I. ELASTIC PROPERTIES

A. SINGLE CRYSTALS

The six components of stress (X) of a perfect homogeneous solid may be related to the elastic deformation (e) by the generalized form of Hook's law (Love 1952):

$$X_x Y_y Z_z Y_z Z_x X_y = |C_{rs}|(e_{xx} e_{yy} e_{zz} e_{zx} e_{zx} e_{xy})$$

where

$$|C_{rs}| = \begin{matrix} C_{11} & C_{12} & C_{13} & C_{14} & C_{15} & C_{16} \\ C_{21} & C_{22} & C_{23} & C_{24} & C_{25} & C_{26} \\ C_{31} & C_{32} & C_{33} & C_{34} & C_{35} & C_{36} \\ C_{41} & C_{42} & C_{43} & C_{44} & C_{45} & C_{46} \\ C_{51} & C_{52} & C_{53} & C_{54} & C_{55} & C_{56} \\ C_{61} & C_{62} & C_{63} & C_{64} & C_{65} & C_{66} \end{matrix} \tag{1}$$

where $C_{rs} = C_{sr}(r, s = 1 \text{ to } 6)$. The twenty-one independent constants C_{rs} are the elastic constants or stiffnesses.

A similar reciprocal relationship relates strain to stress of the form

$$e_{xx} e_{yy} e_{zz} e_{yz} e_{zx} e_{xy} = |S_{rs}| \cdot (X_x Y_y Z_z Y_z Z_x X_y) \tag{2}$$

where S_{rs} are the elastic moduli or compliances.

The structure of graphite is either hexagonal or rhombohedral with the axis of symmetry in the c-axis direction. The symmetry of lattice reduces the number of independent elastic constants to five and the matrix of eqn (2) reduces to

$$\begin{matrix} S_{11} & S_{12} & S_{13} & 0 & 0 & 0 \\ S_{12} & S_{11} & S_{13} & 0 & 0 & 0 \\ S_{13} & S_{13} & S_{33} & 0 & 0 & 0 \\ 0 & 0 & 0 & S_{44} & 0 & 0 \\ 0 & 0 & 0 & 0 & S_{44} & 0 \\ 0 & 0 & 0 & 0 & 0 & \frac{1}{2}(S_{11} - S_{12}) \end{matrix} \tag{3}$$

Large perfect single crystals of graphite do not occur naturally and although recent attempts to synthesize them by pyrolytic methods have met with some success, our knowledge of the elastic constants has largely been derived from measurements of the lattice thermal expansion, specific heat and volume compressibility at very high pressures. These parameters are not dependent on the degree of perfection of the material measured and can be used to derive values for a perfect crystal.

Riley (1945) started from the thermodynamic relationships

$$\left(\frac{\partial v}{\partial T}\right)_p = -\left(\frac{\partial S}{\partial p}\right)_T$$
$$\left(\frac{\partial^2 v}{\partial T^2}\right)_p = -\frac{1}{T}\left(\frac{\partial C_p}{\partial p}\right)_T \tag{4}$$

where V = volume of system, S = entropy, T = absolute temperature, C_p = specific heat at constant pressure, and derived for the graphite crystal

$$\alpha_a = (S_{11}+S_{12})q_x+S_{13}q_z$$
$$\alpha_c = 2S_{13}q_x+S_{33}q_z \tag{5}$$

where α_a = coefficient of linear expansion parallel to the basal planes, α_c = coefficient of linear expansion perpendicular to the basal planes, and q_x and q_z are the thermal pressure coefficients. He determined q_x and q_z from the quantum theory of specific heat to be

$$q_x = \frac{2}{3}\frac{\gamma_x}{v}C_{vx}+\tfrac{2}{3}G_1 T \tag{6}$$
$$q_z = \frac{1}{3}\frac{\gamma_z}{v}C_{vz}+\tfrac{1}{3}G_2 T$$

where γ is a constant (Gruneisen number), C_{vx} the contribution to specific heat from in-plane modes of atom vibration, C_{vz} the contribution to specific heat from out of plane modes of atom vibration, G_1 and G_2 constants independent of volume and temperature.

Combining eqns (5) and (6) gives

$$\alpha_a = \frac{2}{3}\frac{\gamma_x}{v}(S_{11}+S_{12})C_{vx}+\frac{1}{3}\frac{\gamma_z}{v}S_{13}C_{vz}+\tfrac{1}{3}\{2G_1(S_{11}+S_{12})+G_2S_{13}\}T \tag{7}$$
$$\alpha_c = \frac{4}{3}\frac{\gamma_x}{v}S_{13}C_{vx}+\frac{1}{3}\frac{\gamma_z}{v}S_{33}C_{vz}+\tfrac{1}{3}\{4G_1S_{13}+G_2S_{33}\}T.$$

From the experimental values of α_a and α_c over the temperature range 0–800°K of Nelson and Riley (1945) Riley was able to deduce the relationship between $(S_{11}+S_{12})$, S_{13} and S_{33}. Using the additional relationship that the volume compressibility

$$K = 2(S_{11}+S_{12})+4S_{13}+S_{33} \tag{8}$$

he was able to deduce the values of $(S_{11}+S_{12})$, S_{13} and S_{33}. In doing so, he used Basset's (1941) value of $44 \cdot 9 \times 10^{-13}$ cm²/dyne for the compressibility not realizing that Bridgman's (1945) value of $29 \cdot 2 \times 10^{-13}$ cm²/dyne had already been used in deriving the values for the specific heat. If Riley's data is corrected to Bridgman's value, the following values are obtained.

$(S_{11}+S_{12})$	$1 \cdot 20 \times 10^{-13}$ cm^2/dyne
S_{13}	$-2 \cdot 85 \times 10^{-13}$ cm^2/dyne
S_{33}	$38 \cdot 84 \times 10^{-13}$ cm^2/dyne

Bowman and Krumhansl (1958) argued that since the layer plane structure was similar to the benzene ring, the ratio of C_{11} to C_{12} derived from the line spectra of benzene could be applied to graphite. The same authors were able to calculate from the specific heat the value for the C_{44} constant as $2 \cdot 3 \times 10^{10}$ dyne/cm^2. The extremely low value for the C_{44} shows the ease with which the single crystal deforms by relative motion of the layer planes (shear in the a-axis direction).

The elastic constants and moduli for the single crystal are summarized in Table I. The values shown in brackets are those which have been calculated

TABLE I

The Elastic Constants and Moduli for a Graphite Crystal

Elastic constants (dyne/cm² × 10⁻¹²)		Elastic moduli (cm²/dyne × 10¹⁴)	
C_{11}	$(10 \cdot 3)\dagger$	S_{11}	$12 \cdot 1$
C_{12}	$(2 \cdot 1)\dagger$	S_{12}	$-0 \cdot 1$
C_{13}	$(0 \cdot 94)$	S_{13}	$-28 \cdot 5$
C_{33}	$(0 \cdot 40)$	S_{33}	$388 \cdot 4$
C_{44}	$0 \cdot 023$	S_{44}	(4350)

† Calculated assuming $C_{12} = 0 \cdot 25 C_{11}$ from benzene spectra.

to ensure consistency between the elastic constants and moduli according to the relationships:

$$C_{11}+C_{12} = S_{33}/S$$
$$C_{11}-C_{12} = 1/(S_{11}-S_{12})$$
$$C_{13} = S_{13}/S$$
$$C_{33} = (S_{11}+S_{12})/S$$
$$C_{44} = 1/S_{44} \qquad (9)$$

where

$$S = S_{33}(S_{11}+S_{12})-2S_{13}^2.$$

B. NATURAL SINGLE CRYSTALS

The elastic constants given in Table I are those deduced for a perfect hexagonal structured graphite crystal. Naturally occurring single crystals of graphite of the kind found principally in Ceylon, Travancore and at Ticonderoga in the U.S.A. contain a measurable amount of the rhombohedral structure. The two structures are illustrated in Fig. 1. Amelinckx and Delavignette (1960) studied foils cleaved from natural crystals from both Ceylon and Ticonderoga by transmission electron microscopy. Samples

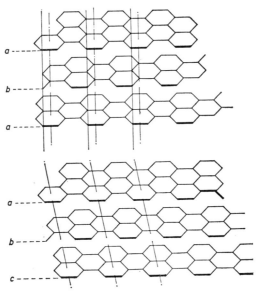

FIG. 1. Two forms of the graphite crystal. (a) The "hexagonal" form of graphite, (b) the "rhombohedral" modification of graphite.

which had been heat treated for a few minutes in a vacuum of 10^{-5} torr at 2500°C exhibited well-developed patterns of dislocation networks. These were shown to be lying in the basal plane with their Burgers vector in this plane. The dislocations were dissociated into ribbons consisting of two partials separated by a stacking fault. Both the dislocations and their networks were very mobile along the basal plane. The stacking fault energy was estimated to be $3–5 \times 10^{-2}$ erg/cm². A typical separation between the partials in a ribbon was 1000 Å. The authors used the relationships of isotropic elasticity to calculate the stacking fault energy and later work by Baker *et al.* (1961) deduced a value of 0·51 erg/cm².

Baker and Kelly (1964) measured the rigidity modulus (G) of a number of natural single crystals of Ticonderoga graphite by a dynamic resonance technique. The samples were heat treated to 3000°C in argon before measurements to purify and anneal them. The beams were vibrated normal to their basal planes. The resonant frequency of a beam is normally determined by the Young's modulus (E) which determines the bending of the beam but the authors were able to show that for a perfect single crystal where $E/G \sim 400$ the effect due to the shear was not negligible. When $E/G = 4000$, the effect is principally due to the shear and the resonant frequency $f = (1/4l)\sqrt{(G/\rho)}$, where l is the length and ρ the density. This compares with $f = (1/2\pi l^2)\sqrt{(EI/\rho)}$ for the case of bending controlled by the Young's modulus. By plotting f against $1/l$ and $1/l^2$, they were able to show that the results conformed more closely to $f \propto 1/l$. The average value for $G(C_{44})$ was 1×10^9 dyne/cm² compared with $2 \cdot 3 \times 10^{10}$ dyne/cm² deduced for the perfect crystal. These experiments show the marked effect of the mobility of the dislocations on the

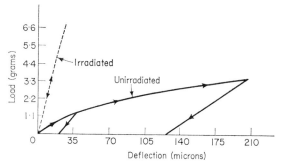

FIG. 2. Load deflection curve for a Ticonderoga graphite crystal. (Reproduced with permission from C. Baker and A. Kelly.)

C_{44} stiffness of natural crystals. Baker and Kelly also measured the static stress–strain diagram for one of their crystals which is reproduced in Fig. 2. Hook's Law is not obeyed and large permanent sets were observed when the load was removed.

After neutron irradiation at 100°C, the crystals were stronger and easier to handle. The resonant frequency was now proportional to $1/l^2$ and the most probable values of $E(1/S_{11})$ and $G(1/S_{44})$ were deduced to be 6×10^{12} dyne/cm² and $2 \cdot 4 \times 10^{10}$ dyne/cm². These compare with $8 \cdot 3 \times 10^{12}$ and $2 \cdot 3 \times 10^{10}$ from Table I. It is apparent that neutron irradiation effectively pins the mobile dislocations in graphite. Irradiation also eliminates the large permanent set observed in the static stress–strain curve as shown in Fig. 2.

C. POLYCRYSTALLINE GRAPHITE

A detailed account of the structure of polycrystalline graphites has been given in Chapter I. To understand their elastic behaviour, these graphites will be considered to consist of three phases:

(a) A phase originating from the original grist particles and composed of small crystallites of an order of 800 Å diameter assembled with some large range order throughout the particle.

(b) A phase originating from the binder, part of which is used to fuse the grist particles together and part to in-fill the pores of the structure.

(c) An additional phase often introduced into these graphites by impregnation with an organic substance which is subsequently carbonized.

The density of the finished product is always appreciably less than the crystal density (2·26 g/cm³) and it will be shown that the resulting porosity has a marked effect on the elastic behaviour.

The room temperature stress–strain relationships for a typical polycrystalline graphite are shown in Fig. 3 (Losty and Orchard 1962). These results were obtained in tension with the stress applied parallel to the axis of extrusion. The loading curves are always convex with respect to the strain axis and if during the test the load is removed before the ultimate tensile stress is reached, the unloading curve is concave with a permanent set at zero stress. The stress–strain curves obtained after a range of pre-stressing up to the failure stress are all parallel at low stress and the value for their slopes

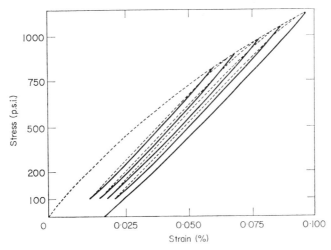

FIG. 3. Typical tensile stress–strain diagram for reactor graphite. Stress parallel to the extrusion axis. —, Loading; -, unloading.

corresponds to the Young's modulus determined by a dynamic measurement with a small strain amplitude. The shape of these curves is similar to that given for a natural crystal although the permanent set is smaller for the poly-crystalline material. The Young's modulus for this particular graphite was 9.6×10^{10} dyne/cm^2 compared with 8.3×10^{12} dyne/cm^2 calculated for a perfect crystal from the data in Table I with the stress parallel to the basal planes and 2.6×10^{11} dyne/cm^2 with the stress normal to the basal planes. The density of this particular graphite which had received at least one impregnation was 1.76 g/cm^3.

This particular graphite exhibited marked anistropy and although the stress–strain curves were similar in shape, the Young's modulus in the direction perpendicular to the axis of extrusion was 4.9×10^{10} dyne/cm^2.

The anistropy of the extruded graphite arises from the lenticular shape of the original coke grains which tend to align themselves during the extrusion process along the axis of extrusion. The coke grains, although composed of crystallites only about 800 Å in diameter, possess some long range order with the a-axis of the crystallites lying along the longest dimension of the particle. A diagrammatic representation of the structure of this graphite is shown in Fig. 4(a) and a simplified diagram of only four particles in Fig. 4(b). The low shear stiffness (C_{44}) between the basal planes of the crystallites allows the coke particles themselves to deform by shear under the resolved components of the tensile stress.

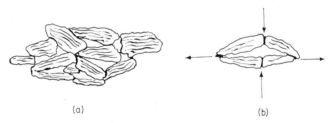

(a)   (b)

FIG. 4. A diagrammatic representation of the grain structure of polycrystalline graphite.

To appreciate the effect of the low shear stiffness on the apparent Young's modulus of polycrystalline graphite it is necessary to deduce an appropriate value for the C_{44} stiffness of the imperfect crystallites of the grains. It must be remembered that the crystallites are smaller than the separation of the partials (1000 Å) responsible for the low shear modules of single crystals. Possible values, therefore, range from the calculated value for the perfect single crystal of 2.3×10^{10} dyne/cm^2 to 10^9 dyne/cm^2 measured for a natural single crystal.

Neutron irradiation of single crystals has been shown in Section B to pin the basal plane dislocations responsible for the low C_{44} stiffness. A similar neutron irradiation of polycrystalline graphite (Losty and Orchard 1962) approximately doubles the apparent Young's modulus in both crystal directions. If it is assumed that the apparent Young's modulus is directly proportional to the C_{44} stiffness, then a reasonable value to assume for the unirradiated value would be about half the theoretical value, i.e. 1×10^{10} dyne/cm^2.

A further difficulty arises in visualizing the effect of the low shear modulus in that although it is relatively easy to consider the coke grains deforming under the resolved components of the tensile stress, it is less easy to see how this applies to the binder and impregnant phases.

A number of workers (Hutcheon and Price 1960; Mrozowski 1956; Losty 1960) have studied the effect of impregnation on the Young's modulus of polycrystalline graphites and their results may be represented by the equation

$$E = k(\rho_B - n) \qquad (10)$$

where E is the Young's modulus, ρ_B the bulk density, and k and n are constants. Typical values for k and n for the particular graphite used as the example in this chapter are 2×10^{11} dyne/cm^2 and $1 \cdot 22$ g/cm^2 (Losty 1962). The impregnant fills the spaces between the coke particles and resists their attempts to change shape by shear deformation. Thus, although the impregnant particles may be isolated from one another, their effect is to provide a second phase which acts in parallel with the first. The Young's modulus of the composite E_c is the sum of the apparent moduli of the grains and of the impregnant. Assuming that the separate apparent moduli are proportional to the weight of each material present, then

$$E_C = E_G W_G + E_I W_I \qquad (11)$$

where W_G and W_I are the weights of each component per unit volume of composite and E_G and E_I their true elastic moduli. Equation (10) confirms that the increase in the modulus due to the impregnant is proportional to the weight of the binder present but tells us nothing about the true value of E_G.

Similar studies on the unimpregnated form of this graphite (Losty and Orchard 1962) cannot completely resolve this situation since this contains some 15 % by weight of binder coke, a large fraction of which is the pores of the graphite and behaves in a similar way to the impregnant. However, if 10 % of the binder is assumed to act as impregnant, then the apparent modulus of the grains is reduced to about 2×10^{10} dyne/cm^2 in the parallel direction and 1×10^{10} in the perpendicular. These values are close to the deduced C_{44} stiffness but their accuracy is not adequate to specify the way the tensile stresses are resolved into shears in the crystallites.

The stress–strain behaviour in compression is illustrated in Fig. 5. Although it is superficially similar to that in tension the strain to fracture is much greater

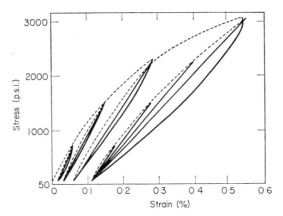

FIG. 5. Compressive stress–strain diagram for reactor graphite. Stress parallel to the extrusion axis. —, Loading; –, unloading.

and the slope of the curves obtained after various levels of pre-stress are no longer parallel at low stress. The curves more closely resemble those of the single crystal (Fig. 2).

The room temperature permanent set induced by stressing a polycrystalline can be recovered by thermal annealing at about 1000°C (Davidson and Losty 1958a). The results of a typical stepwise anneal are shown in Fig. 6. The non-linear deformation of the single crystals were shown in Section B to be associated with the movement of dislocations lying the basal plane. The presence of a permanent set implies that these dislocations are held away

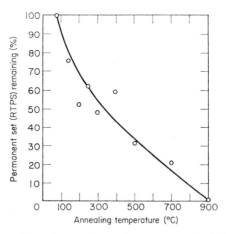

FIG. 6. Thermal annealing of room temperature permanent set (RTPS) for a graphite spring. Specimen W37 strained in the laboratory for six months at room temperature. (Reproduced with permission from Davidson and Losty 1958a.)

from their initial equilibrium position by some albeit temporary pinning points, but retain sufficient memory of their initial state to provide a backstress to act during annealing. The movement of a dislocation implies the generation of the necessary hexagonal to rhombohedral phase change through the graphite structure. Annealing of the permanent set would indicate that this transformation can be thermally activated over a similar temperature range. Confirmation of this arises from the work of Laves and Baskin (1956) who demonstrated that prolonged grinding of natural graphite markedly increased the proportion of rhombohedral to hexagonal phases. They argued that this was the result of excessive shear within the flakes. The transformation back to the original phase ratio could be achieved by thermal annealing and the process was complete after heating to 1300°C.

D. TEMPERATURE COEFFICIENT OF THE ELASTIC MODULI

The elastic moduli of all polycrystalline graphites increase within creasing measurement temperature and reach a maximum at about 2000°C (Malström *et al.* 1951; Davidson and Losty 1958b). Typical results obtained for a variety of polycrystalline graphites are shown in Fig. 7. The maximum increase for graphitizable cokes is of the order of 50%. Graphites made from non-graphitizable cokes show much smaller increases (approx. 10%).

Three possible explanations for the increase in modulus exist:

(a) The micropores which are formed on cooling the graphite from the formation temperature progressively close as the temperature increases causing the stiffness of the structure to increase.

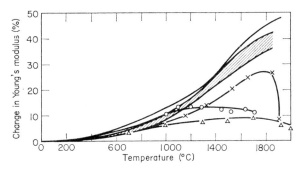

FIG. 7. Variation of modulus with temperature for graphite cantilevers manufactured from a range of raw materials. Band of petroleum coke results included specimens:

1. Calcined coke (30% binder)	4. Calcined coke (33% binder)
2. Calcined coke (30% binder)	5. Calcined coke (33% binder)
3. Calcined coke (30% binder)	6. Uncalcined coke (48% binder)

—, Pitch coke; //, petroleum coke; ×, natural graphite; ○, lamp black; △, cellulose carbon. (Reproduced with permission from Davidson and Losty 1958b.)

(b) The true C_{44} stiffness of the graphite lattice increases over this temperature range.

(c) The reduction of the C_{44} stiffness by dislocation movement is inhibited as the temperature increases.

The increase in stiffness due to void filling can be visualized by reference to Fig. 4(b). If the voids are formed by the internal stress generated on cooling down from graphitizing temperature as suggested by Mrozowski (1956) then they will be in the form of cracks lying parallel to the basal planes. If the four particles shown in Fig. 4(b) are each split into two by cracks running parallel to their basal planes, then the combined stiffness of the unit will be reduced since each limb is now composed of two beams of approximately one-half the original thickness. On re-heating the specimen to its test temperature, some of these cracks will close and thus increase the overall stiffness of the unit.

Davidson and Losty (1958b) demonstrated that the increase in Young's modulus with temperature was greater the larger the crystallite size and the degree of three-dimensional order in the graphite. The thermal expansion of the least graphitic material studied, cellulose carbon, was less than the graphitic materials; therefore the degree of pore generation should be greater than in the non-graphitic material since the thermal expansion of the crystallites has been shown to be independent of their perfections. Thus if pore closure is to be used to explain the increase in Young's modulus for the graphite samples, it is surprising that there is no corresponding increase in the non-graphitic samples. No direct evidence exists for the effect of temperature on either the C_{44} stiffness or the ease with which dislocation can move. However, Kellett and Richards (1964) have shown by X-ray crystallography that the amplitude of the out of plane modes of vibration of the carbon atoms increase at a greater rate than the spacing between the layer planes.

It is significant that the maximum increase in the Young's modulus is large for the more graphitic forms and only small for the disorganized structures. In all cases, the increases are similar to the maximum increases that can be induced by neutron irradiation which pins the dislocation.

It is conceivable that these out of plane modes impede the rapid movement of dislocations although over longer times they would be expected to aid rather than hinder the movement.

II. THERMAL CREEP

When graphite is heated under stress, creep is just detectable at 1200°C and becomes rapid at 2500°C. A number of workers (Malström *et al.* 1951; Wagner *et al.* 1958; Davidson and Losty 1958b; Martens and Jaffe 1960) have studied the creep of polycrystalline graphite. Below 2000°C, the creep consists of a primary creep with a barely detectable secondary component. Davidson and Losty (1958b) were able to represent the creep of a number of graphites in the temperature range 1200–2000°C by the following equation

$$E_t = \sigma \left\{ \frac{1}{M_t} + \frac{C}{M_0} \log_{10} \left(\frac{t}{\tau} + 1 \right) \exp \left(-\frac{E}{RT} \right) + B_0 t \exp \left(-\frac{E^1}{RT} \right) \right\} \quad (12)$$

where E_t = strain at time t (min), τ = constant (1 min), σ = applied stress (dyne/cm^2), $M_0 M_t$ = the appropriate elastic moduli at room temperature and test temperature T (°K) respectively, C = a constant (approximately 13), E, E^1 = energies of activation for the primary and secondary creep 20 and 40 kcal/g mole respectively, B_0 = a constant (approximately 3×10^{11} cm^2/dyne/min), R = the gas constant.

Fischbach (1960) found a similar relationship at higher temperatures although the creep coefficients were no longer directly proportional to the applied stress but to a higher power of approximately two. The proportionality of the primary creep to the room temperature elastic modulus in eqn (12) implies that the creep process is controlled by similar parameters to the elastic moduli. Since it has been argued in this chapter that the elastic deformations are controlled by shear deformations of the grist particle which in turn are in part determined by the basal plane dislocations, the simplest explanation for the transient creep is the thermally activated slip of the basal planes promoted by dislocation movement. The total deformation comprising the elastic deflection at the test temperature plus the transient creep deflection exceeds the elastic deflection measured at room temperature. Thus the suggestion in the previous paragraph that the thermally activated processes aid rather than hinder the dislocation movement over longer times is supported. If the stress is removed at the test temperature, all the primary creep is recovered demonstrating once again the generation of a back stress during the slip process. The secondary creep, however, is not recoverable (Davidson and Losty 1958b).

If the creep experiments are performed close to the highest temperature the graphite has been taken to during manufacture, then very rapid creep occurs. Losty (1960) has demonstrated that the process of ordering which occurs during graphitization can be directed by the application of an external stress to promote large shear deformation. Many of the results reported for high temperature creep in the temperature range 2300–3000°C (Wagner et al. 1958; Martens and Jaffe 1960) have been obtained close to or even exceeding the previous maximum temperature and large creep strains (of the order of 50%) have been reported.

It is difficult in retrospect to decide how much of the creep strain under these conditions was due to stress-directed graphitization processes and how much to genuine creep of an otherwise thermodynamically stable structure.

If these large strains are to occur, then some rearrangement of the junctions between the ordered regions (grain boundaries) must take place. At the highest temperatures studied ($>2500°C$) the activation energy of the creep process is equal to or greater than that for the self-diffusion of a single carbon atom (6·3 eV 140 kcal/g mole) and at intermediate temperatures between 2000 and 2500°C, is greater than that for vacancy diffusion. Thus, reorganization of the grain boundaries is at least theoretically possible although little direct evidence exists.

III. STRENGTH

The breaking strain of graphite in tension is only 0·1 % and it is therefore correctly thought of as a brittle solid. However, the previous section has shown that the stress–strain curve is not linear up to the fracture stress and the influence of this non-linearity, together with the granular nature of the structure on the fracture behaviour, is considered in the following section.

A. TENSILE STRENGTH

To measure the tensile strength of a material with a low breaking strain the test method must avoid bending specimens during test. The author has found that the recommendation in British Standard Specification B.S.S. 18–1950 for the tensile testing of cast iron provides a reasonable basis for such tests. Typical values for a polycrystalline graphite are 0·96 and $1·15 \times 10^8$ dyne/cm^2 in the two principal directions. He also studied the effect of specimen size on the tensile strength (Losty and Orchard 1962) and found no significant effect for diameters ranging from 1·01 to 2·03 cm. The particular graphite used was of the coarse grain variety with maximum particle size of about 0·3 cm and specimens which contained only a few grains across the diameter, that is less than 1·01 cm diameter, failed at a lower stress.

B. FLEXURAL STRENGTH

Because of the difficulties in carrying out a test in pure tension, the strength of many brittle materials is measured in bending and the ultimate strength calculated from the maximum fibre stress in the outer fibres of the beam when failure occurs. The flexural test is usually made on beams whose length is much greater than the specimen thickness. Four-point bending machines are preferred in which the beam is supported on two rollers and a further two rollers are used to apply the load. These rollers need to be free to rotate to avoid friction effects. For a simple Hookean solid, the maximum fibre stress is uniform over the section between the two inner rollers and can be calculated from

$$\sigma = \frac{3P(l-a)}{wh^2} \tag{13}$$

where P = total load at failure, $2l$ = separation of the outer rollers, $2a$ = the separation of the inner layers, w = width of beam, h = thickness of beam.

For graphite, this calculation yields a result which is normally between 1·3 and 1·5 times the result obtained in pure tension. Equation (13) assumes a linear relationship between stress and strain whereas, in both tension and compression, some departure is observed. A number of equations relating stress and strain have been proposed (Jenkins 1962; Wooley 1965) and, of these, the one proposed by Wooley appears to give the best fit to the experimental data. His equation is of the form

$$\sigma = A(1 - e^{-B\varepsilon}) \tag{14}$$

where A and B are constants and ε the strain. The same constants A and B are found in tension and compression and therefore although the stress distribution is altered by the application of eqn (14) the neutral axis is still located in the centre of the beam. If the maximum fibre stress is calculated from this equation, the difference between tension and flexure is approximately halved but not completely eliminated.

C. COMPRESSIVE STRENGTH

When simple cubes are loaded in compression, fracture occurs along the planes of principal shear stress which lie at an angle between 30° and 45° to the line of application. The compressive strength calculated from the specimen area and the load at failure is usually about three times greater than the tensile strength. A typical value is 3.5×10^8 dyne/cm^2. Unlike all the other mechanical properties, very little anisotropy with respect to the extrusion axis is observed.

D. WORK OF FRACTURE

When fracture of a solid occurs, the minimum energy required to produce fracture is that required to produce the two new surfaces. In a perfect brittle solid, this should be equal to the free surface energy of the solid. For graphite, these are reported to be 150 and 5470–6320 erg/cm^2 for surfaces parallel and perpendicular to the basal planes (Mason 1962). Two principal experimental techniques for measuring the energy necessary to propagate a crack in brittle solids have been devised. The first measures directly the work done in causing a crack to travel a known distance through a plate specimen (Obreimoff 1930). The second, using a beam specimen with a triangular notch cut in the centre of the beam, measures the total work done in fracturing the beam through the notched area (Tattersall and Tappin 1966). Both methods in their simplest form rely on the integration of the force–displacement diagram of the machine inducing fracture. When these techniques are applied to graphite, values for the work of fracture, sometimes called the specific fracture energy, of between 1 and 2×10^4 erg/cm^3 are obtained (Blakelock 1967; Davidge and Tappin 1968).

If fracture of the graphite matrix occurs by cleavage of the basal planes, then the work of fracture is some hundred times greater than the free surface energy of the crystallites.

E. NOTCH SENSITIVITY

When a solid under stress contains an abrupt change in cross-section, the stress is concentrated at the discontinuity and exceeds the nominal stress across that section as determined by the load divided by the cross-sectional area. The degree of stress concentration will depend markedly on the sharpness of the discontinuity. Values for stress concentration derived from elastic theory are given by Peterson (1953).

Notch sensitivity may be defined as the ratio of the load per unit area of an unnotched plate to the load per unit area across the remaining sections of a notched plate. Tensile tests performed on 10 cm wide × 6 mm thick graphite plates containing 1·5 and 3 mm wide notches gave a notch sensitivity of 1·5 (Blakelock 1967). This result agrees with data published by the National Carbon Company (1962). Calculation of the elastic stresses would suggest that for the two notch widths used by Blakelock, the notch sensitivity should be 5 and 7 respectively. Alternatively, his results would be consistent with elastic theory if the notch tip radius was approximately 1 cm. Thus, it would appear that the stresses around the notch are being relaxed in such a manner as to raise the crack tip radius appreciably. Similar tensile experiments by Blakelock with sharp cracks in place of machined notches failed to yield a stress concentration as high as two.

F. THE FRACTURE OF POLYCRYSTALLINE GRAPHITE

Any attempt to form a worthwhile hypothesis to explain the fracture of polycrystalline graphite must take account of the three principal features:

 (i) The ultimate tensile strength calculated from a flexural test is always greater than that obtained in pure tension.
 (ii) The notch sensitivity is always less than two.
(iii) The work of fracture is large compared with the free surface energy of the basal planes of the graphite crystallites.

Early workers in the field concentrated on the two-phase nature of the material and related the fracture behaviour to failure in the carbonized pitch binder holding the grist particles together (Mrozowski 1956). The model used

(Kerner 1956) was based on the reduction of the cross-section at the particle joint and ignored the extreme anistropy of the particles themselves.

An alternative view of the role of the binder carbon is that part of it provides an extremely strong junction between the particles and the remainder serves to fill up part of the macroporosity between the particles. It has already been shown that further impregnation with binder carbon serves only to fill the pores and so resists deformation by changes of shape of the pores. If this view is correct, then fracture must originate within the grist particles and ultimate failure occur by the linking of cracks across either the binder junction or the pore walls. The low observed strength of brittle substances was explained by Griffith (1920) by the stress concentration arising around inherent internal effects. He deduced the relationship between the observed strength (S), the free surface energy of the solid (γ), the appropriate elastic modulus (M), and the size of the defect (C_0) to be of the form

$$S^2 = \frac{2\gamma M}{C_0}. \tag{15}$$

Thrower and Reynolds (1963) have shown that the particular polycrystalline graphite used as the example in this chapter contains within its grist particles, micro-cracks lying parallel to the basal planes ranging from 10 to 50 microns in length. Using the C_{44} shear modulus of the crystallites, the basal plane free surface energy and a defect size of 10 microns in eqn (15) yields a tensile strength of 4.7×10^7 dyne/cm^2. When due allowance for the orientation of the particles with the stressing direction is made, this result is in reasonable accord with the measured value for the tensile strength of 11.5×10^7 dyne/cm^2 parallel to the extrusion direction and 9.75×10^7 dyne/cm^2 perpendicular to the extrusion direction (Losty and Orchard 1962). This result implies that stress concentrations can occur on the micro-scale.

Although this simple application of Griffiths' equation correctly predicts the stress at which inherent defects begin to increase in size, the cracks still have to propagate throughout the specimen. In tension, the process can be visualized as a growth of defects in some of the grist particles causing the stress to be transferred at a higher level to other particles until complete fracture of the section occurs.

In the presence of a notch, however, failure does not occur when the stress at the tip reaches this critical stress. As the load on the specimen is gradually increased during the test, the notch tip stress reaches the critical stress and cracks begin to grow in the particles around the tip. As a result of the cracks, the particles themselves become more compliant causing a redistribution of stress around the tip. The boundary between the partially cracked and the uncracked graphite represents the line of the critical stress. As the load on the specimen increases, this boundary enlarges and moves away from the crack tip. In most notch experiments, when the boundary has extended to a radius of about 1 cm, failure occurs. This may arise because the more compliant region is now large enough to contain a crack which satisfies Griffiths' criteria for the bulk material. If the apparent Young's modulus and the measured work of fracture of the bulk material are used in eqn (15), then the critical crack size is indeed between 0·6 and 1·2 cm.

The concept of graphite becoming more compliant as a result of fracture before failure occurs can equally well be applied to the case of graphite beams. In this case, as the stress on the outermost particles reaches the critical stress, fracture occurs. The increased compliance causes a redistribution of stress across the section and the neutral axis moves away from the centre of the beam towards the compressive side. The application of this hypothesis together with the correct use of the non-linear stress–strain characteristics proposed on Section B above can be made to account for all the discrepancies between the tensile fracture stress determined by pure tension and bending (Blakelock 1967).

The events which occur around a notch must also occur during the measurement of the work of fracture of graphite by the cleavage method. Enlargement of a considerable number of the inherent defects will occur in the compliant zone and thus extensive particle cracking will occur over a zone extending 1 cm from either side of the main crack. The density of defects observed by Thrower and Reynolds (1963) is estimated to be of the order of 10^9 microcracks per cm^3. The area of these cracks, assuming them to be disc-shaped with an effective radius of 10 microns, is 3×10^3 cm^2/cm^3. If only 10% of these defects were to be double in area, then, assuming the free surface energy of these cracks to be 150 erg/cm^2, the high work of fracture of the specimen can be explained.

The views given in the preceding paragraphs, are those of the author and are not universally accepted. Their merit is that they permit rationalization of the three principal features of the fracture of graphite. An alternative explanation of the difference between the results obtained in flexure and tension has been put forward by Mason (1962). He applied the extension of Griffiths' theory as proposed by Weibull (1939). This extension is based on the fact that there will be a distribution of inherent defect sizes in any sample under test. Assuming that failure will occur at the weakest link, that is the largest defect, then it can be shown that the chances of the largest defect of the distribution occurring in any given sample will increase with the volume under stress. Thus, the measured fracture stress should decrease with increasing specimen size. A corollary of this theorem is that the standard deviation within a group of samples should decrease as their size increases. Mason's published results support the main theorem but fail to demonstrate the decreasing scatter with increasing specimen size. If two similar specimens are tested in tension and flexure, then the actual volume under stress will be greater in the tensile specimen and thus it should fail at a lower stress as happens in practice. However, the author looked for an effect of specimen size on both tensile and flexural strength (Losty and Orchard 1962) but failed to find one. The Weibull theory requires that once a crack is formed at the weakest link, it must propagate continuously until failure occurs. The explanations for the lack of notch sensitivity and high work of fracture given in this section cannot be modified to allow continuous propagation of a single crack and other hypotheses to explain these events would be required.

If graphite fails because of inherent defects within the grist particles, are there prospects for very much stronger graphites? Bacon (1960) showed that the tensile strength of a graphite whisker formed by vapour phase deposition was $1\cdot4 \times 10^{11}$ dyne/cm^2. In these tests, however, the stress was applied along the axis and thus the shear mode of failure was inhibited. In a polycrystalline graphite, it would be necessary to reduce the size of defects parallel to the basal plane. It is known that these defects arise on cooling down from graphitizing temperature due to the extreme anistropy of the crystal. The larger the difference between the volume thermal expansion of the graphite and the crystallite, the more extensive these basal planes defects will be. Thus, a graphite of high volume expansion would be expected to produce a higher strength. The size of the defects must also be related to the size of the particle in which they are generated, and hence graphites made from finely ground grist should be appreciably stronger than the conventional graphites. The need to allow the decomposition product of the binder to escape from the block during carbonization requires a fairly porous structure and thus prevents the use of fine grist particles when large pieces require to be made.

Both these paths have been followed by the graphite makers whether by accident or design and have led to graphites whose flexural strengths are of the order of 5 ton/in^2. It is unlikely that very much greater improvement in strength can be achieved following the conventional graphite-making process.

G. THE EFFECT OF TEMPERATURE ON THE STRENGTH OF GRAPHITE

The short-term tensile strength of polycrystalline graphites increases with increasing test temperature and reaches a maximum at about 2500°C (Malström et al. 1951; Wagner et al. 1958). The maximum value is about twice that at room temperature and the curves relating strength to temperature are similar to those for Young's modulus.

Equation (15), $S^2 = 2\gamma M/C_0$, has been used to explain the room temperature strength of these graphites. Thus, a doubling of the Young's modulus would be expected to lead to a $1\cdot4$ increase in the strength. The experimental evidence indicates that the strength also doubles which requires some other factor to be evoked. As the test temperature increases, the micro-crack structure progressively closes due to the crystallites expanding at a greater rate than the bulk graphite. Although no direct evidence exists, it is possible that pore closure reduces the effective length of the micro-cracks (C_0) which will further increase the strength.

REFERENCES

Amelinckx, S. and Delavignette, P. (1960). *J. appl. Phys.* **31**, 2126.

Bacon, R. (1960). *J. appl. Phys.* **31**, 283.

Baker, C. and Kelly, A. (1964). *Phil. Mag.* **9**, 927.

Baker, C., Chou, Y. T. and Kelly, A. (1961). *Phil. Mag.* **9**, 927.

Basset, J. (1941). *C.r. hebd. Seanc. Acad. Sci., Paris* **213**, 829.

Blakelock, H. D. (1967). Private communication.

Bowman, J. C. and Krumhansl, J. A. (1958). *J. Phys. Chem. Solids* **6**, 367.

Bridgman, P. W. (1945). *Proc. Am. Acad. Arts Sci.* **76**, 9.

Davidge, R. W. and Tappin, G. (1968). *J. Matls Sc.* **3**, 165.

Davidson, H. W. and Losty, H. H. W. (1958a). *In* "Proceedings 2nd Int. Conf. on Peaceful Uses of Atomic Energy", Paper P/28. United Nations, Geneva.

Davidson, H. W. and Losty, H. H. W. (1958b). "The Mechanical Properties of Non-Metallic Brittle Solids", p. 219. Butterworth, London.

Fischbach, D. B. (1960). *Nature, Lond.* **186**, 795.

Griffith, A. A. (1920). *Phil. Trans. R. Soc.* **221A**, 163.

Hutcheon, J. M. and Price, M. S. T. (1960). *In* "Proceedings of the 4th Conf. on Carbon", pp. 645–656. Pergamon Press, Oxford.

Jenkins, G. M. (1962). *Br. J. appl. Phys.* **13**, 30.

Kellett, E. A. and Richards, B. P. (1964). *J. nucl. Mater.* **12**, 184.

Kerner, E. H. (1956). *Proc. phys. Soc. Lond.* 808.

Laves, F. and Baskin, Y. (1956). *Z. Kristallogr.* **107**, 337.

Losty, H. H. W. (1960). *In* "Proceedings of the 4th Carbon Conf.", pp. 671–674. Pergamon Press, Oxford.

Losty, H. H. W. (1962). *In* "Nuclear Graphite" (R. Nightingale, ed.), p. 157. Academic Press, New York.

Losty, H. H. W. and Orchard, J. S. (1962). *In* "Proceedings of the 5th Carbon Conf.", pp. 519–531. Pergamon Press, Oxford.

Love, A. E. H. (1952). "Mathematical Theory of Elasticity", 4th edition. Cambridge University Press, London.

Malström, C., Keen, R. and Green, L. (1951). *J. appl. Phys.* **22**, 593.

Martens, H. E. and Jaffe, L. D. (1960). *J. appl. Phys.* **31**, 1122.

Mason, I. B. (1962). *In* "Proceedings of the 5th Carbon Conf.", Vol. 2, p. 597. Pergamon Press, Oxford.

Mrozowski, S. (1956). *In* "Proceedings of the 2nd Carbon Conf.", pp. 195–215. Waverley Press, Baltimore.

National Carbon Company. (1962). "The Industrial Graphite Engineering Handbook".

Nelson, J. B. and Riley, D. P. (1945). *Proc. Phys. Soc. Lond.* **57**, 477.

Obreimoff, J. W. (1930). *Proc. R. Soc.* **A127**, 290.

Peterson, R. E. (1953). "Stress Concentration Design Factors". Wiley, New York.

Riley, D. P. (1945). *Proc. Phys. Soc. Lond.* **57,** 486.

Tattersall, H. G. and Tappin, G. (1966). *J. Mater. Sci.* **1,** 296.

Thrower, P. A. and Reynolds, W. N. (1963). *J. nucl. Mater.* **8,** 221.

Wagner, P., Driesner, A. R. and Kmetko, E. A. (1958). *In* "Proceedings 2nd Int. Conf. on Peaceful Uses of Atomic Energy", Paper No. P/702. United Nations, Geneva.

Weibull, W. (1939). *Ing. Vetenskafs. Akad. Handl.,* Nos. 151 and 153.

Wooley, R. L. (1965). *Phil. Mag.* **11,** 799.

Chapter VI

FRICTION AND WEAR

D. V. Badami

Turner Bros. Asbestos Co. Ltd., Rochdale, England

and P. K. C. Wiggs

Morganite Carbon Ltd., London, England

I. INTRODUCTION

Carbon and graphite components are widely used in industry in bearings, seals and other load-carrying applications in which sliding movement takes place. They are in general more expensive than simple lubricated metal parts, and therefore carbon* is employed only where one or more of its special characteristics make its use worthwhile. This is particularly relevant to electrical applications, where current has to be transferred between two bodies in relative motion, such as a motor frame and its revolving armature or between the overhead cable and an electric train. The element carbon exists in many atomic arrangements ranging from amorphous vitreous carbon to crystalline graphite. There is a progression of properties from the amorphous to the fully ordered form. As outlined in a later section there are many variations in raw materials and processes of manufacture, but it is possible, to a first order of approximation, to talk of the percentage graphite content of a carbon material (see Section II). Some characteristics are common to all forms of carbon, while others depend principally on the graphite content. The properties dependent on graphite content are discussed in later sections. Those shown to a significant extent by most carbons are tabulated below.

Mechanical

 Self lubricating
 Non-welding
 Low rates of wear
 Non-abrasive to metal counterface
 Chemical inertness
 High thermal conductivity
 Temperature stability

Electrical

 High electrical conductivity for a non-metal
 High potential drop in sliding contact
 Good resistance to erosion by arcing

A. GENERAL STATE OF KNOWLEDGE

Recent years have seen an increasing amount of work aimed at a better understanding of the complex friction and wear phenomena that occur when carbon is rubbed either against another carbon surface or, more commonly, against a metal surface such as copper or steel. Understanding of the surface phenomena becomes more difficult when an electric current passes across the

---

* To avoid tedious repetition of "carbon and graphite" the simple elemental term "carbon" is used throughout this chapter (including section headings) unless it is wished to draw particular attention to graphite, or to the graphitic component of carbon.

sliding interface. In spite of the upsurge in activity, a full understanding of the many interwoven mechanisms operating has not yet been achieved.

There appear to be two distinct groups of scientific workers, one working with model materials under idealized conditions and the other studying commercial carbon/graphite materials under conditions nearer to operational service. In addition there are the practical technologists and engineers who have succeeded in developing carbons, by semi-empirical methods, to meet many requirements in the mechanical, electrical and chemical fields. These workers have drawn up many classifications of types of carbon, representing the ability of each "grade" to tolerate arduous service of one sort or another. But the relationship of these classifications to each other, to the underlying structure of the carbon and to the influence of porosity and pore structure on properties is only known empirically, and not yet understood in any detail. The position is not made easier by the fact that the manufacturers have been, and still are, reluctant to disclose the detailed processes of manufacture.

It is therefore considered desirable, before discussing the scientific study of the friction and wear process, to indicate briefly the technology of the manufacture of carbon sliding components, their fields of application and the order of magnitude of friction and wear encountered in practical use.

The authors of this chapter do not claim to cover all aspects of the manufacture of carbons and graphite; supporting information is given in Chapter II. It is also not possible to give a complete account of the basic principles of friction and wear, and for these the reader is referred to Bowden and Tabor (1950, 1963), Rabinowicz (1965) and Kragelskii (1965). The book by Shobert (1965) deals with the physics and chemistry of sliding carbon surfaces while Holm's "Electric Contacts" (1967) is the main reference book on the electrical aspects. Braithwaite (1964) has also given a useful basic discussion of the general problems of solid lubricants and surfaces.

II. MANUFACTURE OF COMMERCIAL CARBONS

There are hundreds of grades of carbon/graphite materials for both electrical and mechanical applications. Ward (1964) has described the general flow chart for the manufacture of electrical brushes (Fig. 1) while Shobert (1965) has given a more detailed description of the relevant technology; the general principles are the same for mechanical carbons. A wide range of raw materials is available to achieve the desired variation in properties. Even natural graphites from different sources have different particle shape and size distributions, and these may lead to very different properties in a carbon material. The vast range of raw materials, coupled with the number of stages in processing, explains how it is possible to produce such a variety of carbons and graphites.

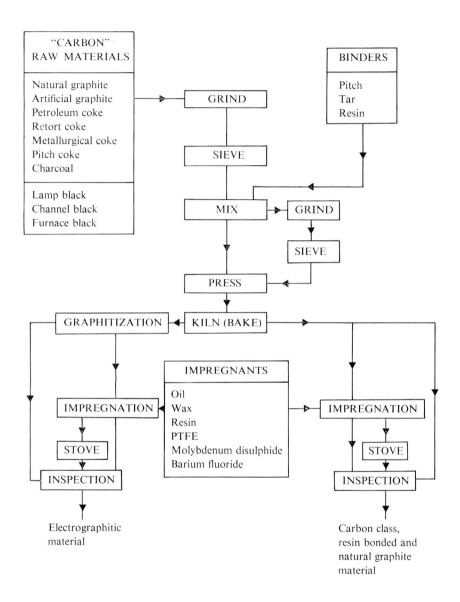

FIG. 1. Flow sheet for the production of non-metallic carbon–graphite brush material. (Reproduced with permission from Ward 1964.)

The desired combination of ground raw materials is blended and mixed with a viscous binder (pitch or tar), reground if necessary and pressed into blocks by hydraulic or mechanical means. These "green" blocks are then heated to about 1200–1300°C with protection from oxidation. This carbonizes the binder leaving a hard, strong material. For some mechanical applications it is usual to employ these "kilned" carbon grades either as they are or after they have been impregnated with resins, waxes, etc. For other applications, however, it is more usual to graphitize the blocks to about 2300–2600°C, again protected by an inert atmosphere or in a packing of carbon dust. Depending on the application there may be a final impregnation with oil, wax, resin or inorganic additive; in some cases the impregnant may have to be set by a further mild heat treatment.

At this stage one may note the confusion that has arisen from the general custom of referring to all materials which have had this high temperature treatment as "electrographite". In fact, depending on the raw materials, they may or may not be very graphitic (Franklin 1951). The term "electrographite" merely indicates a carbon which has been heat treated at least to the temperature which will turn the more readily convertible carbons to graphite. The "graphite content" of an "electrographite" may therefore include both natural graphite, the electrographite added in particle form as raw materials, and also the electrographite formed *in situ* from graphitizable raw materials. In addition to allowing suitable structures to tend towards the three-

TABLE I

The Properties of Two Widely Different Commercial Grades

	A carbon grade	An electrographitic grade
Compressive strength	1600 kg/cm^2	366 kg/cm^2
Transverse bend strength	470 kg/cm^2	206 kg/cm^2
Shear strength	300 kg/cm^2	111 kg/cm^2
Compressive elastic modulus	110 × 10^3 kg/cm^2	28·8 × 10^3 kg/cm^2
Dynamic elastic modulus	150 × 10^3 kg/cm^2	68·0 × 10^3 kg/cm^2
Mechanical resonance (Q) at 8 Hz	670	355
Hardness—scleroscope	90	40
Hardness—rockwell	124 10 mm/60 kg	50 10 mm/60 kg
Bulk density	1·60 g/cm^3	1·59 g/cm^3
Porosity (apparent)	13·0%	20·1%
Specific resistance	48 × 10^{-4} ohm cm	12·0 × 10^{-4} ohm cm
Thermal expansion	4·4 × 10^{-6}/°C	2·6 × 10^{-6}/°C
Thermal conductivity	0·08 W/cm °C	0·53 W/cm °C
Specific heat	0·19	0·20
Coefficient of friction on hard steel	0·3	0·1

dimensionally ordered atomic arrangement of perfect graphite, the heat treatment to above 2300°C tends to purify the materials since most of the impurities are boiled off. As a general rule increasing the "graphite content" leads to lower friction, lower hardness and strength, and lower resistivity. Table I illustrates this by listing the properties for two extremes of commercial carbons.

III. THE APPLICATIONS OF CARBON

A. GENERAL

The principal frictional applications of non-metals are those in which, for one reason or another, oil lubrication of metals is impossible. The decision as to whether to use carbon materials, and then as to the grade of carbon, must be based on a number of factors including cost, life, energy losses and sensitivity to debris.

Unless there is the possibility of mechanical abuse in service, graphitic grades of carbon are almost universally employed for the transfer of electric current to a moving body. (Where this is not possible, for example in collection from the third rail in some electric trains, metals such as cast iron may have to be used, with more rapid wear and increased damage to the countersurface.)

In most applications of carbon in dry (liquid free) running, the surrounding atmosphere is air with a normal level of absolute humidity. However, in some special applications where absolute humidity is low (for instance at high altitude, in polar regions, and occasionally in the tropics), catastrophic wear is liable to occur unless suitable additives are included in the carbon. In the following sections the application of carbon for mechanical and electrical purposes is outlined, together with the principal factors controlling friction and wear.

B. MECHANICAL APPLICATIONS

The most common mechanical applications of carbon are in bearings (either journal or face) or seals. In bearings it is possible to allow channels in the rubbing surfaces by which debris can escape. In seals such channels cannot be permitted. The specific conditions of the application can be expressed in terms of speed, pressure, cooling, operating cycle, etc., and the grade of carbon and the material of the counterface must be chosen to suit the circumstances. For bearings and seals it is usual to employ a strong close-textured carbon with a high graphite content. Friction is seldom of direct importance since adequate torque is available, but the heat produced by frictional work may be critical if the temperature rise causes softening of the metal counterface. It is more usual, however, for the rate of wear of the carbon and counterface to be the limiting factor. In some applications only a slight amount of wear can be tolerated before geometric error (e.g. eccentricity) becomes critical. In others a much larger wear is continuously compensated by movement of a spring-loaded component. In most common applications the metal counterface is both difficult and expensive to change, and must last the lifetime of the machine. The carbon can usually be more easily replaced, and hence may be allowed to wear more rapidly.

C. ELECTRICAL APPLICATIONS

The main electrical application of carbon, in the context of friction and wear, is the carbon brush, which usually runs on a copper or copper-alloy commutator or slip ring. On a slip ring the purpose of the brush is solely to transfer current from a fixed to a moving system, with minimum electrical and mechanical losses, consistent with long brush and ring life. On a commutator the brush has an additional specific electrical function, in that it is required to assist in bringing about the reversal of the current in the armature coil that is at any moment short circuited by the brush. Incomplete reversal when contact with a segment is broken is completed by a spark or arc. The frictional and electrical energy losses at the brush face are converted into heat and cause a temperature rise in brush and metal.

The great variety of electrical machines and of operating conditions necessitated the development of a wide range of carbons for brushes. As in mechanical applications, on some equipment a high rate of brush wear can be tolerated—if changing brushes is little trouble, or if the life of the machine itself is short. In others a very long life is essential. In almost all cases wear of the commutator or slip ring must be kept to a minimum.

Similar considerations apply to the graphite strips on the overhead current collectors on electric locomotives, except that the composition of the graphite for this application can be more standardized.

D. FRICTION IN INDUSTRIAL APPLICATIONS

In mechanical applications friction is seldom important, except insofar as it produces a temperature rise. The value of the coefficient of friction is usually of the order of $0\cdot1$–$0\cdot3$ over a very wide range of load, but at high pressures (say equivalent to 20 atm) heat production may be very rapid with only moderate speeds of the order of 50 cm/sec.

If softening of the metal counterface is the limiting factor in controlling the severity of duty which can be imposed in a given application, then μPV, the product of coefficient of friction, pressure and surface velocity, will have a constant value at the limit, since the frictional wattage is proportional to μPV. The temperature rise will follow the wattage if the cooling does not increase strongly with velocity. However, if the metal counterface is refractory, then temperature will be unimportant, and the limit will be some critical loading pressure. In eccentrically loaded journal bearings, with appreciable diametral clearance, the initial contact will be along a straight line, of width determined by Hertzian elastic theory. Most of the deformation takes place in the graphite, the component of lower modulus (the position of this line on the graphite will oscillate as the bearing rotates) and probably fatigue failure occurs when the local stress in the graphite is of the order of half the tensile strength. If failure does occur deep damage will be produced, and high wear must take place before an equilibrium rate is reached, with a greatly enlarged contact arc.

In electrical applications the value of friction coefficient may vary more widely, from 0·02 to 0·7. Again in most machines the lost power is not important, but the temperature rise may be critical. (Pressures are low, equivalent to 0·1–0·5 atm, but speeds may be very high—7500 cm/sec.) Associated with these extreme values of friction, the electrical characteristics show corresponding variations, as described in a later section. The effect of electric current is in general to reduce friction, and so long as current (of either polarity) passes the friction remains low. On reducing the current near to zero, friction may rise to very high values. This effect does not happen with all grades of carbon, or under all conditions (at low speeds it is not often encountered) but when it does the coefficient of friction may reach unity. The general level of the coefficient of friction, and its changes with speed, pressure and current, depends on the grade of carbon, on the cooling, and on the geometry of the system. In general the electrical contact potential between the brush face and the metal ring or commutator has a value of the order of 1 V, rising only slowly with current between 3 and 17 amp/cm^2, provided that some seconds are allowed at each new current for the voltage to stabilize. If the comparison can be made in milliseconds the contact obeys Ohm's law. The level of contact potential tends to fall as mechanical pressure is increased, and tends to a low value when the coefficient of friction is high, presumably associated with variation in the true area of contact.

Friction may depend on the method of restraint of the brush; any tendency to chatter or vibrate will modify the downward pressure, which will no longer be steady, but may have periods of zero value when the brush is out of contact with the countersurface, compensated by periods of abnormally high pressure. The average friction under these conditions may not be the same as in steady running.

E. WEAR IN INDUSTRIAL APPLICATIONS

In any rubbing process there is a period immediately after the surfaces have been brought into contact during which conditions are unsteady. The surfaces are being worn to conform with each other, a process known as "bedding". The duration of the bedding phase depends on the rapidity of the wear process, and on the accuracy with which the surfaces initially mate with each other. Once the bedding phase is complete, wear normally continues at a constant rate, although in special circumstances a cyclic process can take place.

Wear can be expressed in terms of length per unit time or per unit distance: usually the wear per unit distance is approximately independent of speed and will therefore be adopted as the preferred measure. It is also found for many commercial carbons in mechanical applications that the wear rate is proportional to the applied pressure. These proportionalities apply over a 100 : 1 range in pressure (20–0·2 atm) and over a 200 : 1 range in speed (4000–20 cm/sec). Also in general for a fixed graphite content, the stronger (harder) the carbon the lower the wear rate. Mineral ash in the carbon can cause rapid wear of both carbon and metal. Other things being equal, high graphite content reduces wear. Typical values of wear coefficient are 10^{-10} cm^3/kg cm, indicating that the thickness of the carbon layer removed is 10^{-10} times the distance travelled, under a pressure of 1 kg/cm^2 or 1 atm.

In electrical applications much of the wear is associated with the passage of current and at high current density tends to fall with increasing pressure as the contact improves; at low current densities wear rate increases with pressure as in mechanical applications. The total of mechanical and electrical wear rate remains at a few units of 10^{-11} cm/cm, under pressures from 0·13–0·4 atm, so long as the current density is below 10 amp/cm^2. Above this current density the wear rate may rise as high as 20×10^{-11} cm/cm, when the contact voltage is high, or when sparking takes place. On a commutator brush the wear rate is in general higher than on a slip ring, owing to the sparking caused by the commutation process and displacement of the commutator bars. On small domestic a.c. motors, where sparking is violent, wear may be very rapid, due both to erosion and to roughening of the metal.

In seals in which debris cannot escape, and in brush-commutator or brush–slip ring systems in which current passes, ribbing of the metal and carbon may occur so that a comb-like structure is produced (Fig. 2). The causes and means of prevention of this effect are not fully understood. In other circumstances the wear of the metal may be uniform, although small particles of metal can be transferred and embedded in the carbon, particularly into a negative brush. These particles may also be transported along the metal surface until they reach a slot; there they may adhere to the edge of the slot and form a projecting fillet closing the slot gap. On commutators these two phenomena are known as "copper picking" and "copper drag" respectively, and the latter may cause electrical breakdown.

FIG. 2. Section of brass ring showing serration (threading) produced by several years of running with early copper–graphite brushes.

The rate of wear of the commutator or slip ring is usually very low; in some moderately loaded machines fitted with brushes based on natural graphite, metal wear even after years of running is almost undetectable. In other motors, such as those in electric locomotives, the volumetric metal wear per unit distance travelled may be 20% of that of the carbon; but each point on the metal is in contact with carbon for some 10% of the time, so the nett wear rate is only about 2% of that of the carbon. Low metal wear is associated with a "good" patina or surface film. It is not certain whether this film is a cause or a symptom of the running conditions. If carbon/metal contact occurs only over a small fraction of the surface of the metal, in spots which sweep over the carbon (Stebbens 1964), then the surface film on the metal apparent to the eye mainly covers the area between the spots, and may have only an indirect relation to the wear process. But slowly the topography of the metal is altered by the brushes which run on it, and this topography largely controls the wear of the carbon (Lancaster 1962).

The surface of the carbon is also indicative of the way in which it runs on the metal. Various degrees of polish occur as debris is packed into pores. Finally a condition known as "glazing" occurs, in which the pores are filled with hard packed debris. Wear almost ceases, electrical contact is lost, and chatter and vibration frequently occur with variable friction. This condition, which may possibly be due to a non-permeable brush surface floating on a film of air, is usually associated with zero or low current running.

Under atmospheres containing corrosive gas (e.g. HCl) the transferred film on the copper may disintegrate, leaving bare metal. Rapid wear of brushes and commutator may then occur. Other gases such as H_2S produce a very thick film on copper. In atmospheres of very low absolute humidity (below 3 torr water vapour pressure) catastrophic wear of graphite occurs, with rates a million times higher than normal. This effect can be found in high altitude aircraft, in polar regions and certain other areas, and in special atmospheres such as those maintained round nuclear reactors. The low-humidity wear can be prevented by many adjuvants (additives) in the brush, such as MOS_2, PTFE, heavy metal halides, waxes and varnishes. Also environments of pure oxygen or CO_2 inhibit this form of wear.

IV. THE STRUCTURE OF CARBON

In this section the structure of carbon and graphite is discussed at various levels from local atomic ordering to microscopic geometry. It is not known which level of structure is critical in friction and wear studies.

A. DIFFRACTION STUDIES

Carbon exists in a variety of structural forms, ranging from near-perfect single crystals of graphite and diamond to almost non-crystalline materials. We will now briefly consider some of the various possible departures from such an ideal arrangement. The principal deviation occurs when the carbon atoms are arranged in layers, approximately parallel and equidistant from one another, but with no systematic sequence in their arrangement such as *ABAB* or *ABCABC*. Such an arrangement is referred to as turbostratic (Warren 1941) and is distinguished by the fact that in their diffraction patterns symmetric reflections of the type *(hkO)* and *(hkl)* merge together producing an *(hk)* band; for example (100) and (101) reflections merge to give the (10) band. A further characteristic is that such bands have an asymmetric profile with a steep rise in intensity on the low angle side and a much more gradual fall-off on the high angle side (Fig. 3). This intermediate mesomorphous arrangement can occur in many types of carbons and cokes heat treated to around 1500°C. Many carbon blacks and low temperature pyrolytic graphites also fall into this category. On the other hand, there are certain "non-graphitizing" carbons (for example those produced by the pyrolysis of thermosetting resins) that require temperatures of the order of 2500°C or more to reach even the turbostratic stage.

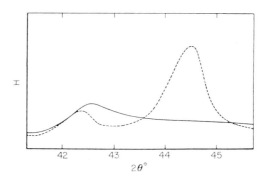

FIG. 3. X-ray diffraction profiles of the asymmetric (10) band from a turbostratic carbon (—) and the (100) and (101) reflections from natural graphite (– –).

It is interesting to note that commercial manufacturers use materials that cover this entire spectrum of atomic arrangement. Natural graphite of high structural perfection, for example, is used either as an additive to other carbons or to sintered metals. The majority of high speed electrographite brushes possess a high proportion of the turbostratic structures. Cellulose carbons, added occasionally to modify the gross structure, remain highly disordered.

B. MORPHOLOGICAL STUDIES

While diffraction studies indicate the degree of atomic ordering, morphological studies give an idea of the extent of ordering and the shape and size of the ordered regions. Such studies can be carried out either in the optical microscope or the electron microscope.

With careful polishing techniques, most carbon/graphite specimens can be examined in the optical microscope. Using polarized light and sensitive tint plates, micrographs of the type shown in Fig. 4(a)–(d) can be obtained. Figures (c) and (d) show the structures of two commercial grades of brush, while (a) and (b) show the structure of a non-graphitizable and graphitizable carbon, both heat treated to 2500°C. The graphitizable carbon shows highly oriented and anisotropic regions several microns in size whereas the non-graphitizable carbons show hardly any sign of ordering at all.

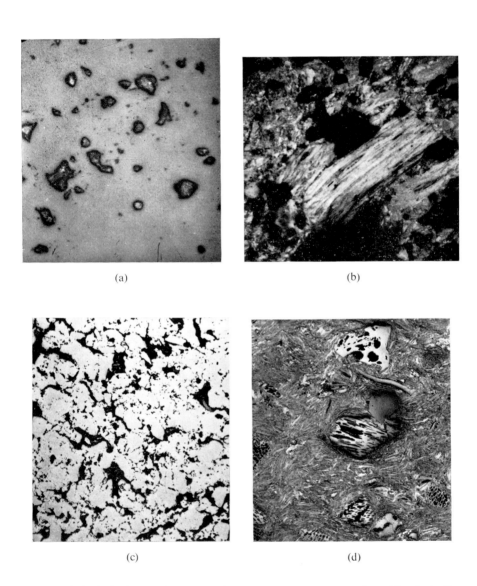

(a)

(b)

(c)

(d)

FIG. 4. Optical micrographs (×100) of carbons (heated to 2300°C) from (a) polyvinylidene chloride, (b) polyvinyl chloride and (c, d) two industrial brush grades.

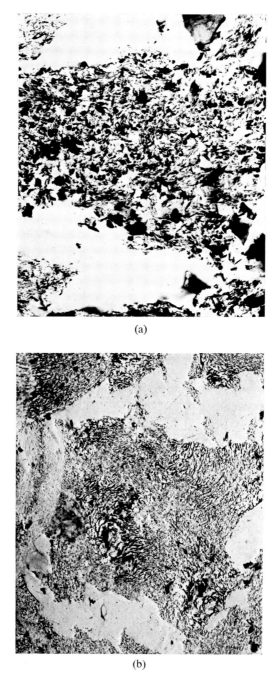

(a)

(b)

FIG. 5. Electron micrographs ($\times 5000$) of a graphitized coke specimen; (a) thin section and (b) replica. (Reproduced with permission from Clinton and Kaye 1965.)

Brush carbons can be examined in the electron microscope by thin sectioning in the ultra-microtome (Clinton and Kaye 1965). Figure 5 shows a section and a replica of a graphitized specimen of pitch-bonded pitch coke. Such studies indicate that these materials are highly porous, with pores ranging from a few angstroms to many microns in size.

C. PORE STRUCTURE

It is still a matter of some controversy whether the pore structure of a brush carbon is an essential requirement or an unavoidable feature. But in general most commercial carbons possess a porosity from 10–25% by volume. The pore distribution can be studied in many ways, for example directly by using microradiographic techniques (Nelson 1961) (Fig. 6) or indirectly by using a mercury porosimeter (Wiggs 1959). Pores formed from various sources can be recognized: mechanically from between the granules during pressing and between fine-ground particles in each granule; in the viscous phases by volatile evolution before carbonization; biologically as in charcoal; and in the atomic structure by impurities and dislocations.

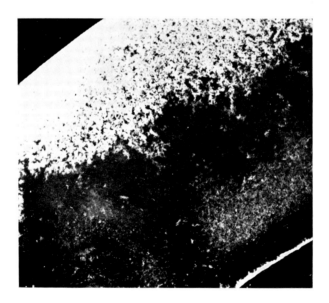

FIG. 6. Microradiograph of a section of a carbon tube impregnated with sulphur. The white areas represent the pores which are accessible to the sulphur (×10). (Reproduced with permission from Nelson 1961.)

V. FRICTION BETWEEN CARBON AND COUNTERFACE

The order of magnitude of coefficient of friction and the main factors controlling it have been outlined in Section IIID. In the following section some of the studies on idealized systems are described, with the conclusions put forward by workers responsible.

A. GENERAL

It is now generally accepted that when two surfaces are brought into contact with each other a small mechanical contact area is generated. The contact area may be made up of both plastically and elastically deformed areas. Shobert (1965) states that in sliding contacts, the mechanically generated area can be five times that in the equivalent static contact, where it is a function of "contact hardness" and compressive strength.

When two metal surfaces are placed in contact they touch only at the tips of asperities and the pressure at these regions may be high enough to produce plastic flow till the true contact area is large enough to support the load. If the load is W and P_0 is the yield pressure and the deformation is perfectly plastic, the area of true contact $A_0 = W/P_0$, so that A_0 is proportional to the load and independent of the shape or sizes of the surfaces in contact. If junctions are formed and sheared during sliding and if S is the specific shearing strength of these junctions, then the frictional force F is given by $F = A_0 S = WS/P_0$. Thus frictional force is proportional to the load and independent of the apparent area or geometry of the surfaces in contact. These are the two basic laws of friction named after Amonton. In practice, between metals, the two laws are closely obeyed. Exceptions to proportionality with load occur when either very hard or very soft materials are involved. In addition to the above adhesion component of friction, there can also be contributions due to the surface roughness and abrasion of the softer surface by the asperities of the harder member. The ploughing component due to abrasion can vary considerably (Avient, Goddard and Wilman, 1960).

B. MECHANISM OF FRICTION OF CARBON

In general, when the load is applied the contact area increases until the forces due to deformation under the true contact areas are sufficient to support the load. The modulus of elasticity of carbon is only some 5% of that of copper, so that normally in carbon/metal systems, the true area of contact is controlled by the carbon rather than the metal. Initially the rough machined surfaces of the carbon and metal interlock and break off the sharper asperities giving a period of high wear with erratic coefficient of friction. With further running-in the surfaces become seated and only elastic deformations occur at the surface.

The coefficient of friction is not constant in carbon/metal systems; as with metals it is taken to depend on the true area of contact and the specific shear strength of the film between the carbon and the metal. This film consists of the wear debris of the carbon/graphite, the oxide layer on the metal counterface, and layers of adsorbed molecules. The friction therefore depends upon the physical and chemical composition of this film and is affected by any factor that modifies this film. The film is probably thinner over the areas of contact than in the gaps between, but it is unlikely that it is entirely removed. The mechanical construction of the brush mounting, temperature, current and atmosphere all affect the film in different ways depending upon the composition and structure of the bulk carbon.

As in metals there seems to be appreciable abrasion, as revealed by optical studies of rubbed surfaces, but very little is known at present as to the relative contributions of abrasion and adhesion to the friction of carbon/ metal systems.

It now appears to be experimentally established that the low friction observed normally for systems including carbon/graphite as a sliding component is not an intrinsic feature of its layer structure but is due to the presence, in minute amounts, of some gases and vapours (see Section VC). There is, however, a controversy about the mechanism by which these vapours produce the low friction.

Savage (1945, 1948, 1951) suggested that the effect of water vapour was to neutralize the free valencies at the edges of the carbon layers by chemisorbing on them and thus reducing the interaction between the free valencies and the counterface. In addition, Savage also postulated a physically adsorbed film which further reduced the interaction between the opposing surfaces. Goodman and Rowe (1957) generally agreed with Savage's findings. McCubbin (1957) correlates the changes in friction with temperature in the range 20–120°C with the mass adsorbed: the changes in adsorption appear to be inversely related to those of friction (Fig. 7a and b). The increase in the middle of the range is attributed to the change from physical to chemical adsorption.

Rowe (1960) suggested that the vapour actually entered the lattice thus reducing the shear strength between the carbon layers. There is also some indirect evidence (Greenhalgh and Tucker, unpublished) for intercalation of water molecules, including the fact that the density of some carbons measured in water is higher than their helium densities. The main objection to the intercalation hypothesis has been that diffraction studies have not so far been able to measure any changes in the interlayer spacing as a result of such intercalation. But Bowden and Tabor (1963) have pointed out that Bacon's (1950) inability to measure any changes in spacing may have been due to insufficient outgassing. There is no clear proof that this possible inter-

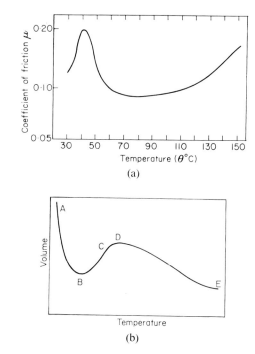

FIG. 7. Dependence of coefficient of friction and volume of adsorbed gas on temperature: (a) experimental values for a copper–graphite system (reproduced with permission from McCubbin 1957); (b) theoretical prediction based on chemisorption (reproduced with permission from Technical Note EL 137, Royal Aircraft Establishment Farnborough, U.K.). Crown copyright reproduced by permission of the Controller of HMSO.

calation is responsible for the low friction of carbon against a counterface, although there is some evidence that intercalation reduces the bonding behaviour between the layers. Cleavage experiments by Bryant *et al.* (1964) indicate that while graphite cleaves easily in air it does so with great difficulty in very high vacuum. Their observed value of the interlayer bonding energy in vacuum is 1750 erg/cm^2 compared with their calculated values of 2500 erg/cm^2 (cf. previous observed and theoretical values of 200–300 erg/cm^2).

The small amount of adsorption required to reduce the friction has been explained by Deacon and Goodman (1958) on the basis that it is merely sufficient to saturate edge groups to lower the friction. A novel explanation has been put forward by Cannon (1964) who has re-interpreted Savage and Shaefer's data (1956). In view of the fact that the critical amount of water vapour is not even sufficient to produce a continuous monolayer, Cannon speculates on the possibility of liquid patching at points of high surface energy such as defects and points of emergence of dislocations. If these patches are mobile, their contribution would be effective until the strain rate exceeded their own mobility.

The technology of carbon is based on the fact that structure and composition can be varied within wide limits and these in turn affect the frictional behaviour under different speeds and pressures. Many of the effects noted in industrial applications become apparent at speeds above 2500 cm/sec, a field in which little work has been published. There is scope for detailed investigation into the effect of small changes in carbon composition and structure, but once again the difficulty in obtaining information on the composition of commercial grades is inherent in the nature of the industry.

Midgley and Teer (1963) studied two commercial mechanical carbons CY9106—a mainly amorphous ungraphitized carbon—and the highly ordered graphitized version of the same material EY9016. Although some slight two-dimensional order exists in the ungraphitized material the layers are not stacked correctly, but in the graphitized material the stacking is much better developed. The specimens were in the form of rings, revolving on a counterface under loads of 13 atm. When the non-graphitic carbon was rubbed at low speed (27 cm/sec) on a counterface of similar material, or on steel, the coefficient of friction varied cyclically from 0·1 to 0·3.

Midgley and Teer suggested that the removal and flattening of asperities and the trapping of a film formed from fine debris temporarily increased the true contact area, leading to high friction; mechanical breakdown of the film restored the original state.

On separation of the two surfaces, blisters formed from compacted debris were also observed. The graphitic carbon did not show the cyclic variation in friction unless high friction and wear were previously induced by evacuating the system or using dry air.

Arnell, Midgley and Teer (1965) attempted to establish directly that the friction of pyrolytic carbon parallel to the deposition plane (i.e. parallel to a high proportion of the layers) was lower than in other directions. Three (0·6 cm) square pegs of pyrolytic carbon were fitted into an annular specimen holder and were rubbed against steel or tungsten carbide annular counterfaces at a speed of 27 cm/sec. The specimens were rubbed in all three orientations (Fig. 8) and the resultant friction and wear were measured in a controlled atmosphere of air of 50% relative humidity. Static friction measurements were also made on the pyrolytic carbon specimens (which had been polished

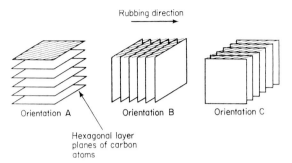

FIG. 8. Rubbing orientations of pyrolytic carbon. (Reproduced with permission after Arnell, Midgley and Teer 1965.)

with successive grades of abrasive down to 0·25 μ diamond paste and finally with γ alumina) against tungsten carbide (surface roughness of ± 250 Å) and the values of friction shown in Table II were observed.

Arnell and co-workers verified by electron diffraction that the preparation of the surfaces did not induce much preferred reorientation of basal planes for specimens with orientations B and C. This provides experimental support for the view that the low shear strength in the plane of the graphitic layers

TABLE II

Orientation A	Orientation B	Orientation C
0·14 ± 0·01	0·15 ± 0·01	0·16 ± 0·01

is not responsible for the observed low values of static friction. The corresponding dynamic frictional coefficients were less reliable indicators of the effect of orientation as the rubbed surfaces rapidly reoriented. All three orientations A, B and C (Fig. 8) showed approximately similar values of friction and wear. There was some variability in the behaviour of similar sets of samples.

Clark and Lancaster (1963) studied the frictional behaviour of a number of carbons, representing different degrees of graphitization, sliding upon similar materials. They used a crossed-cylinders friction machine in which the two cylinders, 0·6 cm diameter, were loaded at right angles to give nominal point contact. One of the cylinders was then moved at 45° with respect to the other, with a load of 1 Kg and a speed of 1 cm/sec, that is at extremely high local pressures and low speed, compared with most practical applications. For each pair of cylinders, a number of successive traversals was made over the same track in one direction of motion only and the friction was measured in every tenth passage. They found that the limiting value of frictional coefficient in all cases lay between 0·11 and 0·13 (Fig. 9). Clark and Lancaster (1963) attributed this to the formation of a film with a micro-hardness of 5–10 Kg/mm² compared to the macroscopic hardness values of 20–100 Kg/mm². These observations require to be established more conclusively as hardness measurements of brittle porous solids are neither easily made nor can they be easily interpreted in terms of the structure. If the surface layers are indeed coherent (if not their micro-hardness measurements would mean little), one then has to find a mechanism for their growth, since bulk carbon does not sinter even at temperatures of 3000°C.

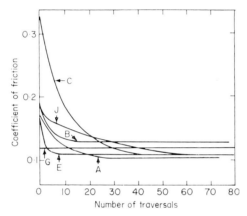

FIG. 9. Variation of friction with number of traversals. Letters indicate different specimens. For details, see Clark and Lancaster (1963).

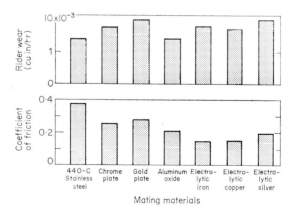

FIG. 10. Effect of mating materials on coefficient of friction and wear of rider (electrographitic carbon) in vacuum (10^{-7} mm Hg), sliding velocity 390 feet per minute and load 1000 g. (Reproduced with permission from Buckley and Johnson 1963.)

Buckley and Johnson (1963) studied the effect of various metal counter-faces on the friction of an electrographitic carbon in vacuum. The specimens were in the form of hemispherically tipped carbon riders (5 mm radius) under a load of 1 Kg, sliding on metal discs rotating at speeds of 200 cm/sec. The results are given in Fig. 10. The friction did not show any particular relation but wear was highest for the gold and silver surfaces which had no transferred graphite film on them. They also studied the effects of changing the content of natural graphite in their carbons and found the relation shown in Fig. 11.

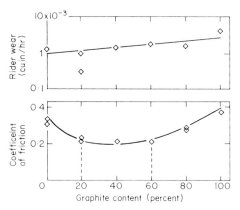

FIG. 11. Effect of graphite content on coefficient of friction and rider wear for various carbon compositions sliding on 440–C stainless steel. (Reproduced with permission from Buckley and Johnson 1963.)

D. SURFACE STRUCTURE UNDER FRICTIONAL CONDITIONS

The earliest attempts to investigate the structure of the surface layers of abraded graphite were by Jenkins (1934). He used reflection electron diffraction techniques to demonstrate that the carbon sheets in a rubbed graphite film were almost parallel to the surface. He also observed that as a result of polishing, the crystallite size in the surface layers was reduced from several hundred angstroms to 25 Å. In 1948 Savage suggested that the alignment of the platelets, due to abrasion, may not be perfectly parallel to the surface but slightly inclined and partially overlapping, thus producing a "shingled layer". He developed this hypothesis to account for a sudden increase in friction when the direction of rubbing was reversed. In later studies Fullam and Savage (1948) used a surface replica technique to obtain electron micrographs which confirmed this hypothesis; by means of stereo-electron microscopy they found that the platelets made angles of up to 90° with the surface but that the majority were at less than 45°.

The first quantitative studies of this angle of tilt were made by Porgess and Wilman (1960) who abraded graphite on emery paper and measured the resultant surface orientation. Figure 12 shows schematically the parameters that can be measured on a reflection diffraction pattern. Porgess and Wilman found that the basal planes were tilted against the direction of abrasion. This is broadly explicable as a compressive texture resulting from the interaction of the load and the frictional force. They also found a

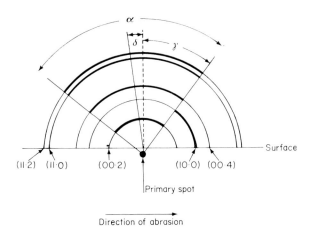

FIG. 12. Schematic diagram showing the angular parameters that can be measured on a reflection electron diffraction pattern from a rubbed surface.

reasonable experimental basis for the relation $\mu = \tan \delta$, where δ is the mean angle of tilt from the surface. Midgley and Teer (1963) extended these observations to cover non-graphitic carbons and found that the preferred orientation was again developed but to a lesser extent.

The surface orientations observed with commercial brushes show a wide variation and Fig. 13 shows two extremes. King and Wilman (1962) have examined by electron diffraction the surface of some commercial carbons and graphites and it was noted that the simple relation $\mu = \tan \delta$, referred to above, was not found to apply in some cases. Clark and Lancaster (1963) suggest that this relationship only applies when the microscopic grain structure is broken down to units comparable to crystallite sizes.

Quinn (1964) carried out an interesting experiment by removing electrolytically the contact film form on copper by sliding a commercial brush grade. He studied this film by transmission electron microscopy and observed a complex distribution of orientation of the graphite crystallites which is best described by a pole figure in which the projection plane is taken to be the sliding plane between the brush and the ring. The poles of the 002 plane (Fig. 14) are not only distributed with an angle of about 22° with respect to the direction of motion but also make angles of $\pm 22°$ on either side of the direction of motion. Quinn suggests that this sliding texture can be explained in terms of the mechanical twinning of the graphite crystallites. The observed texture, however, is a composite one over the whole thickness of the film on the copper and it is not yet clear how this can be related to the texture observed on the surface of the brush itself.

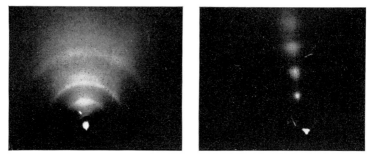

FIG. 13. Reflection electron diffraction patterns from the rubbed surfaces of various carbon graphite compositions.

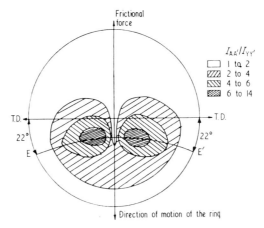

FIG. 14. Approximate pole figure showing the distribution of orientations of the poles associated with the (002) planes of the electrographite crystallites within the contact film. (Reproduced with permission from Quinn 1964.)

E. EFFECT OF CURRENT FLOWING BETWEEN SLIDING SURFACES

In actual applications in motors and generators, the carbon brushes are used essentially for their ability to commutate, that is to control the current pulses that occur during current reversal without damage to the commutator. But as this adds to the complexity of the problem, many investigators tend to use experimental apparatus with only one brush, of either positive or negative polarity, sliding on a metal slip ring, rather than brushes of both polarities on the same track. Davies (1957) studied the effect of passing a current on the friction of a brush (based on natural graphite) in different atmospheres. He found that in general an increase in the magnitude of the current resulted in a decrease in friction.

Lancaster and Stanley (1964) also found that current reduced the friction of several different types of carbons sliding either against themselves or metals (Fig. 15). They attributed this to the change in the carbon surface,

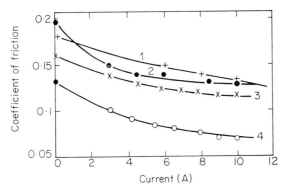

Fig. 15. Variation of friction with current for electrographite C on (1) itself, (2) copper, (3) mild steel, (4) baked carbon A. Load 0.1 kg, speed 500 cm sec^{-1}. (Reproduced with permission from Lancaster and Stanley 1964.)

as the irreversible effect of the passage of current persisted until the surface layer was finally removed by wear. Lancaster and Stanley have postulated that the changes are irreversible and occur when the current exceeds a critical value, leading to a critical contact temperature depending on the degree of graphitization and ranging from 560–1350°C. They believe that this effect is achieved through oxidation of the carbon surface, reducing the total area of contact though increasing the number of individual contacting regions. E. Holm (1962) also attributed the effect of current to the consequent increase in temperature but held that the binding energy between platelets decreased with temperature. This is unlikely to be generally valid as the graphitic structure is very poorly developed in many commercial brushes.

VI. THE WEAR PROCESS

Several of the experiments mentioned in the last section included measurements of wear. The principal conclusions on this topic are outlined below, the main conclusion being that there is very little relation between coefficient of friction and wear rate.

The name "graphite" is derived from the Greek word "graphien" which means "to write" illustrating the ease of transferring a film by rubbing. While wear in natural graphite is high, that of most types of carbon falls to a relatively low value after an initial period of bedding in. A film of the wear debris is transferred to the counterface and may itself form part of the load bearing area.

Figure 16 from Shobert (1965) shows that wear rates of various materials spread over nearly twelve orders of magnitude; those of good electrographite

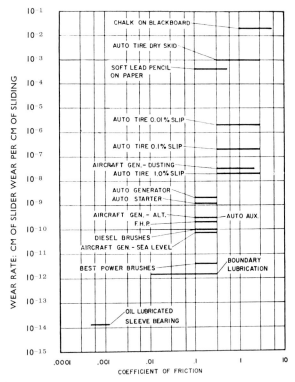

FIG. 16. Schematic representation of friction and wear. (Reproduced with permission from Schobert 1965.)

brushes are almost at the lower end of the range. If a brush with a face 1 cm long in the direction of sliding leaves one layer of atoms on the collector surface as it passes over it once, the rate of wear corresponds approximately to $3 \cdot 5 \times 10^{-8}$ cm/cm. The lowest observed wear rates in brushes is about four orders of magnitude less than this. Stebbens (1964) obtained, by a combination of electrical and optical techniques, a measure of the true (electrical) contact area. This enabled the volumetric wear at each contact to be estimated and hence the true wear rate per contact. Typically, the volumetric wear per centimetre travel for a specimen with a cross-section of $0 \cdot 5$ cm $\times$ $0 \cdot 5$ cm under a load of 90 g is $7 \cdot 5 \times 10^{-12}$ cm^3/cm (linear rate of 3×10^{-11} cm/cm). This corresponds to a uniform loss of material of one atomic layer for each 1200 cm of travel. However, if about 150 contacts per cm^2 are present, at asperites on the metal, each of 2 μ diameter, as Stebbens' electrical measurements indicated, the wear caused by each contact is approximately 6×10^{-6} cm/cm, or one atomic layer in 30 μ of travel. However the wear fragments are much more than one layer thick.

B. EXPERIMENTAL TECHNIQUES

Since the wear rate of carbon is extremely small and is sensitive to conditions of operation as well as the environment, it is found to be very difficult to obtain reproducible results. Much of the work has been done with electrical brushes and this introduces additional effects due to the passage of current. However, work by Clark and Lancaster (1963) and Midgeley and Teer (1963) has provided some data and also models to explain the observed wear rates. The general principle of much of the experimental work has been to examine the surface layers of the carbon and the wear debris to attempt to formulate mechanisms that would account for observed size of the wear debris and the observed rates of wear.

Lancaster has used two experimental arrangements in his friction and wear studies, one a pin and disc type and a second using crossed cylinders: the latter has already been described in Section VC. In the pin and disc type of arrangement, the brush is mounted vertically and is in contact with the horizontal face of a copper disc of diameter 9·2 cm. The disc could be rotated at speeds ranging from 5–5000 cm/sec. The deviations of the copper disc surface from the horizontal plane were approximately $\pm 5 \times 10^{-4}$ cm. In many of the experiments, the end of the brush was machined to a cone with an included angle of 90° and then truncated to a diameter of about 1 mm. The subsequent wear of the brush was determined by measurement of the mean diameter of the worn surface under a travelling microscope. In other experiments using brushes of constant cross-section, the wear was measured by the decrease in depth of the brush, using a Talysurf profilometer and an unworn reference surface on the brush. It is not clear how reproducible such wear measurements were in general, particularly as the studies were usually carried out under ambient conditions of variable temperature and humidity.

C. CARBON–METAL SYSTEMS

In many electrical applications, carbon rubs against a metal counterface, generally copper or steel. The roles of the surface film on the metal, including the metal oxide—and the mechanism of current transfer—are complex and not fully understood, and are outside the scope of this book. However, a brief resumé of some of the salient points concerning such systems is given below.

Lancaster (1962) studied the effect of time or distance travelled on the wear of an electrographitic conical brush. He found that the rate of wear usually decreased to a limiting value, the equilibrium being reached earlier for a heavier load. The rate of wear was unaffected by the following altera-tions to conditions after running a system for about 20 min: (a) stopping the machine and allowing the surface to cool, (b) substitution of the run-in brush by a fresh one, and (c) resurfacing of the brush surface. However, a light abrasion of the copper surface led to an increase in the rate of wear. Lancaster concluded therefore that the reduction in the rate of wear was due to changes in the topography of the copper. It could perhaps also be due to laying down a carbon film on the copper.

Under a load of 50 g, the wear track on the copper appeared tarnished and light brown in colour and electron diffraction showed that although a small amount of graphite was present, the major constituent of the film was Cu_2O. Reflection electron micrographs showed that the copper surface becomes very smooth within a series of shallow grooves. Under 500 g however, a black layer of transferred graphite gradually developed, tending to a limiting thickness. Weighing and profilometer traces led to an estimate of the mass of the film of about 30 µg/cm^2 (1500 Å if a uniform film of graphite). Very little Cu_2O or CuO was present in the layer and the graphite was first deposited in the surface depressions. At heavier loads, after longer times of running, the transferred layer became more uniform and completely masked the underlying surface.

Lancaster suggests that the type of surface film generated determined the magnitude of wear, and that different types of surface films and therefore different rates of wear can be induced by changing the operational conditions. He found two regimes of wear, "mild" and "severe" with the transition occurring at a load of 100 g. In both regimes, the wear was proportional to the load.

D. CARBON–CARBON SYSTEMS

When Midgley and Teer (1963) studied the effect of one piece of carbon sliding on another, they found that the cyclic increase in friction (see Section VC) was accompanied by variations in wear. With non-graphitized carbon, when the friction was low, the wear debris was small in size, a substantial amount being less than 50 Å. During the increase in friction, no wear debris was observed but on separation the surfaces developed "blisters". Similar blisters were also observed with graphitic carbon if dusting wear had been previously induced by low humidity. The authors concluded that the mode of wear of non-graphitic carbon is by brittle failure of surface layers which, combined with the grinding down of larger particles to very fine debris, produced exceptionally smooth surfaces. The compressive stress induced in the layers of packed debris on the surfaces were relieved on separation by the formulation of blisters. In contrast, the graphitic carbon wears by shearing of crystallites, leading to debris in the form of large platelets which do not form a continuous surface film.

Clark and Lancaster (1963) studied the effect of carbons sliding upon themselves using the crossed cylinder arrangement (Section VC). The carbons, covering a wide range of structures from natural graphite to non-graphitic carbon, were all observed to have developed surface films on them. All the surface films appeared to have very low micro-hardness values in spite of the fact that some of the bulk materials were extremely hard. These surface films are believed to play an essential role in the mechanism of wear.

At the initial stages of sliding, Clark and Lancaster found an induction period during which no wear debris was observed but the surfaces became highly polished. This induction period decreased with increasing load and was followed by a period of low wear, approximately 10^{-11} cm^3/Kg cm. Above a critical load "blisters" were formed on the surface, which on breaking led to high values of wear, approximately 10^{-8} cm^3/Kg cm, and also caused severe surface damage. Normal sections through the two carbon surfaces showed the thickness of the surface layers to correspond to the size of the wear fragments, 5 μ at low wear and 50–60 μ at high rates of wear. This indicates that the wear debris originates from the surface layer of the carbon. Clark and Lancaster interpret the critical period before the onset of surface damage to be equivalent to a critical number of deformations at the areas of contact. The graph of the number of cycles required to cause surface failure for a given load resembled characteristic curves for fatigue failure, the number increasing with the strength of the carbon. They also found that the sub-surface showed signs of fracture to about 0·5 mm below the surface film of 60 μ thickness. The two regimes of the carbon–carbon wear are reminiscent of the mild and severe wear of an electrographite on copper (see Section VIC). Non-graphitic carbons behaved differently in that either the degree of structural breakdown required to form a surface layer on the carbon was very high or the rate of breakdown was very low. This was shown by the fact that it was difficult to produce a surface layer even under relatively high loads and the wear rate remained high from the outset at approximately 10^{-6} cm^3/Kg cm.

VII. THE EFFECT OF ATMOSPHERE ON FRICTION AND WEAR

It has been already mentioned in Section VB that the presence of small quantities of various vapours and gases can modify friction, and can multiply the wear rate by a million. The attempts to explain the lowering of friction have been partially successful but there is very little work which relates the presence of the vapours to the mechanisms of wear, except perhaps that of Cannon (1964). This is somewhat surprising in view of the dramatic affect of low humidity on wear (see below).

Savage (1945, 1948) was the first to point out clearly that if graphite was cleaned of its contaminant film by heating in vacuum, then for graphite sliding on graphite, the coefficient of friction rose to 0·5–0·8 compared with approximately 0·1 in the open air. The reason why gross seizure does not occur as in metals in high vacuum is presumably because frictional growth of contact areas does not occur in graphite–metal systems.

It has also been shown that a number of gases and vapours can reduce the wear to normal values, provided they are present above certain critical concentrations. Thus Savage found that whereas water was effective at partial pressures above 3 torr, oxygen was not effective until its partial pressure exceeded 200–400 torr. Carbon dioxide has a strong effect, and ammonia, acetone, benzene, ethanol and hexamethyldisiloxane were also shown to be effective at 5 torr, while hydrogen, nitrogen and carbon monoxide were found to be completely ineffective at all partial pressures. While the actual values reported for the critical pressure vary considerably, for example in the case of water vapour values were reported ranging from 0·6 torr to the value of 3 torr found by Savage, one has to recognize that some of the anomalies observed by workers with other gases and vapour may have been due to the fact that their materials were not as dry or as pure as they believed. There is also the fact that there may have been differences in experimental conditions, such as sliding speed; Savage has observed that the critical pressure of water vapour increased with increasing speed up to 7 torr.

Davies (1957) has studied the effect of water vapour and oxygen on the friction of a natural-graphite based brush rubbing on a copper surface.

With a negative brush, increasing oxygen pressure increased friction, contrary to Rowe's (1960) and Savage's results but in agreement with Buckley and Johnson's (1963) observations on systems without electric current. Under a positive brush water was even found to have a slight detrimental effect on wear. When there is sufficient vapour present, the coefficient of friction is low and the wear of carbons is as described in Section VI. When, however, the vapour pressure drops below the critical value, the moderate increase in the coefficient of friction is accompanied by catastrophic wear. Extremely clean and controlled experimental conditions are necessary to induce the low humidity wear and when it does occur the chamber surrounding the apparatus fills up with a cloud of finely divided carbon, and the wear rate increases by about five orders of magnitude. Typically the rate may rise from 10^{-11} cm/cm to greater than 10^{-6} cm/cm; at this high rate of wear, referred to as dusting, a brush will be worn away in minutes.

In addition to the gases and vapours mentioned, a number of solid additives (adjuvants) to brushes also reduce the wear rate of carbon. CdI_2, $PbCl_2$, $BaCl_2$, BaF_2, MoS_2 and P.T.F.E. are amongst the many that have been found effective. There does not appear to be any agreement however on a universal mechanism; Savage believed that CdI_2 and $BaCl_2$ improved the retention of water vapour by the carbon and so lowered the critical pressure. Lynn and Elsey (1949) postulated that with carbon running on copper, the addition of BaF_2 catalysed the oxidation of the copper to Cu_2O which had less tendency to wear the carbon than bare copper. McCubbin (1957), on the other hand, suggests that BaF_2 is chemisorbed on the copper.

VIII. SUMMARY

Fifty years of engineering experience have confirmed that carbon/graphite compositions can run unlubricated against metal counterfaces with a low wear rate, only moderate friction and little damage to the metal. At the same time a current can be passed across the moving junction without welding or seizure, and with a contact potential sufficient to control commutation in an electric motor or generator.

The wear rate is usually of the order of 10^{-11} cm^3/Kg cm, except in a very dry atmosphere when the rate can increase a million times. This catastrophic increase can be avoided by various additives in the carbon. Under normal humidity but high current density the wear rate may be increased by a factor of ten or more over the zero current value.

The coefficient of friction is usually of the order of 0·2–0·6, but this level is lowered by the passage of current. There is an inverse relationship between potential drop across the faces at a specified current density and coefficient of friction.

The underlying mechanisms controlling friction and wear are not fully understood. There is some evidence that with electrographite there are two wear regimes—"mild" and "severe"—changing over from the first to the second as pressure is increased. In the mild regime a fatigue mechanism is probably involved, controlled by the topography of the metal. The film laid down on the metal is certainly related to the friction and wear process, but whether it is a cause or a symptom is not known.

The suppression of catastrophic wear by traces of water, or of certain other vapours, has been attributed both to the effect of molecules adsorbed on the edges of the crystallites, and to molecules intercalated between the layers. It is possible that both mechanisms can be effective.

Friction is probably a combination of adhesive and ploughing forces, acting over a small fraction of the apparent contact area. Either the true area of contact or the adhesion stress is modified by the passage of electric current: a complete quantitative understanding of the inter-relation of current density, friction force and potential drop would open the door to an explanation of wear and many of the second-order phenomena which occur in service. This understanding has yet to be achieved.

REFERENCES

Arnell, R. D., Midgley, J. W. and Teer, D. G. (1965). In "Proceedings 3rd Lubrication and Wear Convention", p. 62. Inst. Mech. Engrs, London.
Avient, B. W. E., Goddard, J. and Wilman, H. (1960). Proc. R. Soc. A258, 159.
Bacon, G. E. (1950). Acta Cryst. 3, 137.
Bowden, F. P. and Tabor, D. (1950 and 1963). "Friction and Lubrication of Solids", Parts I and II. Oxford University Press, London.
Braithwaite, E. R. (1964). "Solid Lubricants and Surfaces". Pergamon Press, Oxford.
Bryant, P. J., Gutshall, P. L. and Taylor, L. H. (1964). Wear 7, 118.
Buckley, D. H. and Johnson, R. L. (1963). In "Proceedings A.S.L.E. Lubrication Conf.", Paper No. 63.
Cannon, P. (1964). J. appl. Phys. 35, 2928.
Clark, W. T. and Lancaster, J. K. (1963). Wear 6, 467.
Clinton, D. and Kaye, G. (1965). Carbon 2, 341.
Davies, W. (1957). Monograph 271U, I.E.E., London.
Deacon, R. F. and Goodman, J. F. (1958). Proc. R. Soc. A243, 464.
Franklin, R. E. (1951). Proc. R. Soc. A209, 196.
Fullam, E. F. and Savage, R. H. (1948). J. appl. Phys. 19, 654.
Goodman, J. F. and Rowe, G. W. (1957). "Symposium on Chemisorption" (W. E. Garner, ed.), p. 272. Butterworth, London.
Greenhalgh, E. and Tucker, D. J. Unpublished results.
Holm, E. (1962). J. appl. Phys. 33, 156.
Holm, R. (1967). "Electric Contacts". Springer-Verlag, Berlin.
Jenkins, R. O. (1934). Phil. Mag. 17, 457.
King, J. N. and Wilman, H. (1962). Wear 5, 213.

Kragelskii, I. V. (1965). "Friction and Wear". Butterworth, London.

Lancaster, J. K. (1962). *Br. J. appl. Phys.* **13**, 468.

Lancaster, J. K. and Stanley, I. W. (1964). *B. J. appl. Phys.* **15**, 29.

Lynn, C. and Elsey, H. M. (1949). *Trans AIEE*, **68**, 490.

McCubbin, W. L. (1957). Tech. Note EL137, Royal Aircraft Establishment, Farnborough, England.

Midgley, J. W. and Teer, D. G. (1963). *J. bas. Engng* **85**, 488.

Nelson, J. B. (1961). "Proceedings of 5th Conference on Carbon", Vol 1, p. 438. Pergamon, London.

Porgess, P. V. K. and Wilman, H. (1960). *Proc. Phys. Soc. Lond.* **76A**, 513.

Quinn, T. F. J. (1964). *Br. J. appl. Phys.* **15**, 513.

Rabinowicz, E. (1965). "Friction and Wear of Materials", John Wiley, New York.

Rowe, G. W. (1960). *Wear* **3**, 274.

Savage, R. H. (1945). *General Electric Review* **48**, 13.

Savage, R. H. (1948). *J. appl. Phys.* **19**, 1.

Savage, R. H. (1951). *Ann. N.Y. Acad. Sci.* **53**, 862.

Savage, R. H. and Shaefer, D. L. (1956). *J. appl. Phys.* **27**, 136.

Shobert, E. I., Jr. (1965). "The Physics and Chemistry of Sliding Contacts". Chemical Publishing Co. Inc., New York.

Stebbens, A. E. (1964). "I.E.E. Symposium on Commutation", I.E.E., London.

Ward, H. (1964). "I.E.E. Symposium on Commutation", I.E.E., London.

Warren, B. E. (1941). *Phys. Rev.* **59**, 693.

Wiggs, P. K. C. (1959). "Proceedings of 4th Conference on Carbon", p. 639. Pergamon, London.

Chapter VII

INDUSTRIAL APPLICATIONS OF CARBON AND GRAPHITE

A. R. FORD AND E. GREENHALGH

Morganite Carbon Ltd., London, England

I. INTRODUCTION

The applications of carbon and graphite have grown in number and volume since the beginning of the 19th century, and are now many and various. In this chapter a number of the applications of commercial and technical importance are described.

In the commercial context the terms carbon and graphite lose their academic significance and are used to indicate the temperature of heat treatment (carbons ∼ 1000°C, graphites ∼ 2500°C) rather than the degree of crystallinity. It is possible to have carbons in which the main constituent is natural graphite, and conversely to have grades designated as graphite when the crystal structure is very poorly developed.

In keeping with the subject of the book the emphasis of this chapter is on the applications of graphite, but application of carbons are also discussed. This is necessary since for many applications it is impossible to draw a dividing line between carbon and graphite. In some cases, slight changes in operating conditions necessitate the change from one material to the other; in others the preference for one is associated with process economics rather than technical excellence.

For convenience this chapter has been sub-divided into metallurgical, thermal, chemical and miscellaneous applications. Nuclear and electrical brush applications are covered in other chapters. The sub-division is arbitrary but it does make possible the grouping together of applications requiring common characteristics of the material.

A. HISTORICAL BACKGROUND

From the earliest times carbon in the form of wood, wood charcoal and coal has been used as a fuel. Subsequently, charcoal in particular was used as a reducing agent in the manufacture of metals. However, the uses of manufactured carbon and graphite outside these fields did not really begin until the discovery of the voltaic pile and current electricity at the end of the 18th century. From that time the development of applications for carbon and graphite have to a great extent been tied to the development of electrical processes.

One of the earliest applications of manufactured carbon was for arc lamp electrodes. The arc lamp had been demonstrated before 1810 using charcoal electrodes but because of the deficiencies of the natural product, electrodes were developed using pressed and carbonized blocks of powdered charcoal mixed with coal tar. Because of the very limited supply of current electricity the arc lamp did not, at that time, become a commercially important application of manufactured carbon. The alternative method of electrical illumination, the incandescent lamp using a carbonized cellulose filament, did not appear until 1852.

Among the first carbon developments to reach commercial prominence in about 1830 were electrodes for primary batteries, where carbon replaced the copper of the original voltaic cell. These electrodes were made from powdered charcoal or coke bonded with sugar syrup or coal tar, pressed and carbonized.

Even before 1840, the use of electrolytic and electrothermal effects for various chemical and metallurgical processes had been closely investigated, but the absence of any large-scale source of electrical energy precluded further development. It was not until 1870, after the development of the self-excited electric dynamo, that successful attempts were made to utilize the electric arc with carbon electrodes for the bulk melting of metals and for the manufacture of some new materials, such as silicon and calcium carbides. At about this time furnaces were developed in which carbon electrodes were used both to heat the charge and to break it down into its constituent elements. Aluminium extraction is an example of this process. Similarly, electrolytic methods of producing chlorine, caustic soda and other chemicals were also developed.

The period from 1870 to the end of the century saw the birth of many new developments in the use of electrical energy, and a similar number of new applications for carbon. Soon after 1870 the telephone microphone, using the pressure sensitive contact resistance characteristics of carbon granules, was invented. In the subsequent decade the same pressure contact resistivity characteristics of carbon were exploited in carbon pile resistors for dynamo voltage regulation. At about the same time (1890) manufactured carbon and natural graphite were first used to replace copper gauze brushes conveying electric current to and from the rotating surfaces of dynamos and electric motors. The unique combination of self-lubrication, electrical conductivity and non-weldability of carbon and graphite had in this application a profound effect on the development of large and efficient machines.

At the end of the century, Acheson's discovery that artificial graphite could be made from amorphous carbon in an electric furnace was of the utmost importance to the carbon industry. Not only did this lessen the industry's dependence upon natural products, but it also made possible the development of a complete new range of artificial or electrographite materials. These did much to improve the efficiency of many of the processes discovered earlier in the century, and were the basis of many of the new applications of the 20th century.

The early part of this century saw a tremendous growth in the demand for carbon and graphite for the electrothermal and electrical industries for processes discovered previously. Additionally, there were logical developments from some of the existing applications. Current collection from rotating electrical machines was followed by current collection from overhead cables, for example railways and tramways. The carbon arc was brought to a high state of development and played a fundamental part in the growth of the cinema industry. Additionally, the carbon arc was harnessed for welding and cutting metal.

By 1930 the excellent chemical resistance of carbon and graphite had been appreciated, and there was a considerable growth of chemical applications including tank linings and heat exchangers. At about the same time the combination of chemical resistance and self-lubricating properties of carbon and graphite led to the development of mechanical applications of carbon, such as seals, bearings of all types, vanes, gland packings and piston rings.

TABLE I

Annual World Consumption of Carbon and Graphite

Product	Product produced (tons)	Carbon used (tons)	Carbon used (lb/ton)
Carbon			
Aluminium (1962)	6,041,000	3,600,000	1344
Calcium carbide (1963)	5,000,000	110,000	50
Electric ferro alloys (1963)	3,200,000	70,000	50
Blast furnace and chemical carbon bricks (1965)	—	100,000	—
Phosphorus (1964)	800,000	18,000	50
Graphite			
Electric steel (1963)	44,500,000	218,000	11
Chlorine	11,730,000 ⎫	36,700	3
Caustic soda	12,800,000 ⎭		
Magnesium	109,000	10,900	225
Sodium chlorate	500,000	7000	30
Sodium	100,000	900	20
Nuclear graphite	—	9000	—
Carbon and graphite specials			
Electrical	—	40,000	—
Mechanical	—	20,000	—
Chemical	—	10,000	—

Carbon alone	3,898,000 tons
Graphite alone	282,500 tons
Specials	70,000 tons
Total:	4,250,500 tons

The first sustained nuclear chain reaction in 1940 led to a very important new application for graphite. The military and industrial importance of this application, together with the use of graphite nozzles or chokes for solid propellant rocket motors has resulted in the development of many new forms of carbon and graphite, and a much greater understanding of the older forms.

B. WORLD CONSUMPTION OF CARBON AND GRAPHITE

As stated in the previous section, the history of carbon and graphite has been closely associated with the development of electrical power and processes. This pattern still exists today, and the bulk of the demand for the materials, both in terms of tonnage and sales value, is for the electro-chemical and electrothermal industries. However, one must not under-estimate the value to industry of the small tonnage for electrical production predominately brush, mechanical and chemical carbon and graphite. Table I (Smith) shows the annual world consumption in about 1963/64, and this demand is growing at a rate of about 5% compound per annum.

The bulk of the demand is at present in the highly industrialized countries of the world. These countries have both the demand for the products pro-duced and the electrical power available with which to make them. The demand for the less advanced nations can be expected to grow at a rate considerably greater than the average 5% especially where cheap electric power is available.

II. METALLURGICAL APPLICATIONS

A. GENERAL

From the world consumption figures given in Table I it can be seen that metal extraction processes are by far the largest uses to which carbons and graphites are put. Carbon and graphite are chosen for these applications because of their electrical conductivity, ability to withstand high temperatures and thermal shock, and the fact that they are non-wetting and non-reactive towards molten metals and salts. Much the same characteristics are required for the smaller market of casting moulds and hot pressing dies and tools. The relative cheapness and versatility of carbon and graphite ensure that it is used even when its performance may be surpassed by other more expen-sive materials.

The general criteria for selecting a graphite for metallurgical applications are listed below.

1. *Variation of Mechanical and Physical Properties with Temperature*

Graphite is used over the temperature range 300–3000°C. At the higher end of the range care must be exercised in selecting the correct grade, and it is important to consider the system as a whole under these extreme conditions. At high temperatures the thermal conductivity of carbon falls away, and the thermal expansion and the specific heat increase. Contact angles and wetting behaviour of liquid systems at high temperatures cannot be estimated from low temperature data.

2. *Susceptibility to Oxidation*

Above 800°C the rate of oxidation is controlled by diffusion of reactant gases across a stagnant film at the surface of the graphite. The corrosion rate is therefore dependent on the gas flow across the surface of the material. At very high temperatures the oxidation rate of graphite is comparable to that of tungsten and molybdenum (Gulbransen, 1963).

For normal atmosphere use the life of graphite is necessarily short. This can usually be accepted in return for the particular advantages offered. The life may be extended by the application of a suitable surface coating, for example, sprayed with zirconia.

3. *Contact Behaviour*

Table II lists the accepted contact angles for a number of metals under various conditions. Most liquid metals have contact angles greater than 90°. This arises because of the high surface tension of the liquid. It can be seen from Table II that metals unreactive towards graphite do not wet, but those which readily form carbides do. Similarly, molten oxides do not wet. Once

TABLE II

Contact Angles on Graphite

Liquid	Atmosphere	Temp (°C)	Contact angle
Mercury	air	20	164
Silver	vacuum	1200	163
Copper	hydrogen	1100	150
Nickel	hydrogen	1500	68
Iron	hydrogen	1550	37
Silicon	vacuum	1900	15
Zirconium	vacuum	1450	0
Na_2O—$SiO_2(1:2)$	N_2	1000	125
PbO—$B_2O_3(1:1)$	N_2	650	75
CaO—Al_2O_3—$SiO_2(2:1:2)$	N_2	1330	160
CaO—Al_2O_3—$SiO_2(2:1:2)$	N_2	1455	30

again exceptions are found when the possibility of interfacial reactions exist, for example silica/graphite. Similar considerations will apply to halides, borides, silicides, and so on.

Non-wetting can be a very important advantage as it means that the container need not be as pure as the metal being processed, and it need not be free from porosity.

Nearly all commercial carbons and graphites are porous. It may therefore be necessary to choose a graphite having the correct porosity to prevent the liquid metal from permeating through the walls of a container. The pore entry diameters through which liquids will not permeate is given by the relationship:

$$d = \frac{4\sigma \cos \theta}{P}$$

where d is the diameter, σ the surface tension of the liquid, θ the contact angle of the system and P is the applied pressure. Pore size distribution curves are shown in Fig. 1 for four commercial graphites.

For most of the applications considered here the applied pressure is usually no more than that produced by the hydrostatic head of the liquid. However, it is possible for liquids to flood the pores of a graphite such as EY1, and yet this graphite might have ideal thermal properties. A compromise is necessary therefore.

If the additional cost is justified it is possible to make a graphite virtually impermeable by the deposition of carbon in the pores. This also has the advantage of upgrading the thermal properties.

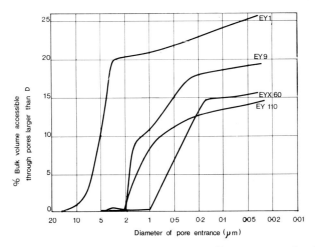

Fig. 1. Cumulative pore volume against pore entry diameter curves for four typical commercial graphites.

4. *Thermal Shock Resistance*

This property is related to the modulus of elasticity and the coefficient of thermal expansion of the graphite. Convenient expressions have been developed which allow a quantitative prediction of thermal shock behaviour. Turner (1958) showed that the product of the modulus of elasticity (E) and the coefficient of thermal expansion (α), both measured for radial orientation, should be as low as possible if the body is to have a good resistance to thermal stresses. Values of this parameter are listed in Table III.

TABLE III

Thermal Stress Resistance of Typical Carbons and Graphites in Terms of the Turner Parameter (αE)†

Grade	Constitution	Texture	αE
EY110	Extruded graphite	Close fine grain	1·57
EY4	Extruded graphite	Medium	1·57
EY9	Extruded graphite	Close fine grain	1·71
EY1	Extruded graphite	Open coarse grain	1·89
EY9106	Press-formed graphite	Medium	2·00
EY106	Extruded graphite	Open coarse grain	2·05
CY9	Extruded carbon	Close fine grain	2·73
CY10	Press-formed carbon	Medium	3·31
CY9106	Press-formed carbon	Medium	4·25

† The lower the value of αE, the better the resistance to thermal stress.

Gangler (1950) had previously shown that the parameter $ks/\alpha E$, where (k) is the thermal conductivity and s is the tensile strength, gave a measure of the thermal and mechanical shock resistance for brittle ceramic materials. Typical values for carbon and graphite are given in Table IV.

5. *Creep Under Load*

This property is not important for graphite below 2000°C, but for carbons the temperature at which non-recovery of deformation sets in is approximately 1200°C.

6. *Dimensional Stability because of Low Thermal Expansion*

The overall expansion of a commercial graphite tends to be low, because the expansion of the crystallites is absorbed in the porosity. This is a very useful effect which can be put to advantage when the graphite is being used for resistor and radio frequency heater-susceptor applications.

TABLE IV

The Shock Resistance of Typical Carbons, Graphites in Terms of the Gangler Parameter $(ks/\alpha E)$†

Grade	Constitution	Texture	$\dfrac{ks\ddagger}{\alpha E}$
EYX244	Extruded graphite, upgraded EY110	Close fine grain	205
EY1	Extruded graphite	Open coarse grain	171
EY110	Extruded graphite	Close fine grain	163
EY106	Extruded graphite	Open coarse grain	136
EY9106	Press-formed graphite	Medium	133
EY4	Extruded graphite	Medium	130
EY9	Extruded graphite	Close fine grain	73
CY9	Extruded carbon	Close fine grain	49

† The larger the value of $ks/\alpha E$, the better the resistance to thermal/mechanical shock.
‡ Arbitrary units.

B. ELECTRODES FOR ALUMINIUM, MAGNESIUM AND SODIUM PRODUCTION

The above metals are produced by the electrolysis of fused salts, and all employ carbon or graphite electrodes in their production.

In terms of tonnage of metal produced, and carbon used, the most important is aluminium production. The starting material is hydrated aluminium oxide in the form of bauxite. The process for the production of aluminium metal consists of electrolysing at 960°C alumina dissolved in molten cryolite (Na_3AlF_6). The liberated metal, having a density of 2·4 g/cm³, collects at the bottom of the cell below the electrolyte of density 2·1. Oxygen is also liberated and this reacts with the carbon anode. Aluminium production cells are generally very large and operate at direct currents of up to 150,000 amp at 4·5 V. The rectangular cells are made of steel, lined with refractory insulating brick with an inner lining of baked carbon or electrographite. This carbon lining serves as both the cathode and as a protection for the refractory brick against the corrosive effects of the molten electrolyte. The cell anodes are of either prebaked carbon, typically 90 × 40 cm cross-section × 50 cm high, or the much larger baked *in situ* Söderberg anodes. The Söderberg anodes are made from a paste of calcined anthracite and petroleum coke with a pitch binder and are baked by the heat from the cell. The anodes are not attacked by the molten electrolyte or the metal, but are consumed at a considerable rate by the oxygen liberated in the cell. Although the efficiency of the cell is high, about 95%, some 60% of the power supplied to the cell is dissipated as Joule heat to maintain the cell at temperature.

Because of the acceptance of, and indeed need for, high Joule losses to maintain the temperature, and the rapid consumption of carbon by oxygen produced during electrolysis, cheap carbon anodes are quite satisfactory and there is no incentive to go to the much more expensive graphite electrodes with their higher electrical conductivity. Graphite electrodes are used, however, in the refining of the 99·6–99·8% purity aluminium produced in the electrolytic cell. This process employs an electrolyte of molten aluminium fluoride, sodium fluoride and barium chloride with an anode layer of molten impure aluminium-copper alloy. The pure aluminium collects at the top of the cell. The cathode in this case is graphite, and the anode is baked carbon. Since little oxygen is liberated in this process, consumption of the graphite cathode is slight. Graphite is preferred to carbon mainly on the grounds of purity, since impurities in a baked carbon anode could easily contaminate the pure metal produced.

In principle the electrolytic method of manufacturing magnesium is very similar to that for aluminium, but there are important practical differences which explain why graphite and not carbon cathodes are used. The electrolyte is a molten mixture of magnesium, calcium and sodium chlorides at 700–750°C. The electrolysis is carried out in a gas-heated cell with the cell acting as the anode. Graphite cathodes, typically 8 in diam × 9 ft long pass through a refractory brick cover and dip into the electrolyte. The 99·9% pure magnesium liberated rises to the top of the cell where it is collected. The chlorine produced is taken away from the cell and used to generate fresh magnesium chloride from magnesium hydroxide precipitated from sea water. In this process no oxygen is liberated to attack the cathode, nor is there any need for a highly resistive cathode for Joule heating of the cell. High purity graphite is therefore preferred to the less pure baked carbon.

For sodium manufacture the electrolyte used is sodium chloride with calcium chloride to reduce the melting point to a practical level. In this case graphite anodes and a steel cathode are used. As in other electrolytic processes described the metal produced rises to the top of the cell and is

TABLE V

Typical Room Temperature Properties of Commercial Carbon and Graphite

	Bulk density (g/cm^3)	Resistivity (ohm cm)	Thermal conductivity $(W/cm\ °C)$	Breaking strength (psi)
Carbon–petroleum coke base	1·55	$6·5 \times 10^{-4}$	0·07	3000
Electrographite–petroleum coke base	1·60	$1·5 \times 10^{-4}$	1·2	2000

collected. The attractions of graphite are its conductivity, temperature stability and its resistance to the very corrosive molten sodium chloride and chlorine gas.

Typical room temperature properties of carbon and graphite electrode materials are given in Table V.

C. ELECTRIC STEEL FURNACE ELECTRODES

After the aluminium industry the second largest user of manufactured carbon and graphite is the steel industry. Here the main demand is for graphite electrodes for three-phase arc furnaces. The use of these furnaces for the production of high quality plain and alloy steels has increased considerably in recent years and now accounts for something like 14% of the world steel production.

The arc furnace process of making steel is basically very simple. It merely employs an electric arc to generate sufficient heat to melt the furnace charge of scrap iron, or blast furnace iron, together with slag forming ingredients and alloying addition elements. An additional effect of the current flow in the arc is the generation of powerful magnetic fields which cause very effective stirring of the melt.

Two forms of arc furnaces are used, the three-phase open arc using graphite electrodes, and the submerged arc furnace often using baked carbon electrodes. With both of these furnace types the steel furnace casing and refractory brick lining are at earth potential and do not carry any current. This makes it possible for a basic or acidic lining to be used as appropriate for the feedstock.

With the submerged arc furnaces three electrodes are used and the arcing takes place below the top of the melt. This is the main source of the heat, but there is some Joule heat supplied by the passage of current through the electrodes. It is for this reason that fairly high resistivity carbon electrodes are acceptable. These electrodes are usually of the prebaked type and vary in size from about 8 in to 60 in diameter but can be up to 100 in in diameter.

With open arc furnaces all the heat required is generated by the three phase arc between graphite electrodes. These electrodes vary in size from a few inches to 45 in diameter and up to 110 in long. Because of the much lower resistivity of the graphite electrodes compared with carbon (1 : 4) they can be operated at a correspondingly higher current density with resultant savings in electrode size. Graphite electrodes have the added advantage of better thermal shock resistance and lower Joule losses outside the furnace. Electrode consumption is small and mainly results from oxidation due to air diffusing into the furnace and to evaporation in the arc.

D. BLAST FURNACE LININGS

The very good resistance of carbon to the corrosive effect of molten metals and fused salts is used to advantage in hearth linings for blast furnaces. The use of carbon blocks in place of ceramic refractories in the lower parts of the furnace, up to the tuyeres or air inlets, greatly increases the furnace life and reduces the chance of dangerous breakouts of iron or slag. The low density of carbon compared with iron introduces problems as the hearth lining tends to float out of place, but this has been overcome by suitable design of interlocking bricks.

E. CASTING MOULDS

Graphite is used in the metallurgical industry for various types of casting processes. These may be conveniently divided into static and dynamic methods.

1. *Static Methods*

The simplest static method is sand casting. Graphite is frequently used as inserts which act as "chills" to even out the temperature gradients across thick sections of the casting. Graphite is not generally used as the mould for simple gravity casting of this type for economic reasons—a life of some 75–100 shots would be required before it became profitable. Recently lives of 150 shots have been achieved in the U.S.A. and these may be extended by spraying the outside with zirconia and the inside with colloidal graphite. Additional incentives to change are associated with the health hazards of sand. Work in the U.K. is currently proceeding on the manufacture of high precision (± 0.0005 in/in) moulds made from a mixture of graphite powder and resin which is first warm pressed to shape and then gas cracked to give strength and imperviousness (see Ministry of Technology report, 1967). The main advantage of this type of system is that the physical properties of the mould can be altered by changing the constituents. Figure 2 shows the degree of detail which can be obtained in castings made from either glass, metal or plastic.

A low-pressure casting technique has been used in the U.S.A. for casting railway wagon wheels. In this case the entire mould is constructed from graphite at least 40 in diameter and 20 in thick.

A slightly more complex type of casting is that known as centrifugal casting. Here, the mould is rotated and the metal is spun out against the wall where it solidifies. In the U.K. graphite is extensively used for all parts of the mould. Owing to the ease of machining of graphite, complex patterns are readily produced on the outside of the casting.

Fig. 2. Medal cast in glass from a carbon mould at Royal Aircraft Establishment. Similar medals have been cast in nimonic and plastic. All reproduce the fine detail of the original. Crown copyright. (Reproduced by permission of Her Majesty's Stationery Office.)

2. *Continuous Casting*

Continuous casting replaces the conventional batch process of the production of rods and tubes for which it is claimed that 45% of the metal is unusable. This arises from the need to machine away surface flaws. In order to produce a sound surface to the casting a number of requirements have to be met by the material of the mould and the die. These are listed in Table VI from which it can be seen that graphite is an ideal material for this application.

F. CARBON FOR HOT PRESSING

For materials with melting point above 1800°C, conventional melting and casting techniques are not suitable for producing high density shapes. Refractory metals and carbides may be compacted as powders and sintered to a high density, but this involves complex heating schedules and the final body usually requires machining.

Hot pressing provides an economical method of forming, heat treating and sizing in one operation. High densities are obtained in shorter time and at lower temperatures than by cold compaction and sintering. An added advantage is that grain growth and phase transformation can be closely

TABLE VI

Specification of Material used for Mould and Die in Continuous Casting and the Suitability of Graphite for this Application

Characteristics	Requirements	Graphite suitability
1. Thermal stability	To maintain shape and configuration at elevated temperatures	Highest temperature stable material known
2. Chemical inertness	To avoid interfacial reaction and contamination of the liquid metal	Does not form carbides with non-ferrous metals at casting temperatures
3. Non-wetting	To avoid "welding" or sticking to the chilling metal	Contact angle of most metal–graphite systems is greater than 90°
4. Thermal shock	To resist rupture as a result of sharp thermal gradients across the die wall	Resistance is in excess of 1500°C/cm wall thickness
5. Thermal conductivity	To permit rapid heat transfer for controlled chilling	Heat transfer rates equivalent to those of metals
6. Frictional properties	To promote free "sliding" in order to avoid rupture of hot short metal and solidus surface	Very low interfacial friction with metals
7. Machinability	To permit economical forming and fine finish	Cuts easily, may be formed or finished to a mirror finish

controlled. Carbon and graphite have the hot strength required for this application. In a non-oxidizing atmosphere at 2000°C the strength may be 50% greater than at room temperature (Malström *et al.*, 1951). All the properties set out at the beginning of this section are extremely important for this type of application.

The pressures used for densification are usually low, and do not normally exceed 4 tons/in². A low pressure is normally used during warm up and the full load only applied when the final temperature is reached. For fuller details the reader is referred to Ford and Campbell (1964).

1. *Ceramics*

At the moment the use of carbon moulds is of limited application and is only suitable for small one-off jobs. Nevertheless, a wide range of borides, carbides, nitrides and oxides have been pressed to near theoretical density without the use of a binder. The interest in this field is such that the hot extrusion of ceramics will probably be developed in the near future.

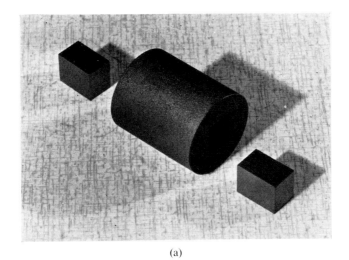

(a)

(b)

FIG. 3. (a) Mould set for producing grinding wheel dressing sticks; Link EY9 is used for the plungers and Link EY1 for the body. (b) Diamond drill core mould. The body is used several times, but the bushing and centre pin are used once only. The body is made from Link EY9 and the bushing and centre pin from Link EY1. (Reproduced by courtesy of J. K. Smit & Sons (Diamond) Tools Ltd.)

2. Diamond Impregnated Tools

The manufacture of rock drills, lapping wheel facings and grinding wheel dressing tools represents the largest single use of hot pressing using graphite mould sets. The mould has a machined cavity, into the walls of which small dimples are cut to hold the diamonds. Alternatively a mixture of diamonds and embedding medium may be used depending on the effect required. Figure 3 shows typical mould sets for this application.

III. CHEMICAL APPLICATIONS

A. GENERAL

Commercial graphites are frequently considered to be chemically inert. This is not strictly true, and there are four basic limitations to their use. These are:

(a) gaseous oxidation,
(b) interstitial formation,
(c) oxidation in solution, and
(d) carbide formation.

1. Gaseous Oxidation

The oxidation rate of pure graphite is remarkably low. Some grades of commercial graphite will not burn on open coal fires. Other graphites are more reactive because of a larger surface area and a higher impurity level. The details of the oxidation mechanism is dealt with in Chapter IV. Here we only discuss those aspects which are relevant to commercial applications.

The effect of purity and surface area on oxidation rates have been extensively studied; Hering *et al.* 1960 have shown that oxidation rates are proportional to the impurity content, and Laine *et al.* 1963 have indicated that the BET surface area is not strictly relevant and that the area available for oxygen sorption gives a better correlation with reaction rates. In Table VII some typical values are given for the oxidation rate of commercial grades used for the manufacture of transistor jigs. The importance of purity is readily seen.

The rate of oxidation may be reduced by the addition of certain borates and phosphates. The mechanism by which these work is not clear. With phosphates it is important to have a low ratio of metal oxide to phosphorous pentoxide (Earp and Hill 1958). Optimum results have been observed with a ratio of 1 : 2 when the rate was reduced to one tenth of its original value. Only trace quantities are required and the phosphate is presumably adsorbed

TABLE VII

Oxidation Characteristics of Transistor Jig Grades

	Grade	Oxidation rate (%/hr at 500°C)	Surface area (B.E.T.) (m²/g)	Purity (% carbon)
	Electrode grade	0·21	0·42	99·5
EY9106	Special coke-based graphite	0·09	0·26	99·9
EYC9106	Special coke-based graphite purified	0·006	0·25	99·99
TY14	Special coke-based graphite densified	0·05	0·23	99·9
TYC14	Special coke-based graphite densified and purified	0·002	0·22	99·99

on reactive sites. In the case of borates it has been shown by Thomas and Roscoe (1965) that when single crystals of natural graphite are oxidized in the presence of boric acid, the etch pit always appears below a boric oxide droplet. The droplets ultimately fall into their own etch pit. This would seem to indicate that oxidation is controlled by the rate of diffusion of gas through the liquid boric oxide, but the mechanism is not understood.

An alternative method of protection is to coat the graphite with a refractory coating. This technique has been extensively used to provide oxidation resistant and ablation resistant materials for space applications. The coating may be applied in a number of ways. Silicon carbide coatings have been produced by the deposition of silicon onto a hot graphite substrate by thermal cracking of trichlorosilane† followed by heat treatment of 2000°C to give a chemically bonded layer of silicon carbide. Alternatively a refractory metal like zirconium can be flame sprayed onto the surface and suitably heat treated to give the carbide.

2. *Interstitial Formation*

The weak bonding in the direction perpendicular to the basal planes make graphite very susceptible to chemical attack by intercalation. Spontaneous lamellar compounds are formed whenever certain elements, metal halides, sulphides and some oxides, either come directly into contact with graphite or are heated with it. They are normally made directly from the vapour, but Hennig (1959) quotes the examples of the intercalation of

† International Rectifier Corporation. French Patent 1,388,539, February 5th, 1965.

potassium from a sodium/potassium solution, and bromine from a solution
in carbon tetrachloride. Figure 4 shows the corrosive effect of aluminium
chloride ($AlCl_3$) on graphite. The tube, originally the shape shown, was
used to bubble chlorine gas into molten aluminium. The graphite bromine

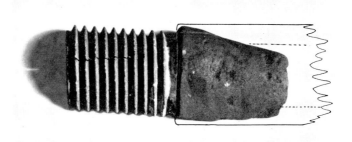

FIG. 4. Corrosion of graphite by aluminium chloride. Test sample screwed to end of
normal chlorine inlet tube. Original shape is indicated.

system has been well characterized because of the similarity of the system
to neutron irradiation damage. The reaction results in a considerable increase
in the lattice in the c-axis direction and only slight changes in the a-axis
dimension. Heat treatment of graphite–bromine compounds results in
explosive exfoliation.

3. Oxidation in Solution

There are two types of oxidation in solution, (a) the almost spontaneous
oxidation by strong oxidizing agents, and (b) anodic oxidation.

(a) *Spontaneous oxidation.* The best known example of this is the formation
of graphitic acid. This is an interlamellar compound of graphite and oxygen
formed by the oxidation of graphite with potassium perchlorate in a mixture
of concentrated nitric and sulphuric acids.

Certain strong acids will react with graphite to form salts, provided that
the graphite is oxidized by these acids. Examples of this are to be found
with nitric, phosphoric, arsenic, selenic, perchloric and sulphuric. Sulphuric
acid reacts to give the well-known bisulphate

$$C + H_2SO_4 \rightarrow C_{24}^+(HSO_4)^- \cdot 2H_2O.$$

Sometimes the reaction proceeds as far as carbon dioxide, and a mixture
of silver dichromate and concentrated sulphuric acid will oxidize graphite
quantitatively to carbon dioxide. This has recently been developed into an
analytical tool for distinguishing between carbon and graphite (Oberlin and
Mering 1964). The more graphitic a material is the more it will intercalate,

and in this particular medium the more readily it will oxidize to carbon dioxide. The reaction is strictly first order and the rate constant for a typical artificial graphite is 1000 times greater than that for a coke heat-treated to 1000°C.

This very large difference between the rates of reaction of graphite and coke suggests an obvious method of protection for certain applications. Figure 5 shows two samples of the same artificial graphite after treatment in

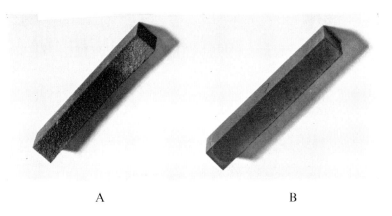

A   B

FIG. 5. Effect of protective carbon coating on corrosion of graphite in silver chromate/ sulphuric acid at 70°C.

silver dichromate/sulphuric acid reagent at 70°C. The surface of sample B was protected by a deposit of pyrolytic carbon, and sample A was untreated. The protected graphite was in contact with the reagent for 60 minutes and no weight loss was observed. The unprotected sample lost 35% of its weight in 2 minutes.

The normal method of protecting graphite against oxidation in liquids is to reduce the porosity by resin impregnation. Figure 6 shows the advantage of a pyrolytic carbon coating over the more traditional protectives.

(b) *Anodic Oxidation.* The anodic oxidation of graphite takes place by the formation of interlammellar compounds of oxyacids according to the scheme:

$$C_n + HA \rightarrow C_n^+ A^- + H^+ + e.$$

Ubbelohde (1964) lists the following acids which have been intercalated during anodic oxidation: H_2SO_4, $ClSO_3H$, FSO_3H, H_2SeO_4, HNO_3, $BF_3(CH_3COOH)_2$, CF_3COOH, H_3PO_4 and H_3AsO_4. He points out that salts of graphite with these acids are probably readily hydrolysed. The initial oxidation and the various side reactions cause the graphite to swell and disrupt. Figure 7 shows a practical example of the corrosion of an anode under conditions of liquid oxidation.

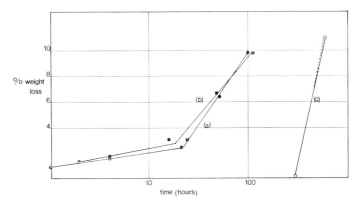

Fig. 6. The effect of impregnation on the oxidation of carbon in nitric acid at 80°C. (a) Natural resin, (b) phenol-formaldehyde, (c) deposit of pyrolytic carbon. Base material: Morganite CY1.

Fig. 7. Anodic corrosion in oxidizing electrolyte.

In principle, it should be possible to protect the graphite anode with a coating of pyrolytic carbon. However, because of the oxidation by hydroxyl radicals or oxygen atoms the problem becomes one of mixed liquid and gaseous oxidation, and complete protection cannot be achieved in practice.

4. Carbide Formation

Graphite will react with a wide range of metals and metal oxides to give carbides (Nightingale 1962). The temperature at which the reaction can be seen to have taken place is normally in excess of 500°C and frequently greater than 1000°C. In the context of this chapter the formation of carbides is mainly important for metallurgical applications of graphite.

B. ELECTRODES FOR CHLORINE CELLS

Chlorine and sodium hydroxide are amongst the most important tonnage chemicals that are manufactured. They are made by the electrolysis of concentrated aqueous brine in either a diaphragm or a mercury cell (Mellor 1956, p. 272 et seq.). In both cases graphite is used as the anode. Chlorine is liberated at the anode and apart from differences in current density which may arise from cell design, the process is the same in both types of cell. In general a 25% aqueous solution of sodium chloride is electrolysed. The reactions which may take place at the anode are:

$$2Cl^- \rightarrow Cl_2 + 2e \tag{1}$$

$$4OH^- \rightarrow 2H_2O + O_2 + 4e \tag{2}$$

$$C + 4OH^- \rightarrow 2H_2O + CO_2 + 4e \tag{3}$$

The quantity of oxygen and carbon dioxide liberated may be as high as 1% of the total gas evolved. This is important as it may represent the main source of graphite corrosion.

The pH in the cell is normally about 4, and the discharge potential of the OH^- ion may be anything between $+1.2$ and $+2.6$ V depending on the overpotential at the anode. This should be compared with the discharge potential of the chlorine ion, $+1.3$ to $+1.4$ V. Therefore, given the right anode, the hydroxyl ion could well discharge preferentially; indeed, theoretically it should. The success of graphite as an anode material depends primarily on the high overpotential for the discharge of hydroxyl ions.

The reversible potential of reaction (3) above, has been calculated to be -0.029 V at pH $= 4$ (Mellor 1956, p. 282). For carbon dioxide to discharge to the extent of only 1% would imply an overpotential of at least 1.3 V. Carbon dioxide probably arises from reaction with oxygen atoms, a process which in the gaseous phase has a very low activation energy and which proceeds at 20°C (Marsh et al. 1965).

It is possible for chlorate ions to be formed in the cell by the following series of reactions:

$$Cl_2 + H_2O \rightarrow H^+ + Cl^- + HOCl$$

$$HOCl \rightarrow H^+ + ClO^-$$

$$Cl_2 + 2OH^- \rightarrow Cl^- + ClO^- + H_2O$$

$$6ClO^- + 3H_2O \rightarrow 2ClO_3^- + 4Cl^- + 6H^+ + 1.5O_2 + 6e.$$

It has been calculated (Mellor 1956, p. 282–285) from the known equilibrium data that the concentration of chlorate ions is low. Nevertheless, the existence of ClO_3^- suggests the possibility of intercalation followed by hydrolysis by OH^- as a contributory process in anode wear.

Graphite has three main advantages over other possible anode materials; price, relative corrosion rate and high overpotential for the discharge of hydroxide ions.

The disadvantages are the slight overpotential for the discharge of Cl^- resulting in a loss of current efficiency, and the fact that the corrosion is

278 A. R. FORD AND E. GREENHALGH

still a serious problem. The latter is normally about 10 lb per ton of chlorine. The graphite anode is being seriously tested by the increasing current densities now being used.

It is claimed that impregnation of the graphite anode reduces the corrosion rate. The principle is to coat the whole of the internal surface and limit the reaction to the outer geometrical surface. In principle this should cut down the wear rate by at least a factor of 100, but set against this is an increase in current density at the external surface, and in addition it is doubtful whether the inner surface is important because of diffusion of reactants and products into and out of the pores.

Linseed oil is the most common impregnant. The complete filling of the pore structure is aimed for. Blocking only the pore entrance is considered insufficient.

C. CHEMICAL-RESISTANT GRAPHITE

The main disadvantages of graphite for chemical applications were discussed at the beginning to this section. Nevertheless, graphite is generally extremely resistant to chemical attack, and this, combined with its high thermal conductivity and resistance to thermal shock, makes it eminently suitable for numerous chemical engineering applications.

Graphites for chemical applications tend to be divided into two classes. First, there is the fine grained close textured graphite which is used for the precision machining of small components such as tiles and segments for the lining of small reactors and pickling tanks, immersion and steam injector heaters, steam ejector components, filter plates and anodes for electro-chemical processes. Secondly, there is the large grained, open texture graphite normally used for applications such as heat exchangers, condensers, cascade coolers, climbing film evaporators, calandrias and large reaction vessels.

The conventional method of fabricating plant in graphite is to machine the components, and then screw or cement them together. In order to contain the chemicals the graphite is normally impregnated with resin to render it impervious. The main disadvantage of this method lies with the chemical resistance of the cement, which is generally more chemically and thermally reactive than the graphite. A further disadvantage is that the cements need to be elastic to stand up to the strains put on the system; they frequently become inelastic as a result of chemical and thermal attack, and then they fail. Carbonaceous cements have recently been introduced and these are more satisfactory from all points of view.

An alternative method of fabricating graphite plant is known as the "Polybloc System" (Hilliard 1957). The basis of this method is the realization that in order fully to exploit the properties of graphite a constructional system must be used which is designed for a weak anisotropic material. As the name implies, blocks of graphite are held together under compression to avoid tensile stresses. The blocks are machined to incorporate their own O-ring sealing ring. If the system is to be used as a heat exchanger, the passages for the fluid are drilled in the appropriate direction to take advantage of the conductivity anisotropy. A typical heat exchange unit is shown in Fig. 8.

The "Polybloc System" appears to be gaining favour and two new applications have recently been described (Hilliard 1965). Both are attempts to incorporate the heat exchanger for which the system was first designed with a particular chemical reaction in which heat is liberated. For example, an integral unit has been produced in which hydrogen and chlorine are burned in the top half, and the hydrogen chloride gas passes into a "Polybloc" unit inside of which it is absorbed in the appropriate liquid. The heat of solution is conducted away to a water cooling jacket.

As already implied, a major use of graphite is in the construction of heat exchangers. Figure 9 shows a typical heat exchanger made from extruded graphite tube. Structures designed in this way need careful treatment and must not be load bearing.

Steam ejectors are simply industrial versions of the laboratory water pump. They are used extensively in the food and chemical industry for such processes as evaporation, condensation, filtration, liquid transfer, and so on. This application is mentioned since carbons and graphites have superseded stainless steel because of their ability to stand up to the corrosive conditions. Steam injectors are similar but are used for heating corrosive liquids with steam. In the case of acidic pickling baths, this is now being done by indirect heating using the "Polybloc" system because of the subsidiary problem of water pollution.

The technique of submerged combustion has been applied to the direct heating of acid pickling baths (Anon 1966). A gas burner is placed directly in the liquid to be heated. A relatively small heater is required since it is claimed that the system is 250 times more efficient than with the conventional heat exchanger. This is achieved by the high surface area of the hot gas bubbles (70,000 ft^2 from 1 ft^3 of hot gases). The burner tubes are made from electrographite and a life of several years is claimed. An additional advantage of this technique is the turbulence in the liquid due to the gas bubbles. This causes the scale to loosen and reduce pickling times by about 25%.

It has already been mentioned that the graphite is normally impregnated with a resin to make it impervious. Table VIII lists typical resins that are used, and Table IX lists a few reagents and conditions in which graphite/resin

(a)

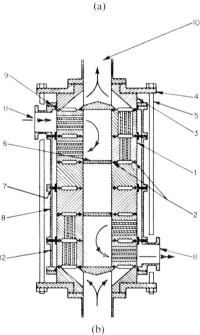

(b)

FIG. 8. (a) Typical heat-exchange constructed in the "Polybloc" system. (b) Flow diagram through polybloc heat exchanger. 1, Monolithic graphite heat exchange blocks; 2, annular gaskets; 3, graphite header block; 4, metal header plate; 5, spring-loaded tie-bars; 6, central baffle discs; 7, peripheral baffle rings; 8, outer shell elements; 9, sliding joint of outer shell; 10, inlet or outlet tube for axial fluid; 11, inlet or outlet tube for radial fluid; 12, outer shell element with inlet or outlet pipe. (Reproduced by courtesy of Le Carbone-Lorraine.)

FIG. 9. Heat-exchanger tube bundle made from extruded tubes.

TABLE VIII

General Classification of Resins Used for Impregnating Carbon and Graphite for Chemical Applications

Commonly used resins:

Description	Operating range (°C)	Stable	Unstable
Phenolic derivatives	0–280	Acids Organic solvents Alkalis up to 20%	
Modified phenolic derivatives	0–240	Acids Alkalis up to 40%	Organic solvents
Furane derivatives	0–170	Alkalis up to 90% Organic solvents Non-oxidizing acids	Oxidizing acids
Linseed oil	0–80	Caustic/chlorine processes Halogen and cyanide reactions	
Paraffin waxes	0–softening point of wax	Alternative to linseed oil	

systems survived for at least three months with a final weight loss of less than 1%.

TABLE IX

Reagents and Conditions in which the Graphite/Resin System Gave a Life of Three Months with a Weight Loss of Less than 1%

Reagent	Concentration	Temp (°C)	Resin
Acetic acid	Glacial	70	Furane derivative
Ammoniacal liquor	Conc.	90	Furane derivative
Chromic acid	3%	20/60	Furane derivative
Caustic potash	$35\frac{1}{2}\%$	90/100	Furane derivative or modified phenolic
Ethylene dichloride	100%	70	Furane derivative
Hydrochloric acid	Conc.	90	Furane derivative
Hydrofluoric acid	40%	90/100	Furane derivative
Methylated spirits	100%	70	Modified phenolic
Sulphuric acid	50%	80/90	Furane derivative

IV. THERMAL APPLICATIONS

A. WELDING CARBONS

Carbon and graphite are used in electric arc welding and cutting, and in resistance welding.

In arc welding, carbon or graphite electrodes can be used for joining most common metals, and are particularly suitable for those applications where it is desired to join two components without any special requirements of strength or ductility. The attraction of carbon electrodes lies in their low cost, compared with covered wire electrodes, for a given length of weld. Furthermore, the workpiece requires the very minimum of preparation before welding. As carbon is carried from the positive to the negative electrode the work must be made positive if excessive amounts of carbon are not to be introduced into the weld.

Carbon electrodes can be used for metal cutting and gouging. For this use very high current densities are required, and sometimes high pressure air jets are used to blast molten metal away from the point of melting.

Graphite covered tips are widely used in resistance welding. The absence of any welding of the graphite tip to the workpiece makes graphite an attractive material for this use.

B. GRAPHITE RESISTOR FURNACES

Under non-oxidizing conditions graphite is the highest temperature-stable solid known. More important from a practical point of view is that it is also far cheaper than any of its competitors. Its good thermal shock resistance coupled with the fact that its electrical resistivity is around 15×10^{-4} ohm cm means that it can be considered as a heating element for high current–low voltage supplies. In order to keep the currents used to acceptable levels, the graphite can be machined to give the highest possible resistance consistent with mechanical strength.

The simplest form of graphite heating element is a tube used in the horizontal direction. In this arrangement the hot zone of the furnace is produced by machining the tube to a thinner wall thickness to increase the resistance. In this way the hot zone can be located anywhere along the length of the tube. The tube is surrounded with carbon black which acts both as a thermal insulation and as a support for the tube. The element is also used as the hearth.

FIG. 10. Interior view of a 800 kW graphite furnace.

Extremely large and complex furnaces can be produced and Fig. 10 shows an interior view of a 800 kilowatt furnace. A furnace of this type has been used for the production of nuclear graphite. Smaller elements are shown in Fig. 11.

FIG. 11. Graphite furnace resistors (background) and thermal assembly jigs (foreground).

The main design features to be followed when designing elements are:

(1) Structures should be self supported and bending moments and tensile stresses should be avoided.
(2) The elements should be allowed to expand and contract freely.
(3) Stresses in the hot zone should be only those arising from the weight of the element.
(4) All graphite parts should be cut so that on assembly they have the same grain orientation. This is important in order to avoid stresses produced by thermal expansion.

Flexible heating elements can be produced from graphite textiles. Graphite cloth and string are readily produced by the controlled carbonization of the appropriate rayon article. Heating elements produced from materials have a low thermal mass thus enabling rapid heating and cooling cycles. Currently, uses are limited to laboratory applications, but it is possible that other uses will be found.

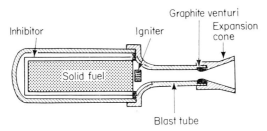

FIG. 12. Typical construction of a solid-fuel rocket motor.

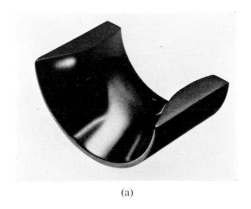

(a)

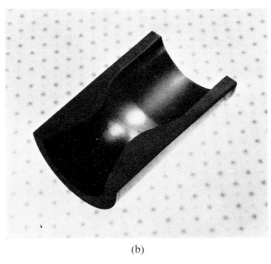

(b)

FIG. 13. Sections of rocket venturi made from graphite.

C. GRAPHITE IN ROCKET MOTORS

The most attractive materials for use in the manufacture of rocket nozzles are either tungsten or graphite. The advantage of graphite lies in the lower density.

A typical solid fuel rocket is outlined in Fig. 12 and sections of graphite nozzles are shown in Fig. 13. The burning of fuel gases in the combustion chamber are constrained by the throat of the nozzle and this causes the pressure to build up. The hot gases accelerate through the throat into the expansion chamber, the design of which is very critical. Erosion of the throat leads to a drop in working pressure and hence thrust.

The erosion rate depends largely on the type of graphite, but also on the nature of the propellant. Table X gives typical test conditions for a small rocket motor. Under these conditions an erosion rate of 0·025 mm/sec would be obtained with a good conventional graphite that had been impregnated with a carbon containing material to increase its strength. Erosion rates several times lower would have been obtained with a pyrographite nozzle.

TABLE X

Typical Test Conditions for Rocket Nozzle

Throat size	0·4 in
Mass flow	4 lb/in^2/sec
Burning time	20 sec
Propellant	Zero aluminium content
Chamber pressure	1600 psia
Chamber temperature	2500°C

There is an established demand for conventional graphite for booster-rocket nozzles in which the burning time is up to one minute and for which a reasonably high erosion rate can be tolerated. Graphite is the best compromise between performance and cost for this application.

D. GRAPHITE IN TRANSISTOR AND SEMICONDUCTOR APPLICATIONS

The growth in the transistor and general semiconductor industry over the last 10–15 years has provided a ready outlet for graphite. These devices are produced under stringent conditions of cleanliness, temperature control and precise positioning. All the properties previously encountered for other applications, together with the fact that graphite can readily be made spectroscopically pure, means that graphite is a natural choice for jigs and moulds.

The manufacture of semiconductors takes place in a number of steps. Here we deal only with those in which graphite is used.

1. *Purification*

In the case of germanium-based devices the commercially pure germanium dioxide is reduced in hydrogen at 650°C and melted at 1000°C in a graphite boat. The purity of the germanium dioxide is better than ten parts per million. However, since the germanium metal does not wet the graphite it is not always necessary that the graphite should be as pure. The germanium metal is then zone refined in a graphite boat.

2. *Single Crystal Growth*

The pure metal ingots are transferred into large single crystals by crystal pulling techniques. Graphite is used for the crucibles and for the radio-frequency susceptors.

3. *Assembly of the Junction*

In order to produce sharply delineated junctions it is essential that the components be located precisely. This is best achieved by locating them in graphite jigs. The ease of machining to close tolerances and an intricate shape make graphite suitable for these applications. Typical jigs are shown in Fig. 13. The jigs are heated and the components diffuse into each other either by liquid or solid state processes.

4. *Encapsulation*

Graphite can be used to produce the metal glass seals for the connector wires. The transistor is placed in a graphite jig with the attached wires passing through small holes. Powdered glass is poured into these holes and the jig is heated to sinter the glass and form a seal.

The disadvantages of graphite are that it wears with continual use and reacts chemically with silicon, a common ingredient in semiconductor devices. Hence, stainless steel jigs are often used, but these are usually mounted in graphite blocks to minimize distortion during heating.

V. MISCELLANEOUS

There are a very large number of technically important applications of carbon and graphite which have small demand and which have not been covered in this or other parts of the book. It is possible to mention only a few of them, and the selection has been made on the basis of characteristics not otherwise discussed.

Graphite is used as anodes in mercury arc rectifiers and in thermionic hard vacuum valves; typical components are shown in Fig. 14. Graphite has replaced metals for these applications because of unique range of properties. In valves of the type mentioned very high wattages are dissipated and the anodes are subjected to fluctuating loads and wide temperature changes. The low coefficient of expansion of graphite means that there are no changes in spacings inside the valve.

FIG. 14. A selection of mercury-arc rectifier components made from graphite.

In the operation of a mercury arc rectifier short circuits occur which cause currents of up to sixty times full load current to flow in the anode. Most metals would melt, but graphite remains relatively unaffected apart from some evaporation. The high radiation emissivity of graphite is also turned to advantage. The radiation emissivity of graphite is quoted as 94% of an ideal black body radiator at 700°C. A molybdenum anode would dissipate by radiation only one quarter of the heat at the same operating temperature. A further advantage is that lower operating temperatures can be used, thus giving a lower electron emission.

On the economic side the sheer size of some of the anodes precludes the use of the refractory metals such as tungsten or molybdenum.

The main disadvantage of the use of graphite for this application is the fact that it is difficult to degas. This is a slow process which can normally be described by an equation of the type

$$V_t = A + B \log t$$

where V_t is the volume of gas at time t, and A and B are constants. The simplest way of overcoming the problem is to degas the graphite in an inert gas steam at temperatures of 1400°C. If the graphite is then stored and handled under low humidity conditions there will be very little pick up of contaminating gases and, provided the component is heat treated again prior to sealing of the valve, it should give little further trouble.

B. CARBON PILE VARIABLE RESISTORS

The carbon pile resistance provides a cheap and convenient form of non-inductive resistor which can be varied, without the use of sliding contacts, over a wide range of ohmic values in a smooth and continuous manner.

The resistor consists of a stack or pile of carbon or graphite plates, discs or rings together with a means of applying a variable force along the axis of the pile. The principle of its operation is that the contact resistance between adjacent elements is sensitive to the mechanical force applied, and the resistance value is obtained merely by altering the value of the force. The resistance level of the pile, its current carrying capacity and its resistance force characteristics are dictated by the grade of carbon of graphite and the number and size of the elements in it.

Semiconducting devices are gradually replacing the carbon pile in many applications, but because of its basic simplicity and reliability carbon continues to be widely used.

C. TELEPHONE ACCESSORIES

Carbon has been used extensively in connection with the telephone. Many of the uses are now being superseded by alternative materials, but the carbon granule is still the only economic means of providing the conversion of sound to electrical energy. Although numerous types of carbon have been tried only heat-treated anthracite appears satisfactory. The main disadvantage of carbon granules is that the modulation efficiency falls off and the resistance of the aggregates increases with use, due to a combination of handling and gas interaction. The change in resistance can not be tolerated on modern lines since this will affect the current flowing through the relays and eventually the relays will not function properly.

As a result of these problems much development work has been carried out into producing a granule with stable properties with respect to time. Considerable success has been achieved by subjecting the granules to several pretreatments, for example vibrating the granules in a controlled gas atmosphere.

D. SPARK MACHINING

Spark machining as a method of cutting and shaping metal has been in use since about 1945. Its importance has increased with the growth in demand for more complex shaped parts, particularly moulds on dies in hardened steels and cemented carbides.

The earliest spark machining equipment was based on simple relaxation circuits, using the discharge of a condenser to generate the spark. Using copper or brass electrodes was effective in machining hard metals, but their rate of cutting was very slow and high electrode wear made dimensional control difficult.

With the development of high frequency square or sine wave pulsed circuit machines using tungsten copper or electrographite electrodes much improved cutting rates, dimensional control and surface finishes were possible. There is no clear evidence why graphite gives such exceptional performance compared with most other electrode materials, nor why particular grades of graphite are so much superior to others; in general it seems that high strength and conductivity are desirable characteristics. The good machineability of relatively low cost of graphite makes it very competitive with other electrode materials.

Precision moulded graphite electrodes are now being produced (see Ministry of Technology report, 1967) to tolerances of ± 0.005 in/in. The advantage of moulded electrodes is that they eliminate the relatively costly machining required with solid graphite. Figure 15 gives some idea of the type of product which can be made in this way.

Fig. 15. Spark-machining electrodes produced by precision moulding techniques. (Reproduced by courtesy of Fordath Ltd.)

ACKNOWLEDGEMENTS

The authors would like to thank all their colleagues who have given advice on the contents of this chapter, in particular J. G. Campbell and M. H Lindsey (Group Technical Editor). They would also like to thank Morganite Carbon Ltd. for permission to use articles appearing in "Carbon and Its Uses" as a basis for this chapter.

REFERENCES

Anon. (1966). *Flambeau* **4**, 20.
Earp, F. K. and Hill, M. W. (1958). *In* "Industrial Carbon and Graphite", p. 328. Soc. Chem. Ind., London.
Ford, A. R. and Campbell, J. G. (1964). *J. Br. Ceram. Soc.* **2**, 68.
Gangler, J. J. (1950). *J. Am. Ceram. Soc.* **33**, 367.
Gulbransen, E. A. (1963). *Nature, Lond.* **198**, 82.
Hennig, G. R. (1959). *In* "Progress in Inorganic Chemistry", Vol. 1, p. 125. Interscience, New York.
Hering, H., Keraudy, S., Lang, F. M. and May, S. (1960). *In* "Proceedings of the 4th Carbon Conference", p. 115. Pergamon Press, Oxford.
Hilliard, A. (1957). *In* "First Conference on Industrial Carbon and Graphite", p. 605. Soc. Chem. Ind., London.
Hilliard, A. (1965). *In* "Second Conference on Industrial Carbon and Graphite", p. 641. Soc. Chem. Ind., London.
Laine, N. R., Vastola, F. J. and Walker, P. L. (1963). *J. phys. Chem.* **67**, 2030.
Malström, C., Keen, R. and Green, L. (1951). *J. appl. Phys.* **22**, 593.
Marsh, H., O'Hair, T. E. and Wynne-Jones, W. F. K. (1965). *Trans. Faraday Soc.* **61**, 274.
Mellor, J. W. (1956). "Comprehensive Treatise on Inorganic and Theoretical Chemistry", Suppl. II, Pt. 1, pp. 272ff. Longmans, London.
Ministry of Technology, London (1967). *New Technol.* **6**, 5.
Nightingale, R. E. (ed.) (1962). "Nuclear Graphite", p. 142. Academic Press, New York.
Oberlin, M. and Mering, J. (1964). *Carbon* **1**, 471.
Smith, M. Anglo Great Lakes Corporation Ltd. Private communication.
Thomas, J. M. and Roscoe, C. (1965). *In* "Proceedings of 2nd Industrial Carbon and Graphite Conference", p. 249. Soc. Chem. Ind., London.
Turner, R. F. (1958) Specification 800–R–3, General Atomic San Diego, California.
Ubbelohde, A. R. (1964). *Carbon* **2**, 23.

AUTHOR INDEX

Numbers in italics refer to pages on which the full reference is given

Corsan, J. M., 120, *126*
Coulson, C. A., 23, 31, *45*, 86, *126*
Cowen, H. C., 73, 74, 76, 136, 183, *191*, *194*
Cowland, F. C., 175, *196*
Croft, R. C., 121, *126*
Cullis, B. D., 172, *190*
Cullis, C. F., 24, *45*
Culver, R. V., 130, 152, *191*
Currie, L. M., 50, 52, *76*

D

Dacey, J. R., 36, 37, *45*
Dahl, R. E., 143, *191*
Darney, A., 53, 72, *76*
Davidge, R. W., 216, *220*
Davidson, H. W., 33, 35, 37, 38, *45*, *47*, 60, 69, *76*, 182, *190*, 210, 211, 212, 213, *220*
Davies, W., 247, 252, *254*
Davy, A. D., 36, *44*
Dawson, I. M., 22, 23, 24, *45*, 148, 182, *190*, *191*
Day, R. J., 143, 187, *191*
Deacon, R. F., 240, *254*
Deitz, V. R., 173, *192*
Delavignette, P., 205, *220*
Dell, M. B., 53, *76*
Démidovitch, G. B., 152, *192*
Denton, W. H., 163, *191*
Derman, B. M., 169, *192*
Devuit, J., 20, *46*
Diamond, R., 32, 33, *45*
Diefendorf, R. J., 105, *126*, *254*
Digonskii, V. V., 23, 24, *45*
Distante, J. M., 68, 69, *75*
Dix, J., 138, 139, 157, *196*
Dollimore, D., 64, *76*
Dollimore, J., 64, *76*
Donald, H. J., 168, *192*
Driesner, A. R., 212, 213, 219, *221*
Dubinin, M. M., 36, *45*
Dresselhaus, M. S., 85, 89, 91, 93, 94, 95, 96, 97, 98, 106, *126*, *127*
Du Chaffaut, F., 26, *47*
Dutta, A. K., 102, *126*
Duval, X., 130, 138, 139, 140, 141, 142, 145, 151, 152, 155, 174, 175, 176, *190*, *191*, *192*, *194*, *199*

E

Earp, F. K., 144, *192*, 272, *291*
Eatherly, W. P., 56, *76*
Edstrom, T., 37, *46*
Eeles, W. T., 16, *45*
Effron, E., 138, 141, *192*
Egerton, J. R., 178, *192*
Eley, D. D., 31, *45*
Elsey, H. M., 253, *255*
Ergun, S., 4, 12, *45*, 159, 161, 166, 169, 171, *192*, *196*
Esaki, L., 120, *126*
Essenhigh, R. M., 138, 188, *192*
Estabrook, J. N., 56, *75*
Evans, E. L., 150, *198*
Evans, T., 130, *192*
Everett, D. H., 19, 36, *44*, *45*
Everett, M. R., 168, 187, *192*
Eyring, H., 139, 169, 177, *190*, *191*

F

Fair, F. V., 18, *45*
Farberov, I. L., 169, *192*
Feates, F. S., 182, 183, *190*, *191*, *192*
Fedorov, G. G., 152, *192*, *199*
Fedoseev, S. D., 171, *192*
Feild, A. L., 188, *193*
Fessler, J. C., 143, *195*
Fialkov, A. S., 24, 25, *45*, 53, 63, 68, 72, *76*
Fillatre, A., 30, 38, *47*, 64, 65, 67, 71, *76*, *77*
Fischbach, D. B., 18, *45*, 213, *220*
Fischer, G., 27, 31, *45*
Fitzer, E., 4, 5, 20, *44*, *45*, 62, 63, *75*
Flinn, R. A., 51, *75*
Floyd, I. J., 175, *196*
Follett, E. A. C., 22, 23, 24, *45*, 148, *191*, *192*
Foner, S., 93, 94, 96, 97, 98, *127*
Ford, A. R., 270, *291*
Fox, B. R., 173, 178, *191*
Frank-Kamenetskii, D. A., 184, *192*
Franklin, R. E., 3, 4, 7, 9, 10, 11, 14, 15, 16, 20, 21, 22, 26, 33, 34, 35, 36, 37, 39, 43, 44, *45*, 227, *254*
Freundlich, J., 159, *192*
Fritz, W., 4, 5, *45*

P

Pacault, A., 19, 28, 29, 30, *46*, *47*
Pallmer, P. G., 143, *197*
Palmer, D. J., 171, *197*
Pandic, B., 9, *47*
Parfitt, G. D., 31, *45*
Parisot, J., 5, *45*, 54, 77, 124, *125*
Parker, W. E., 53, 77, 144, *194*, *197*
Parker, W. G., 37, *47*
Parson, J. L., 41, *45*
Payne, G. L., 51, *78*
Peakall, K. A., 163, *190*
Perels, D. R., 69, 73, *76*
Perrot, J. M., 187, *197*
Perry, M. J., 31, *45*
Petakhova, R. P., 24, 25, *45*
Petersen, E. E., 185, *197*
Peterson, R. E., 216, *221*
Pfister, A. C., 124, *126*
Phaal, C., 130, *192*
Philipp, H. R., 118, *127*
Philippot, J., 56, *76*
Phillips, G., 32, *48*
Phillips, R. H., 130, 133, *193*
Pierce, C., 36, *47*
Pines, D., 118, *127*
Pink, R. C., 121, *126*
Pinnick, H. T., 28, 38, *47*, 101, *126*
Pinto, G., 146, *195*
Pollet, R., 142, *195*
Polley, M. H., 38, 39, *47*
Porgess, P. V. K., 245, *255*
Poston, L. J., 5, 42, *47*
Praddaude, H. C., 119, *127*
Prater, C. D., 184, 185, *199*
Pratt, G. C., 20, *47*
Pregermain, S., 20, *46*
Presland, A. E. B., 24, *45*, 148, *197*
Price, M. S. T., 51, 52, 53, 54, 55, 56, 63, 64, 65, 69, 70, 71, 72, 73, *75*, *76*, 77, 209, *220*
Primak, W., 102, 103, 115, *127*
Pshezhetskii, S. Ya., 183, *199*
Pullman, A., 85, *127*
Pullman, B., 5, 31, *47*, 85, *127*
Pursley, S. A., 168, *197*

Q

Quinn, T. F. J., 245, 246, *255*

R

Raats, E., 73, 74, *78*, 187, *198*
Rabinowicz, E., 225, *255*
Ragoss, A., 62, 63, *75*
Rakszawski, J. F., 20, 24, *48*, 63, 68, 72, *78*, 144, 165, 168, *197*, *198*
Rand, B., 166, *196*
Ranson, H., 56, *75*
Rappeneau, J., 30, 38, *47*, 64, 65, 67, 71, *76*, 77
Read, I. A., 24, *45*
Rebaudieres, P., 135, 138, *193*, *197*
Redman, E., 19, 33, 36, *45*
Redmond, J. P., 24, *47*, 152, 169, *197*
Reed, R., 148, 179, *194*, *196*
Reif, A. E., 159, *197*
Reynolds, W. N., 217, 218, *221*
Richards, B. P., 14, 15, 16, 17, 24, *46*, 67, 77, 212, *220*
Riesz, C. H., 54, 77
Riley, D. L., 41, *46*
Riley, D. P., 70, 77, 203, *220*, *221*
Riley, H. L., 17, 30, 34, 40, *44*, *45*, *47*
Roberts, D. E., 102, *127*
Roberts, F., 70, 71, 77
Roberts, J., 186, *193*
Robson, D., 144, 166, *196*, *197*
des Rochettes, H., 59, *76*
Rogaibin, M. I., 169, *192*
Rogers, J. D., 172, *197*
Rogers, N. W., 56, 77
Römberg, E., 168, 187, *192*
Roosbroeck, W., van, 124, *126*
Roscoe, C., 131, 148, 150, *197*, *198*, 273, *291*
Rosner, D. E., 180, *197*
Rossberg, M., 174, 184, *197*
Rounthwaite, C., 167, 184, *197*
Rowe, G. W., 239, 253, *254*, *255*
Rüdorff, W., 121, *127*
Ruland, W., 32, 37, *47*
Rushbrooke, G. S., 23, 31, *45*
Rusinko, F., 20, 24, *48*, 53, 63, 64, 65, 68, 72, 73, 74, *77*, *78*, 130, 144, 152, 159, 165, 167, 169, 171, 173, 174, 184, 186, 187, *197*, *198*
Russell, C. C., 33, *47*
Ruston, W. R., 168, *197*

S

Sach, R. S., 182, *190*, *192*
Sato, H., 39, *48*, 49, 60, *78*, 153, *197*
Saunders, G. A., 88, 99, 100, 103, 104, 105, 107, 108, 109, 111, 112, 113, 114, 115, 116, 117, 124, *125*, *127*
Savage, R. H., 239, 240, 244, 252, *254*, *255*
Scala, S. M., 189, *197*
Schaad, L. J., 31, *45*
Schaeffer, W. D., 38, 39, *47*
Schiller, C., 26, *47*
Schmidt, L., 40, *47*
Schmidt, P., 123, *126*
Scholten, J. J. F., 137, *197*
Schulze, E., 121, *127*
Schulze, V., 144, 159, 164, *194*
Scott, C. B., 51, *77*
Scott, D. S., 169, *195*
Seeley, S. B., 56, *78*
Sekiguchi, A., 18, *47*
Sekiya, T., 34, *47*
Seldin, E. J., 69, 73, *77*
Sella, C., 150, 151, 160, *195*
Sesonski, A., 172, *197*
Shaefer, D. L., 240, *255*
Shahin, M. M., 181, *197*
Sharman, S. A., 33, 36, *45*
Sharratt, E. W., 136, *191*
Shelef, M., 144, 157, 163, *197*, *198*
Sherwood, J. N., 20, 24, 25, 26, 27, 36, 41, *45*, *46*
Shobert, E. I., Jr., 225, 238, 248, *255*
Shooter, P. V., 20, 24, 25, 26, 27, 33, 36, 41, *46*
Short, M. A., 4, 20, *47*, *48*
Simbeck, L., 4, *47*, 70, *77*
Simmons, J. H. W., 70, 71, 72, *77*
Sleightholm, P., 161, *192*
Slonczewski, J. C., 85, 88, 89, *127*
Slysh, R. S., 37, *45*, *46*
Smirnov, B. N., 24, 25, *45*
Smith, G. E., 110, 119, *127*
Smith, L. B., 93, 94, 99, *126*, *127*
Smith, M., 261, *291*
Smith, R. C., 35, *47*
Smith, R. N., 36, *47*, 152, *197*
Smith, W. R., 38, 39, *47*
Snowdon, R. A., 167, 184, *197*
Sosin, A., 22, *45*

Soule, D. E., 87, 93, 94, 96, 97, 98, 99, 102, 103, 104, 105, 106, 107, 109, 124, 125, *127*
Spain, I. L., 96, 97, 98, 103, 105, 109, 115, 116, *127*
Spangler, C. W., 173, *197*
Spencer, D. H. T., 133, 136, 152, *191*, *196*, *197*
Spurrier, P. L., 169, *196*
Squires, R. L., 167, 184, *191*
Stacy, W. O., 133, *197*
Stadler, H. P., 21, 22, 32, *47*
Standring, J., 74, *77*, 183, *197*
Stanley, I. W., 247, *255*
Stebbens, A. E., 232, 249, *255*
Sterling, E., 161, *197*
Stevens, J. A., 136, *196*
Steward, E. G., 16, 37, 38, *47*, 70, *77*, 78
Stokes, A. R., 2, *46*
Strange, J. F., 163, *198*
Stranks, D. R., 182, *190*
Straub, W. D., 88, 105, *126*
Streeter, E., 40, *44*
Streznewski, J., 178, *198*
Strickland-Constable, R. F., 169, 174, 175, 176, 177, 183, *191*, *196*, *198*, *199*
Surma, M., 119, *127*
Susman, S., 54, *77*
Sutherland, J. W., 160, *191*
Sutter, P. H., 108, *126*
Sutton, A. L., 25, *47*, 71, 72, *78*
Sutton, J., 152, 157, *194*
Sykes, K. W., 144, 159, 161, 165, 169, *192*, *196*, *198*
Szwarc, M., 37, *47*

T

Tabor, D., 225, 239, *254*
Taft, E. A., 118, *127*
Tait, J. N., 74, *77*
Takahashi, H., 9, 10, 14, 15, 17, *44*, 47
Takegami, Y., 33, *48*
Takeuchi, Y., 66, 69, *77*
Tang, M. M., 34, 35, *44*, *47*
Tappin, G., 216, 220, *221*
Tattersall, H. G., 216, *221*

SUBJECT INDEX

A

a-Axis electron transport properties in graphite, 98
Acetylene soot
  crystallite dimensions, 7
  layer-plane spacing, 7
Alfvén wave propagation, 119
Aluminium chloride-graphite, 123
Aluminium, production, 265, 266
Anthracite
  carbonization, 62, 65
  heat treatment, 21
  reaction with carbon dioxide, 166
Applications of carbon, 228
Aromatic hydrocarbons forming soft carbons, 32
Asphalt coke, in graphite manufacture, 52, 132

B

Band structure of graphite, 81
Benzene carbon, magnetic susceptibility, 28
Bernal structure, 88 *et seq.*
Bitumen coke
  in graphite manufacture, 52
  magnetoresistance, 120
Blast furnace linings, 268
Boron, presence in graphite, 58, 99, 117, 124, 142, 148
Boudouard reaction, 158, 168
Brillouin zone, 83 *et seq.*
Butane carbon, magnetic susceptibility, 28

C

c-Axis electron transport properties in graphite, 114
Carbon
  activated, 160

Carbon (*continued*)
  anisotropy, 62, 71
  breaking strength, 266
  chemical reactivity, 74
  classification, 3, 4, 225
  coefficient of friction, 230, 243
  creep under load, 264
  crystal, 62, 70, 71
  crystallography, 130
  density, 266
  distinguishing from graphite test, 274
  effect of current on friction, 247
  electrical properties, 224
  electrical resistivity, 5, 20
  electron spin resonance, 5
  electron transport in, 79 *et seq.*
  elemental analysis, 5
  Fermi surface, 101
  friction and wear properties, 224 *et seq.*
  from naphthalene, 183
  from polyfurfuryl alcohol, 166
  granules, 289
  graphitizing, 3
  hard, 3, 62, 73
  hardness, 5
  heat treatment, 50, 68, 101, 227, 228
  industrial applications, 257 *et seq.*
  isotropy, 62
  macroscopic hardness, 243
  magnetic susceptibility, 5, 19, 28
  manufacture, 49 *et seq.*, 225 *et seq.*
  mechanical properties, 224, 227
  micro-hardness, 243
  microporosity, 5
  microradiograph, 237
  non-graphitizing, 3, 70
  oxidation, 136
  oxygen absorption, 152
  permeability, 73
  phase rule diagram, 50
  pore structure, 136, 137, 237
  production, 49, 131 *et seq.*

D

Degreee of graphitization, 9
Delayed coking process, 51, 52
Diamond
  conversion into graphite, 130
  heat of combustion, 130
  reaction with atomic oxygen, 178
  reaction with carbon dioxide, 165
  thermal gas reactions, 130
  structure, 233
Dibenzanthrone carbon, magnetic susceptibility, 28
Diffraction studies on carbon, 233
Divinylbenzene, in graphite manufacture, 56
Doped graphites, electron transport properties, 124, 125
Dragon reactor, 168

E

Effect of atmosphere on friction and wear of graphite, 252
Effect of composition and structure of carbon on friction, 241
Effect of current on friction of carbon, 147
Elastic moduli, 211 et seq.
Elastic properties, 201 et seq.
Elastic properties of graphite, 202
Electric steel furnace electrodes, 267
Electrical applications of carbon, 229
Electrical brushes
  coefficient of friction, 243, 253
  contact area, 249
  contact film structure, 245, 246
  "copper drag", 231
  "copper picking", 231
  critical contact temperature, 247
  crystal orientation of contact film, 246
  effect of additives on wear, 233, 253
  effect of current on friction, 247
  effect of gases and vapours on wear, 251, 252, 253
  electrical contact potential, 230
  friction, 230, 253, 254
  "glazing", 232
  low-humidity wear, 233
  manufacture, 225, 226
  properties, 229

Electrical brushes (*continued*)
  sliding texture, 246
  structure by electron microscopy, 236, 237, 246
  structure by optical microscopy, 234, 235
  surface orientation on abrasion, 245
  turbostratic structure, 234
  variation of friction with current, 247
  wear debris, 249
  wear rate, 231, 232, 233, 249, 250, 253, 254
Electrical properties of graphite compounds, 120
Electrical resistivity, 102 et seq.
Electrodes
  amorphous carbon, 52
  baked, 52
  for aluminium production, 265
  for magnesium production, 265
  for sodium production, 265
  for steel production, 267
  graphite, 132
  pre-baked, 265
  Söderberg, 265
Electrodes for aluminium, magnesium and sodium production, 265
Electrodes for chlorine cells, 276
Electrographite, 227
  breaking strength, 266
  coefficient of friction, 243, 244, 247
  density, 266
  effect of current on friction, 247
  effect of metal counterfaces, 243, 244
  rate of wear, 248, 249
  resistivity, 266
  thermal conductivity, 266
Electron microscopy, 22, 31, 38, 42, 71, 134, 146, 148, 179, 205, 234, 236, 237, 242, 245
Electron transport in graphites and carbons, 79
Electronic properties, 28

F

Fermi surface, 80 et seq.
Flavanthrone structure on heat treatment, 21, 22
Flexural strength of graphite, 214